MW01139613

THE WHITES OF THEIR EYES

The Life of Revolutionary War Hero Israel Putnam
from Rogers' Rangers to Bunker Hill

MICHAEL E. SHAY

STACKPOLE BOOKS

Essex, Connecticut
Blue Ridge Summit, Pennsylvania

STACKPOLE BOOKS

An imprint of Globe Pequot, the trade division of
The Rowman & Littlefield Publishing Group, Inc.
4501 Forbes Blvd., Ste. 200
Lanham, MD 20706
www.rowman.com

Distributed by NATIONAL BOOK NETWORK

British Library Cataloguing in Publication Information available

Library of Congress Cataloging-in-Publication Data

Names: Shay, Michael E., author.
Title: The whites of their eyes : the life of Revolutionary war hero Israel
   Putnam from Rogers' Rangers to Bunker Hill / Michael E. Shay.
Other titles: Life of Revolutionary war hero Israel Putnam from Rogers'
   Rangers to Bunker Hill
Description: Essex, Connecticut : Stackpole Books, [2023] | Includes
   bibliographical references and index.
Identifiers: LCCN 2023008674 (print) | LCCN 2023008675 (ebook) | ISBN
   9780811773515 (cloth ; alk. paper) | ISBN 9780811773522 (electronic)
Subjects: LCSH: Putnam, Israel, 1718-1790. | Generals—United
   States—Biography. | United States. Continental Army—Biography. |
   United States—History—Revolution, 1775-1783—Campaigns. | United
   States—History—French and Indian War, 1754-1763—Campaigns. | Rogers'
   Rangers—Biography. | Brooklyn (Conn.)—Biography.
Classification: LCC E207.P9 S43 2023 (print) | LCC E207.P9 (ebook) | DDC
   355.0092 [B]—dc23/eng/20230428
LC record available at https://lccn.loc.gov/2023008674
LC ebook record available at https://lccn.loc.gov/2023008675

*For 1st Lt. Robert E. Scott, 69th Tank Battalion,
6th Armored Division, World War II,
and Marion Pauline ("Polly") Scott, she kept the home fires burning;
And in honor of all the citizen-soldiers, past, present, and future,
for their service and sacrifice on behalf of their country.*

Contents

Maps and Illustrations

Map 1. Ft. Miller to Crown Point, 1755–1759.

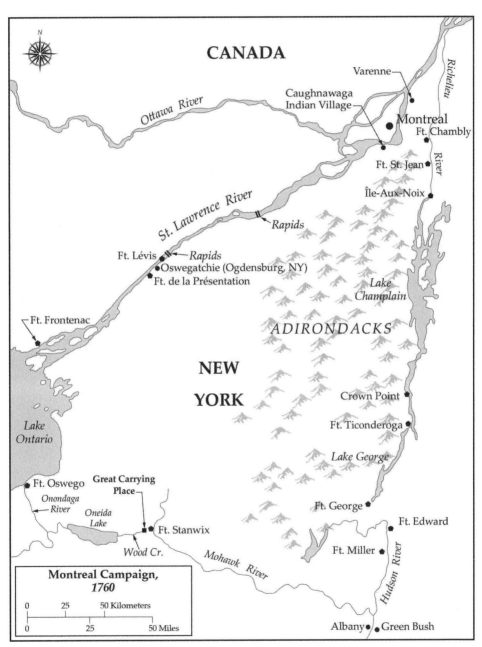

Map 2. Montreal Campaign, 1760.

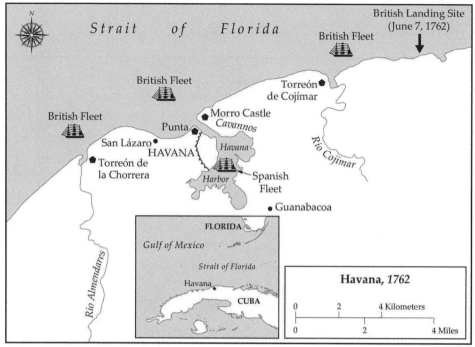

Map 3.   Havana, 1762.

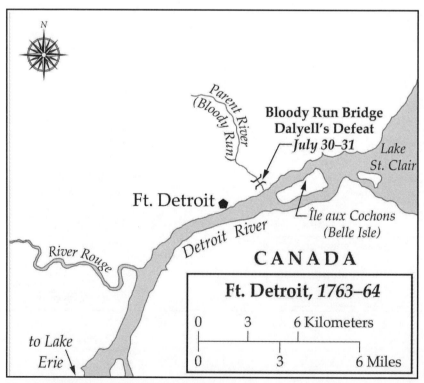

Map 4.   Ft. Detroit, 1763–1764.

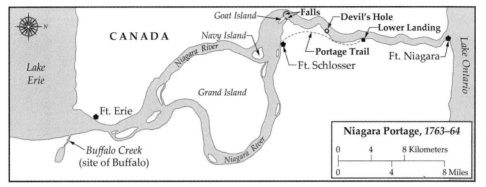

Map 5. Niagara Portage, 1763–1764.

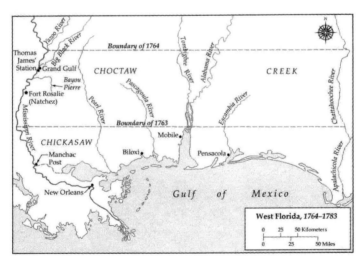

Map 6. West Florida, 1764–1783.

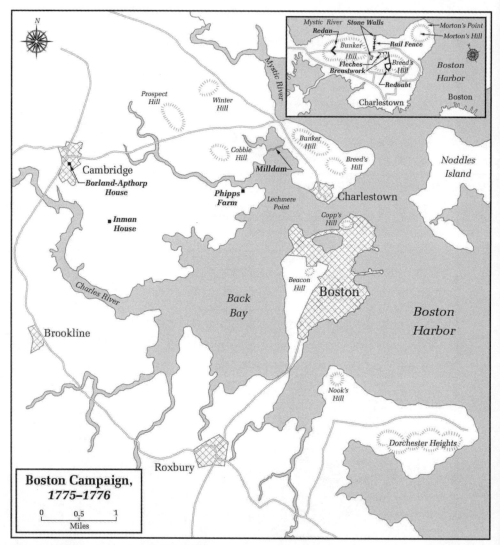

Map 7.   Boston Campaign, 1775–1776.

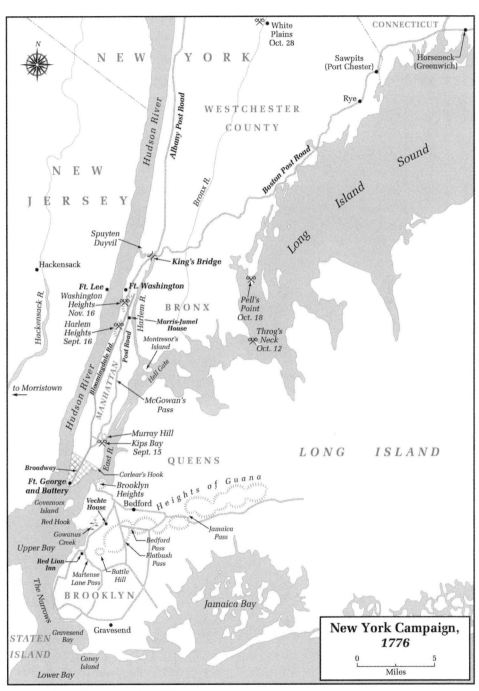

Map 8.   New York Campaign, 1776.

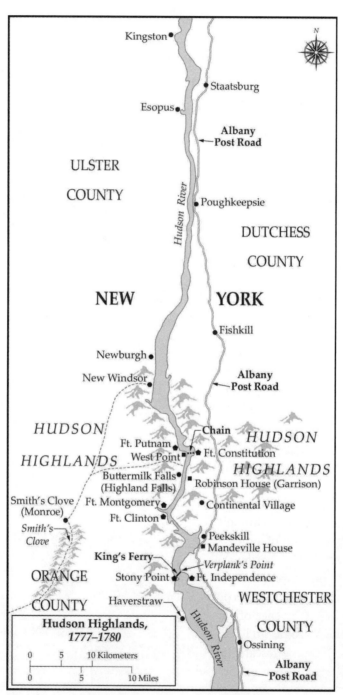

Map 9.   Hudson Highlands, 1777–1780.

PREFACE

As do all historians, we "stand on the shoulders of those who came before." To David Humphreys we owe a debt of gratitude for the firsthand glimpse of the life of Israel Putnam—farmer, soldier, and adventurer. Putnam was a man with little formal education, but with boundless strength, energy, and, above all, courage. With him, there were no halfway measures. Humphreys' account is based upon his personal knowledge, having served as Putnam's aide-de-camp, and on at least one interview with the general in his later years. He also had the benefit of the firsthand knowledge of Putnam's earlier life gleaned from Putnam himself by his friend Dr. Albigence Waldo, also a Revolutionary War veteran. Humphreys' account was first published a year before Putnam died and reprinted in several later versions. His monograph, and that of the well-researched biography by William Farrand Livingston in 1901, remain important sources for the several full-length biographies that have followed, once every succeeding generation. Most of them have covered the same ground, presenting a mostly accurate chronological account, while blending firsthand sources with some exaggerated, if not apocryphal, tales. However, a biographical narrative without context remains just that, a chronological account.

The function of a biographer is, as the late Jim Croce would say, like "saving time in a bottle." Which is another way of saying that context matters. The subject must be judged by the standard of his day and the actions of himself and his peers. When it is done, the distillate remaining should be the essence of who the subject was as a person. In most cases, a biographer comes to like and admire the subject (or why else spend the time and energy researching the person). Ideally, one should tease out of the subject's own words, and those of other contemporary voices, as accurate a picture of the person as possible, "warts and all." To do less is to do a disservice to the person, and to do more risks straying into the realm of hagiography. A biography should not only inform, but also should demonstrate the relevance of the subject to the reader. That is my hope.

During his lifetime, Israel Putnam was a prisoner of his own fame. One prominent historian observed that Putnam, "never achieved the success that was expected of this most famous veteran of the French and Indian War."[1] As time passes, Putnam's reputation has suffered, as he fades more and more into the status of a historical footnote. He becomes less the energetic, inspirational leader that he was, and is summarily associated with the loss at Brooklyn and Forts Clinton and Montgomery in the New York Highlands. For some, he continues to be judged by his admittedly atrocious spelling, while ignoring his native intelligence. Without a doubt, Putnam had his limits, as George Washington came to know, but until his untimely stroke, he remained an integral part of Washington's efforts in New York, New Jersey, and Connecticut. Some might argue that Putnam's story has already been told and retold so many times that there is little more to tell. However, I would argue that is not the case, and, moreover, that fact, in and of itself, makes it important to introduce a new generation of readers to this true American hero.

Part of Washington's genius was that he was able to get the most out of those he trusted, and at the same time, bearing in mind his own limitations, he made allowances for theirs. Major General John Sullivan is a case in point. In initially evaluating him for congressional consideration for appointment as a general officer, George Washington confessed that, "his [Sullivan's] wants are common to us all; the want of experience to move upon a large scale; for the limited, and contracted knowledge which any of us have in Military Matters stands in very little stead." He went on to say that Sullivan had an "enterprising genius" that made up for his limitations. No doubt, the same could be said for Israel Putnam. Contemporary historian Stephen Taaffe sums it up best when he said of Putnam, and many of his fellow generals, that "they demonstrated more courage than skill."[2]

Fortunately, in this time of COVID-19 and the limitations imposed by the pandemic, archivists and scholars have made readily accessible a digital trove of original documents, many in Putnam's own hand. One such source, a collaboration between the University of Virginia and the National Archives, called Founders Online, makes available the papers of George Washington, John Adams, Alexander Hamilton, John Jay, and others, many of whom exchanged correspondence with Putnam during the period leading up to and during the American Revolution. Another source has resulted from the collaboration of Google with a consortium of first-rank universities, such as the University of Michigan, Yale University, the University of California, and others, who have digitalized hundreds if not thousands of relevant out-of-print works, like the *American Archives*, that had lain moldering in their libraries and are now instantly accessible to the historical researcher. My apologies to the purists for those instances in the text where I have adopted modern spelling and punctuation for the sake of clarity, without changing the words themselves.

No author can take full credit for a work of history or biography. I have, once again, relied upon the generosity and help of many persons, including: Susan Bigelow and Christine Pittsley, Connecticut State Library & Archives, Hartford, Connecticut; Jessica Becker and Michael Frost, Manuscripts and Archives, Sterling Library, Yale University; Elaine Heavy and Sara Georgini, Massachusetts Historical Society, Boston, Massachusetts; Linda Hocking, Litchfield Historical Society, Litchfield, Connecticut; Miranda Peters and Richard M. Strum, Fort Ticonderoga Museum, Fort Ticonderoga, New York; Katy Scullin, Special Collections, Legacy Library at Marietta College, Marietta, Ohio; Stacey Stachow and Allen Phillips, Wadsworth Atheneum Museum of Art, Hartford, Connecticut; Catherine Steele, Wilton Library Association, Wilton, Connecticut; Wendy Taylor, Kent Memorial Library, Suffield, Connecticut; and Michelle Tom, Windsor Historical Society, Windsor, Connecticut.

Thanks to my brother Pat, and sons Ted and Kevin, as well as Robby and Annie for reading portions of the manuscript and offering corrections and suggestions. My colleague Ed Krumeich has proven a font of all things Greenwich. The book is all the better for their input. Once again, Chris Robinson's wonderful maps have dovetailed with the text and will enhance the reader's experience.

My wife, Marilyn, remains my rock, as she has supported and encouraged my efforts from the beginning. She is a good sport and a great traveling companion, not to mention researcher and photographer. We have hit the road once again with our newest family member, "Baxter," enjoying the sights and tastes of this big, beautiful country and hoping to leave the COVID-19 scourge safely in the rearview mirror.

Author's Note

IN READING THE LETTERS AND DIARIES OF THE PARTICIPANTS IN THESE historic events, I have, as I am sure most researchers have, found the spelling and grammar, as well as the lack of punctuation, have made the task all the more difficult. To leave the original spelling untouched yields an authentic voice, particularly when read out loud. However, rather than test the patience of the modern reader, I have in most places opted to use the more modern spelling, grammar, punctuation, and so on.

The diaries and memoirs also present added challenges, particularly as to the chronology. Many were written or published years after the events chronicled. Humphreys' account was written based upon Putnam's decades-old memories. Rogers' journal was published nearly a decade after the events. Wherever possible, I have tried to rely upon the most contemporary version, particularly where there is some corroboration, and the sources are cited in the notes.

What creature walks about on four legs at dawn; two legs at mid-day; and three legs at sunset?

—THE RIDDLE OF THE SPHINX

. . . a man whose generosity was singular; whose honesty was proverbial; who raised himself to universal esteem and offices of eminent distinction by personal worth and a useful life.

—EXTRACT OF EPITAPH FROM HIS ORIGINAL GRAVESTONE, AND LATER ENGRAVED ON THE BASE OF ISRAEL PUTNAM'S STATUE MARKING HIS GRAVE AT BROOKLYN, CONNECTICUT

CHAPTER ONE

The Early Years

BROOKLYN, CONNECTICUT, 1787

A FIRE CRACKLED IN THE HEARTH, TAKING THE AUTUMN CHILL OFF. THE old man paused briefly, closed his light blue eyes, looking for just the right word, then managed a crooked smile as he leaned a little forward, while gripping the top of his ivory-handled Havana cane for support, and went on with his story. Although a stroke eight years before had left him partially paralyzed and his speech somewhat slurred, his mind remained sharp. Moreover, here, within the safe confines of his own home, in the company of his good friend, he shared with him, for perhaps the last time, the details of a long life, full of drama and adventure. No doubt, the listener had heard many of the stories before, dating from a time when they had served together with General Washington, but David Humphreys had traveled here to Brooklyn, Connecticut, from his home in Ansonia, to gather them together in hopes of presenting them to the public at large in a more formal tribute to the old citizen-soldier.[1]

∞ ∞ ∞ ∞ ∞

EARLY YEARS

On January 7, 1718,[2] in Salem Village,[3] in the province of Massachusetts Bay, Capt. Joseph Putnam paced anxiously back and forth across the sitting room of his home awaiting the by now familiar first sounds from the inner chamber warmed by a fire.[4] One would think he would have been used to the process by this time, his wife having delivered ten previous children. Nevertheless, childbirth was fraught with danger for both mother and child, as he and most of his neighbors well knew. Soon the cries of the newborn could be heard, and Joseph sighed with relief. Elizabeth had delivered a healthy baby boy, and, the Lord be praised, she had come through the ordeal once more. The couple named the child Israel. He was baptized by the Rev. Peter Clark on February 2.[5]

The members of the large, extended Putnam family were a prosperous and important part of the community, surviving the perilous years of the early settlement and, more recently, the hysteria of the previous generation, when twenty of their neighbors had been tried, convicted, and executed for witchcraft. For their part, Joseph and Elizabeth were outspoken critics, even though other family members had played a prominent role in that American tragedy. Joseph died in 1723, leaving Elizabeth a widow with a house full of children.

Figure 1.   Putnam Birthplace, Danvers, Massachusetts
COURTESY OF THE LIBRARY OF CONGRESS

Young Israel grew to manhood in the Salem Village community, and at the age of twenty, he started farming on land there that he had inherited from his father. At between five feet six and five feet eight inches tall, Putnam was slightly below middle height, and he had what could be described as a robust constitution. He did not shirk hard work, and as a result, he, in turn, achieved a degree of success. Along the way, he more than likely received a typical, but minimal, education at home, so that he could read and write, although his spelling was always notoriously poor, even in an age before Noah Webster began to standardize it.[6]

When it came time to marry, he chose a local girl to share his life—eighteen-year-old Hannah Pope, the daughter of Joseph and Mehitable. The Popes were another prosperous and prominent local family. The wedding took place on July 19, 1739. Hannah was three months pregnant at the time. The young couple moved into a small home that Israel had previously built on his farm, and on January 28 of the following year, they welcomed their first child into the world. They named him Israel.[7]

In the meantime, Putnam heard of a large tract of land for sale in the northeast corner of the Connecticut colony, perhaps from the owner himself, the Massachusetts governor, Jonathan Belcher. It is likely that he went to view the property first, and obviously liked what he saw. Israel sold a portion of his inherited land, and he joined forces with his brother-in-law, Joseph Pope, and with the help of a mortgage, in March 1739 they purchased just more than 514 acres in what was then called the Mortlake District near Pomfret, Connecticut, in the Valley of the Quinebaug River. In 1740, Israel, Hannah, and the baby traveled down the well-worn Connecticut Path, or one of its many alternates, to their new home.[8]

Undeterred by arduous work, Israel built a home, began to clear the land of trees and stones, and planted an apple orchard. He set about to raise sheep and some cattle. For some men, the way to prosperity was through land speculation, but for Israel, the work was its own reward. He had a natural affinity for farming, and soon, with the profits from his farm and the sale of additional inherited property in Salem Village, by June of 1741, he was able to buy Hannah's brother out and pay off his mortgage to Governor Belcher.[9]

ISRAEL AND THE WOLF

For sheep farmers like Israel Putnam, wolves were problematic, attacking their flocks almost at will, particularly the newborns. This was especially true for those like him, newly arrived and just starting to increase their flocks. For them, it could be devastating. Neighbors helped neighbors, trapping and killing the predators. By early 1743, they had successfully rid the area of most of the wolf population, that is except for one wily old female and her pups. That winter Israel and five other men set out in alternating pairs to track the small pack. Soon, all the pups were caught, but the she-wolf continued to elude the searchers. Finally, two members of the party tracked her to a cave, the entrance to which was only three to four feet around. One of the men went to find Putnam, while the other kept watch at the entrance. By midmorning, Putnam arrived with his "servant" and bloodhound, as did a large group of neighbors and their hounds.

At first, the dogs were sent into the cave, but the wolf bested them all. The hounds slunk back to their masters all scratched and bloodied, so cowed that no amount of coaxing or remonstration succeeded in getting a single dog to re-enter the cave. The men also attempted, without success, to smoke the animal out. From that failure, they reasoned that the wolf's den must be deep within the narrow cave. As a last resort, they concluded that someone would have to crawl in to investigate. Putnam volunteered to do so after his "servant" had also emphatically declined.[10]

It was ten o'clock that evening when Putnam removed his jacket and vest and the party tied a sturdy rope around his legs so that, if necessary, upon a given signal, they could pull him out quickly. In he went, crawling slowly on all fours along the narrow stone passage of unknown length, holding a smoking birch torch in front of him. At first the passage went downward for about fifteen feet, at which point it leveled off for ten more feet before finally inclining upward sixteen feet or so to the beast's lair.

As Putnam shimmied his way along, alone with his thoughts, he most certainly realized his vulnerability to a sudden attack by the cornered she-wolf, as well as his limited options should that occur. The closer he got, he could hear the low, guttural warning sounds of the beast and smell the foul air of her lair. Although the confrontation was anticipated by both man and animal, when Putnam finally reached the end of the

Figure 2. The Wolf's Den, Pomfret, Connecticut

passage, both became startled. The wolf growled loudly and bared her teeth, while Putnam, heart pounding, began to back away, jerking his legs as a signal to pull him out. So vigorously did his friends yank and tug on the rope that Putnam emerged from the cave with numerous cuts and scratches and his shirt pulled over his head.[11]

Once back in the open air, Putnam caught his breath, adjusted his shirt, and quickly assessed the situation with his companions. After loading his musket with several balls, and with a fresh torch, he entered the cave once more. The young man crawled along the passage, more slowly this time as both hands were engaged, and as he got closer to the den, the wolf began to howl and growl more loudly. Finally, face-to-face, he took aim, and likely closed his eyes just as he discharged his weapon. The noise was deafening, and the tunnel quickly filled with the acrid smoke and smell from the powder. His colleagues, hearing the reverberations from the musket shot, pulled him out, no doubt this time more deliberately. He assured them that he had killed the beast, but they all knew that there was only one way to be certain.

Once again, Putnam entered the cave, crawling, torch in hand, through the now familiar passageway. When he reached the lair, he saw that the wolf lay motionless. Just to be sure, he touched the torch to her nose, and she did not move. He then pulled on her ears. Thus reassured, Putnam dragged the carcass out of the tunnel. When Israel emerged for the final time, his friends and neighbors cheered and clapped him on the back. The wolf's body was carried to a nearby farm, where it was hung from the rafter of the barn, on display for all the neighborhood to see. For Putnam, his reputation in the community was assured.[12]

YEOMAN FARMER

The incident behind him, Israel Putnam continued his husbandry and tended to his orchard. He took considerable pride in the results of his hard work, particularly his Roxbury Russet trees, the fruit long prized for its keeping qualities and cider.[13] For the next two decades, he and Hannah enjoyed the fruits of their labors, and she delivered four more children. Their growing brood helped with the chores. As the years passed, his family grew, and the young farmer began to play an increasingly larger role in the life of the community. From time to time, Putnam would serve the town as a selectman. Moreover, he was looked upon as a man who could be counted on in times of crisis, and one whose advice was frequently sought.[14]

Of Human Bondage

While it is not clear at what point Putnam began to use slave labor, it was undoubtedly quite early. At any one time, Putnam, whose holdings were more than five hundred acres, owned at least one or two slaves, often referred to euphemistically as "servants," to help with the farm or around the house. There is no evidence that Putnam was overtly wanton or cruel to his slaves; that would not be in his nature. However, at this stage, it is unlikely that he gave the fundamental moral issue much thought, as his situation was no different from many of his neighbors.[15]

Slaveholding was quite common in Connecticut, and, for that matter, all throughout New England, beginning in the mid-seventeenth century. At that time, many prominent families became wealthy transporting Indian captives to the sugar plantations in the Caribbean, and later in the African slave trade. The practice was an integral part of the colonial economy until the late eighteenth and early nineteenth centuries, when it became less profitable with the advent of gradual abolition. Access would have been easy for Putnam, as nearby Norwich, Stonington, and New London were active ports for merchants engaged in the trafficking in captive human beings.

For a long time, it had been assumed that the practice was limited to individual tradesmen and farmers, like Putnam, who held only one or two slaves, yet recent studies have found evidence that there were several large plantations in Connecticut and Rhode Island, each with one thousand or more acres, where it was common to find more than two dozen slaves performing the menial labor. In fact, Putnam's next-door neighbor, Godfrey Malbone, was thought to be the largest slaveholder in Connecticut. Clearly, Putnam's use of slave labor made an important contribution to his growing prosperity.[16]

CHAPTER TWO

The French and Indian War

For King and Country

CONNECTICUT ANSWERS THE CALL

FOR FIFTEEN YEARS, PUTNAM HAD LIVED THE LIFE OF A PROSPEROUS farmer, blessed with a loving wife and a growing family. As a mark of that success and to accommodate them all, he had built a larger home near the old one. His routine pastoral life, no doubt, passed in rhythm with the seasons. That all changed after the war broke out with France in 1754 and the call for volunteers went out to each province the following spring. Connecticut responded promptly on March 13, 1755, at which time the General Assembly, sitting in Hartford, voted to raise one thousand men to be divided into two regiments, each comprised of six companies. In addition, in anticipation of the possible need for a further call for troops, the General Assembly authorized the raising of an additional five hundred men as a reserve in that event. These Provincial troops were separate from Militia, in that they were called upon to serve outside the colony. Substitutes, including free Blacks and Indians, could serve.[1]

Though most of the volunteers could not be called soldiers, per se, the men of New England were well-used to the Militia tradition, where each able-bodied man was required to turn out on a regular basis for drill on the town green. At those times, each man was expected to provide his own musket and kit, that is, powder and lead. So, no one was surprised when Gov. William Shirley of Massachusetts, then commander in chief of his majesty's forces in North America, ordered those volunteers to so equip themselves "under penalty of a fine." Although each Connecticut volunteer was paid a bonus of thirty shillings and encouraged to turn out with a serviceable "firelock, sword or hatchet," along with a blanket, "belt and cartridge box," no penalty was imposed for not doing so. In fact, those who were not able to do so were issued these items, but they were required to return them at the end of their enlistment. Failure to do so would result in a deduction from their pay. As a further incentive, those who were able to provide for themselves were given an additional payment of up to another thirty shillings. If a weapon or blanket were "lost or spoilt" during their service, their owner would be reimbursed by the colony.[2]

Appointed a major general to lead the 1st Regiment was Phineas Lyman. The thirty-nine-year-old Lyman was a native of Durham, Connecticut, and was a distinguished Yale graduate, who was a tutor first and later a practicing lawyer. He opened a law school in what was then Suffield, Massachusetts. After Suffield was annexed by Connecticut in 1752, Lyman served in the General Assembly, as well as various public offices in Connecticut, as he had previously done in Massachusetts. In addition, he was a successful businessman. Phineas and Eleanor Dwight were the parents of eight children. His father-in-law, the Rev. Timothy Dwight, would later serve as his chaplain, and Eleanor's brother Timothy Jr., also a clergyman, would serve as chaplain to a Connecticut regiment in the Revolution. Later in life, Lyman became friends with Eleazar Wheelock, and he supported the latter's efforts to establish a school for Indians.[3]

PRELUDE

In early July 1755, Lyman led his roughly five-hundred-man regiment north to a staging area at Green Bush (now Rensselaer) just across the Hudson River from Albany, New York, where they rendezvoused with other Provincial regiments raised in Massachusetts and New York. Soon after, Sir William Johnson, who had been designated by Governor Shirley to lead the expedition, arrived there with a contingent of three hundred Mohawk Indians under the leadership of the venerable old warrior Hendrick.[4]

The objective of Johnson's force was the capture of the French outpost called Fort Saint Frédéric at Crown Point situated on a promontory on the west shore, at the southerly end of Lake Champlain, roughly one hundred miles north of Albany. It was part of a four-part English strategy to defeat the French. The area was situated on a direct water route to Montreal, and, more important, it was the locus of two critical portages that were natural choke points. However, by late summer, word had already reached Johnson that one important prong, the expedition to capture Fort Duquesne, had ended in abject failure, as Gen. Edward Braddock suffered a devastating defeat nearby on July 9. Notwithstanding this news, the spirits among the soldiers of Johnson's small army were high.[5]

On July 17, while Johnson and his Mohawks remained behind in Albany to arrange for wagons and supplies, the Provincial regiments under General Lyman trudged north along the upper Hudson River until they reached a point the Indians called the Great Carrying Place, a fourteen-mile portage to Lac Saint Sacrement (later Lake George). In 1709, during Queen Anne's War, it was the site of Fort Nicholson, since abandoned. In 1731, a Dutch fur trader from Albany by the name of John Henry Lydius built a trading post there that operated for about fifteen years. Now the site would be occupied once again as a military installation. For the next three weeks following their arrival, Lyman set his men to work cutting trees and laying out a storehouse and fort, initially called Fort Lyman. In addition, his troops began to cut a thirty-foot-wide road northeast toward Wood Creek over the length of an old road, now overgrown. However, the effort was abandoned after eight miles when it was decided that the better route led directly from the new fort to the lake. That post would serve as a base of supply for the expedition, and for their protection in the event of a French attack. For a brief time, at the height of activity during 1758 and 1759, the population of what would later be named Fort Edward was exceeded only by that of the cities of New York and Philadelphia.[6]

Word reached Johnson through his Indian scouts that Maréchal-de-Camp Jean-Armand, Baron de Dieskau, was leading a large mixed force, consisting of French regulars and Canadian militia, along with their Indian allies, south to attack Fort Lyman, and Johnson decided to meet the threat head on. Earlier, after joining the main body at Fort Lyman, Johnson had led two thousand men and their Indian allies north toward Lac Saint Sacrement on August 26. Axmen prepared the way, cutting a rough road through the forest. Following the main body were the teamsters. Johnson left a five-hundred-man contingent of New Hampshire men behind at Fort Lyman. Inexplicably, once the main body arrived at Lac Saint Sacrement, the pace seemed to slow, although Johnson did send out scouting parties. Johnson assessed the immediate threat from Dieskau based upon the scouting reports, and he asked the provinces for reinforcements.[7]

VOLUNTEER

Once again, on August 27, in response to Johnson's call, coupled with correspondence from General Lyman earlier that month, Connecticut began the enlistment process for the 500 men previously authorized in the spring. In addition, the Connecticut General Assembly voted to raise two additional regiments of 750 men with nine companies each. The deadline to fill the quota was September 8, and in the event his enlistments were slow, each company commander was authorized to impress or draft enough men to meet it. All volunteers were given a thirty-shilling bounty, and, in addition, all the draftees who agreed to sign on within twenty-four hours of their selection were also given the same.[8]

It was in response to that second call-up that Israel Putnam, now thirty-seven years old and in excellent physical condition, volunteered to serve. At that time, Hannah Putnam was pregnant with their seventh child. Given his age, his growing family, the oldest of whom was only fifteen, and the hard work related to running his large farm, one must ask why he would have volunteered to serve. Putnam, himself, leaves no written record of his decision. While it is only speculation, more than likely it is a combination of the fact that he was a man his community frequently looked to and he wished to set an example and that, given his abundant, restless energy, he sought a new adventure. Moreover, he was a responsible person, and he would not have risked jeopardizing his family's security and the fruits of his hard work for the previous fifteen years without knowing that his farm and orchard would be well looked after in his absence, no doubt by Hannah and the older children, with the help of his slaves, which would have salved whatever qualms he may have had on that score.

Given his rising standing in the community, it was no surprise that Putnam received a commission as a second lieutenant in the Sixth Company of the Third Regiment, despite an ostensible lack of active military service. That was how most officers were selected. Moreover, the social gap helped with recruiting, as well as providing a sense of good order and discipline. His company commander, John Grosvenor, was from Pomfret and a delegate to the General Assembly. The Third Regiment was led by Col. Samuel Talcott. Within "a few days" of muster, Putnam's company was on its way north, though too late, it would turn out, to join in the impending fight. Putnam himself may well have hurried on ahead, not wanting to be left out of the action.[9]

The "Bloody Morning Scout"

At eight o'clock on the morning of Monday, September 8, after having consulted with his officers and Chief Hendrick earlier that day, Johnson split his force. He remained behind at the lake, designating Col. Ephraim Williams to lead approximately twelve hundred men, including about two hundred Mohawks, up the portage road toward Fort Lyman to meet Dieskau. Two days before, Dieskau, whose original intention was to attack that post, had left his boats at South Bay with a small guard while he and the main body marched south through the woods, skirting the many swampy areas. Along the way, Dieskau's Indian allies expressed reluctance to attack Fort Lyman, as they had heard that it had cannon, and he quickly changed the objective to Johnson's camp at the lake. In the meantime, on September 8 his scouts had brought him word about Williams' force, and he laid an ambush along the portage road about three miles south of the lake, where the road passed through a narrow ravine. The attack would look very much like the one that had caught Braddock by surprise.[10]

The ensuing fight proved bloody and costly, as a deadly fire from the French and their allies poured into Williams' van from three sides. The toll in dead and wounded quickly mounted, particularly among the leading elements, who initially stood their ground and returned fire. Among those killed were Col. Ephraim Williams himself and the old warrior, Hendrick. At first, the ferocity of the fight favored the French, and the rear ranks of the Provincials began to break. Many of the wounded were left to the tender mercies of Dieskau's Indians. However, a small but valiant rear guard, led by Lt. Col. Nathan Whiting of New Haven and a contingent of Connecticut and Rhode Island men, exacted a heavy toll on Dieskau's force, and what could well have been a rout turned into a fighting withdrawal. Lieutenant Colonel Seth Pomeroy from Northampton, Massachusetts, called it a "handsome retreat," as the Provincials began to fight back, stopping to fire from behind trees and logs, then moving back slowly, only to repeat the process. The affair would come to be known as the "Bloody Morning Scout."[11]

Meanwhile, after hearing the sounds from the nearby battle, Johnson dispatched a small relief force and at the same time placed the balance of his men behind hastily formed barriers, anything from logs to upturned wagons and bateaux, with Lyman's Connecticut regiment to the left center. Johnson also placed three of his four field pieces in the center of the line, and the fourth on some higher ground. Soon, the remnants of Colonel Whiting's party began to filter back and join the defenders, some in orderly formations and others singly or in small groups, carrying what wounded they could. The French paused to regroup.[12]

Between eleven and twelve o'clock, Dieskau renewed his attack in earnest. His Canadians and Indians stormed the right flank "helter skelter" using the woods and rough terrain to their advantage, while the French regulars came forward in perfect formation, first trying their luck against Johnson's right and center and, failing that after numerous volleys, then the left. Lieutenant Colonel Pomeroy compared the bullets to "hailstones from heaven." After Johnson was slightly wounded in the thigh and left the field, General Lyman took command, deliberately moving up and down the line, encouraging his troops. At first, the fighting was intense, and although his regulars maintained their discipline, the rest of Dieskau's forces, once again, became disbursed and engaged in individual sniping contests. The shooting gradually tapered off and finally stopped late that afternoon when the baron was wounded in the leg, and he and his aide were captured. His troops retreated to Ticonderoga to reconstitute. As the French withdrew, the Provincials were quick to follow. "Our men sprang over the breastwork," wrote Lyman, "and followed them like lions, and made terrible havoc." Johnson would claim credit for the victory, but Lyman had distinguished himself during the heat of the battle. Moreover, the battle would have ended differently if Whiting's gallant retreat had not slowed Dieskau down, thus giving Johnson more time to arrange his forces. Pomeroy wrote that Lyman "behaved with steadiness and resolution." In turn, Lyman was proud of his men and heaped praise on them with justifiable hyperbole. "Never any army in the world exceeded them in valor, courage and bravery," he told his wife. Dieskau would later comment on the fighting qualities of the Provincials: "In the morning they fought like good boys, at noon like men, and in the afternoon like devils."[13]

In a bloody postscript, as some of Dieskau's Canadians and Indians paused in their retreat to loot the dead at the site of the morning's fight, they were surprised by a small scouting party of New Hampshire woodsmen from Fort Lyman. Many more of the enemy were killed and their bodies dumped unceremoniously in a nearby pond, which became known as the "Bloody Pond."[14]

In the aftermath of the fight, in what can only be described as currying favor with the king, Johnson renamed Lac Saint Sacrement as Lake George, Fort Lyman as Fort Edward, and his new post at the lake, Fort William Henry, all after the king or his relations. Hence, the fight later became known as the Battle of Lake George. For most of the survivors, it was their first trial by fire, and they had stood the test. The invaluable lesson they learned was that Militia, when well-led and fighting from behind barriers, were more than a match for any regular troops.

Lieutenant Colonel Pomeroy led a large burial detail on September 10, and on that day alone, buried the bodies of 136 of their comrades, including his own brother, Daniel. Other than small skirmishes by scouts, the battle ended any large-scale fighting for the season, and the troops were soon divided and assigned to garrison duties at either Fort William Henry or Fort Edward. General Johnson called a council of war on October 9. Although the main objective remained the capture of Crown Point, to the disgust of Lyman and other officers, instead of pursuing the defeated French, Johnson issued orders to build a fort near the site of his victory. For the soldiers themselves, the fighting was done, and they wanted to go home. Some of them did just that. In addition, there were shortages of food, blankets, and even tools. Morale sunk. As a result, Johnson had trouble putting together daily work details to build his fort.[15]

PUTNAM ARRIVES AT LAKE GEORGE

The record is incomplete, but Putnam may have arrived at the Lake George area on his own, as a volunteer, sometime in mid-September. It is clear from Humphreys' account that Putnam did not participate in the Battle of Lake George on September 8. On the other hand, that same account states that "he was appointed to the command of a company in Lyman's regiment of Provincials." There is a brief reference in the Connecticut records to Captain Putnam's company being "paid from Sept." Perhaps General Lyman commissioned him to replace a wounded or deceased officer in his regiment. According to Seth Pomeroy's journal, the Third and Fourth Connecticut Regiments, including the Sixth Company, in which Putnam had been commissioned a second lieutenant, did not arrive at Fort Edward until October 9, not only late in the season, but also far too late to participate in the battle. Putnam was not on hand there to greet Captain Grosvenor, his company commander, as he had already been assigned to duty with Robert Rogers to scout the area around Ticonderoga, from which he would not return for two more days. Moreover, he is referred to throughout Rogers' journal as "Captain Putnam." In any event, it is unlikely that he ever served in Captain Grosvenor's company, since it is apparent that he was already leading his own.[16]

ROGERS' RANGERS

Shortly after his arrival at the encampment at Lake George, Putnam had the good fortune to meet and become friends with Capt. Robert Rogers, the leader of a company of irregular fighters called Rangers, who were used primarily as long-range scouts. Initially, this unit was part of the New Hampshire Provincial Regiment led by Col. Joseph Blanchard. Later, it would become an independent Ranger corps, with more than one company, all under the leadership of Rogers. How exactly it is that Putnam came to fight with the Rangers is not certain. It is easy to envision a scene in which a natural bond might develop between two men swapping tales around a fire on chilly fall evenings. Such a scenario is even more likely when the two men share many of the same attributes. In this case, "a capacity for physical endurance and instinctive bravery" were common to both. Rogers had spent much of his life in the woods interacting with the native population, while Putnam was a farmer-turned-soldier who had a natural affinity for this unconventional form of warfare. In any event, the relationship between Putnam and Rogers, and their joint service that followed, would later separate Putnam from the conventional veteran and come to form a large part of his reputation for the balance of his life. Rogers' reports, and his later autobiography, are detailed and contain several references to Putnam during this period.[17]

The use of Rogers' Ranger company, and others like it, was the brain-child of Massachusetts governor William Shirley, who saw such units as a counterweight to the superior woodland experience of the French Canadians and their Indian allies. The best known of those partisan bands operating in the region was led by Joseph Marin de la Malgue ("Marin"), who proved time and again to be a deadly and effective opponent. As a result, Ranger companies initially consisted of experienced backwoodsmen, later augmented by recruits like Putnam. Out of all these units, it was Rogers and his men who would garner the largest place in history.[18]

The son of recent Scottish immigrants, James and Mary Rogers, Robert Rogers was born in Methuen, Massachusetts, on November 7, 1731. The family would soon move to Great Meadows near what is now Concord, New Hampshire. The young boy grew to manhood immersed in the lore of the forest, as well as the lessons he learned from his father and the Native Americans who dwelled nearby. Later, as a young man, he roamed the forests of New York and New England not only to acquaint himself with the area and its inhabitants, both French and English, but also, in his words, to "inure me to hardships and . . . to qualify" for his later service as a Ranger. In addition, he picked up some French along the way. Rogers learned his lessons well and had come to General Johnson highly recommended for his woodland skills. That said, there was a cloud over his reputation back home in New Hampshire, as he had recently been involved in a scheme to pass counterfeit currency there, and Francis Parkman hints at his engaging in the "smuggling trade" with Canada.[19]

At first, the Rangers camped at Lake George. Later, during the summer of 1756, Rogers established what was initially a seasonal camp for his Rangers in the middle of a fifty-acre island separated from Fort Edward proper by a narrow channel of the Hudson River. The northern part of the island was occupied by a scattering of small Dutch farmers. In the ensuing years, the island became the site of a large barracks occupied by British regulars, as well as a sutler's camp, a cemetery, and, at the lower end, a smallpox hospital surrounded by a palisade. For the most part, the Rangers and other Provincial troops were quartered in rows of tents or log huts of their own construction. The latter were approximately sixteen feet square with crude fireplaces, and each housed more than twelve men, who shared the space two to three men to a bunk. In time, some of the huts took on an air of permanency, as many of the more skilled Provincials built cabins, complete with brick fireplaces. The island was reached by way of a pontoon bridge. Today, Rogers Island is often referred to as the birthplace of the U.S. Army Special Forces.[20]

In the Ranging Service

The Iroquois called it *tekontaró:ken*, or "the place where two waters meet," while to the English ear it sounded like Ticonderoga. It was aptly named, as it was, in fact, a point of land at the juncture of Lake Champlain, Wood Creek, and the three-and-one-half-mile-long La Chute River that drains Lake George. Over its short length, that river falls two hundred feet in elevation over a series of rapids and five impassable cascades. Accordingly, Ticonderoga was also at the terminus of another important portage. The first European to view the area was Samuel Champlain in July 1609. He and his Indigenous allies had a sharp fight there that resulted in the death of fifty Mohawks.[21]

The first recorded instance of Putnam's service with the Rangers occurred on October 7, 1755, when he joined a long-range scout organized by Rogers on orders from General Johnson. On that cool, crisp fall evening, Rogers led a party of between forty and fifty men from the encampment at Lake George to reconnoiter the French activity near

Ticonderoga. The night was dark, and it was difficult to keep all the boats together. From time to time, the Rangers could see the flickering lights from lone campfires on both shores, a clear sign that the French and Indians were active. After rowing their bateaux about sixteen miles, Rogers put in at a point of land on the eastern shore. His party waited and watched there throughout the following day, seeing nothing suspicious. That night they took to the boats again. On passing a small island, another campfire was spotted, and Rogers sent some men in a canoe to reconnoiter. On approach to the island, the canoe was seen, as the fire was quickly extinguished, and the campsite abandoned. Meanwhile, Rogers' party rowed on for several more miles, and, this time, put in on a point of land on the western shore. There they concealed the boats and made camp.[22]

On the morning of October 9, Rogers sent three small teams to scout the area of the portage. As one of the teams, Putnam and a companion hiked seven or eight miles north until they came to a heavily wooded hill (most likely Bare Mountain) located just across from the point where the outflow of Lake George enters the La Chute River. Captain Samuel Hunt and two other men accompanied Putnam to this point, then returned to Rogers to make a report. Although the view from the top was partly obstructed by trees and bushes, Putnam and the remaining Ranger heard and observed much activity carried on by a large body of Indians and French soldiers on both sides of the narrows that sounded like the cutting and hewing of timber, the firing of guns, and the howling of dogs. Deeming it too dangerous to move on to Ticonderoga by daylight, they waited until dark and counted the campfires. Based upon their observation, Putnam estimated both work camps to contain a total of six hundred to seven hundred men. He and his companion pulled their blankets around themselves, and no doubt huddled together to stay warm. The two started back to Rogers' camp in the morning. Along the way, a small party of Indians passed close to them, heading in the same direction. The Rangers paused briefly to let the warriors pass and then hurried to find Rogers and warn him.[23]

As Putnam and his companion approached the rendezvous point, they saw another large party of French and Indians on the lake, and upon arrival at the boats, Putnam warned Rogers of the enemy's approach.

Rogers' first impulse was to attack, and he sent out a small party in the canoe as a decoy to lure the enemy. However, he quickly thought better of it when he realized the size of the party he proposed to attack. The Rangers prudently broke off the contest and beat a hasty retreat. They rowed fifteen miles and made camp on an island for the night of October 10. In the morning, Rogers and his party rowed the rest of the way to the encampment at Lake George, arriving there on October 11. By then, the weather had turned bitterly cold with blowing snow.[24]

Putnam continued to accompany Rogers on other scouts, and he did not have long to wait for more action. On the night of October 14, Rogers left camp at Lake George with four other men, one of whom was Putnam. The objective of the mission was to secure a French prisoner from the works at Crown Point. The scouting party went partway by canoe and landed at a point on the western shore, twenty-five miles down the lake. Concealing their canoes, they hiked north through the thick forest toward Crown Point and arrived at a mountain just to the west of the fort on October 18. Rogers and his men took up positions on the top and waited all that night and the following day, observing the comings and goings from the fort. On the evening of October 19, Rogers led his party to a cluster of houses built on the shore of Lake Champlain south of the fort. He left three of his men hiding in a barn full of wheat while he and Putnam went to find a good ambush site.

Upon finding a willow thicket about one hundred yards from the fort, the two returned to the barn, collected the three others, and returned to prepare an ambush. Rogers crept forward to a large pine log, holding some brush in front of him for cover. There the Rangers remained throughout the night and waited for their opportunity to seize a prisoner. About midmorning the next day, a solitary French soldier left the fort and unknowingly walked directly toward the concealed positions of Rogers and his men. When the Frenchman got close enough, Rogers jumped up and demanded his surrender, at the same time pulling his pistol. The startled man grabbed hold of Rogers' gun, crying out for help, while at the same time drawing a knife, he attempted to stab Rogers. As the two men struggled, Putnam, seeing that Rogers was in trouble, rushed from his hiding place and struck the man a blow on the head, killing him.

Rogers promptly scalped him. It is likely that Rogers' gun discharged during the scuffle, which took place in plain view of the fort, as the alarm was raised. Rogers and his party quickly retreated without a prisoner. The Rangers traveled south toward Ticonderoga, where they observed an estimated two thousand of the enemy encamped there. After that, they retrieved their canoes, and all returned safely to the encampment at Lake George during the evening of October 21.[25]

On October 29, Rogers led another scouting party to spy on the French activity near Ticonderoga. The party included about thirty-two men in four bateaux, each mounted with two wall pieces, large-caliber smoothbore muskets. Once again, Putnam was included. On the night of October 31, as the party approached the lower end of Lake George, they saw in the distance flickering campfires on a point of land jutting out from the west side of the lake and pulled their bateaux upon the shore for the night.

The next morning, while he waited with the main body, Rogers sent Putnam and two others, Lt. Robert Durkee from Windham, Connecticut, and Capt. John Fletcher, to reconnoiter the enemy camp. Fletcher returned to report that he had seen four tents and the remains of numerous campfires. Putnam and Durkee continued the scout in the direction of Ticonderoga. In the meantime, Rogers sent Captain Fletcher back to Fort William Henry with a report to General Johnson, along with a request for reinforcements. Fletcher took with him one bateau with thirteen men, six of them too ill to continue. Not content with Fletcher's report, Rogers took a bateau and five men to see for himself. There he discovered a small log fort, palisaded on three sides and open along the lakefront. After Rogers had returned safely to camp, he learned that Putnam and Durkee had not yet reported back.[26]

Meanwhile, Putnam and Durkee pressed on toward the French camp and waited until dark when they could get a closer look than had Rogers and Fletcher. Unlike the British, the French sentries maintained their posts outside the circle of light thrown off by the campfires. Wanting to get a better look at the camp, Putnam crawled slowly through the underbrush until he came within fifteen feet of an alert sentry, only to be discovered, no doubt, with the rustle of leaves or the snap of a twig. The sentry quickly raised the alarm and shot wildly in the direction of Putnam and Durkee. The dark woods quickly exploded in a cacophony of shouts, whoops, and musket fire. Both men were by now in full flight in the darkness, zigzagging to avoid looming trees and jumping over fallen logs.

At some point Putnam turned to fire on his pursuers but lost his balance, and, in the darkness, toppled into an open claypit, the bottom of which had several inches of standing water, which soaked both him and his firelock, making it unusable. Durkee, who had been close by, tumbled in on top of Putnam, who mistook his friend for one of their pursuers. As he instinctively raised his hatchet to strike, Putnam recognized Durkee's voice, who was just as surprised to find himself in the hole and must have uttered a curse. Both men crawled out of the pit and continued their retreat, finally finding cover behind a large fallen tree. Putnam offered Durkee a swig of rum from his canteen, only to find it empty, having been perforated by several bullets. Both men laughed. It was a small price to pay. He would later find that his blanket roll had been pierced by fourteen bullets. The pursuit finally ended for the night, and the forest became still. Wet and cold, the two Rangers spent the night huddled together in fitful sleep.[27]

In the morning, the French pursuit was renewed, and Putnam and Durkee ran as fast as they could back to Rogers' camp, the enemy close on their heels. Now, with knowledge of the location of Rogers' camp, the French and their Native allies quickly formed a plan to attack it from both the water and the land, and it could well have succeeded, but for a breathless Putnam issuing his warning.

Rogers' plan was bold: Row out to meet the waterborne threat first, making use of the two wall pieces, while Putnam defended the camp. Rogers decoyed the French toward the shore, where they received a "galling fire" from both his wall guns as well as from Putnam and his men. The plan worked. After the remaining enemy boats were in retreat, Rogers returned to the shore and, with Putnam, drove off the remaining French. However, realizing the recently augmented enemy force had overwhelming superiority, Rogers ordered his party back to the encampment at Lake George.[28]

Halfway back they met a flotilla of bateaux led by Capt. Roger Billings, who had been sent to relieve Rogers. After a brief discussion, it was decided to return to the encampment at Lake George, and, except for one wounded man, all arrived there safely on November 8.[29]

WINTER QUARTERS

Other than leading a scout two weeks later, Putnam's duty with the Rangers ended for the season. He was transferred back to Fort Edward and parted with Rogers and his Ranger company, who had remained behind at the nascent Fort William Henry. By mid-October, the weather had turned cold and rainy, with an occasional blast of early snow. Many of the Provincials, who lacked blankets and proper clothing, had become sick with fevers. The miserable men "grew more and more unruly" and close to mutiny. Some simply slipped out of camp and headed for home.[30]

Plans were made for a contingent of Provincial troops to remain behind to man Forts Edward and William Henry throughout the coming winter, while the remainder would be discharged and free to return home. Accordingly, in late November, a composite regiment was formed by drawing from the existing Massachusetts, Connecticut, New Hampshire, and Rhode Island troops, all of whom would serve under the command of Col. Jonathan Bagley of Massachusetts. His second-in-command was Col. Nathan Whiting of New Haven, Connecticut. On November 25, Putnam volunteered for the duty with that regiment, and he was appointed a captain of a company slated to remain at Fort Edward. Soon, he settled into the dull routine of the post that winter, boredom occasionally broken by a scouting mission.[31]

In April 1756, a party from Putnam's company was escorting Ebenezer Dyer of New Haven, the fort major and commissary, south toward Saratoga when they were ambushed and carried off into captivity. Hearing the report, Putnam led a relief force, which arrived one day too late. He later reported that the ground was littered with torn paper currency, in his words, "wholly made useless."[32]

Putnam's enlistment was slated to expire on May 30. However, early in the new year word reached him that the General Assembly was raising regiments for the upcoming summer offensive. In fact, in February 1756, that body had authorized four regiments, with a combined total of 2,500 men. Each regiment would have eight companies. Once again, Phineas Lyman would command the 1st Regiment, and Israel Putnam would command the 4th Company in that regiment. Contrary to most accounts, Putnam did not return home, but he conducted a recruiting drive from among his company at Fort Edward. The remainder of his new company was raised in Connecticut by his lieutenants, Thomas Gallup of Plainfield and George Crary (sometimes spelled Creary) of Voluntown. His company would later join him at Fort Edward.[33]

During Putnam's absence, Hannah gave birth to another child, a daughter Eunice, on January 10, 1756, and at its May Session, the Connecticut General Assembly voted to award Putnam fifty gold "Spanish-milled" dollars for his service as a Ranger and scout during the previous winter. After only his first campaign, the farmer from Pomfret had established a province-wide reputation for courage and service.[34]

CHAPTER THREE

The French and Indian War

The Long Haul

CHANGES (1756)

THE YEAR 1756 BROUGHT MAJOR CHANGES IN COMMAND. BEFORE HE himself was relieved, Gov. William Shirley appointed Maj. Gen. John Winslow of Massachusetts to overall command of the forces for the planned attack on the French post at Crown Point later that summer. General Lyman would be next in command. Lord Loudoun succeeded Governor Shirley in overall command, and his second-in-command was Maj. Gen. James Abercromby, an able administrator but, as it would turn out, an indecisive field commander. Also traveling with Loudoun was Brig. Gen. Daniel Webb. He, too, would prove to be an ineffectual leader. Abercromby arrived that summer with a contingent of British regulars.[1]

Given Rogers' success as a scout, his force was augmented, and he was authorized to raise new Ranger companies, including one led by his brother Richard. As a second lieutenant in his own company, Rogers chose another New Hampshire man, John Stark from Londonderry. Stark would prove to be an excellent choice.[2]

"BLOOD FLYING AT EVERY STROKE"

The effort to better integrate the Provincial forces with the British regulars meant that the former became subject to the Articles of War, including the harsh corporal punishment meted out for anything from desertion to trivial breaches of military discipline. Though the independent-minded Provincials must have bristled, relying upon their contract of service, nevertheless, such measures were regularly administered in

25

public at a whipping post erected for that purpose. Fifty lashes were not an uncommon punishment for sleeping on guard, up to hundreds of lashes, or even death for desertion. Other punishments included the wooden horse, where a man was made to straddle a narrow board for hours while heavy objects were tied to his feet. For many Provincials, it would be the first time such discipline was imposed.[3]

The gauntlet was particularly brutal, as described by Luke Gridley of Farmington, then serving as a private in Maj. Nathan Payson's company in Lyman's regiment. Daniel Bogue of Gallup's company had been caught sleeping on guard and was made to run the gauntlet between thirty men pummeling him at every step. The unfortunate soldier cried, "Lord, God have mercy on me," Gridley noted in his diary, with "blood flying [at] every stroke." The diarist added that, "this was a sorrowful sight."[4]

UP CLOSE AND PERSONAL

That summer the opposing forces played a deadly game of "cat and mouse," each looking for prisoners and information. Putnam was a "hands-on" type of leader, willing and able to perform any task he asked his men to do. As a case in point, after several sentinels from his company had been killed while on guard duty, Putnam himself took a turn at night watch. He remained alert, and his effort was not in vain, as he caught and killed the stealthy intruder, and the problem was solved, at least in the short run.[5]

His time was also spent training his company in the woodcraft that he had gained with Rogers during the previous year. It was war in a non-traditional sense, as it involved patience, stealth, endurance, and self-reliance; it was most often up close and personal. Putnam soon discovered that the training of inexperienced men could often be just as dangerous as being in a full-fledged fight.

One day, on orders from General Webb, Putnam took five men from his company into the woods to capture a prisoner and to teach them cover and concealment in the process. During the exercise, several of the group broke cover too soon and received a stern rebuke. Sometime later, two of the enemy passed along the trail, a French soldier with an Indian in the lead. Putnam started after the last man, fully expecting his men to follow. No doubt still smarting from the scolding, they did not, and this left him exposed. By the time he finally realized that he was alone, he had nearly caught up with the Frenchman, when he pointed his pistol and boldly demanded that the man surrender. The pistol misfired, and Putnam beat a hasty retreat, the Frenchman close upon his heels, at which time his men finally came alive. Seeing that he was outnumbered, the pursuer escaped into the woods. Putnam was so upset with his trainees that he struck them from consideration as Rangers.[6]

BACK WITH ROGERS

The summer of 1756 found Putnam back with Robert Rogers following an attack on a British supply train by a large body of French and Indians. The attack took place at Halfway Brook along the trail from Fort Edward to Fort William Henry, sometimes referred to as the "Upper Fort." The enemy escaped laden with their captured goods and headed for their bateaux, which were concealed at the narrow part of Wood Creek near where it joins South Bay. General Webb ordered Rogers to overtake the enemy before they reached Fort Carillon. Rogers, along with Putnam and a party of one hundred men, rowed most of the way down Lake George and then landed on the eastern shore, where they concealed their boats and left a small guard. The pursuers hastened overland to prepare an ambush on the banks of Wood Creek, anticipating that the enemy boats would pass by on their return to Fort Carillon. They did not have long to wait.

The enemy raiders, weighed down with their booty, were caught totally by surprise by the murderous fire from Rogers and his men. Some of the raiders escaped to nearby Fort Carillon and gave the alarm, while other boats were driven by the wind into South Bay and out of musket range. Now the tables were turned, and it became a foot race, as Rogers and his party ran back to where their boats were hidden. They reached the shore of the lake that night and were relieved to find no enemy waiting in ambush. Wasting no time, Rogers and his party launched their boats and rowed all night, reaching Sabbath Day Point on the western shore by the following morning. Meanwhile, the French had finally caught up with them, and the two groups collided in a small naval battle. Fortunately,

Rogers had brought with him two wall guns and two blunderbusses, and with their fire he was able to drive the enemy away. Afterwards, Rogers and Putnam returned to Fort William Henry, having sustained the loss of only one man killed and two wounded.[7]

"BLUNT AND STURDY" (FALL 1756)

The anticipated attack on Crown Point was postponed after it was learned that the critical supply depot of Fort Oswego and its outlying posts, located in western New York where the Oswego River enters Lake Ontario, was lost when the garrison was overwhelmed in mid-August by an attack directed by the Marquis de Montcalm and a three-thousand-man force made up of French regulars and Canadian Militia, along with their Indian allies. Montcalm had promised to provide safe conduct for the British and Provincial soldiers. However, in a grim foreshadowing, to his mortification as an honorable soldier, Montcalm's Indian allies killed several dozen of the English garrison, including the helpless wounded, and carried off many more to Canada as prisoners to be exchanged for ransom. One of the latter was Col. Peter Schuyler of the New Jersey Blues. By coincidence, Brigadier General Webb was leading a contingent of reinforcements for Fort Ontario when, halfway there, he learned about the loss of the post. He simply turned his troops around and marched them back to Albany. Afterward, Montcalm returned to Fort Carillon at Ticonderoga, where he continued the task of strengthening the works there.[8]

In early October, General Winslow, who was visiting Fort William Henry, ordered Putnam to conduct a scout near Fort Carillon and report to him the current state of the works there. Putnam and six men rowed a whaleboat partway down Lake George about ten miles above Sabbath Day Point. Hiding their boat on the eastern shore, Putnam and his Rangers proceeded on foot to the vicinity of Ticonderoga, where they climbed a mountain (later called Mount Defiance) that had a clear view of the fort. Putnam took detailed mental notes of the French fort and its outposts. Briefly crossing over to the other side to get a closer look, he and his party very nearly caught three French soldiers, who barely escaped capture by fleeing through the gate. Putnam and the Rangers returned to Fort William Henry, where he made his report. General Winslow praised

Putnam's actions and for the thoroughness of his report, calling Putnam a "man of strict truth" and entirely trustworthy. Throughout the rest of the fall, Putnam and his company conducted similar scouts.[9]

GARRISON DUTY

Once again, by November the fighting season was over. Most of the British regulars were sent to winter quarters in Philadelphia, Boston, or New York. In New York and Philadelphia, local leaders balked at the quartering of troops, acquiescing only after coercive threats by Loudoun. The Provincial troops, their enlistments over, were sent home. Putnam returned home at this time after more than a year away from his family. A small contingent of regulars, however, was held over to garrison both Forts Edward and William Henry during the winter. At his headquarters in Albany, Lord Loudoun made his plans for the following year. As part of that process, he sent a request to the colonial governors for a new levy of 4,000 troops, of which Connecticut was expected to furnish 1,400.[10]

SPRING 1757

In February 1757, in anticipation of a renewed attack on the French posts in New York, the Connecticut General Assembly authorized the enlistment of 1,400 men to be part of a single regiment consisting of fourteen companies. Once again, Maj. Gen. Lyman was placed in overall command. However, five of the companies under the command of Lt. Col. Nathan Whiting were sent to man the Fort at Number 4 on the Connecticut River. The other nine companies, under Lyman, were sent to Fort Edward. Spring found Captain Putnam and his company back at Fort Edward in advance of the anticipated fighting. His company (4th Company) was part of General Lyman's regiment. Also at the fort then was a tall, thin, dark-haired sixteen-year-old recruit from Ashford in Capt. John Slapp's 8th Company by the name of Thomas Knowlton. He would go on to serve in the following five campaigns, rising from the ranks to the grade of second lieutenant, before eventually returning to his family farm.[11]

For the time being, Lord Loudoun's primary focus was on what turned out to be an abortive attempt to capture the fortress at Louisbourg on Cape Breton Island, while at the same time, Montcalm had other plans closer to Fort Carillon. In the interim, in addition to a wound to his hand that would not heal properly, in late January, Rogers contracted scurvy and spent the next several months in Albany recuperating in a military hospital, where he caught smallpox. When Rogers had sufficiently recovered, Loudoun ordered him and three companies of his Rangers to accompany his expedition to Nova Scotia. Rogers' absence during most of 1757, and the death of his brother Richard from smallpox, meant that Webb would be increasingly reliant upon the Provincial Ranger companies like Putnam's for intelligence.[12]

PUTNAM'S RANGERS

On Thursday, May 19, 1757, on the west side of the Hudson, seven Indians came across a young boy hunting pigeon. They immediately gave chase with the intention of killing and scalping him. Nearby were one hundred Dutch carpenters, who, frightened by the Indians, stood by and watched the scene play out, swinging their hats to catch the attention of the soldiers across the river. Finally, one of their number went to the boy's aid, and the Indians, seeing the other men, gave up the chase. However, enough of a concern was raised to send Putnam and his Rangers, along with thirty men drafted from Maj. Nathan Payson's 3rd Company, to cross the river to guard the carpenters.[13]

Prior to his death, Richard Rogers had met with Lord Loudoun in Boston and convinced him to increase the size of Ranger companies to one hundred men. In late May, Putnam began to recruit men to augment his company of Rangers, starting with men from his own company of Provincials, including his first lieutenant, George Creary (sometimes spelled Crary), with the rest drawn from several other Connecticut companies. The balance of Putnam's 4th Company, approximately sixty men, remained under the day-to-day command of 2nd Lt. Samuel Porter and Ens. Benjamin Hayward.[14]

In early June, there were reports of a large body of French in the vicinity of Fort William Henry. On June 6, 1757, Putnam and his Rangers, along with several men from Maj. Nathan Payson's company, set off on a scout near "The Narrows" on Lake George. Meanwhile, on June 10, while Putnam was away, a large party of French and Indians attacked a work detail a short distance outside Fort Edward and captured four men from Connecticut. General Lyman himself led the pursuit with a small party of about twenty men. After an eight- to ten-mile chase, he finally caught up with the attackers and fired upon them, but they managed to escape with their prisoners. Lyman returned to Fort Edward with some weapons and other equipment discarded by the fleeing French and Indians, in addition to some captive Mohawk allies that he had freed.[15]

On June 15, a regiment of eighteen hundred Provincials from Massachusetts under the command of Col. Joseph Frye encamped at Fort Edward following a six-week journey. The forty-seven-year-old Frye, from Andover, was a veteran and considered a "capable and competent officer." He had served as an ensign in a Provincial regiment during the Louisburg campaign in 1744–1745, and with the outbreak of the French and Indian War, he rejoined the ranks, serving with John Winslow at Kennebec in 1754 and with William Shirley in Nova Scotia in 1755–1756.[16]

One of the soldiers in Frye's regiment, then serving in Capt. Ebenezer Learned's company, was a tall, nineteen-year-old private from Brookfield, Massachusetts, by the name of Rufus Putnam, a distant cousin of Israel Putnam. Whether they had met before is uncertain; however, the fact that the younger man refers to the elder in his diary indicates that they at least knew of each other. In time, despite the twenty-year difference in ages, they and their families would develop a strong relationship that endured through future war and peace.[17]

Putnam returned to Fort Edward from his scout with a French prisoner in tow on June 16. When he was interrogated, the prisoner told Putnam that the four captives had been taken to Fort Carillon and the French had lost seven men in the skirmish. In addition, he told him the French had two battalions of regulars at Carillon and that the main army was at Fort Saint Frédéric (Crown Point).[18]

By Saturday, June 25, Putnam and his Rangers were back in action when they were ordered to reconnoiter the area around Wood Creek Falls (present-day Whitehall, New York) and South Bay and to intercept any enemy scouting parties. He and his roughly sixty-man party left Fort Edward that morning. There was a steady rain that afternoon, and the night turned cold. The rain continued the following day, adding to the misery. The bad weather finally let up. In the interim, Putnam sent fifteen men too ill to fight back to Fort Edward. Unsure if their provisions would last, he took a calculated risk and shot a deer. In time, his patience was rewarded.[19]

During the clear, moonlit night of Thursday, June 30, Putnam and his remaining forty-plus men lay in wait for the enemy behind a rough stone barrier, thirty feet long and camouflaged with brush, that they had constructed along a low ledge above the shore of Wood Creek, just north of its juncture with South Bay. Earlier that same day, a large party of more than two hundred Indians, mostly from the upper Midwest, along with ten Canadians and two dozen Abenaki and Caughnawaga scouts, led by the well-known partisan leader Joseph Marin, left Fort Saint Frédéric at Crown Point and rowed south. Their canoes glided smoothly along Wood Creek close to the shore, unaware of the ambush that awaited them. Sometime between ten and eleven o'clock that night, as the party neared Putnam's position, a careless Ranger, in anticipation of the fight, accidently brushed his firelock against a rock, breaking the eerie silence. Putnam ordered his men to open fire.[20]

At first, the sudden volley of buckshot caught the enemy by surprise, but given the size of the raiding party, many turned their canoes and started to row toward shore, all the while firing back. The Rangers' fire, while effective in preventing an immediate landing, could not prevent others from attempting to flank them from above and below and to cut off their avenue of retreat. Twice Putnam detached small parties, one led by Robert Durkee, to stave off these attempts; twice with success. However, by dawn, the third such attempt to overwhelm the Rangers was simply too large to stop.[21]

About 4:00 a.m., realizing that he was overmatched, Putnam ordered a retreat. At the same time, he left a fifteen-man detail behind to assist his three wounded to get away, but with a such large party of the enemy in pursuit, they were either unable or unwilling to do so and, after a short while, left their wounded comrades to their fate. On the way back, Putnam and his party crossed paths with another friendly scouting party of Provincials that had set out from Fort Edward two days earlier, who mistook them for the enemy and fired. A brisk firefight ensued. One of the

Provincial officers cried out frantically that "they were all friends." It was too late to save one of Putnam's men, Elijah Sweetland, who was fatally wounded before the error was discovered and the shooting stopped. Putnam was so angered that he was said to have sarcastically retorted: "Friends or enemies, they all deserve to be hanged for not killing more when they had so fair a shot!" Putnam arrived at Fort Edward at seven o'clock that evening.[22]

Meanwhile, at noon on that same day, two of the men whom Putnam had detailed to help the wounded reached Fort Edward and explained the situation. General Lyman led a large relief force to aid Putnam and to recover the three wounded men. They were disappointed to discover that two of the men had been carried off as captives and horrified to find the third, Henry Shuntup, likely a Mohegan Indian, scalped, horribly mutilated, and burned alive. The scene must have been jarring for many of the newer men, and it may well have dampened their enthusiasm for this type of soldiering. Lyman and his party returned four days later.[23]

Given the overall success of Captain Rogers, and the fame that came with it, the formation of six Provincial Ranger companies was officially authorized on July 5, 1757, including the one led by Putnam, thus confirming what had long been a fait accompli. The Ranger companies had already established their camp on Rogers Island, as had Putnam and his Provincials. Putnam had learned his lessons well, and in Rogers' absence he had proven himself to be a reliable and resourceful leader. Apart from Robert Rogers, no one held as high a reputation among the soldiers for daring and intrepidity than Israel Putnam, and he had no trouble enticing recruits to join him. That was not the case with some of the other companies. Initially, prospective recruits were enticed to join the more elite Ranger units with the promise that they would escape all other company duties except the admittedly dangerous duty of scouting. However, for many that simply was not enough, and, as a further incentive, an extra rum ration was offered along with $3.00 a month in pay. Although the rum was forthcoming, the money never was.[24]

Early on Wednesday, July 13, Putnam led a large, one-hundred-man scouting party from Fort Edward. Several hours later he sent a runner back to report to General Webb that he had sighted twenty-five of the enemy wading through a swamp about four miles from the fort. Later that morning, Putnam and his patrol returned empty-handed, the enemy having eluded their pursuit.[25]

FORT EDWARD—ATTACK ON A WORKING PARTY

One did not always have to go looking for trouble in the forests and glades of the upper Hudson River Valley; it quite often found you when you least expected it. That was the case when at about 8:00 a.m. on Saturday, July 23, a working party from Fort Edward was fired on by a party of about two hundred Indians, all within a quarter mile of the walls. Guarding the party was a small contingent of British regulars. Following the initial confusion, the first on the scene to come to the relief of the beleaguered detail, many of whom had scattered into a nearby swamp, was a company of Provincials led by Capt. Ebenezer Learned, which quickly engaged the enemy. Next to arrive was Captain Putnam with his Ranger company, who first had to cross the pontoon bridge spanning the channel separating the main fort on the east bank from their encampment on Rogers Island.

The fighting was desperate, but the defenders were determined, and the tide soon turned. When the attackers withdrew to the swamp and resumed their firing, Putnam led a charge and put them to flight. As a result of the fight, more than a dozen men had been killed, several more were wounded, and one was missing and presumed captured. After viewing the dead for the first time, a private in Learned's company observed: "This was the first sight I had of Indians' butchering, and it was not very agreeable to the feelings of a young soldier. I think there are few if any who can view such scenes with indifference." Later that day, at the head of three companies, Putnam followed the trail for ten miles as far as the former site of Fort Anne, where they found the remains of a large camp with five or six hundred of the enemy. Putnam was aggressive, but at the same time he was a cautious leader. As he was about to return to Fort Edward with the main body, as a precaution, he ordered his cousin Rufus and two others to hang back and follow the Indian trail for a short distance to make sure that the raiders had not backtracked.[26]

The Tragedy at Fort William Henry

If it seemed to some that Loudoun and Abercromby had chosen to ignore the situation in New York, Montcalm certainly did not. That summer, he planned a campaign to capture both Forts William Henry and Edward in that order. At that time, Fort William Henry was garrisoned by a mix of approximately eleven hundred regulars and Provincials under the command of fifty-seven-year-old Lt. Col. George Monro of the 35th Foot, a career officer with limited field service. Monro was understandably nervous, as he well knew that his command was a likely target for an imminent French attack. An earlier attack in March had failed because the attackers brought no cannon, and the defense of the fort was expertly overseen by its designer, Maj. William Eyre. Monro was certain that Montcalm would appear with overwhelming numbers this time. He was right.[27]

Fort William Henry consisted of two fortified sections separated by a swampy area over which there was a small bridge linking them. The main fort was a more typical structure situated on a low plateau nearer the lake, with gravel embankments surmounted by a log rampart and bastions at all four corners. The second was an earthen enclosure, called the "Retrenched Camp." It was situated on a nearby hill called Titcomb's Mount and was the larger of the two. The complex was not an easy one to defend.[28]

Monro wanted to be proactive and forestall an attack on his post, or at the very least, have an advance warning. Accordingly, in addition to some smaller scouting parties, in late July, he sent a large scouting party up Lake George composed of about four hundred New Jersey Provincials ("New Jersey Blues") in about two dozen bateaux under the command of Col. John Parker. On Saturday, July 23, that force was ambushed and virtually wiped out by a large party of French and Indians near Sabbath Day Point on the western shore of Lake George. It was a bitter prelude to worse things to come.[29]

On July 25, General Webb traveled to Fort William Henry, escorted by a two-hundred-man contingent led by Captain Putnam. Webb wished to see for himself the state of the garrison. While there, Webb sent Putnam on a daring daylight scout down Lake George. Putnam soon returned with word of some French troops on an island, but more important, that a large waterborne body was rowing toward Fort William Henry. Webb gave the order to Putnam to prepare to return to Fort Edward. Sensing Webb's reluctance to meet the enemy, the aggressive Putnam asked the general directly, did he intend "to neglect so fair an opportunity of giving battle should the enemy chose to land here?" Webb replied, no doubt with a shrug: "What do you think we should do here?" Webb and his party set out from Fort William Henry on July 29, accompanied by Col. James Montresor, an engineer, and they arrived at Fort Edward the following day. On the same day that Webb left Fort William Henry, at Monro's direction, "all of the carpenters and bateaux men in the camp set out to work at Lake George" to strengthen the defenses.[30]

Before parting from Lt. Col. Monro, Webb promised to come to his aid in the event of an attack. Once back at Fort Edward, he had second thoughts and instead ordered Colonel Frye and 823 Massachusetts Provincials, along with 100 Royal Americans led by Lt. Col. John Young and Capt. Rudolphus Faesch and an equal number of Independents from New York under Capt. Charles Cruikshanks, to Fort William Henry to bolster the garrison there. Frye set out on the morning of August 2 and arrived at Fort William Henry at sunset that same day. Too late, in fact, to set up a proper camp except for a couple of tents, so most of the men wrapped themselves in their blankets and slept on the bare ground. A slower contingent hauling five whaleboats arrived even later. In addition to the reinforcements, a small contingent of specialized troops and eight field pieces had already been sent ahead under the command of Capt. William McLeod of the Royal Artillery. Upon his arrival, Monro ordered Frye to occupy Retrenched Camp with him.[31]

Early the next morning, the English awoke to the sight of the approaching French flotilla of more than three hundred boats, which had been first spotted by Putnam several days earlier. Montcalm began the siege on August 3 with a demand for surrender that was quickly rejected by Monro. Over the course of the next six days, Montcalm gradually brought pressure to bear upon the fort by daily increasing the number of artillery batteries, including from cannons mounted on platforms on boats lashed together. That day at Fort Edward, cannon fire could be heard from Fort William Henry, fourteen miles away, a clear sign that the attack had begun. Rogers was still in Nova Scotia with Lord Loudoun, and Webb relied upon Putnam, who sent out three small scouting parties. Two of Putnam's scouts were able to enter the beleaguered fort and return with firsthand information.[32]

Over the next several days, Monro also sent runners to Webb describing the situation at the lake. Webb sent communications in reply. Not all messengers would arrive safely, as the French and their Indian allies had effectively blocked the road to Fort Edward. One letter in particular, a message from Webb to Monro dated August 4, suggesting that he consider a surrender, was taken from the body of a dead Ranger the following day, and two days later, at Montcalm's direction, shown to Monro, who then knew that no help would be forthcoming. On August 3, Monro sought to test the effectiveness of Montcalm's cordon, and he sent out a one-hundred-man detail under Capt. Richard Saltonstall of the Massachusetts Provincials, which was quickly overpowered and forced to retreat after sustaining the loss of eighteen dead and several wounded.[33]

To the consternation of all, including Putnam, Webb did nothing further to help lift the siege. According to Sgt. Jabez Fitch Jr., many of the soldiers at Fort Edward were "extreme[ly] resolute to go to relieve our people, but never could by any means get orders." Webb used the excuse that he first needed reinforcements from the various colonial governments. Just days earlier, he had written to the respective governors asking for more troops. This was patently hypocritical, since there was no real chance that the messages would even reach the governors in time, let alone for the legislatures to act.[34]

Amid the crisis, on Saturday, August 6, 1757, Brig. Gen. George Augustus, Viscount Howe ("Lord Howe"), then serving as Lt. Gen. James Abercromby's deputy, arrived at Fort Edward from Boston. The thirty-four-year-old Howe was a very brave and capable young officer, a soldier's soldier, and he had become interested in the Ranger units that had been operating so effectively. European armies were familiar with the so-called *petite guerre* conducted by irregular units, and Howe was in America to view those that had been formed in order to adapt to fighting in the northern forests of America. As a result, in Rogers' absence, Howe spent much of his time on scouting missions with such Provincial Ranger companies as Putnam's, and the two men came to know each other well.[35]

In Webb's defense, he had, as a practical matter, done all that he could when he sent Frye and the other troops to Monro on August 2. To his credit, on August 8, Webb, along with Lord Howe and Colonel Montresor, surveyed the high ground just north of Fort Edward for suitable places to dig an entrenchment and set an abatis if Montcalm attacked them. Even so, by then, many soldiers had lost confidence in Webb and thought him a coward. As a result of Webb's inaction, some men deserted. Even Putnam's cousin Rufus had to be talked out of leaving. Finally, on August 9, no distant sounds could be heard, and all knew that Fort William Henry had fallen.[36]

"The Regiment was thereby tore to pieces."

During the siege, Montcalm focused most of his attention on the small fort and its 400- to 500-man garrison, pounding it relentlessly with artillery. The bulk of Monro's troops were in the Retrenched Camp and engaged their attackers with muskets and a few artillery pieces. At one point, Montcalm's troops threatened the water supply of the defenders. Monro promptly ordered one hundred Massachusetts Provincial troops under Captain Waldo to drive them away. Waldo was successful, but he was gravely wounded in the process. Over time, the siege began to take its toll, as one by one, Monro's overworked guns began to split open and, worse, explode, killing and maiming their crews. The number of dead and wounded began to mount. Moreover, it was clear that no further help would be forthcoming, and on August 9, Monro bowed to the inevitable.[37]

Montcalm recognized Colonel Monro's honorable defense, and in the European tradition, he allowed the defenders to march out with their colors under the safe escort of French soldiers. Unfortunately, Montcalm's Indian allies were not satisfied, particularly those who had been recruited from the Great Lakes region with promises of plunder. Fearing that the French had deceived them, they began to loot and menace the Massachusetts troops in the entrenched camp. The French suggested appeasement by giving them their packs and other baggage, but that proved insufficient. At first, Monro suggested that they leave the fort that night, before further and, perhaps, worse damage was done. That idea was rejected when it was learned the Indians had plans to attack the convoy in such event.

Accordingly, on the morning of August 10, the defenders were ordered to form ranks, regulars in front, followed by the Provincials, and then the women and children at the rear. Understandably anxious to begin with, the soldiers in the stationary column became agitated when the Indians began to strip them of their clothing and personal effects. All Black soldiers and Indian allies were immediately taken from the ranks as prisoners. The slaughter itself began at the back of the column among the women and children. Many were killed and scalped right in front of the French soldiers, most of whom stood by and watched, unmoved. Concern turned to outright panic as the rear of the column pushed forward to escape the carnage. Some of the guards shouted to the English to flee to the relative safety of the woods. Many of those who failed to flee or who had not already been killed were carried off into captivity as slaves or for later ransom before order could be restored. The ragged remainder were marched off toward Halfway Brook under the protection of the French, where they were turned over to a waiting British escort.[38]

At Fort Edward, Webb ordered the signal gun be fired at intervals so that, hopefully, those wandering in the woods could orient themselves. Most of those who fled, including Colonel Frye, ultimately made their way to Fort Edward after days of aimless wandering, tired, delirious, hungry, and barely clothed, some stark naked. Back at Fort William Henry, by the time some semblance of order had been restored, there were hundreds of casualties, including 185 dead and between 300 and 500 captives. Over the course of the next year or so, many of these would be returned through purchase or exchange. As for Lt. Col. Monro, he, too, survived the massacre only to die suddenly in Albany three months later. Later, "A brief Account of the Military Services of Joseph Frye," written by the colonel himself, or perhaps his son or grandson, aptly summed up the tragedy at Fort William Henry by commenting that, "the Regiment was thereby tore to pieces."[39]

The stories of the "massacre" grew with the telling, and, as bad as it was, it was nowhere near the extent of the exaggerated tales. In fact, when word reached Montcalm that the killing was taking place, he personally intervened to restore order and sent his disgruntled Indian allies away from the scene. In addition, some fortunate officers were hurried off to the safety of the fort by compassionate French soldiers. Furthermore, Montcalm took the time to write to General Webb that he had organized another escort to meet their counterparts at the halfway point to safely deliver the survivors. Webb placed Fort Edward on alert, anticipating an attack by the French, which ultimately did not happen.[40]

In the aftermath of the attack on Fort William Henry, the inhabitants of Fort Edward were understandably on edge, knowing that they would likely be next. On the morning of Sunday, August 21, Putnam led a contingent on a long scout to the area around Ticonderoga to check out any French activity. Accompanying him were Lt. John Durkee and Ens. Eleazer Tracy. He and his party approached the site of Fort William Henry shortly after the last of the French had departed. They were shocked by the extent of the devastation. Aside from the still smoldering ruins of the fort, worse yet was the sight of the unburied bodies of the men, women, and children who had been slaughtered in a most horrible manner and left to the animals and the elements. One soldier viewing the scene shortly after the massacre thought Webb lacking in humanity when "he took no care to bury the men butchered . . . or seek after the wounded should there be any lying among the dead." On August 26, some of Putnam's men brought back a British deserter, and the following day four more of his men, two of them sick, returned and reported that they had found "no signs of French or Indians" in the vicinity of Ticonderoga. Montcalm had retreated to Crown Point. Fort Edward was safe for the time being.[41]

Putnam returned with the main body to Fort Edward on August 30, still without having sighted any of the enemy; however, he had to leave behind one of his party, a Black man who had become ill and unable to travel. He did leave two Indian allies to watch him while he recovered enough to travel, but they also abandoned him when they became frightened by the appearance of some French soldiers and ran away. A search party later brought the man in on September 3. On September 20, Major Rogers finally returned to Fort Edward with his Rangers, having spent the summer with Lord Loudoun in Halifax, Nova Scotia.[42]

ANOTHER WINTER AT FORT EDWARD

On October 13, Putnam and several other officers went hunting, and they returned with nine deer and a bear. Four days later, on Major Rogers' orders, Putnam sent seven of his men on an eight-day scout.[43]

When Loudoun himself returned to Fort Edward on November 7, 1757, he discharged the bulk of the Provincial troops. Although their enlistments did not expire until the following March, they were, no doubt, happy not to spend the winter in northern New York. Loudoun did, however, demand that Governor Fitch leave behind a contingent of 280 Rangers, culled from the ranks of the Connecticut troops at both Fort Edward and the Fort at Number 4, and Israel Putnam was designated to command the contingent remaining at the former. To that end, on November 9, on orders from General Lyman, twelve men were selected from those troops slated to go home to fill the quota. Those who volunteered were allotted a bonus of three pounds, and those drafted were given thirty shillings. Each of these payments was on top of their normal wage. In addition, the men were to be provided "suitable cloth and coating, duffield blankets, good flannen shirts, yarn hose, and good shoes" for the winter service.[44]

Lieutenant Colonel William Haviland of the 27th Foot was in command of Fort Edward that winter. He was a stickler for discipline and entered orders strictly prohibiting the theft of firewood or vegetables from the post garden on Rogers Island, threatening punishment of the "utmost severity." His command included the Rangers on Rogers Island, and he was unwilling to make allowances when those special troops exhibited unruly behavior. One day, a group of Rangers turned into a small mob, cut down the whipping post on the island, and stormed the guardhouse, demanding the release of two of their own being held there on Haviland's orders. Quick action by their officers, John Stark and Charles Buckley, stopped the near mutiny in its tracks. Informed of the incident, Haviland ordered Rogers to seize the ringleaders. He did so, and six Rangers spent the night in the guardhouse awaiting the inevitable imposition of discipline.[45]

Aside from one or two scouting missions, the normally dull routine of garrison duty was suddenly disturbed during the early evening of

December 25, when a large fire started in the barracks near the northwest bastion, which quickly spread toward that part of the fort that contained the powder magazine some twelve feet away. At that time, Putnam and his Rangers were in their encampment on Rogers Island opposite the fort proper. When he received word of the fire, he rushed quickly to the scene, and, taking charge of the bucket brigade, he mounted a ladder leaning against the barracks and poured bucket after bucket of water and snow on the flames. For more than an hour, Putnam's efforts to put out the fire went above and beyond, and it inspired Haviland and the other men to redouble their efforts. Although successful, because of his continuous proximity to the flames, Putnam suffered serious burns on his hands and other parts of his body. He spent two weeks in quarters recuperating. No doubt Haviland had a better appreciation for Putnam and the Rangers that night.[46]

In addition to the usual winter hardships endured in northern New York, the Hudson River normally overflowed during a late winter or early spring thaw, flooding two-thirds of Rogers Island, including the Ranger encampment, thus adding to the collective misery. This winter was no exception. On January 3, the river overflowed, flooding some huts waist-deep with water. Many of the huts filled with mud and silt, and the outhouses were carried away. The water did not begin to recede until January 6. That day, Putnam and some other officers went hunting again to supplement their rations.[47]

On a cold, snowy January 10, 1758, Putnam asked Sgt. Jabez Fitch to come to his quarters. He was taking a short leave of absence to go back home, and he needed the young man to handle some paperwork before he left. His business done, Putnam dismissed Fitch, and he set out to cross the Hudson to bring the men who had been on a detail at the brick kilns back to Fort Edward. However, he was unable to do so as the ice flows were too thick.

Putnam left Fort Edward for home two days later, bearing letters for Sergeant Fitch's father and brothers who lived nearby in Norwich, Connecticut. Putnam returned to Rogers Island by February 21; at which time he handed Fitch a letter from a friend back home. He also returned to find the soldiers very discontented and ready to go home. At roll call that evening, Putnam tried to calm the roiling waters, telling the assembly about the support of the Connecticut authorities for the war effort that he had found during his recent visit. According to Sergeant Fitch, the talk only "increased their rage."[48]

Lieutenant Colonel Haviland ordered Putnam to reconnoiter the area around Ticonderoga in advance of a large strike on Fort Carillon that had already been planned by Rogers. On February 28, Putnam set out from Fort Edward at 1:00 p.m. with a large party consisting of 115 officers and men. They came within eight miles of the French works at Ticonderoga, when Putnam sent out several smaller scouting parties. One of those parties reported that they had sighted six hundred Indians encamped at Ticonderoga. Putnam and his party returned to Fort Edward several days later and Putnam made his report. Unfortunately, along the way, one of his men deserted to the French. Rogers expressed concern that since the details of his large upcoming raid were well-known throughout the camp,

Figure 3.   Putnam Homestead, Brooklyn, Connecticut
COURTESY OF MARILYN SHAY

the recent capture of the sutler to the Rangers and Putnam's deserter could well have compromised that mission.[49]

When spring came, Putnam was discharged, and he made his way home to Brooklyn.[50]

CHAPTER FOUR

The French and Indian War

The Tide Slowly Turns

THE KING'S SHILLING

THE BRITISH WERE SLOW TO COME TO THE REALIZATION THAT 150 years and three thousand miles had brought about changes to their rough Provincial allies. The colonists were British citizens to be sure, but their experience was quite different from their cousins back in England. There were no press-gangs here, and, for the most part, men volunteered for duty, and, moreover, brought their own kit. True, some men hired substitutes, and at times, when the quota was not initially met with paid volunteers, bonuses were offered, and as a last resort, the levy. When their term of service was done, or in their minds the mission was over or the planting had to be done, men simply walked out of camp and headed for home. That was the contract.[1]

The Provincial soldier took umbrage at the application of the same harsh discipline imposed upon the regular British soldier as a matter of course. So, too, with the colonial governors and legislators. Used to debate, they bristled at the demand for troops and the quartering of regulars without so much as a please and thank you. Although they would be eventually reimbursed, the high cost associated with the levies was viewed as an unwanted burden on the citizenry. That burden fell heavily on New York and New England, particularly Connecticut and Massachusetts.[2]

The year 1758 would bring yet more change. The incoming Pitt government recalled Loudoun, leaving Abercromby in place for the time being. Aggressive plans were made to finally take both Louisbourg and Fort Carillon. The Pitt government also initiated some changes in its approach to the colonies. First, with an eye toward integrating the regulars and the Provincial troops, no longer would the provisions of the Proclamation of November 12, 1754, apply to the effect that the most junior regular officer outranked every Provincial officer regardless of grade. Hereafter, while a regular officer of equal rank would always outrank his Provincial counterpart, Provincial officers from the grade of colonel on down would outrank a British regular of lesser rank. This was logical, as many officers like Putnam had gained considerable experience fighting side by side with the British for the past three years.[3]

Second, appeals for troop levies would now be couched not as demands, but rather requests to the various governors and legislatures. This at the very least gave the appearance of deference. Despite the changes, the seeds of independence had been planted long ago; the British government simply did not fully appreciate the signs.

CONNECTICUT STRETCHES

In March 1758, the Connecticut General Assembly held their legislative session in New Haven. Among the items considered was the request for five thousand Provincial troops to take part in the upcoming campaign. In approving the request, Governor Fitch noted that it would further strain the colony's finances and manpower. The new levy was divided into four regiments with twelve companies in each. Putnam was assigned to 3rd Company in Col. Eleazer Fitch's Third Regiment. At the same time, he received a commission as a major. The troops began their trek to Albany, and then on to Lake George in late spring. Once again, while at Fort Edward, Putnam would form a Ranger company.[4]

TICONDEROGA

Summer brought a marked increase in activity from Albany to Fort Edward, as Maj. Gen. James Abercromby prepared for the launch of the long-awaited attack on Fort Carillon. It was expected that Lord Howe, his deputy, would direct the effort on the ground. To stage the attack, the general had assembled at a camp near the site of the former Fort William Henry some 6,000 regulars and 9,000 Provincials, along with 600 Rangers under Robert Rogers, engineers, and assorted support troops.

Included in that number were Major Putnam and his company, who had been ordered to the camp at Lake George.[5]

Sometime after midnight on July 5, the silent sea of canvas at the head of Lake George stirred slowly with signs of life, as sergeants and corporals roused the sleepy soldiers and ordered them to dress, pack their kits, and strike the tents. The sounds grew louder as breakfasts were hastily eaten. The heavier baggage had been loaded the night before, and at the same time, the men had been issued thirty-six rounds of ammunition each, as well as nine days of provisions, which they were ordered to boil. Louder still were the drums beating and the urgent orders barked by the officers, as the soldiers began to board more than a thousand whaleboats and bateaux.[6]

For the thirty-five-mile trip down Lake George, the large flotilla would be under the direct command of the quartermaster, Lt. Col. John Bradstreet. The forty-four-year-old Jean-Baptiste Bradstreet was born in Nova Scotia, and he had, from an early age, made the army his life. His driving ambition, combined with the good fortune to be favorably treated by both Governor Shirley and Lord Loudoun, brought him quick promotion. However, he could be quick-tempered and stubborn, and unafraid to speak his mind to power. Historian Francis Parkman described him as "a man of more activity than judgment, self-willed, vain, and eager for notoriety." More important, he was not a favorite of the troops. Rufus Putnam would later write that "the furious Bradstreet was hated by all the Army."[7]

The first units pushed off in the pre-dawn hours, and the embarkation was completed between 7:00 and 8:00 a.m. The armada reached Sabbath Day Point that evening, where it paused briefly for the men to stretch their legs and for the artillery barges to catch up, before continuing the journey throughout the balance of the night. The following morning, July 6, the flotilla reached a peninsular on the western shore, at the outlet of the lake, where it pours into the rapid-filled La Chute River. Before landing the army, a group of Rangers, including Putnam and Rogers, along with Lord Howe, were detached to reconnoiter the immediate area, and they easily drove off a small party of the enemy that had been observing from the shore. At that, Abercromby began to disembark his troops and made camp. In the process, they drove off an even larger French advance post nearby, which was vacated so hastily that some equipment was left behind.[8]

Meanwhile, in anticipation of just such an expedition, Montcalm was not idle. His many scouting parties brought him word of Abercromby's progress, and he was busy with his defensive preparations. Montcalm planned to block the only land approach to Fort Carillon with the erection of a massive breastwork on the slightly higher ground across the width of the neck of land on which the fort was built. The wall itself was built using felled trees laid end to end and on top of each other, to a height of eight feet or more. In front of the wall was an impenetrable tangle of the top branches of the felled trees, with the tips of the exposed branches sharpened, thus forming a natural abatis.

In short, the wall was virtually impossible to surmount or penetrate without artillery to blast gaps in it. Moreover, the ground in front of the position was now denuded and created a wide-open field of fire for the French. In addition, the French established fortified picket positions in front to keep British scouts from getting a close look, and they masked parts of the wall with "living trees and fir boughs entwined throughout its structure" to deceive any long-distance viewers. Amazingly, this defensive position was virtually all built within the space of two days. Montcalm placed his defenders behind this natural curtain wall and waited. He did not have long.[9]

A LOSS KEENLY FELT

Meanwhile, on July 6, Abercromby set his army in motion with Lyman and Fitch's Connecticut regiments in the lead, followed by the regulars and the remainder of the Provincials. Israel Putnam and a two-hundred-man contingent of his Rangers were in the vanguard of the main force. Lord Howe, who was Abercromby's second-in-command and the de facto leader of the expedition, accompanied Putnam. Rogers and a party of Rangers had already gone ahead on a scout to Bare Mountain (now Cook Mountain, elevation 1,213 feet), where they had an unobstructed view of the sawmill and French activities near Ticonderoga. Since the French had burned the bridge across La Chute that led to the established portage trail, Abercromby opted to traverse the heavily wooded western side of the La Chute River.

Abercromby's decision soon proved problematic. The woods were very thick, so dense in fact that even the Rangers had difficulty getting their bearings, and many units became intermixed. At the same time, by coincidence, a large contingent of 300 to 400 French and Indian scouts had been shadowing Abercromby, at least as far back as Roger's Rock on Lake George. They, too, had become hopelessly lost and soon found themselves between Lyman and Fitch's Provincials on the one hand and the main body on the other, which led to an inevitable clash. When the muffled sounds of gunfire could be heard through the forest, Howe told Putnam to face-about and that they needed to quickly get to the scene of the action. A hasty dialogue followed, where Putnam suggested that Howe remain where he was, as he would be too valuable to lose. The intrepid brigadier replied: "Putnam, your life is as dear to you as mine is to me; I am determined to go."[10]

Within minutes of his arriving at the fighting, Howe was shot dead. His loss was keenly felt throughout the army. The initial surprise gave the French an early advantage, but that was soon overcome by a coordinated charge by the Connecticut regiments, led by Putnam and his Rangers, along with a contingent of British regular light infantry led by Capt. James Dalyell. The victory was further marred by friendly fire, as more British and Provincial units pushed through the dense woods toward the fighting, and Putnam's men were mistaken for the enemy by some British regulars, resulting in several deaths. According to one account, the tension was so high that when a lone Indian war cry was heard coming from within the dense woods, it triggered an uncoordinated burst of firing all up and down the line. The firing stopped only after Putnam rushed head-long toward the source, bellowing, "cease fire" at the top of his lungs.[11]

That night the combatants "slept on their arms" in the woods where the skirmish had taken place. The French casualties were high, including about 167 officers and men, many of whom were wounded. In the aftermath, Putnam made it a point to personally tend to the wounded Frenchmen, and he gave them assurances that they would be well cared for. The following morning, as the prisoners were about to be marched back to the British camp, in sharp contrast to Putnam's kindness, one by one, Rogers calmly killed all the seriously wounded Frenchman who were "unable to help themselves." When he heard the report, Putnam was appalled. He would later tell Humphreys that both British and other Provincial officers who heard the news "were struck with inexpressible horror."[12]

Perhaps stunned by the loss of Lord Howe, as well as the sudden ferocity of the engagement, early the following morning, July 7, Abercromby withdrew the army to the camp at the outlet of the lake and regrouped. The events of the next day and a half would prove critical to Abercromby's decision to stage his attack on Montcalm's fortified position without benefit of artillery. At the morning officer's meeting, Bradstreet pressed Abercromby to let him take four thousand to five thousand troops to advance up the east side of the La Chute River to the sawmill at the falls to, in effect, conduct a reconnaissance in force. Anticipating Abercromby's assent, the aggressive lieutenant colonel had, on his own initiative during the night before, erected a bridge across the outlet from Lake George near the Portage Road. The general approved the plan, and Bradstreet set out late that same morning. His force consisted of the 44th Foot, six companies from the 1st Battalion of the 60th Royal Americans, Capt. John Stark's company of Rangers, along with two regiments of Massachusetts Provincials. He also had two small field pieces. After his command reached the damaged sawmill, Bradstreet's engineers rebuilt the nearby bridge, a critical link to Ticonderoga. Abercromby followed later that day with the rest of the army, including Lyman's Provincials.[13]

Later that same day, Abercromby's chief engineer, Lt. Col. Matthew Clerk (pronounced Clark), along with the general's aide, Capt. James Abercrombie of the 42nd Foot (no relation to the general), escorted by Capt. John Stark and a detail of Rangers, performed his own reconnaissance from the top of Rattlesnake Mountain (later called Mount Defiance). From that vantage point, some 850 feet high, he had a clear view of Fort Carillon across the outlet from La Chute, as well as the fortified wall that Montcalm's men were constructing. He made his report to Abercromby, who by late afternoon or evening had established his headquarters at the damaged sawmill. Lieutenant Colonel Clerk told the general that the works were still under construction. His report would have been at best incomplete or at worst, unintentionally misleading, due to Montcalm's efforts to camouflage the wall.[14]

The following day, July 8, Clerk conducted another reconnaissance. From the mountaintop the day before, he ascertained that if artillery could be properly sited, fire could be effectively directed upon the fortification in flank, making it more difficult for Montcalm to defend it. He must have convinced Abercromby to have four field pieces (two more had been brought forward on July 7 by Col. Nathan Whiting's 2nd Connecticut) loaded on rafts pulled by whaleboats or bateaux to the falls of the La Chute River. Unfortunately, the French guns spotted the attempt and drove the boats back before Clerk could situate the guns, and, worse, at some point during that day Lieutenant Colonel Clerk was killed.[15]

By July 8, Abercromby had received erroneous reports from French prisoners that Montcalm had a force of 6,000 men, with more on the way, when, in fact, he had only approximately 3,600, and no reinforcements coming. These false reports could well have created a sense of urgency in the general. Meanwhile, Bradstreet conducted his own reconnaissance that morning, crossing the La Chute River with another unidentified "foreign" engineer to get a closer look. In that engineer's judgment, an immediate attack was recommended, based upon the mistaken impression that the works were still not finished. It would have been in reliance upon this report, and not Clerk's, that Abercromby ordered an immediate attack, even though he had not brought up his artillery train. In doing so, he had chosen to ignore the warnings of Putnam and others who had scouted the area, and who had assured him that the fortifications were, in fact, complete.[16]

"THEY WERE THEIR OWN GENERALS"

Early on the morning of July 8, Abercromby ordered Phineas Lyman's regiment, along with a regiment from Massachusetts led by Col. Timothy Ruggles, to dig a breastwork near the sawmill in case the army was attacked from the rear. No doubt Putnam, anxious to get in the action, was disappointed at this turn of events. Meanwhile, Robert Rogers was ordered to probe the defenses, when his advance guard under John Stark was ambushed by about two hundred French. Rogers rushed forward with the rest of his Rangers, followed by some light infantry that had formed on his right flank and his bateaux men on the left. The three nearby Provincial regiments formed up in the rear. The French were driven off, and British pickets as well as grenadiers passed through Rogers' ranks. The fighting began in earnest, and the British soldiers quickly realized that the defensive position of the French was both high and solid.[17]

Starting between 1:00 and 2:00 p.m., the first wave of the main attack went forward without benefit of artillery to soften up the defenses. Again, Lyman and Fitch's regiments, including Putnam's Rangers, were at the front on the right flank, along with regulars, who actually bore the brunt of the initial attack, without making any appreciable headway. Abercromby ordered five successive assaults with the same result. As the day wore on, he began to feed the Provincials into the fight. About 3:00 p.m. it was the turn of Lyman's regiment. Clearly in his element, Major Putnam was everywhere, as he moved from unit to unit along the front, inserting men here and encouraging them there. The soldiers, both regular and Provincial, displayed tremendous courage throughout the day. During the last assault around 7:00 p.m., some soldiers had managed to partially cut their way through the breastwork in a few spots, but it was not enough.[18]

A participant that day was Capt. Charles Lee of the 44th Foot, an experienced, but opinionated young officer. Lee led his company forward that afternoon, passing through the ranks of a Provincial regiment, clambering over and through the treacherous abatis, and, resolutely, with bayonets fixed, marching directly into the hail of fire from behind Montcalm's defensive wall. "The fire was prodigiously hot," he wrote, "the slaughter of the officers very great, almost all wounded, the men still furiously rushing forwards." He continued: "For five hours they persisted in this diabolical attempt," before being forced to retreat in good order, despite their losses. He offered high praise, as much as a lament, for the conduct of his soldiers, saying, "they were their own generals."[19]

THE GRIM AFTERMATH

Two thousand dead and wounded littered the field when the order to withdraw was given. One Provincial soldier would later write that it was "the most injudicious and wanton sacrifice of men that ever came within my knowledge." Israel Putnam and his Ranger company helped to cover the retreat.[20]

Captain Lee himself was one of the casualties, knocked "senseless" when a bullet passed through his body, breaking two ribs in the process. He lay on the battlefield in great pain until his servant was able to carry him to safety. He would spend more than two months recuperating in a hospital at Albany.[21]

In his report to William Pitt, Abercromby was quick to unfairly place the blame for the defeat on Lieutenant Colonel Clerk, a convenient scapegoat, now that he was dead and could not defend himself. The general correctly told Pitt that he had sent Clerk to reconnoiter the entrenchments, however, that was on July 7, the day before the attack. The general went on to write that, "upon his return and favorable Report of the practicality of carrying those Works, if attacked before they were finished, it was agreed to storm them that very Day." Clerk was elsewhere on the morning of July 8, in a frustrated effort to locate a favorable spot to place his ordnance, clearly supporting the argument that he would not recommend a direct attack without some artillery in support. In the aftermath, the inaccurate story spread among the officers and men, all of whom had gallantly surged forward in the attack, and who would naturally have asked why their and their comrades' sacrifices had all been for naught. Even Captain Lee, no fan of Abercromby, passed the story on, calling Clerk a mere "Stripling who had never seen the least service." History has been unkind to Clerk, and the unfortunate officer's reputation has continued to suffer.[22]

It was a humiliated army that reached the English camp later that night. The troops, some angry, many demoralized, embarked the following morning for the head of the lake. They arrived there that evening. On August 1, at the camp at Lake George, an obviously discouraged Col. Phineas Lyman wrote a letter to his friend Col. Jonathan Trumbull back home in Connecticut. The failed attack behind them, and some half measures being taken for a further attempt, Lyman had his doubts. "I can't say my confidence of going forward is great," he wrote, "for I really fear I must again bear the mortification of returning to my friends

without a conquest over the enemy, but I hope to the contrary." He asked
his friend to keep these thoughts to himself, and that he would talk more
freely when he came home. He added a final observation: "I am sure that
nothing extraordinary can ever be expected in the way we are in, and I
think the governments are flinging away their money."[23]

A Close Call

In July following the return of the army from Ticonderoga, Putnam was
scouting the area along the Hudson River south of Fort Edward near
Fort Miller, a supply depot on the west bank. The area was called the
"Little Carrying Place" due to the impassable falls and rapids there that
required a portage. His party was separated into two small bands, one
on each side of the river. Putnam was on the east side above the rapids
when he was signaled from across the river that a large enemy party was
closing in on him. The decision was either to fight or to chance the rapids.
Putnam and his men chose the latter, and, without a moment to spare,
he and his men quickly pushed their boats into the swirling waters. All
but one of his party was able to get away, and that man, who had been
separated from the rest, was killed. The swift current soon carried them
well beyond the hail of bullets fired by their disappointed but astonished
pursuers. Although the descent was hair-raising, all the boats safely nav-
igated the roiling rapids. Once more on dry land downstream, Putnam
and his men no doubt breathed a sigh of relief, as the alternative could
well have been much grimmer.[24]

Back in the Ranging Service

On the morning of July 27, the French attacked and overcame a large
supply train along the road to Fort Edward, and, lingering just long
enough to consume a large quantity of liquor, they set off toward Ticonderoga loaded down with their plunder. Word reached Abercromby
at 9:00 p.m., at which time he ordered Rogers and Putnam to form a
large pursuit force. At 2:00 a.m., seven hundred men set out from their
encampment at Lake George, including Rogers' Rangers, Putnam's company of Provincials, and some regular light infantry under the command
of Capt. James Dalyell. Rowing bateaux twelve miles down the lake to

the Narrows, and then cutting east cross-country toward South Bay, they very nearly caught up with the raiders. However, the enemy had narrowly escaped, their campfires still warm. Meanwhile, other scouts had reported to Abercromby about a large French party operating in the vicinity of Fort Edward. Understandably anxious, Abercromby sent a messenger to Rogers, who reached him on July 31, with orders to deal with the threat. For a week, Rogers combed the area without incident. August 7 found his party camped at the site of the former Fort Anne. Frustrated with the lack of any contact with the French, a large number of the regular contingent were sent back to Fort Edward.[25]

"Putnam Leads"

Early on the morning of August 8, Rogers engaged in a shooting contest with one of the British officers. This was either an uncharacteristically rash breach of Ranger discipline or a shrewd gamble to draw out the French, which, in either event, it did. Later that morning Rogers divided his force, with Putnam and his contingent of Provincials in front, Dalyell and his regular light infantry in the middle, and his Rangers in the rear. They marched out of camp toward Fort Edward single file, in a mile-long column. Within a short distance, Putnam walked right into a hastily organized ambush by the well-known partisan Joseph Marin, his men disposed in a horseshoe, well-concealed by the heavy underbrush lining the trail.[26]

Once the firing commenced, Putnam sent word to Captain Dalyell to bring up his men in support, which he did promptly. The fighting was in Humphreys' words, "obstinate," and the tide of battle flowed back and forth several times. At some point early in the fighting, Putnam and a small group of his men became isolated, and he was overcome and captured by one of Marin's Indians. Without leadership, Putnam's men began to scatter, and the fighting became between individuals or small clusters. Meanwhile, his captor stripped Putnam of his shoes and outer garments, tied him to a tree, and returned to the fight. From time to time Putnam was taunted and threatened with death by both the French partisans and his captor, who repeatedly threw his tomahawk at the tree. At some point, one of his tormentors, a Frenchman, struck him in the jaw with his pistol butt in frustration after it had misfired. Worse, his captor cut him with his tomahawk, leaving a scar along Putnam's left jaw that he carried the rest of his life. During several stages of the fight, the prisoner wound up between the two sides, as bullets whizzed past him from all directions.[27]

In the end, Rogers held the field, as the French and Indians retreated in small groups with their captives, including Putnam, in tow, making it difficult to follow them. The French got the worst of the fight, losing approximately 169 killed, while the British losses were considerably fewer. Among the wounded in Putnam's Rangers were Lemuel Dean of Plainfield, Caleb Atwater of Wallingford, and Ens. Peter Wooster of Derby. The latter was wounded, scalped, and left for dead. Killed outright was Dana Benjamin Jr. Rufus Chapman of New London was captured and taken to Canada along with Putnam. He would later be redeemed.[28]

Although Putnam never did, some would later criticize Rogers for not coming quickly to Putnam's aid, but the fact remains that the latter was a mile behind, and Putnam was already a captive. Nevertheless, a saying arose that Putnam "dared to lead where any dared to follow."[29]

Prisoner of War

After his captors felt that they had traveled a safe distance from the battle, Putnam was stripped naked and tied to a large tree, where sticks and brush were piled at his feet and lit on fire, with the intention of burning him alive. No doubt thoughts of home and family flooded his mind as the smoke began to choke him and the flames scorched his skin. While he could not have known it, on the very day of his capture, his son Daniel, age seventeen, died at the family home in Brooklyn. But for the timely intervention of Marin himself, who kicked aside the burning brush and untied him, it would also have been the day of Putnam's own death.[30]

Perhaps sensing some unrest among his Indian allies, Marin directed his party to turn south toward Fort Carillon, which they had passed earlier. Once again, fate intervened to relieve Putnam of some of his suffering when a kindly Caughnawaga Mohawk chief compelled his captor to feed and minimally clothe him, at which time he was given moccasins and a blanket, and he was no longer made to carry heavy loads. At Carillon, he was brought before General Montcalm, who must have wondered why such a miserable wretch could command such a soldierly reputation. Montcalm ordered that Putnam be escorted to Montreal by a French officer. Thereafter, although he was still treated as a prisoner, he received food and water to sustain him during the long journey to Montreal. Each night he was bound tightly to prevent escape.[31]

Putnam arrived at Montreal dirty, unshaven, footsore, and all scratched up. He was taken to the home where Col. Peter Schuyler of New Jersey was being held as a prisoner. It was yet another stroke of good fortune. Schuyler was a wealthy member of a prominent family with connections to New York. After a shave and a bath, good food, and a clean bed, Putnam's spirits revived. He was given the liberty of the city. Soon, however, he was transferred to Quebec City.[32]

CHANGES AT THE TOP

The debacle at Ticonderoga would be cause for one more major change. In September 1758, Prime Minister Pitt recalled Major General Abercromby as commander in chief and replaced him with Maj. Gen. Jeffery Amherst. In a brief letter to the unfortunate general, Pitt's choice of words left no doubt about the loss of confidence in Abercromby: "The King saw, with much Concern, that an Enterprize of the greatest Importance, had unhappily miscarried, with so considerable a Loss of Brave Officers and Soldiers. At the same time, the great Spirit, with which the Troops shew'd in this unfortunate Attempt, gives the King just room to hope for future Successes."[33]

Before the word of his relief had reached Abercromby, the general would make a crucial decision, one that would, in time, affect Putnam. Shortly after the army's return to the camp at Lake George, Bradstreet convinced Abercromby of the necessity of seizing Fort Frontenac at the outlet of Lake Ontario, where it entered the St. Lawrence River. More important, he induced the general to let him lead the effort.

Accordingly, in late July, Bradstreet set out from Albany up the Mohawk River Valley with a force of 5,600 men, mostly Provincials, to rebuild a fort at the Great Carrying Place. It was there that the true purpose of his mission was revealed. The expedition reached Fort Frontenac on August 26, and Bradstreet quickly invested the works. The fort capitulated the following day, short on defenders but rich in stores. Bradstreet loaded his bateaux with what they could carry and destroyed the fortification. He returned to Albany. His thirst for glory unslaked, Bradstreet immediately lobbied Abercromby again, this time in vain, for permission to lead an expedition against Fort Niagara. Bradstreet was vocal in his criticism of that decision.[34]

The British scored another significant victory in 1758, as Fort Duquesne was abandoned and destroyed by the French on November 23, as a British army was within striking distance. The tide was certainly beginning to turn.[35]

Free at Last

With the capture of Fort Frontenac by Bradstreet on August 27, an opportunity was presented for the two sides to exchange prisoners. Abercromby authorized Colonel Schuyler to handle the negotiations with Governor Vaudreuil. To that end, lists of prisoners were compiled. Putnam was not originally on a list to be exchanged, but Schuyler was so taken by his story, he asked that Putnam be added to the list, and he even suggested that a younger, unmarried man be held back instead.[36]

Colonel Schuyler's efforts were successful. He had also taken under his wing a certain Mrs. Jemima Howe, widowed in an Indian raid on the Fort at Number 4 in 1755. She and her surviving children were taken into captivity in Canada. Mrs. Howe and three of her sons were placed in Putnam's charge for the homeward journey. The party and their French escort arrived at Fort Edward on November 11, 1758. From there, Putnam and the newly released prisoners parted ways and made their way back to their respective homes.[37]

In his absence, Israel Putnam had missed the death of his son Daniel, and the news must have tinged his return with a measure of sadness. Overall, he was happy to be back with his family again, much relieved that his ordeal was over. Certainly, there was much to do about his farm.

Call of Duty

The war dragged on, and it was clearly taking its toll on the citizenry and fiscal well-being of the colony of Connecticut. In a long letter to William Pitt acknowledging compliance with the demand for more troops for the upcoming campaign, Gov. Thomas Fitch outlined his current concerns: "It being also considered that the loss of men, and the disappointments with the last campaign not only had weakened the Government but seemed in some measure to have abated the vigor and spirit of the people . . . I beg leave also to acquaint you that the Colony could devise no means for answering the expense occasioned by the preparations for the ensuing campaign but having recourse to a further use of credit to the amount of sixty thousand pounds on interest in addition to their former debts, which were very great, and to laying heavy taxes on the people."[38]

Earlier, at its legislative session in March 1759, the Connecticut General Assembly had met at Hartford to consider the latest request for troops for the forthcoming campaign. Although stretched thin by previous losses, the delegates had voted to raise 3,600 officers and men and "gave further encouragements" or bonuses for 400 more. The troops were divided into four regiments, with ten companies in each. Each company would be made up of no more than 100 men. For men who had been in service during the past year, they were to receive pay retroactive to the previous December 1, and for new recruits, the sum of four pounds. If the ranks were not filled by April 16, all able-bodied men were to assemble and be subject to impressment. There would be no fixed term of enlistment. Rather, service was to be "no longer than is necessary for the ensuing campaign."[39]

The levy did not go as smoothly as hoped. Enlistments were slow in coming, not only in Connecticut, but also all throughout the Northeast. In May, the General Assembly voted to provide "encouragements" for the enlistment of an additional one thousand men. As a result, the bonus for new recruits was raised to seven pounds. Those able-bodied men who still declined to enlist could pay the sum of ten pounds to avoid service. The need to continue to offer bonuses was a clear indication that there were more concerns about meeting the quota, as it was already known that, over the winter, many veteran Connecticut Provincials had enlisted in the British army or with the regiments of other colonies.[40]

Parkman would later astutely observe that, "there were those among [the Rangers] for whom this stern life had a fascination that made all other existence tame." Despite the love of his family and farm, and his recent ordeal, Putnam must have loved the excitement and the action, as well as the soldierly comradery, more, as he enlisted once again. He was appointed a lieutenant colonel in Eleazer Fitch's Fourth Regiment and assigned to command the 2nd Company. His friend John Durkee of Norwich, with whom Putnam had served at Fort Edward during the previous winter, was appointed a major in the regiment and assigned to command the 3rd Company. Once again, Maj. Gen. Phineas Lyman would be in overall command of the Connecticut troops. As Putnam and his regiment set off for Albany, Hannah was pregnant with another child.[41]

THE FALL OF FORT CARILLON (JULY 26, 1759)

The fall of Fort Carillon was anticlimactic, as the bulk of the French forces had already withdrawn to Crown Point and farther north, leaving only a token force to temporarily hold the British at bay. However, this was unknown to Amherst at the time. Determined not to make the same mistakes as Abercromby, Amherst made careful preparations for a successful siege. In July, he began to assemble his army and an enormous stockpile of powder and stores in careful stages, moving from Fort Edward to the head of Lake George over a period of several weeks. At the same time, he began construction of a new fort near the site of the former Fort William Henry. The new fort would be called Fort George.[42]

By July 21, Amherst was ready. Between 2:00 and 3:00 a.m., the troops were awakened and ordered to strike tents, and two hours later the drummers beat "assembly." The first casualties of the expedition were two ten-inch mortars, sunk when the dock gave way under their weight. Anxious to start, Amherst left his artillery behind to catch up later, and at 6:00 a.m. he started his ten-thousand-man force forward. It was a mix of regulars and Provincials, along with nine companies of Rangers. It rained off and on throughout the day, adding a touch of misery to the already strenuous exercise. The army stopped for the night at the Narrows, midway down the lake, and it resumed its movement in the morning.[43]

After landing at the north end of Lake George, Amherst found the portage road blocked by numerous felled trees that had to be cleared, a task that Amherst found the "Provincials did vastly well." All along the route, danger lurked in the woods, and several unfortunate individuals who had strayed from the main body, as well as inattentive sentries, were killed or captured. Once opposite Fort Carillon, cannon were sited, fascines made, and trenches dug. At the same time, the sawmill that had been burnt the previous year was rebuilt.[44]

The attack commenced in earnest on July 23 and was over four days later, with virtually no loss of life, after Amherst had brought forward some artillery and commenced to fire at the fort. Sometime during the late evening of July 26 or early morning hours of July 27, the French blew up the magazine and abandoned Fort Carillon, and as they retreated to the northern end of Lake Champlain, along the way they also abandoned Fort Saint Frédéric (Crown Point). Sergeant Robert Webster of Eleazer Fitch's regiment noted in his diary that the French escaped from the fort as the fire lit up the night sky. The fire would burn for two days before it was finally extinguished.[45]

For Putnam and his company, the capture of Fort Carillon (Ticonderoga) and, a short time later, Fort Saint Frédéric (Crown Point) meant that duty at either would involve some scouting missions, but for the most part, would consist of work details to cut timber, make hay, plant gardens, and make repairs to the damaged Fort Ticonderoga, as well as the construction of a new fort at Crown Point, after it, too, had been partially blown up. He and his company arrived at the latter on August 4. By mid-August, Sergeant Webster noted in his diary that the men in the work detail were all well but exhausted. On August 9, Putnam was ordered to take a work party of 331 men, along with tents and four days' provisions, across the lake just after reveille and to establish a work camp. On August 22, Amherst visited Putnam at his post five miles down the lake to observe his timber-cutting operation. Otherwise, the Provincial soldiers remaining at Crown Point enjoyed the dull routine of camp life, the monotony of which was occasionally relieved with some fishing and hunting to supplement the usual army rations.[46]

The Beginning of the End

Fort Niagara surrendered on July 25, 1759, following a two-week siege. The British commander of the assault, Brig. Gen. John Prideaux, died a grisly death when his head was blown off as he stepped in front of a mortar just as it was being fired while he inspected the battery. The loss of the fort deprived the French of control of a vital portage and a key to the supply of its western posts. Of more significance, the French garrison at Quebec surrendered on September 18, 1759, and with that city in British hands, the fate of French Canada was sealed. Any further attacks were put off until the following year.[47]

An Infrastructure Project

Amherst also took measures to protect his supply line with the construction of a blockhouse at Half-way Brook. In addition, on August 8, he ordered a party of two hundred Rangers, led by Capt. John Stark, to start to rough out a new seventy- to eighty-mile road from Crown Point to the Fort at Number 4, located along the Connecticut River in Cambridge, New Hampshire. Built around 1740, that post was really a fortified settlement, where several farmers had joined their houses together with lean-tos and a log stockade for their individual protection and that of their small community. The stated purpose of the road was to "open a communication from the Massachusetts and New Hampshire governments to Crown Point." It would also shorten the distance that New England troops would have to travel coming and going. A month later, on September 9, Stark's detail returned from the Fort at Number 4, having measured the route and found it to be seventy-seven-and-one-half miles long. On October 26, Amherst sent a 250-man detail, "with proper tools," under the command of a Maj. John Hawks, along with Lt. John Small, to build the road. Later, a spur would be added connecting the road to Fort Ticonderoga.[48]

By late October, the weather took a turn for the worse, and the usual spate of illness turned into a serious outbreak of typhus or camp fever, as hundreds sickened and dozens died. The outbreak was so bad that on October 25 hundreds of men were transported to Fort Edward or the army hospital in Albany to be treated and hopefully recover. The remaining Provincials became restless, and even the daily rum ration was not enough to quell the growing call to go home. As a result, on November 1, a small number of New Jersey and Massachusetts Provincials staged mutinies, quickly suppressed by regular troops.[49]

When the term of their enlistments was up, Colonel Fitch's Fourth Regiment, along with the other New England Provincials, would be sent home by way of the Fort at Number 4, by turns, along the newly cut road. Typical was Sergeant Webster's company, which left Crown Point on October 26, as part of Major Hawke's detail, and along the way built numerous bridges and made other road improvements. Their journey home would take a little longer. At one point, their rations ran out, and they staged a work stoppage, until Lieutenant Small and a contingent of regulars from Crown Point delivered bread to the hungry men.[50]

November 24 was a bitterly cold day, and a new snow fell on the now frozen ground. The men of Col. Eleazar Fitch's regiment were the last remaining Provincial troops held at Crown Point, when orders were finally issued that day ordering them home. Putnam and his company crossed Lake Champlain the following day and arrived at the Fort at Number 4 sometime before December 2. In his absence from home, another son was born on November 18, 1759. The baby was given the name Daniel, in memory of his older brother who had died in August of the previous year.[51]

A BATTLE OF WILLS (1760)

After five years of war, the colony of Connecticut was fiscally exhausted and at the limit of its martial spirit. The same was true for the other colonies in the Northeast. As a result, Amherst's troop request in February 1760, though not unexpected, certainly gave Governor Fitch pause. Amherst had asked Connecticut to match its levy of five thousand men from the previous year, thus harkening back to the enormous problems encountered recruiting men during the spring of 1759. Moreover, Connecticut was expected to clothe and provision them, at least until some reimbursement could be voted on by Parliament in the future. The troops were to be ready to march and assemble at Albany by April 10, in time for the new campaign to commence around May 1.[52]

The Connecticut General Assembly met in a Special Session in Hartford held on March 13 and voted to meet Amherst's request by "voluntary enlistments," and offering by way of bonuses, referred to as "encouragements," that differed depending on whether the volunteer was a veteran or a new recruit. The troops were to be divided into four regiments of twelve companies each. As was the case the previous year, there would be no fixed term of enlistment, which would be limited to the end of the forthcoming campaign. Once again, Israel Putnam answered the call of duty. He was appointed to the rank of lieutenant colonel, and once again, he was given command of the 2nd Company in Eleazar Fitch's Fourth Regiment. John Durkee was appointed a major and as captain of the 3rd Company. Governor Fitch notified Amherst of the General Assembly's vote, and the general's response was one of great pleasure.[53]

Amherst's sources informed him that Connecticut was having difficulty meeting its quota and the recruits were unlikely to reach Albany in time. Much to the general's frustration, the situation was the same in the neighboring colonies. Amherst's tone changed markedly, and he became more demanding of Fitch. First, he suggested that Fitch call the General Assembly back into session and that the governor institute the equivalent of a draft if the quota was not met in time. "If you find there is no prospect of immediately completing the numbers . . . [s]ummon the Assembly to meet before the time above mentioned, in order to resolve upon an impress." Amherst did move the deadline for the troops to meet at Albany to the second Thursday in May.[54]

Presented with this demand, Fitch temporized: "If only Amherst's letter had reached him earlier, before the legislative session had ended and the new Assembly elected."

Besides, he observed, the new session was only a couple of weeks away. Moreover, he wrote, "I have never known the Old Members to be summoned to meet," and therefore, "I must be obliged to wait till the stated session of the Assembly, when I will take the first opportunity to communicate your proposal for impressing men to complete out levies." Amherst had also asked that Fitch send a small contingent of 150 men and wagons to Albany, and Fitch told him he would be only happy to oblige.[55]

Amherst appeared almost convinced by Fitch's argument. Nevertheless, he became adamant. "I trust, your hopes, that most if not all of your companies will be in a great measure, full and ready to march, at that time, will be accomplished," he wrote. "If not, I must renew my instances, that you then move the Assembly, to consent to complete your levies by impress." When Amherst reached Albany on May 8, none of the Provincial forces had arrived. He was clearly frustrated with the situation. Once again, Fitch made the case as to why impressment should not be used, not the least of which it had been tried unsuccessfully before, but more important, the General Assembly had considered that option, and "considering the many difficulties and very great inquietudes attending such a method of proceeding . . . judged that some further encouragements would not only better attain the end proposed, but prevent the difficulties consequent thereon, and better promote His Majesty's Service." To that end, the General Assembly voted for further bonuses.[56]

In the end, despite the substantial "encouragements," few new recruits signed up, and the company quotas were finally met by individual commanders, like Putnam, who were able to convince many of those veterans who had served before to re-up. As an example, of the eighty enlistees in Putnam's company, only fifteen were new recruits. The Connecticut troops reached Albany in batches starting on May 31 and ending on June 22, when Fitch's regiment arrived. Amherst, who had gone ahead and reached Oswego on July 9, well in advance of the Provincial levies, blamed the expedition's late start on the "sloth of the Colonies in raising their troops and sending them to their rendez-vous" at Crown Point and Fort Oswego.[57]

A Three-Pronged Plan of Attack

A three-pronged attack was planned to take Montreal and the remaining French posts along the St. Lawrence River during the summer of 1760. One column under Brig. Gen. James Murray would drive up the St. Lawrence from Quebec, while another column, under now Brig. Gen. William Haviland, would drive north from Crown Point to Île-aux-Noix near the outlet of Lake Champlain, and then on to Montreal via the Richelieu River. Putnam joined the third column under the direct command of Brig. Gen. Thomas Gage. Major General Amherst accompanied this force, which was ordered to proceed up the Mohawk River by whaleboat and bateau, across western New York to Lake Ontario,

Figure 4.   Ruined Barracks at Crown Point, New York
COURTESY OF THE LIBRARY OF CONGRESS

and then down the St. Lawrence. All three armies were to converge near Montreal, ideally at the same time.[58]

After leaving Albany, the columns were strung out for miles along the Mohawk Valley, first in bateaux and whaleboats, and later as the waters became shallow or dried up, slogging along portage trails, and, in some cases, dragging the fully loaded boats over log rollers. The four Connecticut regiments arrived at Oswego on July 22. Final preparations were made there for the expedition, while some men were put to work repairing Fort Oswego.[59]

Reveille was sounded at daybreak on August 10, and a half-hour later the flotilla left Oswego. The next several days were marked by high winds, swamping several boats along the way. Amherst reached Fort de la Présentation, a Catholic mission in the vicinity of Oswegatchie (Ogdensburg, New York), on August 15. There the way was blocked by the French brig *Ottawa* and another smaller vessel. Amherst's own warships had not yet arrived from Fort Niagara, and the French ships were a serious threat to his small watercraft. According to Humphreys' account, Putnam devised a plan to disable the unnamed vessel by stealthily approaching its stern and jamming the rudder with wedges. Amherst approved, and Putnam and a select group performed the daring maneuver, and the smaller ship soon ran aground. As to the second vessel, after a brisk fight, the *Ottawa* surrendered on August 17.[60]

Slightly farther downstream at the head of a series of rapids in the St. Lawrence, the French had built Fort Lévis on one of a group of small islands near present-day Ogdensburg, New York. The fort presented a new set of problems for Amherst, principally the deadly abatis that surrounded it, not to mention its guns, which could disrupt his continued passage. Amherst could have simply bypassed the fort with a minimum of casualties. The French counted on him to do the opposite, to buy time for them to improve Montreal's defenses. Amherst obliged them, brought up two armed sloops, the *Mohawk* and the *Onondaga*, placed artillery batteries on two nearby islands and on the south bank, and began his costly nine-day siege on August 18.[61]

Once again, according to Humphreys, after several days, Putnam devised yet another stratagem, this one to overcome the fort's defenses. He fitted out several bateaux with large planks that could be dropped from the bow, thus forming a bridge for the soldiers to cross the deadly abatis. Upon seeing the modified bateaux approach, and after having suffered the crippling effects of the devastating bombardment from Amherst's guns, the fort surrendered on August 26, without either side incurring further casualties in a costly infantry attack.[62]

On August 31, the flotilla resumed its journey downriver, safely passing through a series of rapids. However, on September 4, upon reaching an obviously dangerous stretch of water, as a precaution, Amherst ordered that the bulk of his force disembark before running the rapids. At first, some may have questioned the need, as the first of several rapids had been passed without much difficulty. Amherst tackled this, the most dangerous, section of rapids with the help of some Caughnawaga Mohawks, whose settlement was near Montreal. These Indians were realists and wanted to be on the winning side. However, even with their assistance, eighty-four men drowned in the rapids called, in turn, the Cedars, the

Buisson, and the Cascades, as dozens of boats were swamped, wrecked, or otherwise damaged in the deadly turbulence.[63]

Amherst's army reached the outskirts of Montreal on September 6 and made camp. Meanwhile, as if on cue, the following day, both Murray and Haviland arrived at the same time. Shortly thereafter, the campaign ended with the French surrender on September 8. The hard rain that day did nothing to dampen the spirits.[64]

Once Montreal was in British hands, Putnam visited the nearby Caughnawaga Indian settlement, where he became reacquainted with the Indian chief who had treated him so kindly during the first few days of his captivity. Now that the tables were turned, Putnam was able to offer the Indian the same protection. On September 11, Putnam and his company were homeward bound.[65]

ANOTHER TOUR OF DUTY
At the special legislative session held at New Haven on March 26, 1761, the Connecticut General Assembly voted to raise 2,800 men, to be divided into two regiments of twelve companies each. Recruiting went slowly, and the first Connecticut soldiers did not begin to arrive in Albany until June 8. Once again, Putnam would volunteer, however, not initially. No doubt he was ready to tend his orchard and fields that he had long neglected. However, fate took a hand when Lt. Col. Nathan Payson died suddenly in Hartford at the age of forty-one, and the General Assembly reached out to Putnam. He accepted a commission as a lieutenant colonel, and he was assigned to command the 2nd Company in General Lyman's First Regiment that had originally been Payson's. This would be his seventh deployment in as many years. As was so often the case, Hannah was again with child.[66]

The summer found Putnam and his company once again around Fort Ticonderoga and Crown Point. Their duties were not particularly taxing or, for that matter, interesting, and comprised construction and repair of the fortifications.

In October, already situated in his comfortable winter quarters on Staten Island, Amherst renewed his request for a large contingent of Connecticut men to winter over at Crown Point. In fact, he sought 323 men divided into three companies. So far, Governor Fitch had ignored the demand. Now that it was near the end of the season, in his reply, Fitch took the opportunity to ask Amherst to make sure that the Connecticut troops left before the snow and extreme cold settled into northern New York. In previous years, he pointed out, a late start home had resulted in many unnecessary casualties, a fact that concerned Fitch. Amherst made short shrift of the governor's request and patronizingly told Fitch that, "you may be assured the rest of the Troops shall not be kept a day longer than the Season will Admit of their Carrying on the Works; and that they shall be Discharged before the Weather becomes Rigorous."[67]

Putnam and his company marched to the Fort at Number 4 in New Hampshire, where on November 23, they were mustered for the final time before heading home. In his absence, a son, David, had been born on October 19, but he died on November 21, while Putnam was still in New Hampshire. Four days later, his Black slave, Peggy, also died at the family farm.[68]

LESSONS LEARNED

After six years of constant war, Putnam the farmer had become a seasoned warrior and a leader of men under fire, now outside of the shadow of Robert Rogers, respected by both those whom he led as well as his superiors. He was bold and aggressive without being reckless; patient in ambush; and relentless in pursuit. He was also quick to size up a situation and to react, as with the fire near the powder magazine, and during the attack on the work party outside Fort Edward. Putnam also learned that no matter how much he demonized the enemy, both French and Indian, when the fighting stopped, there was often a measure of decency and humanity shown, if only a glimmer, as he experienced with the actions of the skilled partisan leader Marin and the kindly Caughnawaga chief.

Finally, the gregarious Putnam, who made friends easily, maintained long-standing friendships with many regular British officers with whom he had served or served under. Years later, during the American Revolution, when he encountered them as the enemy, he was able to maintain those cordial relationships with the men themselves, while at the same time remaining loyal to the "Glorious Cause." This would be a source of some talk and consternation among those who disparaged him.

CHAPTER FIVE

Cuba

"THE JEWELL OF THE ANTILLES"

IN EARLY 1762, AS ANTICIPATED, SPAIN INVADED PORTUGAL, AN ALLY OF Britain. It was surely the last gasp of the Seven Years' War, as the various participants, their armies decimated and their treasuries exhausted, looked for ways to end the conflict. Britain successfully countered the Spanish attack on its ally, and, at the same time, staged an all-out effort to take Havana, Cuba. Not only was the island considered the jewel in the Spanish crown, the city itself was also a major port and a transshipment hub for the minerals and produce from Spain's American colonies.

The harbor behind the city of Havana was large, deep, and well-sheltered from the frequent tropical storms and hurricanes, especially in the late summer and fall. The narrow entrance to the harbor was guarded by two fortresses, Castillo de Los Tres Reyes del Morro ("Morro Castle") on the east and Castillo de San Salvador de la Punta ("Punta") on the west. The walled city of Havana was adjacent to the Punta. The New England colonies would, once again, be asked to raise troops to assist Britain in this effort.[1]

"ONCE MORE UNTO THE BREACH"

On March 4, 1762, at a special legislative session, the Connecticut General Assembly voted to authorize the raising of 2,800 officers and men "to march to such places in North America as his Majesty's said Commander-in-Chief shall appoint." They would be divided into two regiments, with twelve companies in each. Bounties were offered to entice the enlistment of an additional 575 men to supplement the ranks of the British regulars.

The First Regiment, composed of one thousand men, would be commanded by Maj. Gen. Phineas Lyman, and it would take part in the invasion of Cuba. Lieutenant Colonel Putnam would serve as Lyman's second-in-command and lead the 2nd Company in the First Regiment. At some point, the 10th Company, led by Capt. Hugh Ledlie, was detached and added to the Second Regiment, where it would serve at Crown Point. The second lieutenant of the 10th Company was Thomas Knowlton of Ashford. After Lyman was named overall commander of the Provincials, Putnam would, in effect, command the regiment.

There were several familiar faces among the officers in the First Regiment, including John Durkee of Norwich, who was appointed the regimental major, as well as captain of the 3rd Company. Also appointed was Roger Enos of Windsor, who served first as regimental adjutant and later as captain of the 1st Company. Captain Robert Durkee of Windham would command the 9th Company. He and Putnam had had a hairbreadth escape from a large party of French and Indians while on a scouting mission with Major Rogers near Ticonderoga seven years before. Among the British contingent were Maj. John Small, Col. William Howe, and Brig. Gen. William Haviland, with whom Putnam had also previously served.[2]

The first of the Connecticut troops arrived in New York City on May 24, led by Major Durkee. The balance arrived over the next two days. There, Putnam and his regiment assembled along with smaller contingents from New York, New Jersey, Massachusetts, and an equal number of other assorted regular troops, in all, about four thousand strong. The troops were awaiting the arrival of their transports and, for the Provincials, the issuance of arms. Prior to sailing, by day, troops were taken to Nutten Island (renamed Governors Island) for target practice, and at night they were confined to their ships due to an outbreak of smallpox in the city.[3]

HAVANA

The British expedition, led by Gen. George Keppel, earl of Albemarle, set out from Portsmouth, England, on March 6, 1762. His force consisted of four regiments of regular troops, siege artillery, and a group of French Protestants, prisoners who had offered to serve. They were joined enroute by another force under Brig. Gen. Robert Monkton, who had lately been stationed in Martinique. Overall, Keppel's army amounted to approximately twelve thousand men. Although he was expecting additional troops, including Lyman's Provincials, he deemed his present force adequate to conduct a successful siege. Moreover, as the fleet approached, the Spanish garrison was unaware that war had been declared between England and Spain.[4]

At daylight on June 7, strong winds and currents initially impeded the scheduled landing, until all the ships were finally able to rendezvous. However, from about 9:00 a.m. through 3:00 p.m., the British troops came ashore in waves without incident, five or six miles east of Morro Castle, and easily brushed aside token resistance on the part of the

Figure 5.   Havana Harbor circa 1762
COURTESY OF THE LIBRARY OF CONGRESS

Spanish. Advancing west along the shore, they came to the Torreón de Cojímar, a small fortress guarding the crossing at the mouth of the Río Cojímar, defended by six hundred of the enemy. The assistance of the naval warship *Dragon* was enlisted, and, after a vigorous bombardment, the fortress was overcome by a large contingent of Royal Marines. The British forces continued their march to within two-and-one-half miles of Morro Castle and made camp in the pouring rain, which would continue for the better part of the week, impeding the work.[5]

Albemarle prepared for a formal siege of Morro Castle, and he began by seizing the high ground along the east side of the harbor called Cavannos, which was accomplished by Col. Guy Carlton after a sharp fight on June 11. He also sent Lt. Gen. George Augustus Elliot and a large force to establish a position at Guanabacoa near the head of the harbor to prevent any attack from the interior and to send foraging parties into the hinterland. In the meantime, the navy was hard at work landing cannons and supplies, while the soldiers prepared fascines and dug parallels in front of Morro Castle. The latter proved difficult, as there was only a thin layer of topsoil covering the underlying rock in that area.[6]

In the interim, on June 10, Albemarle ordered the naval bombardment of the Torreón de la Chorrera, a small fort guarding the mouth of the Río Almendares west of Havana. Not only was it a good anchorage, but also a source of fresh water. After the navy finished its work, a small contingent of Marines subdued the defenders. On June 14, Col. William Howe and eighteen hundred men were landed at Chorrera to pressure the Spanish in Havana and the adjacent Punta. In time, this force would suffer the same fate as those attacking Morro Castle, as disease and heat exhaustion began to take their toll.[7]

According to one diarist, "the Morro was found to be tuffer work, and the Spaniards more resolute than was at first imagined." On June 27, Maj. Alexander Moneypenny skirmished with some Spanish cavalry, and two days later, the Spanish mounted a large attack on the British batteries. They were repulsed with severe losses. Of the 600 Spanish taking part, 220 of them lay dead on the field. To soften up Morro Castle, Albemarle ordered several warships to sail close to the fort, but in doing so he had not counted on the accuracy of the Spanish gunners from both Morro

Castle and the Punta. While the mission was accomplished, the effort resulted in many casualties, including the death of Capt. William Goostrey of the *Cambridge*, not to mention severe damage to the warships. The dead and wounded amounted to 157 British seamen.[8]

Many men, unused to working in the tropics, soon succumbed to the heat, humidity, and a lack of potable water, as well as tropical diseases. At first it was two to three a day, however, as those numbers climbed steadily, Albemarle began to worry that his initial estimates were overly optimistic and that he should have waited for his reinforcements to arrive. By July 5, many more men had succumbed to "fevers and fluxes," and Albemarle withdrew 400 Marines from Howe, as well as 300 seamen from Adm. George Pocock, all to supplement the work parties. Several days later a diarist described "infinite numbers of sick." Through it all, the work continued with the help of 500 Black slaves from Martinique and Antigua purchased by Albemarle. By the last week in July, an estimated 5,000 troops were incapacitated, along with 3,000 seamen, and it had reached a point where there were not enough men to mount the regular guard.[9]

Near Chorrera, despite the loss of more than a quarter of his force, and with the help from some sailors, Howe built a battery composed of three cannons and two sea mortars to fire on the Punta. However, within a week, in a surprise attack on July 18, the Spanish were able to spike the cannons but were driven off before they could damage the mortars. A gunner from the *Dragon* restored the cannons, and the battery was soon operational once again. Four days later, a force of 1,200 to 1,500 Spanish attacked several areas of Colonel Carlton's position at Cavannos, but they were driven back with large losses. Carlton was wounded in the effort. The Spanish still had some bite.[10]

THE RELIEF FORCE

The first of two relief convoys sailed from New York on Friday, June 11, 1762. It consisted of sixteen troop transports escorted by the *Intrepid* and *Chesterfield*, in all approximately 2,500 men, including General Lyman's First Connecticut Regiment. First Lieutenant William Starr, of Capt. Timothy Hierlihy's (in other sources spelled Herlihy) 6th Company in that regiment, kept a diary of the voyage aboard the transport *Swallow* and of his service in the Cuban campaign. With fair winds and clear sailing, the convoy reached Cape Samaná at the northeastern tip of Hispaniola (now the Dominican Republic) thirty-five days later. From there, the ships turned northwest, sailing along the coasts of Hispaniola and Cuba.[11]

The first hint of trouble came during the night of July 19 when part of the convoy became trapped in a large bay on the northeast coast of Cuba during a storm and had to ride it out. The following morning, Starr observed two transports in trouble. The *Masquerade*, with her top mast gone, was barely holding her own in the high swells, while the transport *Juno* had washed up on shore. Aboard the *Juno* were Putnam and five hundred Connecticut Provincials.[12]

Humphreys described the harrowing tale of the *Juno* and Lieutenant Colonel Putnam's role in the catastrophe, when during the early morning hours, it became apparent that the ship would ultimately either founder and sink or smash itself on the rocky shore. Seamen and soldiers pulled together in a race to save themselves. Putnam quickly tapped the ship's stores for lumber and rope, and he had the men build crude rafts. Though soaked through by the rough sea, all made it safely to land. Once ashore, Putnam directed the men to build a fortified camp using the lumber from the rafts until they could get their bearings, and, more important, before the Spanish got wind of their difficult circumstances.[13]

For the next two days the marooned men watched anxiously as all attempts to rescue them failed due to the high swells. Then their spirits sank as the *Masquerade* finally made it out of the bay and joined the rest of the fleet as it sailed away westward late in the afternoon of July 22. The transport *Falls* remained behind, waiting for the seas to calm, so that another rescue attempt could be made. Eventually, Putnam and his men were taken on board; however, by the time they reached Havana about August 6, Morro Castle had been taken.[14]

MORRO CASTLE FALLS

The hard work of the chief engineer, Col. Patrick McKellar, and that of his sappers eventually paid off. On July 30, at 2:00 p.m., after weeks of tireless digging, explosives planted beneath the walls of Morro Castle ripped open a large breach. That, in turn, led to its ultimate fall, as hundreds of British soldiers alertly stormed through the opening. The fighting was intense, but it was over quickly. One hundred and thirty Spaniards were killed within the fortress, while dozens more drowned or were killed while attempting to escape across the harbor by boat. The British casualties amounted to just more than thirty. The fighting yielded four hundred prisoners. With the tables turned, the Spanish trained their guns on Morro Castle to deprive the British of its use.[15]

ANOTHER SHIPWRECK

Disaster followed upon disaster for the first relief convoy. On July 23, *Chesterfield*, and at least four transports, including the *Swallow*, struck a reef and sank in shallow waters near Sugar Key off Cayo Confites. Private Levi Proctor described the island as a "barren desert, without . . . a drop of fresh water . . . nor was there a tree to overshadow us from the . . . scorching rays of the sun by day." It would be days before the men would be rescued. In the meantime, escorted by the *Intrepid*, the balance of the first convoy sailed on, and to the "greatest joy" of Albemarle and his diminished forces, those surviving troopships arrived offshore on the morning of July 28. Brigadier General Ralph Burton and approximately fourteen hundred of those newly arrived troops were immediately landed at Chorrera to bolster the effort by Colonel Howe, whose own forces had also been reduced by illness and Spanish attacks.[16]

The second relief convoy set sail from New York on the afternoon of July 4, and it arrived at Havana on August 2. It, too, had suffered some serious losses, as sometime during the week before, off the coast of Hispaniola, several transports had been seized by French men-of-war, resulting in the capture of five hundred sorely needed soldiers, regulars from the 58th Foot and Provincials from New York.[17]

Finally, on August 4, the remainder of the first convoy, including General Lyman and four hundred Connecticut Provincials, were taken off Sugar Key and arrived at Chorrera, where they disembarked on August 9, just in time to take part in the final attack on Havana.[18]

THE FALL OF HAVANA

With the seizure of Morro Castle, the focus shifted to the west of the harbor, to the Punta and to the city of Havana itself. Albemarle himself went over there to reconnoiter and plan an attack. Between August 1 and 10, the artillery array at Cavannos was built up to include more than forty heavy cannons, along with an assortment of mortars, howitzers, and cohorns. In anticipation of the forthcoming assault, Colonel Howe's force, now augmented by General Burton's newcomers, razed and burned many small villages and any freestanding structures outside the walls of Havana that could provide cover for the enemy. The Spanish did the same. On August 5, in anticipation of the final attack, Albemarle moved his headquarters to the west side of the harbor.[19]

General Lyman had established a camp for the Connecticut regiment at San Lázaro, just to the east of Chorrera. In the effort to capture Havana and the Punta, the Provincial forces, including Putnam's, lent a hand. For example, on August 10, Lieutenant Swann and his company were ordered forward to help dig a redoubt about five hundred yards from the city walls. They labored from 6:00 p.m. all through the night, at times under a short but fierce barrage of grapeshot from the Spanish guns.[20]

On August 10, with all his guns in place, Albemarle offered the Spanish an opportunity to surrender without further bloodshed. The offer was spurned, and, in fact, the Spanish started firing their cannons before Albemarle's envoys had returned to headquarters. The British commenced firing on August 11, and within a short time, the Punta was reduced to rubble, its garrison seen fleeing toward the city. Havana suffered damage, and the Spanish commander quickly sent word that he was now willing to listen to terms of surrender. The city of Havana finally capitulated on August 13.[21]

To the Victor, the Spoils

Albemarle was determined to conduct the occupation of Havana with a light hand. He issued orders that his troops treat the occupants with courtesy and that they respect the religious practices of the inhabitants. He also imposed a curfew for any soldier not on duty. Lieutenant Colonel Putnam maintained an orderly book detailing the latter part of the expedition during the occupation. The orderly book offers a window into conditions facing the British and Provincial troops following the capture of Havana. It also reflects the sheer dullness of the daily routine.[22]

At some point just prior to sailing home, a partial distribution of the prize money was made in pound sterling to all the soldiers and seamen from the highest ranks to the lowest, regulars and Provincials alike. It was heavily weighted toward the officers, a fact that would cause some to become disgruntled. It is estimated that a private soldier would receive anywhere from £1 to £4, while officers, like Putnam, were said to have been well-rewarded. As a field officer, Putnam received more than £500. The real controversy arose years later regarding the division of the remainder of the booty, such as ships and military stores, which had been taken to England to be sold at auction.[23]

THE "TYRANT HAND"

It was not the casualties inflicted by Spanish forces, which were light, that proved more costly. Rather, disease stalked the allied ranks, from dysentery and typhus to malaria and yellow fever, slowly at first, then in increasingly greater numbers, enough to cause alarm. The conditions in the camps were so bad that they became breeding grounds for pestilence.[24]

Reverend John Graham was chaplain to Lyman's forces, and he maintained a vivid account of the unfolding tragedy. In dramatic prose, he described the grim scene: "Thus with our melancholy Camp a fatal disease enters tent after tent, and with irresistible force strikes hands with soldier after soldier, and with hostile violence seizes the brave, the bold the hearty and the strong . . . no skill of Physicians can free from the Tyrant hand, but death cruel death that stands just behind . . . and at once throws his fatal dart, and fast binds them in Iron Chains." Putnam's orderly book details the frequent reassignment of officers to replace those who had fallen ill or had died. Of the latter, auctions were held to dispose of their personal effects. At some point, the growing sick roll became so large that sentries were told that if they became sick while on duty, they were to immediately request relief.[25]

No one was immune, including Nathaniel Hubbard, the regimental surgeon's mate, who died on September 30. Despite his normally robust constitution, Putnam fell gravely ill on September 25. The Reverend Graham described the patient as "seized with Cold Chills that pass through every part, throws all nature into violent agitation and Shakes the whole frame." This was followed by a high fever and feebleness in his limbs. He went on to describe Putnam's normally "ruddy Countenance" as taking on a "languid hue." Putnam survived this bout, but many others did not.[26]

With the growing sick list, it became increasingly important that the army obtain fresh fruit and vegetables, as well as poultry to supplement the regular army diet. This was especially so since army provisions spoiled quickly in the heat. On several occasions, Putnam himself, now recovered, accompanied by his quartermaster, 2nd Lieutenant Moses Park, went out into the countryside to purchase such items. In addition, from time to time, small advances were paid to the soldiers so that they could purchase fruit, vegetables, and meat from the local vendors. At one point, they were even authorized to swap their salt rations for fresh fruit and vegetables. However, the troops were not allowed to either purchase or swap rations for hard liquor under pain of severe punishment. Regular patrols were detailed throughout the city to prevent the sale of hard liquor.[27]

TALE OF A CANE

In the years following Putnam's death, many tales were told of his exploits and adventures, some fact-based and others fictional. All were meant to exemplify some notable attribute, such as his courage or compassion. The true tale of how he acquired his walking stick, along with a slave, a Black man by the name of Dick, is typical.

One day during the occupancy of Havana, while Putnam was walking in the city, he saw a local man beating his Black slave with a bamboo walking stick. He immediately confronted the man, who told him to mind his own business. Putnam wrested the cane away so that he could not hit the helpless man again. Meanwhile an unfriendly crowd of Cubans had gathered. All alone and unarmed, Putnam saw immediately that trouble was brewing, and he ran off down a nearby alley, cane in hand and the Black man in tow. The man, whom he called "Dick," would accompany Putnam to Brooklyn and attend him for the rest of his life. While most accounts refer to Dick as a servant, he remained a slave. The cane became a cherished possession of Putnam's, and later, in his old age, a necessity. No doubt, he told the tale of the cane countless times. On October 3,

1789, shortly before his death he wrote: "Walked out today supported by my Havana cane, which is a necessity in my present infirmity, and which I never carry without a remembrance of that day when I seized it."[28]

After the fall of Havana, other members of the Connecticut regiment, including Capt. John Durkee, Lt. Moses Park, and Lt. Jedidiah Hyde, had also taken one or more Black men into their camp at San Lázaro, most likely to act as servants. Prior to sailing, General Lyman ordered that all such slaves be rounded up in one place and returned to Havana, or the members of the regiment would forfeit a substantial penalty, no doubt from their share of the prize money, for each slave concealed. At that time, Durkee and Hyde complied with the order, but fearing that Dick would be mistreated if returned to his owner, Putnam did not.[29] Neither did Moses Park.

RENDERING UNTO GOD

Bored and sick, tired of the heat, the rain, and the general misery, no longer feeling the urgency or importance of the mission, the troops clamored to go home. Nothing else seemed to matter to them, not even Sunday church services. At first surprised and later discouraged by the sparse attendance at his religious services, Reverend Graham noted in his journal that, "God and religion, Christ and Salvation are disregarded, contemn'd and despised, and we live as tho there was no God, no future Judgment." On Sunday, October 7, Graham posed a question to Putnam. Was there anything "to hinder public [religious] Service?" he asked. "No," replied Putnam, "nothing in the world to hinder it, but there will be but few to attend, there's so many sick, and so many to attend the sick, that there could be a great many [missing]." Graham persisted, saying that it was not so much the number that was important, citing Christ's presence when even only two or three persons gather in His Name. Putnam admitted that that was true, but he sensed that the conversation was going nowhere. Hoping to mollify the discouraged chaplain, he walked away, at the same time telling him that he would speak to General Lyman. The situation remained unchanged one week later.[30]

HOMEWARD BOUND

On or about October 11, the Provincial troops were notified that they were scheduled to embark for home on October 19, 1762. Right on schedule, the troops boarded their transports. When it came time to sail, Lieutenant Park conspired with Captain Chadwick, the master of the transport taking them home, to sneak six slaves on board, including (unbeknownst to them) one each originally found by Durkee and Hyde, all of them, like Dick, concealed below decks contrary to General Lyman's explicit orders. Two days later, the convoy of six troopships sailed from Havana escorted by the *Intrepid*. Lieutenant Colonel Israel Putnam and his friend, Maj. John Durkee, sailed from Havana harbor aboard the transport *Jane & Elizabeth*, both with much-reduced companies. Out of the original 96 men in Putnam's company alone, 76 would die, 15 of them aboard ship, and another 12 in the hospital in New York. Of the latter, Putnam took a special interest in young Ens. Isaac Dana, who died there on December 23. The lieutenant colonel paid more than £51 for Dana's care out of his own pocket.[31]

The convoy arrived in New York on November 22. From there, more than likely Putnam and Durkee caught a coastal vessel to take them and their companies to New London or Norwich. They all made their way home from there.[32]

The British would occupy their conquest for a mere six months, sailing home with a substantially smaller force, ravaged by disease. Under the terms of the Treaty of Paris signed in February 1763, Britain ceded hard-won Havana and its environs back to Spain, in return for her interests in East and West Florida. While the politicians had achieved a diplomatic masterstroke; as is always the case, the common soldiers had paid the price.[33]

Shortly after landing, Park and Chadwick sold the smuggled slaves to buyers in Connecticut. Later, when Durkee and Hyde found out about the secret arrangement, they each sued for the return of their "property" and won. In a sad irony, in the case of Dick, Putnam was quick to put a stop to the physical cruelty of his former master, yet he failed to recognize the inherent cruelty of the bondage itself and perpetuated it.[34]

CHAPTER SIX

The Bradstreet Expedition

THE TREATY OF PARIS IN 1763

THE TREATY OF PARIS IN FEBRUARY 1763 BROUGHT AN END TO THE Seven Years' War in Europe, and with it came a major realignment of territorial claims in North America. Except for Saint-Pierre and Mique-lon, two small islands off the coast of Newfoundland, and the retention of fishing rights, France ceded to Britain all of Canada and most of the land west of the Allegheny Mountains, all the way to the Mississippi River, excluding the city of New Orleans. Spain, a late entry into the war on the side of France, gave up its claims to the Floridas in a swap for the return of Havana and its environs. Under the terms of the separate Treaty of San Ildefonso, Spain, in turn, was awarded French claims to New Orleans and Louisiana.[1]

THE COMPANY OF MILITARY ADVENTURERS

For some time, Phineas Lyman had been enamored with the idea that the Provincial soldiers, who had sacrificed so much for the Crown since 1755, should be rewarded with a grant of land in either Nova Scotia or the area around Crown Point, or, ideally, in the vast trans-Appalachian lands. Given the severe economic slowdown that had followed the war, the idea gave Lyman a new sense of purpose. As a result, shortly after his return from Cuba, he had floated that idea in an exchange of correspondence with Jeffery Amherst, going as far as to suggest that he could plead the case himself while in England, since he would already be there on behalf of the Provincials trying to collect the final installment of the Cuban prize money. Perhaps having a better handle on the political winds then blowing in England, Amherst discouraged the trip and suggested a written plea instead. Lyman would not be deterred.[2]

In due course, Lyman brought together fifty-five cash-strapped veterans in Hartford, Connecticut, on June 15, 1763, to form an organization called the Company of Military Adventurers. The objective was to obtain land grants in the "conquered" lands for Provincial veterans of the French and Indian War. The financial stress was most keenly felt in New England due to a growing population and a shrinking amount of good land. Some of the veterans intended to resettle on the new lands and get a fresh start toward a better life for themselves and their families. While others, no doubt, like so many of their compatriots, considered speculation in land as the route to fortune. Whatever the reason, some two thousand veterans, mostly from Connecticut, would sign on, about five hundred of whom paid a modest subscription fee to the organization in hopes of receiving some benefit.[3]

There were many familiar faces among the attendees at Hartford that day besides General Lyman, who was unanimously chosen to chair the meeting. Captain Timothy Hierlihy of Middletown was elected clerk, and Capt. Hugh Ledlie of Hartford as treasurer. In addition, a standing committee was appointed that included Col. Nathan Whiting of New Haven and Col. Eleazer Fitch of Windham, as well as Maj. John Durkee of Norwich and Lt. Moses Park, the former quartermaster. Other subscribers to the organization included Israel Putnam and Capt. Roger Enos of Windsor. That day in Hartford, many argued for a settlement on the St. John River in Nova Scotia, while Lyman made the case for Ohio.[4]

The meeting voted to make Phineas Lyman their representative in England, with instructions to plead their case. Lyman was a man they all trusted, as he had led them throughout the fighting in the upper Hudson River Valley, in Canada, and in Cuba. At the same time, he would also attempt to sort out the issue of the remaining prize money. The Hartford meeting adjourned until August 10, although there is no evidence of what, if any, business was conducted then. Lyman sailed to England from New York aboard the *Pitt Packet* (*Pitt*), an eight-gun cutter, in late July.[5]

THE PROCLAMATION OF 1763

While in England, Lyman labored in a diligent but often frustrating and dispiriting effort, calling upon British officers with whom he had served and frequenting many government offices. At times he received encouragement, and at other times, utter rejection. His task became all the harder when, in October 1763, King George III issued a proclamation that, among other things, prohibited most settlement west of the Appalachians to mollify the restless Native American population living there and to manage Britain's recently acquired territory. The government adamantly opposed any such expansion and strictly enforced its provisions. Exempted from the prohibition were Canada and East and West Florida. Initially, the governors in those provinces were given wide latitude to award grants of land to individuals within their own boundaries. This restrictive policy would hopefully buy some time to formulate a coherent strategy, one that not only protected Indian rights, but also eventually allowed for regulated settlement.[6]

As a reward for their service, at the same time, Britain adopted the ancient Roman practice of awarding land grants to its former soldiers. It was an inexpensive gesture that also assured that the far-flung frontier colonies would be populated by loyal men, who could, if necessary, defend them. Accordingly, that restrictive Proclamation of 1763 also provided land grants based upon a veteran's rank—fifty acres for privates and up to five thousand acres for those with the rank of major or above. In return for a ten-year moratorium on the payment of a quitrent, each settler was required to cultivate and improve the land. Initially, there was a question as to whether the land grants would apply to Provincial veterans.[7]

By this time, there had already been some intrepid individuals and clusters of restless folks seeking something more. In 1750, Dr. Thomas Walker from Virginia had led a group of settlers across the Appalachians through the Cumberland Gap and into an area of rich grasslands and abundant game that would later become the state of Kentucky. Daniel Boone and others followed in his footsteps. These and the increasing number of other settlers upset the Indigenous peoples, diminished the game that sustained them, and encroached upon their traditional habitat. Increasingly violent clashes became the norm, and Britain did not have the manpower to keep the peace. It was easier, so the theory went, to stop the settlements for now before the situation turned into an unmanageable flood. In short, the acquisition of the additional territory was a lot for Britain to absorb all at once.[8]

Pontiac's Rebellion

This major shift in control of the region left many of the Native peoples, particularly in the Great Lakes region and the Ohio River Valley, restless given the new uncertainty. The French had governed with a light hand, often integrating their traders into Indian society through marriage and trade relations. On the other hand, the British seemed obsessed with actual control of the land itself, and with it the inevitable upset of normal hunting patterns and traditional alliances with other tribes. In addition, Amherst had stopped the French practice of giving presents, including gunpowder, to the Indians, as well as provisions in times of need. Why, he reasoned, should Britain incur this unnecessary expense? Soon after the fall of Quebec and Montreal, red-coated soldiers began to replace the French at a dozen forts throughout the northwest, from Fort Duquesne (now Fort Pitt) to Detroit.[9]

The situation came to a head in 1763 when an Ottawa chief by the name of Pontiac took matters into his own hands. Born in an Ottawa village on the west bank of the Detroit River about fifty years before, Pontiac thought that he had the answer—unite the tribes with a common goal to return to the traditional ways and to strike a death blow to the English before it became too late. Pontiac had a commanding presence and excellent oratorical skills, and he had already earned the reputation as a brave warrior when he had fought as an ally of the French and was said to have led a band of Ottawa against the ill-fated Braddock expedition. When Pontiac sent his emissaries to the various northern tribes, the response was overwhelming, and a formidable alliance was formed.[10]

One by one, Pontiac and his allies easily picked off or forced the abandonment of eight critical British posts, leaving only Fort Niagara, as well as Forts Pitt and Detroit, both of which were also under a lengthy siege. The fighting at each was desperate, and each was in danger of falling in the absence of immediate relief. Detroit was particularly vulnerable, being the farthest away, despite the heroic efforts of its commander, Maj. Henry Gladwin.[11]

SIEGE OF FORT DETROIT

At his headquarters in New York City, Maj. Gen. Jeffrey Amherst, whose disdain for the Native Americans was matched only by his arrogance, dispatched his aide, Capt. James Dalyell, to Detroit via Fort Niagara with orders to gather a sufficiently powerful force along the way from Albany through western New York. Described as "ambitious and impulsive," Dalyell was always looking to advance his career. He was a friend of Putnam's, having served with him during the late war, including the day of his capture. Overall, Dalyell's force was made up of approximately 260 men, including a contingent of Rangers under Robert Rogers. From Fort Niagara, the soldiers traveled slowly by boat across Lakes Ontario and Erie and up the Detroit River. The small force, which reached the fort on July 28, was a welcome addition to Gladwin's command.[12]

Within days of his arrival, the young officer convinced an initially reluctant Gladwin to approve his plan to surprise Pontiac in his camp located two miles north by means of a nighttime attack. In the early morning hours of July 30/31, 1763, Dalyell and about 250 men ventured out of the safe confines of the fort, secure in the arrogant assumption that British regulars were more than a match for mere savages. Unknown to Dalyell was the fact that the plan had already been leaked to Pontiac by a French habitant, and thus the tables were turned on the young officer. The result was a complete disaster. After a sharp fight in the darkness, as his losses mounted, Dalyell ordered his men to fall back to the fort. Seeing a wounded comrade, he went to his aid but was shot dead in the process. In all, 19 members of the force were killed, 39 wounded, 3 of whom would later die from their wounds, and 100 captured. The survivors made their way back to the fort, shocked but no doubt relieved to be safe. The encounter was aptly called "Bloody Run."[13]

The siege of Fort Detroit continued throughout the fall, after which Pontiac called a temporary pause during the winter months, with every intention of resuming the fight during the following spring. When word finally reached Putnam of Dalyell's death, the news must have saddened him.[14]

On November 17, Amherst wrote to both Sir William Johnson and Colonel Bradstreet to meet him in Albany to plan a three-thousand-man expedition "for the punishment of the Indians who have committed hostilities." Amherst, however, would no longer be in charge. After his conference, he sailed for England aboard the sloop *Weasle* on November 30. He was relieved of command and replaced by Maj. Gen. Thomas Gage, who was familiar with the North American scene, having served with Braddock. Gage had an American wife, and he has been described as "cautious and lacking in imagination." Based upon reports from both Forts Pitt and Detroit, Gage immediately sent a request to the New England governors for another troop levy. Connecticut's allocation was five hundred men. Reluctantly at first, the various legislatures complied, but with far fewer men than Gage had hoped for.[15]

THE ELUSIVE PRIZE MONIES

Lyman's sojourn in London was frustrating on two counts. As if it was not enough that he had his share of troubles in England, trouble soon erupted back in Connecticut. On November 3, 1763, Lyman wrote to John Durkee that the authorities stood ready to make the distribution, but only if the applicants and the representatives of the estates of deceased soldiers provided written powers of attorney. Otherwise, without them, those persons "must expect to lose their money." He sent the blank forms to Durkee, and he urged him to try to obtain the executed documents. That should have ended the matter.[16]

Two months later, in January 1764, Jonathan Trumbull's son, Joseph, met General Lyman in London. The latter told Trumbull the same thing he had told Durkee. Young Trumbull passed this on to his father, who, in turn, told Hugh Ledlie. Somehow the message must have struck Ledlie the wrong way, and he as much as accused Lyman of pocketing the funds, or at the very least allowing the wrong persons to do so. Why Ledlie had become so exorcised is strange, since he did not serve in the Cuban campaign. Nevertheless, he spread the rumor that soon reached Putnam and Durkee. Although they both should have known better, particularly the former, they became incensed with the apparent lapse by their friend and colleague. Enough so to write Lyman a letter threatening to come to London themselves and to bring Lyman's alleged conduct to the attention of the authorities. Meanwhile, Ledlie also threatened to go to London. Putnam and Durkee soon calmed down after they had thought things through. Somehow Lyman was able to calm the waters, and the distribution was made. By then, however, things had taken a new course for Putnam, who was once again in uniform.[17]

BRADSTREET'S EXPEDITION

On March 8, 1764, the Connecticut General Assembly met in Hartford and appointed Israel Putnam as a major in charge of a battalion composed of five companies. Their term of enlistment was to run no longer than the following November 1. The recruits were to be between the ages of twenty-one and fifty and found to be "able-bodied and effective." Putnam was then at home in Brooklyn enjoying the past year's respite, tending to his farm and orchard following his return from Cuba. In addition to personal affairs, he had served a term as a selectman in the town of Pomfret, the first of several times during his adult life. After accepting his appointment to command the battalion, Putnam and the Connecticut troops made their way to Albany to join Bradstreet's force assembling there. Once again, he had left Hannah, now pregnant, and his family to serve his king and colony. In May, just before Putnam left home, the General Assembly met at Hartford once again and appointed him a lieutenant colonel and placed him in charge of all the Connecticut troops.[18]

Gage ordered Col. John Bradstreet to assemble a large relief force composed of regulars and Provincials. Many of Bradstreet's force, regular and Provincial alike, were recently returned veterans of the Cuban expedition, many still not fully recovered from the ravages of disease. Gage had no choice, as he had reached the limits of his available manpower. Bradstreet and twelve hundred men marched out from Albany at the end of June 1764 bound for Fort Ontario near Oswego, New York, which they reached several days later. Lieutenant John Montresor, an army engineer, was a member of the expedition and kept a diary during the entire time. Putnam had served with him and his father, Col. James Montresor, also an engineer, at Fort Edward in 1757. At Fort Ontario Bradstreet was met by Sir William Johnson and six hundred Indian warriors, including a large contingent of Caughnawaga led by the kindly Indian chief who had intervened to help Putnam after his capture in 1758. By coincidence, it was Bradstreet who indirectly secured Putnam's eventual freedom in a prisoner exchange because of his capture of Fort Frontenac. Putnam and the Indian had remained friends ever since.[19]

The relief force set out along the southern shore of Lake Ontario in a large flotilla consisting of two sloops, along with "seventy-five whaleboats, numerous canoes and other craft." They soon encountered a storm that could well have scattered them, but all arrived safely several days later at Fort Niagara located at the mouth of the Niagara River some eighteen miles downriver from Niagara Falls. Five years earlier, Capt. Charles Lee had been present at the siege of Fort Niagara. Aside from the falls being "the most stupendous Cataract in the known World," Lee also wrote that the area abounded in fish and game, and that "the situation of this place [Fort Niagara] and the country round it are certainly most magnificent." Upon their arrival, the scenery quickly gave way to the scene, as Putnam and his Provincials found an enormous assemblage of Indigenous people, summoned there for a council by Sir William Johnson. As a result of the deliberations, the Ojibway gave permission to build a fort at the outlet of Lake Erie.[20]

It was a short distance upriver from Fort Niagara to the Lower Landing situated on what is now the American side, two miles below Niagara Falls. That landing was the northern terminus of the portage road to Lake Erie, known to the Native Americans as the "Carrying Place," that bypassed the falls and the rapids below. The route was critical to the regular supply of the western posts. The French knew it, the Native Americans knew it, and so did the British, particularly after suffering a defeat by Pontiac's allies midway along the road where it overlooked the gorge at a place called the Devil's Hole. There, on September 14, 1763, when Lieutenant Campbell and his small contingent of British soldiers came to the aid of some teamsters, they were attacked by a large party of Seneca and virtually wiped out. Bradstreet was determined to secure his supply line, and he ordered the construction of a series of small block-houses along the route. He also sent Lieutenant Montresor ahead, along with a work detachment of approximately five hundred men, including Putnam and his battalion, to build the new fort.[21]

On July 17, Putnam and his men set out at first light along the portage road. They were part of the entire work detachment, taking with them two boats and several bateaux, all towed by oxen. Through heavy winds and a driving rain, the detachment reached Fort Schlosser at the southern, or upper, end of the portage, just above the falls, around two o'clock that afternoon. Montresor launched the boats on the Niagara River, and the troops rowed a short distance across to Navy Island, where they made camp that night. The following day, once again through heavy rains, the work detachment rowed another short distance upriver to the worksite on the western shore.[22]

Putnam and his battalion spent the next three weeks cutting timber, burning brush, and otherwise clearing the site for what would become Fort Erie. The woods were full of good hardwood species, so there was plenty to do. Putnam directed his working parties. The work was hard and sometimes dangerous, and the inevitable accidents occurred through carelessness and inattention. Many of Putnam's men came down with fevers and diarrhea. From time to time, smaller work details were called upon to load vessels bound for Detroit. On July 24, the men set aside their axes and were put to work building a stone revetment on the lakeshore to protect the walls of the new fort. At the same time, as the clearing progressed, Montresor laid out the plans for the walls and barracks. For those tasks, he had sent for artificers, including "carpenters, masons, brickmakers, lime burners, shingle makers, and sawyers." Throughout the period, there were days of heavy rain and gale-force winds, strong enough to raise the water along the shore by two feet, thus swamping any longboats beached there.[23]

Finally, on August 8, Bradstreet arrived at Fort Erie with the balance of his force, joining Putnam and his men. The large flotilla set out for Detroit the following day, hugging the southern shoreline of Lake Erie as it made its way west. The expedition camped nightly along the shore, when convenient at the mouth of a river. On the first night, at a place called L'Anse-aux-Feuilles, they were joined by a delegation of Iroquois, Delaware, and Shawnee, emissaries from their respective tribes, who had come to press Bradstreet not to attack them. Putnam and others urged the colonel to use caution when dealing with the visitors. Nevertheless, Bradstreet reached an agreement with this delegation on the condition that they meet him just more than three weeks later near Sandusky and bring with them white prisoners who had been seized by those tribes.[24]

On learning of the agreement, General Gage upbraided Bradstreet. "You have concluded a peace with people who were daily murdering us," he wrote. Gage immediately tore up the treaty; however, that word did not reach the colonel until September 25 at the time that he was in the middle of further negotiations at Sandusky.[25]

By the time the flotilla had reached the Cuyahoga River, they were greeted by another delegation of Indians, this time composed of Wyandot, Ottawa, and Miami. Putnam suspected an attack, and he alerted his battalion. The message from the delegation was the same as before—they feared an attack by Bradstreet's large force, and they were prepared to follow him to Fort Detroit and sign a treaty. Bradstreet believed that the group was sincere, and he held off any plan to attack them. The relief force arrived at Fort Detroit on August 27.[26]

Bradstreet encamped just north of Fort Detroit and set Lieutenant Montresor to work building more permanent improvements to the post. To that end, on August 31 he ordered Putnam and a two-hundred-man battalion, equipped with narrow axes, to row over to the Île aux Cochons ("Isle of Pigs") to cut timber for the construction of barracks to accommodate four hundred men. They returned to Fort Detroit on September 7. As work on the improvements progressed, Bradstreet replaced the fort's defenders with some of his fresher troops.[27]

More of the Same

As it turned out, Bradstreet's force was more than adequate to break the siege without further bloodshed. In keeping with his earlier arrangement, on September 14, Bradstreet first took his force to Sandusky for a council with the various area tribes, many of whom had been investing Fort Detroit. Once again, Putnam and his battalion were set to work building a new fort there near the ruins of an earlier one destroyed by the Indians.[28]

Bradstreet had sent emissaries to the various tribes, many leery of the British intentions, inviting them to the conference. These brave men were in Putnam's words, "illy used." One of them, a Capt. Thomas Morris of the 17th Foot, was "much abused, and stripped and whipped and threatened to be tomahawked" if he dared come back to the tribe. The conference took place, and after days of speeches, a treaty was signed. Accepting reality, Pontiac and his allies slowly disengaged and gradually returned to their respective homelands.[29]

On October 7, while in camp at Sandusky, Putnam wrote a letter to Major Durkee, his friend from their long service together in northern New York and Cuba. It was one of several that he had written to family and friends while he served in Bradstreet's expedition, and the only one that has survived. He begins the letter with a humorous swipe at Durkee and the erstwhile recipients of his correspondence. "According to your desire I have wrote to you several times," he began, "but I have had no answer from you, nor anybody since I left home; nor don't know but you are all dead."

Although he had not heard directly from his friend, no doubt he had received word of a meeting of the Company of Military Adventurers that had taken place on August 22 at David Bull's Tavern in Hartford, where those assembled had received an overly optimistic report from General Lyman. As a result, the right to subscribe was extended to men from the neighboring colonies. No doubt, with an eye toward future settlement, Putnam took in the northern Ohio scene with the eye of a farmer and husbandman. He described for Durkee large open spaces of ten thousand to twenty thousand acres, each having "not a bush nor twigg on it, but all covered with grass so big and high that it is very difficult to travel." The soil, he noted was "all as good plow-land, as you ever saw." Putnam found it would be perfect to raise hemp, a cash crop, but for the thousands of birds that would be attracted to the seeds, thus "making it very unhealthy to live among."

Aside from his description of the land, Putnam wrote about the Indian situation and Bradstreet's efforts, as well as that of the punitive expedition that had set out from Fort Pitt under Col. Henry Bouquet. Finally, no doubt eager to go home, he ends the letter with a typical soldier's lament. "And here we are," he wrote, "and for what I know not; nor when we are to leave it."[30]

Once more, on October 18, Bradstreet's force took to their boats and headed along the southern shore of Lake Erie. This time they were going home. The regulars and the sick were loaded on sailing vessels, while the Provincials like Putnam used longboats and bateaux. The late fall weather did not cooperate. Wind and rain slowed the progress, while high waves swamped many longboats. As there was no room in the other boats, the bedraggled survivors were compelled to make their way to Niagara, or worse, back to Detroit, on foot along the shore. Some of them would not survive the ordeal. Worse yet, rations ran low for the remainder of Bradstreet's fleet. Overall, the experience was one of profound misery.[31]

The flotilla finally reached Fort Schlosser at 11:00 a.m. on November 3, where, hungry and exhausted, the men made camp. The following morning, the regulars marched straight to Fort Niagara. There the fortunate ones found room in the barracks, while the remainder camped on the sloping glacis outside the walls. Bradstreet ordered some oxen killed to feed the hungry regulars. Meanwhile, Putnam and the Provincials remained behind at Fort Schlosser, cold and hungry, while blanketed by a light snowfall.[32]

Over the course of November 7 and 8, Putnam and his battalion, along with the remaining Provincials and Canadians, made their way to Fort Niagara, slowly hauling their longboats and bateaux over the portage road. Once at Niagara, the boats were loaded with provisions for the journey to Fort Ontario. All departed midmorning on November 9, the regular troops on board three sloops, and the remainder in the longboats and bateaux. For the better part of three days, the flotilla braved wind, rain, and high swells before finally arriving at their destination at sunset on November 11. Fortunately, they found shelter when they did, as later that night, the men were subjected to a bone-chilling cold, amidst a howling wind and drifting lake-effect snow.[33]

Bradstreet did not linger at Fort Ontario, and he led his troops on the last leg of the journey home, retracing their steps through western New York and the Mohawk Valley. All arrived in Albany on November 19, where the regulars settled into winter quarters, and the Provincials and

Canadians were discharged. Putnam made his way back to Connecticut, and he arrived home by December 1.[34]

Putnam had served his king and colony for nine out of the previous ten years, neglecting his farm and family much of the time. Along the way, he had learned to be a soldier, particularly, an officer who could lead from the front, and at the same time to be solicitous of the welfare of his men and merciful toward his defeated enemies. Blunt and affable, Putnam also made many friends among those with whom he had served, including the British officers. He came home in late 1764 with a wealth of experience and a well-burnished reputation. As for the Provincial soldiers, those years would prove to be an incubator of sorts for many of them also, shaping their actions a decade or so later. According to historian Fred Anderson, the greatest impact was felt in New England, "where between 40 and 50 percent of the men in the prime military age range would pass through the provincial forces before peace finally returned." That is something that should have given Great Britain pause.[35]

CHAPTER SEVEN

The Middle Years

CITIZEN PUTNAM

Upon his return to Brooklyn, Putnam, now almost forty-seven years old, embraced his family and began to reintegrate himself into the life of a prosperous farmer and nurseryman. If he suffered any ill effects from his decade of often hard service, other than his obvious physical scars, there is no evidence that he displayed them publicly. Surveying his acres, especially his orchard, and inspecting the flock, Putnam could see that his sons, particularly Israel, his eldest, now married to Sarah Waldo, had taken good care of things during his many absences. Nevertheless, given Putnam's restless, ever-present energy, he surely had ideas for improvements. Hannah was eight months pregnant with their tenth child, and to him, life must have seemed like it had returned to normal.

On December 31, 1764, Hannah delivered a healthy baby boy, whom the couple named Peter Schuyler Putnam, after Col. Peter Schuyler of New Jersey, who had come to Putnam's aid when he had been taken to Montreal as a prisoner in 1758. The initial joy turned to sadness when Putnam's daughter Elizabeth died at the age of seventeen on January 24, 1765. That sadness turned to gloom when, nearly three months later, on April 6, Hannah died at the age of forty-four, perhaps from lingering complications from her pregnancy. Putnam was left a widower with five children still at home, the youngest, Peter Schuyler, just three months old.[1]

In 1765 Putnam could easily have turned inward and raged at the heavens at his losses, yet on May 19, within weeks after Hannah's death, he publicly embraced his faith by joining the Congregational Church. He also became more active in his community, serving his second term as a Pomfret selectman.[2]

STAMP ACT CRISIS

Meanwhile, on the other side of the Atlantic, the British government sought ways to replenish its depleted treasury following a successful conclusion to the Seven Years' War. As a result of the treaties, all of Canada and Florida, as well as millions of acres of land beyond the Alleghenies, all the way to the Mississippi River, was now within her control. The British government intended to leave troops behind to man the various posts and forts scattered throughout the new territory. This, too, would add to the already staggering financial burden.

Although many believed Britain had absorbed the entire cost for the war, that simply was not the case. True, during the conflict Britain had partially reimbursed the colonies through subsidies, but the fact is that much of the cost was paid from the individual colony's own revenues, in equipping, supplying, and paying the soldiers raised by each of them to meet Britain's demands. This was particularly true for Massachusetts and Connecticut, especially during the late stages of the war. Colonel Nathan Whiting told Rev. Ezra Stiles that he estimated that between 1755 and 1760, some forty-three thousand New England Provincials had served in the field. All of this was in addition to the incalculable losses in lives and limbs among the Provincial levies, not to mention the productive time lost while absent from their shops and farms. Shortsightedly, Britain ignored these contributions and became focused only with the past and future costs, and how to pay them.[3]

It began quietly enough in 1764 with the passage of the American Duties Act, otherwise known as the "Sugar Act," which levied a small tax on foreign sugar, as well as Madeira wine, in addition to tightening the loose enforcement of customs duties imposed by the Molasses Act of 1733. Also passed at the same time was the "Currency Act," which banned colonial paper as legal tender. Those acts had been implemented with only a mild protest at first. More ominous was George Grenville's quiet hint that a Stamp Act was soon to follow, which is just what happened. Following a vigorous debate, Parliament passed the Stamp Act on

March 22, 1765, to take effect on November 1, by which all manner of paper, from newspapers to legal documents, would carry a modest tax.[4]

Little could those ministers and parliamentarians have imagined the firestorm of protests engendered by this one ill-conceived act. Implementation of the law had both fiscal and political consequences. First, and perhaps the most obvious, it was the economic aspects of the tax that affected most of the people. Parliament had declared that the tax had to be paid in hard currency, specifically silver. The problem was that there was a dearth of hard currency in the colonies. Colonial merchants primarily used it to settle their own accounts in England. The tax was also an assault on the fundamental tools that drove the colonial economy. Most ordinary citizens had long-standing arrangements with local merchants and neighbors that did not involve hard cash. While farmers like Putnam had come to rely upon paper money, a simple handwritten promise to pay a debt, or a handshake, to conduct their routine daily business was sufficient. More complicated matters such as land surveys, transfers of real property, and the filing of lawsuits, along with the many attendant legal pleadings, would all now cost money that many did not have. Something as important as the drafting of a Last Will and Testament would bear added cost. George Washington predicted that, "our Courts of Judicature must inevitably be shut up; for it is impossible (or next of kin to it) under our present Circumstances that the Act of Parliament can be complyd with were we ever so willing to enforce the execution . . . we have not the money to pay the Stamps."[5]

The furor should not have come as a total surprise to the British Parliament, as ample writing had been circulating during the lead-up to the passage of the bill. In 1764, Connecticut governor Thomas Fitch published a long, well-reasoned argument against passage of the stamp tax, entitled "Reasons Why the British Colonies in America Should not be Charged with Internal Taxes by Authority of Parliament." He touched on both adverse aspects of the proposed legislation: "It must be supposed that the People in America will buy and sell their lands, nay in a Multitude of Instances, they would not know how to subsist without such Dispositions. They will also be necessitated to give and take Obligations, and to use Paper for various other Purposes, or there will be of Course, so great a Stagnation of Business as almost to bring on a Dissolution of their civil and political existence. These things will be found as necessary as the Use of Agriculture itself."[6]

Invoking the fundamental right of all Englishmen to be bound only by taxes enacted by their own representatives in assembly, Fitch sent a warning to the Crown: "If these Taxations take Place, and the Principles upon which they must be founded, are adopted and carried into Execution, the Colonies will have no more than a Shew of Legislation left, nor the King's Subjects in them, any more than the Shadow of true *English* Liberty; for the same Principles which will justify such a Tax of a Penny, will warrant a Tax of a Pound, an hundred, or a thousand Pounds, and so on without Limitation; and if they will warrant a Tax on one Article, they will support one on as many Particulars as shall be thought necessary to raise any Sum proposed" (emphasis in the original). He went on to observe that should that happen, the colonists "will no longer enjoy that fundamental Privilege of *Englishmen*, whereby, in special, they are denominated a free People" (emphasis in the original). John Dickinson expressed that sentiment more bluntly in his *Letters from a Farmer in Pennsylvania*. "Those who are taxed without their consent, expressed by themselves or their representatives," he declared, "are slaves."[7]

Fitch sent copies to Jared Ingersoll, the colonial agent, with instructions to pass them along to members of Parliament in hopes of changing their positions. According to Ingersoll, three minor changes were made due to his persistence: an exemption for marriage licenses, appointments of justices of the peace, and personal notes given for small sums. However, in the end the effort was in vain, as the legislation passed with overwhelming support.[8]

Benjamin Franklin was also in England at this time, serving as the agent for the colony of Pennsylvania. While closely following the debate in Parliament, Franklin predicted to his friends that passage would be a mistake. From his personal experience as a printer, he offered the observation that "it will affect Printers more than anybody." No truer words were spoken. Printers were at the intersection of the fiscal effects of the act with the political opposition to it, particularly those who published newspapers and pamphlets. They envisioned a substantial loss of revenue and became quite vocal in their opposition to the act. Historian Jeffrey Pasley concludes that for most printers, the adoption of "zealous patriotism was the most prudent and profitable course."[9]

The marriage of the press and the political partisans proved to be a potent, if not irresistible, combination. What followed was a string of events that eventually led to revolution and a permanent break from Britain, or as John Adams wrote, "the child Independence was born."[10]

Putnam had not been home for many months before he would be drawn into the controversy. Hard currency had always been in short supply in colonial America, particularly for farmers such as himself, and the industrious and inventive inhabitants found many ways to sustain a viable economy, including barter and the evasion of import duties through smuggling. In addition, the land itself was in the mix. One measure of a man's wealth was his acreage; however, if one could not afford the tax imposed to buy or sell land, the delicate economic balance would be upset. However, it was not simply the cost of the tax that bothered the colonists. For many it was the fact that the individual colonies, self-governing for more than a century, had not had a say in the decision to lay what they referred to as an "internal" tax on them.[11]

Protests erupted all throughout the colonies, some violent, as stamp agents were harassed and intimidated and their materials destroyed. Israel Putnam quickly responded to the crisis by meeting with his neighbors, and an ever-expanding group of protestors, his large home no doubt the venue for many gatherings. These informal groups soon became more well-organized, eventually taking the name "Sons of Liberty," a phrase coined by parliamentarian Isaac Barré as he exchanged sharp words in debate with Charles Townshend.[12]

On October 28, Cadwallader Colden, the governor of New York, advised Jared Ingersoll, the stamp agent for Connecticut, that a ship had arrived bearing three packages of stamped paper "marked for Connecticut," which he had taken to his home at the fort in Lower Manhattan for safekeeping. At the same time, he said, that the Revenue Cutter *Gaspee* "is now here and it is a very fit vessel for carrying the Papers to you if you can prevail upon Captain Kennedy in order to do it." Colden also informed him that three more ships with stamped paper were expected any day.[13]

Connecticut's governor, Thomas Fitch, was now in an awkward position. Despite his earlier argument against the passage of the act, and, no doubt, his continuing belief in the premise that an internal tax must emanate from the lawful representatives of the people, he was the chief executive officer of the colony, and his duty was to execute the law. In late 1765, Putnam was appointed head of a small delegation sent to meet with Governor Fitch in Hartford, at which time the governor asked Putnam what would happen if the stamped paper made its way to Connecticut by order of the king. His answer direct and to the point, Putnam told the governor that he should lock it up, and that he and his friends would come back for a visit. "And what will you do then?" queried the governor. Putnam replied: "We expect you to give us the key of the room where it [the stamped paper] is deposited." He added that the governor could protect himself from accusations of dereliction by ordering Putnam not to enter the room. "What will you do then?" asked Fitch. "Send it safely back again," he replied. Finally, the governor asked what would happen if he refused to let Putnam and his men into his home. Putnam's reply was chillingly blunt: "In such a case, your house will be leveled with the dust in five minutes."[14]

THE "PUMPKIN GENTRY"

Canterbury, Connecticut, was the site of a meeting of the Windham County Sons of Liberty, held on Tuesday, March 4, 1766. At that time, Israel Putnam and Hugh Ledlie were appointed as a Committee of Correspondence to share like-minded ideas and information with the "neighboring provinces." Later that same month, the Sons of Liberty held a general meeting in Hartford on March 25. Although intended as a statewide gathering, the attendees were predominantly from Windham and New London Counties. That, and given Putnam's already being a member of a Committee of Correspondence for Windham County, he was chosen as the chairman of the Committee of Correspondence, along with members John Durkee and Hugh Ledlie. These secret bodies were initially formed to share news and like-minded ideas with similar committees in Connecticut and neighboring colonies in opposition to the Stamp Act. Those who did not agree with Putnam and the other Sons of Liberty referred to them sarcastically as the "Pumpkin Gentry."[15]

Putnam eagerly approached his new responsibilities, carrying on a regular correspondence. He also traveled from town to town throughout eastern Connecticut and into Rhode Island organizing those citizens ready, willing, and able to fight, if necessary. The resistance in Connecticut was so effective that not a single stamp reached the colony during the crisis, and all such materials remained locked up in the fort in New York City. Moreover, it was said that Connecticut was so well-prepared that a magazine for arms and powder had been established, and that Putnam had organized ten thousand men to react with force at a moment's notice should that become necessary.[16]

All during the crisis, work went on at the Putnam farm. He was also elected to serve as a delegate to the General Assembly from Pomfret in the spring of 1766. That year he attended the first session in Hartford in May, and again in October in New Haven. Other than the scar on his face, through nearly ten years of war, Putnam was never wounded or suffered any severe injury. However, it was during this time that he lost the top section of his right thumb, more than likely due to an accident at the farm. For a while, he stayed close to home as he recuperated, but he was soon up and about, only to suffer an even more serious accident when he received a compound fracture of his right thigh, more than likely from a fall from a horse. Although he recovered, the injury left his right leg about one inch shorter than the left, and he walked with a limp for the balance of his life.[17]

By February 1766, Putnam had already extended the reach of his correspondence to the leaders of the Sons of Liberty in New York City, assuring them that "he would assist them with their Militia to the utmost lives and fortunes to prevent the stamp act being enforced in New York, or for that matter, in any other province." Unknown to Putnam at that time was that the battle had already been won, as Parliament had repealed the Stamp Act on January 29, to take effect in March. When all was said and done, the act was a failure, as a total of only £45 was collected, and that was from the colony of Georgia alone. The more important upshot was the fact that strong intercolonial bonds had been forged, ready to meet the next crisis, and Putnam was no longer just a simple Connecticut farmer.[18]

A WIDOWER NO LONGER

In the meantime, Putnam was re-elected to the General Assembly in 1767. He attended the first two sessions in Hartford in January and May, respectively. After the close of the May Session, he returned to Pomfret, where he married forty-five-year-old Deborah Lothrop Gardiner on June 3. Some years later, after meeting her in Boston, Mercy Otis Warren would describe Deborah as a good, simple woman, lacking some of the social graces or a brilliant wit, yet having an "honest, unornamented, plain friendliness." Deborah Gardiner and Putnam had become reacquainted sometime around 1764 after she had been widowed for the second time. Putnam had known Deborah when her first husband, the Rev. Ephraim Avery, was the minister of the Second Church in Brooklyn. Reverend Avery died in 1754, along with their young son Septimus, during an outbreak of a virulent type of dysentery. This left the mother of seven surviving children a widow for the first time. The Reverend Avery also

Figure 6. "General Wolfe" Tavern sign
COURTESY OF THE CONNECTICUT HISTORICAL SOCIETY

left her their substantial home on the Green in Brooklyn. The following year, Deborah married John Gardiner, and she and her younger children moved to his large estate on Gardiner's Island in New York. There, she had two more children, one she named Septimus in honor of her previous child who had died young. She was widowed once again after Gardiner died in 1764.[19]

It was shortly after the wedding that Putnam and his now blended family reordered their living arrangements. First, his son Israel and his family moved into the Putnam homestead, where he would continue to manage the farm. His daughters, Mehitable, Mary, and Eunice, would move between homes, and Putnam, along with his sons Daniel and Peter Schuyler, moved in with Deborah and her younger children, Hannah and Septimus, in her large farmhouse on the Green in Brooklyn, Connecticut. There, he and Deborah established an inn, which they called "The General Wolfe." It was a popular stop, frequented by travelers and locals alike, where the gregarious ex-soldier swapped tales of his many adventures. More important, like most inns, it was also a place where news and local gossip was shared and issues like the widening breach with England were discussed. Still a delegate to the General Assembly, later that same year Putnam attended the October Session in New Haven.[20]

In the ensuing years, Putnam continued to play an active role in his community. He was elected once again as a selectman in 1772. Putnam vigorously pushed for the construction of a new church building, and he took on different roles within the Brooklyn Society, from lay deputy to sexton. From time to time, he was called upon to serve on various committees.[21]

In 1772, at the May Session, the General Assembly appointed him to a committee to rebuild Lovett's Bridge over the Shetucket River in Norwich, which had been carried away by "flood and ice" the previous winter. One of his fellow committeemen was former sergeant Jabez Fitch, who had helped him with some paperwork at Fort Edward during the winter of 1757–1758. The selectmen of Norwich were given until August 1 to complete the work, or the committee were given the authority to have the work performed at the expense of the town.[22]

Rumblings of Discontent

During this time in New England, discontent continued to bubble beneath the surface, erupting into violent clashes from time to time. Parliament continued to stir the pot. As a case in point, immediately following the effective date of the Townshend Acts on November 20, 1767, Boston merchants began a campaign to ban the importation of British goods and manufactures. The non-importation agreement spread throughout the colonies with mixed results. Some argued that the ban would boost local manufacturing and industry and send a message to Britain. By 1770, however, most merchants had begun to yield to pent-up demand and a surplus stock of goods in their warehouses.

In August 1770, a group of prosperous merchants and landowners from Norwich, New London, and New Haven met at the latter place to discuss the continuation of the non-importation agreement. Their list of specifically prohibited items exceeded thirty items and included sugar and "spiritous liquors," gold and silver buttons, and women's hats. At the same time, Putnam presided over a meeting at Woodstock. There the more self-reliant assembled farmers had no trouble excluding "all imported articles," except those considered "positive necessities, that one could not live decently without." Theirs was a brief list and included "Bibles, pins, needles, gunpowder, lead, flints, German steel, apothecary's drugs, spices, and window glass."[23]

CHAPTER EIGHT

West Florida and Natchez

GEOPOLITICS

In addition to the trans-Appalachian settlement ban, the Proclamation of 1763 also established three new provinces: Canada, East Florida, and West Florida. Contrary to the situation west of the new proclamation line, these areas were open for settlement, something initially encouraged by Britain. Moreover, the royal governors of these new provinces were eventually empowered to award head rights and land grants and to collect quitrents within their territorial boundaries. Yet, for many restless Americans, the so-called boundary was nothing more than an arbitrary line on a map, which they simply chose to ignore.[1]

The original boundary of the province of West Florida began at the Apalachicola River on the east and ran west along the Gulf of Mexico to the Mississippi River, excluding New Orleans. The northern boundary was arbitrarily set at the 31st parallel, in the belief that it would be enough to separate the new and existing white settlements in the province from the unorganized Indian lands to the north. However, that soon changed when it became known that there already were established pockets of French and Spanish settlers, with an occasional Englishman, living along the Mississippi River well north of that line. More important, there was a realization that not only did a portion of the lucrative fur trade pass down the Mississippi to New Orleans, but also that the soil in the region was rich. Moreover, many of the king's friends were looking to cash in on the post-war speculative fever, and that became a source of several large grants of prime land along the Mississippi north of the line.[2]

107

Accordingly, in May 1764, the northern boundary was reset to run due east along a line beginning at the confluence of the Yazoo River with the Mississippi all the way to the Apalachicola and Chattahoochee Rivers. The glaring irony in this change was that it violated the very purpose of the Royal Proclamation of October 7, 1763. For the Native peoples, the Choctaw, Chickasaw, and Creek, the change was not welcome.[3]

THE COMPANY OF MILITARY ADVENTURERS AGAIN

By 1770, Phineas Lyman was ultimately successful in obtaining the promise of a grant of twenty thousand acres in West Florida for himself, but he was unable get a firm commitment from Lord Hillsborough, secretary of state for the colonies, on behalf of the Company of Military Adventurers. The secretary was reluctant to authorize large migrations, or any migration for that matter, to areas west of the proclamation line. Hillsborough's views were more sophisticated than his colleagues, as he was concerned not only with the unregulated growth in the trans-Appalachian region, but also with the negative effects of the large ongoing population drain on Britain itself. Finding no support, he resigned his position in August 1772. He was succeeded by Lord Dartmouth, who was more sympathetic to Lyman's application.[4]

Author Horace Walpole, son of the former prime minister, wrote a letter to Dartmouth in August 1772 that was remarkable for its boldness and its prescience. He was at once concerned with massive grants of land to political favorites and the inevitable drain on the population of "Scotland, Ireland, and Britain," but also as to the practicality of settlements along the Mississippi River. He observed that the policy had the "tendency not only to hurt Great Britain but the Colonies, by granting upwards of twenty million acres in the inland parts of America, on the banks of the Mississippi, where neither our ships of war or troops can visit the inhabitants, either to give them aid, or keep them within bounds." Walpole added: "It is true 'tis a fine country and climate, but so distant from the sea, it never can be of any utility to Great Britain, therefore a very dangerous, unprofitable grant, take it in all its views."[5]

Concerned for her husband's well-being, Eleanor Lyman had sent her son Thaddeus to England to bring his father home. Lyman returned to America in September 1772, after nine years in England, "disappointed and in debt." He had received a small pension of £200 per year, as well as a gift of £500, arranged by his friends there, who were no doubt fully aware of his circumstances. In a testimonial on his behalf, Lt. Gen. Daniel Webb wrote that he had reason to believe that Lyman was "much distressed." In late January of that same year, a visitor to his flat in London commented upon the straightened circumstances of Lyman and his guest, John Henry Lydius. The latter was a former Indian trader from Albany whose then-defunct trading post at the Great Carrying Place had become the site of Fort Lyman (later renamed Fort Edward) in 1755. Lyman would need the pension, at a minimum, as his once thriving law practice in Suffield was no more.[6]

If nothing else, Lyman still held on to the dream of a settlement of former soldiers, but with an added sense of urgency. Except for the issue of the Cuban prize monies, the Company of Military Adventurers had been relatively inactive for several years. Word of Lyman's arrival must have spread quickly, as a small group of a dozen subscribers, including Israel Putnam and Roger Enos, met with him in Hartford on October 16 to plan the next steps. As a result, Lyman and the others issued a call for a meeting to take place at the courthouse in Hartford starting on November 18, 1772, and to continue for the following two days.[7]

Without any documentation in hand to substantiate his assertion, he reported to those assembled, including Israel and Rufus Putnam, that with the departure of Lord Hillsborough, he had secured assurances from Lord Dartmouth, the new secretary of state for the colonies, that the benefits available to regular British veterans would also be extended to former Provincial soldiers who had fought so bravely alongside British regulars.[8]

The next step for the Company of Military Adventurers was to conduct a survey of the putative grant in what was then West Florida and to decide how to fund it. First, the actual composition of the explorers had to be decided upon. After several different proposals, the meeting finally settled upon their ultimate choices. Israel and Rufus Putnam were selected to head a so-called "Exploratory Committee." The former was chosen for his well-known intrepidity, and the latter for his skills as a surveyor. The two men then assembled the rest of the small party that included Israel's thirteen-year-old son Daniel, along with Thaddeus Lyman, the general's son, and Capt. Roger Enos of Windsor, who had served with Israel in northern New York and Cuba. Rounding out the group was William Davis, a hired hand. The meeting had already voted that the voyage commence on December 10.[9]

Bound Away

The Exploratory Committee gathered at Israel Putnam's home in the village of Brooklyn on December 11, 1772. Other than church services in Windham on the thirteenth, the men took the next four days making their preparations for the voyage. Finally, on Wednesday, December 16, they made their way on horseback, followed by at least two wagons or carts full of their gear and supplies, twenty-one miles south to Norwich, where they spent the night at the Widow Bushnell's home. In the morning, the party trekked to the landing and loaded their stores on Capt. Samuel Champlin's boat, and when that was done, immediately sailed down the Thames River thirteen miles to New London, where they spent the night as guests of Capt. William Coit at his home on Cove Street, then facing Bream Cove.[10]

The following morning, Israel Putnam arranged passage with Capt. Wait Goodrich, first to carry the party to New York City and then to West Florida. He also purchased a whaleboat for future use on the Mississippi if needed. It was then lashed to the side of the small sloop *Mississippi*, which would take them to New York the next day. All arrived safely at noon on Sunday, December 20, after a harrowing passage through the treacherous Hell Gate, made even more so by an incompetent pilot. While in New York, Putnam's party lodged at Richard Waldron's Inn. That afternoon, Putnam attended church services at the First Presbyterian Church, where he heard a sermon by the Rev. John Rogers. No doubt, he gave thanks for the recent preservation of his party.[11]

The following three weeks were spent completing the preparations for the voyage. When the weather, which for the most part was cold and rainy, permitted, the explorers purchased livestock, armaments, and other provisions and went about rigging and making the necessary repairs to the vessel. They also installed a capstan to assist in sailing the ship up the Mississippi River against the current. When not at work, Putnam dined with acquaintances and attended church services. He was not particular about the denomination, only the quality of the sermon. However, since smallpox was prevalent in the city at this time, many spare hours were spent in their lodgings. All was in order by January 9, 1773; however, the wind would not cooperate that day. Putnam and his party re-boarded the sloop *Mississippi* the following day, and Captain Goodrich set sail that noon.[12]

THE VOYAGE

Goodrich charted the course of the *Mississippi* south to the island of Hispaniola (Haiti and the Dominican Republic). Rufus Putnam complained of "amazing" seasickness for much of the early days, leaving him weak, having lost "much flesh and strength." The ship made a brief stop at Mole Saint Nicholas on the north coast of Hispaniola and then headed for Montego Bay in Jamaica, arriving there in the late morning on Monday, February 8.[13]

During the brief stopover, Israel and the others received a tour of a nearby plantation and sugar mill, where the cane was ground and eventually made into rum and molasses. Suddenly, a ferocious dog attacked Mr. Barnard, the plantation manager, and in the scuffle Israel was knocked into a vat of the cane liquor used to distill rum. Everyone had a good laugh, but seeing his guest thoroughly drenched from head to toe, the manager lent Putnam a change of clothing. When the travelers found out that smallpox was prevalent on the island, all who had never had it went back on board ship and stayed there. The following morning, Israel walked back to the plantation and changed back into his own clothes, all washed and dried. Following dinner on board ship that evening, Captain Goodrich weighed anchor and sailed out of Montego Bay.[14]

The *Mississippi* sailed through the Winward Passage and west along the southern coast of Cuba. Along the way, the ship nearly grounded on a small, bare island called Grand Commanders. On February 17, they rounded Cabo Corrientes, and the following day they passed Cabo San Antonio at the western end of Cuba. The next week was marked by violent wind and rain squalls. Through a fortunate turn, the party arrived safely at the port of Pensacola on March 1, 1773.[15]

Pensacola, the capital of West Florida, was a well-established town dating from the Spanish occupation, with about 150 homes and businesses, a government building, a good harbor, and a small, stockaded fort. Although Gov. Peter Chester welcomed them warmly, nevertheless, the encounter proved embarrassing. While the governor could conduct smaller land transactions, he had not yet received authority to honor the larger land grants, like Lyman's, and Putnam had no written evidence of Lyman's grant in hand. Perhaps, suggested Chester, it was too soon, as Lord Dartmouth had only recently been appointed.[16]

Governor Chester had assumed his authority in August 1770, and he soon heard reports of the fertility of the soil along the Mississippi River near Natchez, and the eagerness of settlers from Pennsylvania and Virginia to come there, provided they receive protection from the government. When Chester asked Gen. Frederick Haldimand, the military authority, if he could provide that protection, he was told that Gen. Thomas Gage had strictly forbidden the movement of any troops to that area. The regiment would, he said, remain in garrison at Pensacola. Notwithstanding this disappointment, the governor remained enthusiastic about such settlements, and when approached by the Putnams in March 1773, he was willing to give them the benefit of the doubt, telling them that ["I will] do everything that [is] in [my] power to promote the settlement."[17]

Accordingly, on the strength of the "possibility" that the appropriate authority might reach Pensacola, Governor Chester gave them permission to "reconnoiter" the area along the Mississippi and to "make such surveys as [they] might think proper." The governor also gave them permission to "take up lands" below the Yazoo River that were unclaimed and limited settlement to no more than five townships. Rufus was commissioned as a deputy surveyor for West Florida. As a further measure, the governor agreed to hold their claim open until the following March 1. Israel negotiated a reduction of the purchase fees per ten thousand acres, although not as low as he would have liked.[18]

In the days that followed their arrival, in addition to their official business, the group explored the countryside around the town. The woods were primarily pine, and the soil sandy and not well suited to traditional agriculture. There were scattered swamps and two lagoons, which were "well stocked with small fish and oysters and clams." Israel did, however, write that he had eaten some good locally grown oranges. They staged a couple of deer hunts, largely unsuccessful, although they did manage to shoot a wild turkey. For the most part, while in Pensacola the explorers maintained their living quarters on board the *Mississippi*, but they enjoyed a daily round of dinners on shore. Israel and Rufus did spend the night of March 5 as guests of a Mr. Livingston. In their spare time, they wrote letters home, to be carried back by returning ships. Colonel Putnam renewed his acquaintance with Gen. Frederick Haldimand, and his Scottish friend, Maj. John Small, with whom he had previously served. On March 8, Putnam sat up all night with Small, who had taken ill.[19]

Israel and his party were ready to set sail for the Mississippi River on March 15, but contrary winds prevented them from doing so until March 18. On board was a Monsieur Caters, a Frenchman, who had been hired by a group of German investors to explore the region along the Mississippi River north of New Orleans. The following day, the sloop approached the mouth of the great river, which was distinguishable by a large plume of fresh, brown water extending more than six miles out into the Gulf of Mexico. Because of its color, it was first mistaken for a large sandbar. The ship dropped anchor just off Mud Island, however, strong contrary winds pushed them back out to sea. Finally, after a long night, the ship was able to claw its way back and to rest at anchor where it started. A Spanish sloop pulled alongside and begged provisions, having had a similar but more difficult time, as the crew had just spent forty days simply trying to safely anchor there only to be driven farther offshore all the way to the Yucatán Peninsular.[20]

Between March 22 and March 30, wind permitting, and when not, by kedging, the sloop slowly made its way to an anchorage eleven miles above a sharp bend in the river called English Reach, and about three miles below New Orleans. There they found several British merchant ships forced to anchor, as the Spanish authorities would not allow them to do so at New Orleans. Captain Goodrich sought the assistance of a Captain Ladlee, who was more familiar with the Mississippi River.

Along the way, Israel, Rufus, and some of the others used the whaleboat to explore the delta as well as the tributary rivers and streams along the course of the great river. In the process, they shot three alligators and were able to harvest some oysters. They also found time to visit some small plantations owned by French settlers along both sides of the river, where they purchased milk, butter, and other fresh foods. Israel Putnam's journal ends without explanation at this point.[21]

On March 31 Israel took the whaleboat and rowed to New Orleans, where he presented a letter of introduction from Governor Chester to the Spanish governor. Rufus wrote that his cousin was "received coldly." The following day, in what could very well have stymied the Adventurers, Captain Goodrich refused to take the sloop *Mississippi* farther up the river, saying that he needed to finish his trading. This was clearly a breach of their original agreement. Rufus Putnam expressed his understandable frustration by noting in his journal that if the Military Adventurers were to fulfill their exploratory mission, they would now be "obliged to row themselves 100 leagues against the current in an open boat."[22]

GETTING THERE
Since Captain Goodrich had refused to take them farther up the Mississippi, the resourceful Colonel Putnam arranged for the installation of a sail on the whaleboat, if needed, to help carry them the rest of the way upriver to their destination. However, on the downside, they found that the whaleboat could not carry them and, at the same time, enough supplies to complete the exploration. Moreover, they were advised that the whaleboat was too fragile, given the many snags and hidden dangers lurking just under the river's surface carried along by its tremendous current. As a result, on April 2, the explorers met with Captain Goodrich to express their displeasure. They made it clear to him that they were not leaving the vessel voluntarily and suggested that, under the circumstances, he would have to justify his actions to the Company of Adventurers at home. Goodrich relented and, the following day, told the Putnams that they could leave the whaleboat behind and he would sail upriver as far as he could when the winds were right. This was agreeable to the Adventurers. However, after several days of inaction, even when the winds were

clearly favorable, and, in fact after several other sloops had already sailed upriver, it was apparent that Goodrich had led them on. Finally, Israel had had enough of the captain's equivocation, and he, Rufus, and Roger Enos walked four miles above the city to see a Mr. Willey and arranged for use of a bateau, a shallower draft vessel better suited to the river and its tributaries than the more fragile whaleboat. As it turned out, the boat belonged to Lt. Gov. Elias Durnford.[23]

In the meantime, on April 6, while waiting for Goodrich to make up his mind, Israel went ashore in New Orleans. As he walked along, he became aware that several homes on that street had caught fire and there was a good chance that the conflagration would spread to other structures. Never one to sit idly by in a crisis, without any hesitation, Putnam stepped in and took charge of the effort, and, according to his cousin, "many more [houses] would in all probability been consumed had it not been for Colonel Putnam who happened to be there." When the crisis had passed, Putnam must have recalled the fire at Fort Edward on Christmas Day sixteen years before.[24]

Putnam and his party, including Monsieur Caters, set out on the Mississippi River on Thursday, April 8, and they made excellent time, rowing about eighteen miles up the river that first day. The following day, they attached a rudder and a mast to the bateau, and from that point on, hoisted the sail whenever the wind seemed favorable. Day by day as they worked their way north along the twisting course of the river, kedging around the sharp bends, the party saw evidence of civilization on both banks. They stopped at several plantations owned by Englishmen, growing grains and flax; two or three Indian villages of various sizes (Houma and Tunica); a prosperous settlement of Acadians from Nova Scotia, dispossessed by the British in 1755; and a group of Frenchmen, former prisoners from the last war that had been held in the Carolinas. In all, the party averaged more than fifteen miles a day for the first eighteen days.[25]

On Monday, April 26, they reached the ruins of Fort Rosalie built by the French high on the bluff at present-day Natchez. Rufus estimated that the group had traveled 388 miles north from the mouth of the Mississippi. For the next three days, the Adventurers explored the immediate area to obtain more supplies and gather information, particularly about the soil and water. They spent a fair amount of time speaking with a Mr. Thomson at his plantation. Rufus took some time himself to examine the ruins of the fort.[26]

The Adventurers set out to fulfill the purpose of their enterprise on April 28. That afternoon, prior to making camp, they rowed just more than eight miles toward Bayou Pierre to begin their exploration there, as they learned that all the best lands below that point had already been surveyed and some were already occupied. The mighty river continued to twist and turn, and all along its sinuous course it was fed by many creeks and rivers. From time to time, the men stopped to explore the immediate countryside, continuing to assess the types of soil and the vegetation. They were also interested in whether the land was subject to flooding in the spring and, on the other hand, if there was enough fresh water year-round to drink and to power a mill. Along the way, they found evidence of recent settlement activity. On Saturday, May 1, they met Maj. Luke Collins, who had led a group of a dozen settlers from Redstone, Pennsylvania. They had already started to work the land in hopes of obtaining a grant for it. Farther on, they found a rude hut with three men and a woman. Close to the mouth of Bayou Pierre they encountered yet another recent immigrant from Pennsylvania breaking ground, as well as several Choctaws, one of whom agreed to join them in their bateau. All this activity must have fed the Adventurers' sense of urgency.[27]

BAYOU PIERRE

Bayou Pierre enters the Mississippi River across from present-day St. Joseph, Louisiana. It is a long, languid stream with many smaller branches, twisting and turning over its ninety-five-mile course through southwestern Mississippi. Early French explorers found that the stream-bed was composed of gravel and stones (the French for stone being "pierre"), and referred to it as a "bayou," adapted from the Choctaw word for stream.

The Adventurers decided to explore the area with the friendly Choctaw as their guide. For a start, on May 3 they rowed some seventeen miles up Bayou Pierre to a fork in the river and made a camp. From there, over the next two days, they broke into small parties and explored the area on foot. Satisfied with what they found, from the quality of the soil to fine stands of hardwood, Rufus Putnam made the first of his survey marks on a large black oak near their camp at the forks. They all returned to the mouth of the bayou on May 5. Along the way, their Choctaw guide's dog treed a bear, but it escaped before anyone could get off a shot.[28]

Once back on the Mississippi, the party rowed north nine miles to present-day Grand Gulf, where they met with Thomas James, an Indian trader, at his station. Through the auspices of James, and over Rufus Putnam's objections, they hired another Choctaw Indian guide called "Sam" who knew the area, and whose presence would hopefully allay any fears his fellow tribesmen might have regarding the intrusion into their territory. They asked James to tell the Indian that the men were only interested in seeing the area and not settling on it. Rufus was rightfully skeptical, and he was certain that their guide would soon glean the true purpose of the exploration, despite the misinformation. The entire party then rowed north three miles to the mouth of the Big Black River.[29]

On May 6, the Adventurers rowed past two stone quarries and the home of a Captain Barber before reaching the mouth of the Big Black River, some one hundred feet across. At this point, Roger Enos, Monsieur Caters, and the Choctaw set off on foot to explore the land along the river. The rest rowed another fifteen miles upstream before making camp. Along the way, they observed that the Mississippi shore was made up of some high ground mixed with cypress swamp. The following day, they met Jacob Winfrey encamped on an island. Winfrey was the leader of a group of families from Virginia, one hundred or so persons in all, including fifteen or sixteen of his slaves. It was their stated intention to settle lands farther south along the river. May 8 was more of the same. They met Col. Anthony Hutchins, another transplant, born in New Jersey, but a recent emigrant from South Carolina, at his large plantation. Hutchins would play an influential role in the region for decades to come. They also had a strange encounter with William Burns, a native of Ipswich, Massachusetts, who had been captured by Mohawks almost two decades before, and who had been a prisoner in Illinois for nine years. The company also managed to kill a bear. Roger Enos and his party rejoined the group later that day. All along the route, the company continued to encounter groups of new settlers. The country was on the move.[30]

On May 9, Captain Enos and his party set out once again to see the high ground near the Yazoo River that had once been a French settlement. The rest of the explorers rowed to the mouth of the Yazoo and camped. There, their Choctaw friends parted with them, wishing them well and "happy times" at home. The following day, the company started up the Yazoo River. Rufus described it as a wide, sluggish stream, with stagnant water, its banks swarming with alligators. He also noted that it was apparent that the high water in the Mississippi during the spring floods the area and forced its way for many miles upstream. Captain Enos and his party rejoined the company once again, but they had other visitors as well, who brought the first hint of trouble. Seven Choctaw Indians appeared at the camp with "sowered countenances" to warn the company off. This was their, and that of the Chickasaw, remaining hunting grounds, they explained, diminished by settlement and white hunters, some of whom had built huts there. Given the range of their ages, it was clear from the deference shown by the younger men that three of the older visitors were chiefs. Coincidently, Rufus had taken some measurements earlier that day, and he determined that the company was about three miles above the northerly boundary line. The Indians went away "cheerful" after they were told that the company was only trying to see the country and that they were going back. In fact, the company prudently turned right around and rowed about six miles downstream and made camp. The following two days were spent taking short solitary tramps to see the surrounding area.[31]

Israel, along with Thaddeus Lyman, had intended to explore the lands along the so-called "Chickasaw Path" to the Black River, however, considering the previous day's confrontation, their guide flatly refused to lead them, explaining that earlier he had met two Choctaw chiefs, both of whom were opposed to any settlement in the Yazoo country, and limited such to lands south of the Yazoo River. Undeterred, starting on May 13 and over the next two days both Rufus and Israel, along with Thaddeus Lyman, set out to explore the land near the mouth of the Yazoo. The three encountered cypress swamps and dense, impenetrable canebrakes, full of tall, tough vegetation, with soils of varying quality. So thick were the canebrakes in places, that from time to time both Israel and Rufus had to climb tall trees to get their bearings, and they were forced to stay on the existing rough paths. At one point, without any evidence of a path, the cane became so dense that it took them two hours to travel fifteen hundred feet! It is interesting to picture Israel, the former Ranger, now fifty-five years old, but still vigorous, pulling on an oar for days at a time, climbing tall trees, and tramping tirelessly for miles through swamps and over broken ground. The three returned to a rendezvous with Captain Enos and the rest of their company who had rowed the bateau south from the mouth of the Yazoo.[32]

Rufus and Thaddeus made a short scout on May 15, but they soon returned to the camp after their guide, Sam, told them that their proposed route south was virtually impassable. Short of provisions, the whole party returned to Mr. James' station on May 16.[33]

On May 17, both Putnams and Thaddeus Lyman returned to the Big Black, rowing the bateau upstream some fourteen miles from its mouth and past McClure's trading post. It would prove to be the most productive exploration, as they found the lands farther up the Big Black promising. However, that was not the case during the first day. They made camp for the night, and in the morning continued their exploration. The following day was much the same; however, at some point Israel came across a small Choctaw hunting party in camp, who graciously invited him and the others to partake in their feast of bear meat and venison jerky. Putnam reciprocated with a gift of biscuit. The three returned to where they left the boat and made camp that night. The following day, Wednesday, May 19, they rowed another twelve miles upriver and noticed a change in the land for the better. There was an abundance of game, and good hardwoods in the uplands. In addition, there the river flowed swiftly over a solid ledge, suitable for the erection of a mill, and, most important, in the bottomlands away from the river they found that the soil was rich. Since it was late in the day, they rowed back downriver to their previous night's campsite.[34]

The following day, Thursday, May 20, the company was reunited at Thomas James' station. There they were greeted by yet another Choctaw chief, who showed them his commission from the British government, and who reiterated the threat that there could be no settlement north of the Yazoo. Late the next day the group bid Mr. James good-bye and set off downriver. By June 3, the company had traveled downstream where they first met up with Captain Ladlee, whom they took on board as supercargo, and, much later, their sloop *Mississippi* some forty miles below Manchac. As they came in sight, Captain Goodrich saluted the weary travelers with the boat's swivel gun. The men stored their gear on board. Once all was settled, with a touch of sarcasm, Colonel Putnam asked Goodrich if he was ready to sail home. Not surprisingly, the captain answered yes, but only, he replied, after he had finished some business with Ladlee. Rufus does not record his cousin's response, but one can imagine that it was all Putnam could do to keep his temper. The party spent just more than two weeks at and near New Orleans making repairs and taking supplies on board. The *Mississippi* set sail for Pensacola before dawn on Wednesday, June 30.[35]

MAKING THEIR CASE

Once again, headwinds slowed their progress, but they finally reached Pensacola on the evening of July 5. Soon after their arrival, the band's spirits must have been dampened when they learned that still no authority had yet reached the governor. Nevertheless, Israel and Rufus took their proposal for a grant before Governor Chester and his council. Questions were raised, and Rufus was asked to make changes in his drawings. They registered nineteen townships of 20,000 acres each that they had surveyed in the area below the Yazoo and near the Big Black, a remarkable 380,000 acres in total. That done, the best the governor and council would do at that time was to give permission to all members of the Company of Military Adventurers to settle on any "unoccupied" land surveyed by Putnam within the province, on the condition that it be done before March 1, 1774. Putnam and the others asked that the time be extended to give the potential settlers enough time to give notice of their intent to purchase; sell their homes, farms, and possessions; and take passage to West Florida. The governor's council was adamant. Though disappointed, the Exploratory Committee realized that it was the best they could accomplish.[36]

Israel Putnam and his party set sail for New York on July 11 and arrived there on August 6, after an unremarkable voyage. He, his son Daniel, and Rufus booked passage on a coastal vessel to take them to Norwich and put their baggage on board. Israel and Daniel were back home in Brooklyn on August 12.[37]

"THE WILDERNESS OF AMERICA IS ALL ALIVE"

At a meeting of the Company of Military Adventurers, Putnam explained the limited success of their trip to West Florida. He had no reason to hang his head, for as it turned out, hundreds of its members were just waiting for some hopeful word to start the process of relocating with their families. Notices were published in newspapers all over New England, together with Pennsylvania and New York. Foremost among those waiting for word was General Lyman, whose enthusiasm for the project never waned. However, unbeknownst to the Military Adventurers, in October 1773, Governor Chester received orders from the king in council that placed a moratorium on all further grants in West Florida. By the following February, a new order required that all public lands be first surveyed then sold in small lots, not large grants.[38]

Ten years after the Proclamation of 1763, Rev. Ezra Stiles simply stated the obvious when he observed that, "the Wilderness of America is all alive with the Travels of Settlers." New land and a fresh start were the drivers, and the Natchez region was no exception. Putnam brought back a letter written by an anonymous traveler while at Pensacola, dated July 12, 1773. The writer praised the Military Adventurers as "indefatigable in the Execution of their Commission" and went on to describe the present settlement activity in the region: "The settlement of that Part of the Country contiguous to Natchez goes on with incredible Rapidity; exclusive of about 200 Families that within the last six weeks have come down the Ohio from Virginia and the Carolinas, no less than four Vessels have arrived from North Carolina . . . filled with Inhabitants. Parson Sweezy [Swayze] with his little party from New Jersey are safely arrived and begun their Settlement on the lands reserved for them." The migration to West Florida from the East Coast accelerated in 1776, after the commencement of the American Revolution.[39]

Despite the glowing reports of the region, commerce and family migration on the lower Mississippi River was not without its challenges. Since the early days of the French and Spanish rule, pirates and other cutthroats preyed upon the numerous flatboats and keelboats plying the river. If they were fortunate, some helpless travelers were merely forced to pay a tribute to the ruffians before moving on. However, many more were simply killed outright and their cargoes or possessions stolen. Upon their return to Connecticut, Roger Enos and Thaddeus Lyman described the murderous activities of a particularly vicious gang of river pirates who sought to blame their actions on the local Indian population. The two Adventurers felt that it was best to set the record straight and expose the criminals by name. Despite efforts by the authorities to stop these activities, piracy remained a problem through the early decades of the next century.[40]

Four hundred families joined the migration from New England, beginning with General Lyman himself and twenty-nine others on December 19, 1773, aboard the sloop *Adventurer*. By coincidence, the master of the vessel was the same Capt. Wait Goodrich who had carried Israel Putnam south earlier in the year. They sailed from Middletown, Connecticut, and after a brief layover in New York, to pick up an additional twenty passengers and so that Lyman could conduct some personal business, the *Adventurer* arrived at Pensacola on March 3. The passengers were described as "in perfect health and high spirits."[41]

Two of Lyman's sons, Phineas and Thaddeus, and eight slaves and dozens more settlers left New London on December 17, 1773, and made a brief stop at Stonington, Connecticut, prior to sailing for the Mississippi River. Except for a brief chance meeting on the high seas near Florida, the two vessels would not meet again until both reached New Orleans sometime in late March or early April and there joined forces. Prior to that meeting, the general had landed at Pensacola on March 3, 1774, where he met with Governor Chester to secure the proper titles to the property. He left for the Mississippi River on or about March 14. As his consolidated party reached Natchez, Phineas Junior developed a fever and died. The settlers went on to locate and develop their grant on the Big Black River near its junction with the Mississippi. The general himself succumbed to fever on October 10, 1774. Eleanor Lyman, now a widow, and her brother Timothy Dwight sailed from Middletown with a group of settlers from Massachusetts on May 1, 1776. Within days after her arrival at the plantation, she suffered the same fate as her husband.[42]

Phineas Lyman had a vision of a successful colony, which he called "Georgiana" after the king. Given the rich soil and the industriousness of the migrants, he was certain of its success. However, for him the dream would be short-lived. Upon hearing the news of Lyman's death, in a sad postscript, the Reverend Stiles summed up the general's life as, "in the middle of it honorable, but for the last ten years very inglorious." The patent granted by the Crown was finally issued on February 2, 1775, but only after the general's death. It was registered in the name of Thaddeus and his siblings.[43]

All seemed well with Lyman's colony at first. However, within a short time, things took a tragic turn. In addition to Lyman's colonists, hundreds of others settled lands all along the Mississippi from New Orleans to the Yazoo near Natchez. During the American Revolution most of them remained loyal to the Crown. At some point during their occupancy of West Florida, the British had withdrawn all troops from Natchez, as a cost-saving measure, or else as a practical matter since the distance and lack of a decent military road from Pensacola made resupply or support difficult. In either event, the garrison remained at Pensacola, thus leaving the region without an adequate defense.

Consequently, when Spain entered the war as an ally on the Patriot side, the area became ripe for the picking. On October 5, 1779, Spanish forces took over Fort Panmure (formerly Fort Rosalie) at Natchez, thus establishing a foothold in the western portion of West Florida. Despite the light hand of the Spanish, tension gradually rose to the point that in April 1781 a group of two hundred Loyalists led by Thaddeus Lyman and other prominent landowners with British sympathies, including Jacob Winfrey, John Blomart, and Col. Anthony Hutchins, staged a revolt. They surrounded the Spanish garrison at Natchez and, by means of a ruse, forced the Spanish surrender on April 29. The victory was short-lived, as Governor Chester surrendered Pensacola ten days later, and in June, Col. Carlos de Grand Pré led a large Spanish force that retook the lost area, including Fort Panmure. Some rebels, including Thaddeus Lyman, were forced to flee, never to return, and saw their grants forfeit, at least in part. Many simply surrendered and retook their oaths to the king of Spain and resumed life as usual. Colonel Anthony Hutchins, too, emerged unscathed, and in fact, after his return to the territory, the Spanish enlarged his holdings.[44]

Neither Israel nor his cousin Rufus ever returned to West Florida, where they each had played such an instrumental role in its development. According to Humphreys' account, Israel Putnam sent some men with provisions and farm implements to the area on his behalf to secure a claim. Even if that were the case, nothing ever came of it. Much later, Rufus Putnam would come the closest to fulfilling Phineas Lyman's original dream when he became an original pioneer in the first permanent settlement in the Northwest Territory at Marietta.[45]

CHAPTER NINE

The American Revolution

The Fuse Is Lit

"THE WEED OF SLAVERY" (DECEMBER 1773 TO AUGUST 1774)

IF THINGS WERE QUIET FOR PUTNAM AT HOME IN BROOKLYN, IT WAS not so elsewhere in New England. While the citizens of Boston continued to carry on their daily lives, ignoring the presence of British troops, it was at best an affront to their sensibilities to see hundreds of "lobster backs" roaming the streets at will. Boston was a cauldron of warm water at near boil. Some among the population simply turned up the heat.

One dramatic act of defiance occurred during the night of December 16, 1773, when approximately fifty men disguised as Indians took it upon themselves to board three British merchantmen, *Dartmouth*, *Eleanor*, and *Beaver*, all recently arrived in port, each carrying chests of tea, property of the East India Company. Without damage to the vessels, the intrepid party seized and dumped the contents of the more than three hundred chests into Boston Harbor. The incident became known as the Boston Tea Party. Although the miscreants were never caught, the authorities had a good idea who the likely ringleaders were.[1]

The king and Parliament were angered because of this action, and the Boston Port Bill and the Regulating Act were passed, two in a series of laws otherwise known as the "Intolerable Acts," in short, closing the port of Boston and abrogating the Massachusetts Charter. General Gage became the governor, and once again, British troops were quartered in town and freely roamed the streets. Salem became the new capital, and Marblehead the official port of entry. The response throughout New England and the other colonies was swift. Committees of

Correspondence were formed to share the news, and gifts of money, livestock, and food were sent to Boston. The farmers of the town of Windham, Connecticut, supplied a flock of 258 sheep. Other Connecticut towns made similar efforts. The town of Salem, Massachusetts, too, long a problem for Gage, opened its port to ships otherwise barred from Boston, thus easing the strain on the residents of the beleaguered town.[2]

In Connecticut, Brooklyn Parish named Israel Putnam as chairman, along with Joseph Holland and Putnam's son-in-law, Daniel Tyler III, as a Committee of Correspondence. As such, on August 11, 1774, they drafted a letter to Samuel Adams, chairman of the Boston Committee of Correspondence, expressing their support and advising him of their intention to send a gift of 125 sheep from the citizens of Brooklyn for the benefit of the poor of Boston. The letter is an eloquent testament to the depth of their commitment to the fight. "With our hearts deeply impressed with the feelings of humanity to our near and dear brethren of Boston," it begins, "who are now suffering under a ministerial, revengeful hand, and at the same time full of gratitude to the patriotic inhabitants, for the noble stand which they have made against all oppressive innovations." The letter continues: "We send you one hundred and twenty-five sheep, as a present from the inhabitants of Brooklyn, hoping thereby you may be enabled to stand more firm (if possible) in the glorious cause in which you are embarked." Lest Adams question the commitment of this one small town, they wrote: "In zeal in our country's cause, we are exceeded by none; but our abilities and opportunities do not admit of our being of that weight in the American scale as we would to God we were." Using a Biblical metaphor, the trio continued: "We mean in the first place to attempt to appease the fire . . . of an ambitious and vindictive minister, by the blood of lambs and of rams; if that do not answer the end, we are ready to march in the van, and to sprinkle the American altars with our heart's blood, if occasion should be." In sum, they emphasized the importance of the Cause: "Here we have an unbounded, fertile country, worth contending for with blood."[3]

The committee delegated Putnam to deliver the sheep to Boston and the letter to Samuel Adams. As a farmer, Israel Putnam frequently traveled to Boston over the course of many years, no doubt where he found a ready market for his wool and other produce. This time was different. He arrived in Boston on Monday, August 15, 1774. While in the city, Putnam was a guest in the home of Dr. Joseph Warren, who referred to him as the "celebrated Colonel Putnam." He remained in Boston for several days, and as in the past, he visited with friends and acquaintances, as well as many of the British officers with whom he had served, including General Gage and other members of his staff, such as Maj. John Small and Maj. Thomas Moncrieffe. Small, along with Maj. Gen. Frederick Haldimand, had recently returned from West Florida.[4]

According to Dr. Thomas Young, a member of the local Committee of Correspondence, Putnam's discussions with Small were often spirited, with the former always getting the better of the cut and thrust. If the conversations became lively, they did not turn unpleasant. "What side will you take in the event the dispute should proceed to hostilities?" the officers would ask. "With my country," Putnam would respond, and "whatever happens, I will abide the consequences." His inquisitors were incredulous. "Haven't you seen firsthand our fleets and witnessed the victories of our armies?" they pressed. Putnam could not help but poke a little fun at their arrogance. "If it took six years to conquer a less populated Canada," he rejoined, "how long do you think it would take to subdue the American colonies that are so much stronger?" They persisted—perhaps Maj. Gen. James Grant himself repeated his earlier boast to Parliament. Would Putnam not concede that five thousand British regulars "could march unimpeded through the colonies?" "No doubt," Putnam answered, "if they behaved civilly, and paid well for everything they wanted." Then, just for fun he added with a smile: "If they should attempt it in a hostile manner, the women, with their ladles and broomsticks, would knock them all on the head before they got halfway through."[5]

Some British officers, such as Capt. John Montresor, had a more cynical view. He thought that former Provincial officers like Putnam could be cheaply bought, and he lamented that Gage had been remiss in not attempting to do so. It was a "blunder," he said, "not purchasing the Rebel Generals; even Israel Putnam, of Connecticut, might have been bought to my certain knowledge, for one dollar per day, or eight shillings New York currency." At the end of the day, Montresor misjudged his man, as Putnam remained steadfast in his resolve to support his fellow Americans.[6]

Doctor Young went on to discuss the visit and the visitor: "He cannot get away, he is so much caressed, both by the officers and citizens. . . . He looks fresh and hearty, and on an emergency, would be as likely to do good business as ever."[7]

"POWDER ALARM" (SEPTEMBER 1, 1774)

Shortly after Putnam had reached his home in Brooklyn, the city of Boston erupted once again with violent protests. On September 1, General Gage had staged a dawn raid on the Provincial Powder House on Quarry Hill in Cambridge (present-day Somerville). His troops seized the remaining 250 half-barrels of gunpowder stored there and brought them to Castle William in the harbor for safekeeping. While the raid took the citizens completely by surprise, it could have been much worse, if little by little over the previous weeks the Militias of each of the surrounding towns had not already quietly removed their own powder stored there, leaving only the Provincial supply.[8]

Facts merged with rumors and spread like wildfire all that day and night after the seizure had been discovered, resulting in what has been called the "Powder Alarm." The following day thousands of armed men rushed to Boston, some from as far away as the Connecticut River Valley, demonstrating and intimidating prominent Tories. More important, the response grabbed Gage's attention. He was surprised by the swift, overwhelming reaction to the seizure, and, although he conducted similar raids elsewhere in the colony, he cancelled a planned raid farther west in Worcester. He also asked for more troops to supplement his three-thousand-man garrison. Cooler heads prevailed, and both sides learned a lesson that day, particularly General Gage, who finally came to realize the depth of American resolve.[9]

In the meantime, by the time word of the raid reached Putnam in Connecticut, on Saturday, September 3, the facts had given way to hysteria. That day, an express rider by the name of Keyes arrived at Putnam's door with a letter from his correspondent in Oxford, Massachusetts, with a wildly exaggerated story, by now at least third hand, to the effect that the British had killed six people and that Boston was in flames. As a member of the Committee of Correspondence, Putnam sent a letter to Aaron Cleveland in nearby Canterbury that repeated the sensational tale and, through the various Committees of Correspondence, ultimately made its way to Philadelphia. Putnam then backed those words up with action. Within hours, thousands of fully armed Connecticut Militia, including Putnam himself, had crossed into Massachusetts before the true facts became known. Silas Deane, a delegate to a session of the First Continental Congress in Philadelphia, unfairly blamed Putnam for the false alarm, calling it a "blundering story."[10]

Putnam vigorously defended his actions, and he published an open letter dated October 3, detailing the chain of events that led to his decision. Eventually, most people forgave his hasty action and credited his ability to raise so many men so quickly. However, for some, it only served to feed the narrative of Putnam's impulsivity. Not everyone found fault with Putnam's actions. William Cooper, clerk of the Boston Committee of Correspondence, expressed their appreciation. "We cannot but admire at the generous, brave, and patriotic spirit which actuated our noble friends in Connecticut on this occasion," he wrote. "The hour of vengeance comes lowering on," he added, "repress your ardor, but let us adjure you do not smother it."[11]

During the week of September 4, as chairman of the Committee of Correspondence, Putnam received a letter from Dr. Thomas Young, his counterpart in Boston, informing him that thirty-three chests of tea had arrived at Salem aboard two ships, consigned to certain merchants. No doubt fearing retribution, one of the merchants had quickly attempted to arrange for the return of the tea. More tea was expected shortly at Portsmouth, New Hampshire. More disturbing was the fact that one hundred British soldiers were also aboard one of the ships. Dr. Young lamented that, "nothing but a non-consumption agreement can save America." Putnam duly passed the information along as a part of his "indispensable duty."[12]

"THE SHOT HEARD ROUND THE WORLD" (APRIL 1775)

During the evening hours of April 18, 1775, approximately six hundred British troops under Lt. Col. Francis Smith (10th Foot) and Maj. John

Pitcairn (Royal Marines) left their barracks in Boston bound for Concord, where they hoped to seize additional arms and military stores hidden there by the Provincial Militia. In addition, they had received word that John Hancock and Samuel Adams were staying overnight in Lexington, and Gage wanted the arch troublemakers captured and brought before him. Fortunately for the two, word of the raid had been leaked and they made a hairbreadth escape, carrying their important papers. Several riders, including Paul Revere, had set out to sound the alarm the night before, and as the British soldiers entered the center of Lexington, they were surprised to see a group of local Militiamen led by Capt. John Parker already assembled in formation on the Green. Ignoring an order to disburse, the initial standoff became a short but brisk fight after someone fired a shot, and when it was done, eight Militiamen lay dead and another nine wounded. One man in the 10th Foot was wounded. The bloody day, though, had just begun.[13]

The British continued their march toward Concord, where they found a mere fraction of the stores they had expected hidden there, and in the process, found the way contested by hundreds of armed Militiamen assembled at a small wooden bridge over the Concord River. Another sharp fight occurred, and British soldiers died.[14]

Thousands of men answered the alarm, some from as far away as Framingham and beyond. What followed for the British was a long, bloody retreat to Boston, with heavy casualties inflicted by large and small bands of Militia firing from inside homes and behind stone walls along the route. As bad as things were, they could well have been worse had not help arrived in the form of Lord Hugh Percy and the 1st Brigade. Amos Farnsworth of the Groton (Massachusetts) Militia, one of hundreds, was making his way to Boston later that day and described the scene: "I saw many Ded Regulars along the way. [I] went into a house whare Blud was half over [my] shoes."[15]

Word of the fights at Lexington and Concord reached Brooklyn, Connecticut, by express rider at 11:00 a.m. the following day. Humphreys says that, like Cincinnatus, Putnam was plowing a field with his son Daniel when he heard the news. This is a wonderful image, yet entirely possible, as Putnam was an active farmer, and it was spring. Nevertheless, whether literally or figuratively, Daniel Putnam recounts the fact that when his father received the news, he "tarried not" and "left me, the driver of his team."[16]

No doubt with the memory of the recent Powder Alarm fresh in his mind, this time Putnam's reaction was more measured, as he went first to meet with the town leaders and Militia officers. By mid-afternoon, as he was heading home from his meetings, he stopped to address the hundreds of local men milling about the Green awaiting some direction. He told them to go home and to prepare to receive official orders. In the meantime, he saddled his horse and set out for Boston that evening along a by now familiar route.[17]

"RABBLE IN ARMS"

When Putnam reached the outskirts of Boston on April 21, he was greeted by the remarkable sight of thousands of fellow citizens, like him, all bearing arms and ready to fight. It was, as Gen. John Burgoyne would later be quoted as saying, "a rabble in arms." More important, he realized that the British, who had fortified Boston Neck, were penned up in the city, along with thousands of its residents. While there, he attended a council of war in Cambridge. From Concord that evening, Putnam wrote a brief letter to Col. Ebenezer Williams in Pomfret. The accounts of the battle were "much as represented at Pomfret" he wrote. Though, he added, those accounts were "confused" as to the exact number of casualties. Putnam was informed that Connecticut would be expected to furnish six thousand fully equipped men, including "Commissary together with Provisions and sufficiency of ammunition." He asked that a copy of his letter be sent to Governor Trumbull, and he made plans to return home promptly to help raise a regiment.[18]

Israel Putnam was not alone in his response to the alarm, as many Connecticut towns mustered their Militia. Windham County raised a regiment, including a company from Mansfield led by Experience Storrs, a leading citizen of the town, and, at that time, a delegate to the Connecticut General Assembly. On April 20, Storrs noted in his diary of hearing the "Mallencolly Tidings" of the fights at Lexington and Concord. That night he traveled to Windham to meet with Jedediah

Elderkin, the colonel of his Militia regiment. The following morning his company was mustered and set out for Boston on April 22, reaching Pomfret that evening.[19]

By that time, the forty-year-old Storrs experienced a personal crisis: Should he continue to lead his company to Boston or could he best serve the Cause by taking his seat in the General Assembly? At Woodstock, the regiment was culled of every fifth man, who was sent home, and reconstituted into three new companies. Storrs broached the subject of his rejoining the General Assembly with his officers, "who strongly urged" him to continue with his company. He did so, but by the following day, after the company had reached Dudley, Massachusetts, he had convinced them otherwise. He left his company at noon that day and set off for home, which he reached during the evening of April 24. While attending the General Assembly, he continued to work tirelessly for the benefit of the Connecticut troops.[20]

One of the many companies arriving at Cambridge shortly after the alarm was an independent Militia company from Wethersfield led by Capt. John Chester. A member of the company was Chester's brother-in-law, Ens. Samuel Blachley Webb, who was also the stepson of Silas Deane, a prominent Wethersfield merchant, then serving in the Second Continental Congress in Philadelphia. Resplendent in their blue coats with red facing, the company was soon selected by General Ward as his personal guard. Young Webb would quickly distinguish himself in service and, in addition, over time amass a large collection of correspondence and official papers, which are a veritable trove for historians.[21]

Connecticut Answers the Call

On April 26, Gov. Jonathan Trumbull called the General Assembly into special session to deal with the situation in Boston. One of its first actions was to select the senior leadership of the Connecticut troops. David Wooster was appointed as a major general, Joseph Spencer as the senior brigadier general, and Israel Putnam as the second brigadier. No one thought anything of it at the time, but this action would later be cause for some bruised egos in July.[22]

In addition, the General Assembly called for the raising of six regiments with ten companies in each. Putnam, age fifty-seven and considerably heavier, his full head of unruly hair now snow white, was appointed to command the Third Regiment, as well as the First Company in it. Experience Storrs was appointed as the regiment's lieutenant colonel and in command of the Second Company. Putnam's friend and colleague, John Durkee from Norwich, was appointed as major and given command of the Third Company. The Tenth Company was led by Captain Israel Putnam Jr., who would later serve as his father's aide-de-camp. Nine companies of the regiment were raised from Windham County, along with Durkee's company from New London County. The month of May was spent raising and equipping the companies. The regiment marched by companies to Boston by the last week of the month. Without so much as a second thought, Putnam had gone off to war again.[23]

SETTLING IN

After reaching Boston, Putnam encamped his regiment, along with two formerly independent companies, that of Capt. John Chester (now the Ninth Company in Col. Joseph Spencer's 2nd Connecticut Regiment), and that of William Coit (now the Fourth Company in Col. Samuel H. Parson's 6th Connecticut Regiment), all in tents "on the high ground" at the David Phipps farm near Lechmere Point. Two Massachusetts regiments were also attached to Putnam's command: Col. Paul Dudley Sargent's 8th Massachusetts Regiment was camped in the outbuildings at Ralph Inman's farm in an area that would come to be known as Cambridgeport, and Col. John Paterson's regiment of infantry was camped near Lechmere Point. Inman was a prominent Tory merchant. Fearing for his life, he had fled to the safety of Boston, leaving his wife, Elizabeth, a nephew, and their servants behind. Throughout his stay in Cambridge, Putnam treated Mrs. Inman with the utmost courtesy, and, after a couple of minor incidents involving the troops billeted in an outbuilding there, he ordered Colonel Sargent to mount a guard at the home. He also left his son Daniel, then serving as an aide, to sleep there. In the meantime, the Borland House in Cambridge (also known as the "Apthorp House") was chosen as his residence and headquarters. John Borland was another Tory merchant who had abandoned his home for the safety of Boston.[24]

Once at Cambridge, the more experienced men, like Putnam and Artemas Ward, took an active hand in bringing order out of chaos. According to Col. Jedediah Huntington, "they have, both of them, too much business upon their shoulders." Perhaps harkening back to his service with the Rangers, as did many Militia officers, Putnam mingled freely with the men of his regiment, and on occasion, even cooking his own meat alongside them.[25]

As the bulk of the assembled forces were from Massachusetts, and as he was the most senior Militiaman, Seth Pomeroy, a sixty-nine-year-old gunsmith from Northampton, was initially chosen by the Congress in Watertown to take command. Putnam and Pomeroy had served together during the French and Indian War. Soon, the daily grind became too much for the old soldier, and in early June he went home for a short, but much-needed rest. He arrived at Northampton on the evening of June 15. Pomeroy was replaced by Artemas Ward, another older veteran.[26]

SPOILING FOR A FIGHT

From long experience, Putnam realized that idle soldiers spelled trouble. Moreover, with Militia, it was even more important to keep them occupied, if only to keep their minds off their farms and families back home. Many must have thought, "What am I doing here, when I could be home getting the spring planting done." His son Daniel recalled that one of his father's sayings was that "it is better to dig a ditch every morning and fill it up at evening than to have the men idle." Putnam, himself, had an aggressive spirit, and idleness did not suit him either. Accordingly, early on, he had suggested an attack on the Boston Neck using bales of hay as cover. On May 12 at a council of war, which included members of the Committee of Safety, he suggested that the heights at Charlestown be fortified, to "draw the enemy from Boston where we might meet them on equal terms." His proposal was rejected as too risky. The following day, just for show, he marched his regiment up nearby Bunker and Breed's Hills, paraded them through Charlestown in full view of the British, and then marched them back to Cambridge. In addition, he set the men to building floating artillery batteries. Putnam would soon get his chance to fight.[27]

"THE REIVERS" (THE BATTLE OF CHELSEA CREEK)

The people of Boston had long grazed their animals on many of the thirty islands in and around Boston Harbor. It was practical, as there were no fences to mend, and the principal islands, Hog and Noddle's (now part of modern-day Chelsea and East Boston), could be easily reached at low tide. Shortly after the hostilities began, it became apparent that unless the animals still grazing there were removed, they would be subject to seizure by the British, which would become increasingly likely the longer the siege continued to choke off the normal farm trade with the city. In fact, the British already successfully removed hay from Grape Island on May 21, narrowly escaping the fury of the swiftly assembled Militia. However, they had hoped to remove seventy tons of hay but were only able to retrieve seven to eight tons before the Militia arrived and burned the rest.[28]

A prosperous farmer and friend of the Patriots, Henry Howell Williams, lived at the lower end of Noddle's Island. In addition, the British grazed some of their animals on the island and used the existing buildings there for storage of wood and naval stores to repair their leaky warships. Admiral Samuel Graves had stationed a small number of Marines to guard them. Accordingly, in late May a plan was hatched by the Committee of Safety to preemptively burn the hay and seize the grazing stock there.

On Saturday, May 27, at approximately 11:00 a.m., a small group of farmers and herdsmen were recruited to remove their stock currently grazing on both islands. Backed by a body of more than three hundred Militia under the joint command of John Nixon of Sudbury, Massachusetts, and John Stark, a native of Dunbarton, New Hampshire, and a former Ranger with Robert Rogers, they waded across the mud flats at low tide to Hog Island. After successfully removing hundreds of animals from Hog Island, they moved over to nearby Noddle's Island. A small contingent of British Marines on duty there, seeing what was occurring, began to fire on the intruders. Despite the opposition, the raiders were able to retrieve a fair number of animals, including two British horses, and to burn some hay and grain before retreating to Hog Island. Unfortunately, they also became carried away and plundered the Martin farm, while at the same time, inexplicably, leaving much of Admiral Graves' stores intact. The British, now fully aware of the circumstances and seeing the billowing smoke from the burning buildings, dispatched more Marines in longboats from several warships at anchor in the harbor, as well as from a sloop, and the schooner *Diana*, which had just returned from a cruise along the Maine coast. The Americans dug in and returned fire for the balance of the afternoon, killing two Marines and wounding two others, one fatally. According to one of the raiders, Amos Farnsworth of Groton, Massachusetts, the "bullets flew very thick yet there was not a man of us killed." About sunset, Farnsworth and his comrades withdrew to Chelsea, but they continued to draw heavy fire from the two vessels.[29]

Help came in the form of Israel Putnam at the head of a party of three hundred men, along with two cannons. Dr. Warren, who had become close to Putnam, volunteered to accompany Putnam as an ordinary soldier. Putnam arrived around 9:00 p.m. and immediately hailed the schooner, which by then had grounded in the shallow waters, and he demanded its surrender. The vessel's crew responded with shot, as did British Marines with cannon fire from Noddle's Island. Thus began an extended exchange of fire. Amos Farnsworth had remained for the fight and wrote how "the balls sung like bees round our heads." At some point during the night, the *Diana* began to list very badly, and the crew abandoned ship. By early Sunday morning when the tide was low, Putnam and his men waded out to the ship carrying bunches of hay that they placed beneath the vessel and set her afire. At the same time, he and his men also removed two cannons, several swivel guns, and assorted booty. Four Patriots were wounded, one of whom later died.[30]

Wet and muddy, but exhilarated, Putnam returned to his Charlestown headquarters at the Borland House later that morning, where he found Dr. Warren, who had gone on before, and General Ward. He briefed them on the night's activities, and he told General Ward that, "I wish we could have something of this kind to do every day." That way, he reasoned, they could harass the enemy, and at the same time, give his men the experience of acting under fire. Ward replied that such actions would surely undermine any hope that America could reconcile with England. Putnam was having none of that. "You know, Dr. Warren," he rejoined, "we shall have no peace worth anything till we gain it by the sword." Warren calmly told Putnam: "I admire your spirit and respect General Ward's prudence, both will be necessary for us, and one must temper the other." Despite Warren's wise observation, Putnam's spirit remained undimmed. Later, in retelling the story of the fight at Noddle's Island, he was heard to say that "there was nothing between us and the fire of the enemy but pure air." In her history of the American Revolution, Mercy Otis Warren praised Putnam for this exploit as "an officer of courage and experience."[31]

THE TRUCE

On June 6, a truce was arranged to exchange prisoners. Israel Putnam and Dr. Warren were chosen to cross the lines to oversee the operation. Both men maintained cordial relations with many of the British officers then stationed in Boston, particularly Putnam through his past association. The exchange took place in Charlestown at the home of a Dr. Foster. The companies of Capt. William Coit, from New London, and Capt. John Chester of Wethersfield were selected as an escort. For Putnam and many of the British officers present, including Maj. Thomas Moncrieffe, it would be an emotional reunion. Aside from the bear hugs and friendly greetings, many, including Putnam, looked back nostalgically on a decade of service together. He and Warren hosted a reception for the officers, and when it was over, both sides returned to their respective lines and resumed their previous postures.[32]

A RECURRING THEME

Many veterans of the French and Indian War, like Generals Putnam and Pomeroy and Col. William Prescott, maintained an aggressive spirit, and the idea of fortifying the heights at Charlestown kept coming up. Others, on both the Committee of Safety and the council of war, which was "in continual session," opposed the idea as too risky. At one session, when someone suggested that there was not enough powder, Pomeroy exploded, "I will fight the enemy with but five cartridges apiece!" Generals Ward and Warren were afraid that fortifying the heights at Charlestown would "bring on a general engagement." Putnam's response provides a valuable insight into how and why the events of June 17 unfolded as they did. For him, at this stage, the fight itself was more important than a win. "We will risk only two thousand men," he said, [and] "we will go on with these and defend ourselves as long as possible, and, if driven to retreat, we are more active than the enemy," and as such, we will extract a high price. Moreover, he added that if surrounded and we cannot retreat, "we will set an example of which it shall not be ashamed and teach mercenaries what men can do determined to live or die free." Warren told him that he was "almost convinced," but that if Putnam's position prevailed, he would, once again, fight at his side as a common soldier. Putnam told him bluntly that he was too valuable to the Cause to risk his life now.[33]

THE "DECISIVE DAY" (THE BATTLE OF BUNKER HILL)

After they received word that the British intended to occupy the Charlestown peninsular, the Massachusetts Committee of Safety did an about-face on June 15 and decided that the time was ripe to beat them to it, and they recommended that the council of war follow through with a plan to do so. Accordingly, the council directed General Ward to use two thousand men to seize and fortify Bunker Hill, the high ground closest to the Charlestown Neck. Putnam was pleased that the council had finally come around, and, with tongue in cheek, he expressed his confidence in the men taking part. "The Americans are not at all afraid of their heads, though very much afraid of their legs," he pronounced, "if you cover those, they will fight forever."[34]

To that end, during the afternoon of June 16, all Connecticut regiments were ordered to cull from each company 31 men, 28 privates and 3 noncommissioned officers. These men, along with a larger contingent from Massachusetts, would be the nucleus of the 1,000- to 1,200-man force under the direct command of Col. William Prescott, who was ordered to carry out the plan. The balance of the troops were to remain in Cambridge as a reserve.[35]

Putnam's younger son, Daniel, then sixteen years old, was serving as a volunteer aide on his staff. At sunset, just before he left headquarters,

Putnam called Daniel aside and said: "You will go up to Mrs. Inman's tonight as usual; stay there tomorrow, if they find it necessary to leave town, you must go with them." Knowing that his father was going to a fight, Daniel pleaded with him to let him go too: "You . . . may need my assistance more than Mrs. Inman. . . . Let me go where you are going." Putnam was firm. "No, no," he told him, "do as I have bid you." The father's eyes welled up, and he told his son that he "could do little where I am going," and besides, "there will be enough to take care of me." Daniel did as he was told. The arrangement pleased Mrs. Inman, who, after she heard, tightly hugged the young man when he returned that evening, and she exclaimed: "Oh happy General Putnam in such a son!"[36]

That same evening around 8:00 p.m., after assembling on the Cambridge Green, the selected troops marched off with their muskets, along with about a thousand picks and shovels they had loaded on carts. Once across the narrow Charlestown Neck, Brigadier General Putnam, who had command of the sector, Colonel Prescott, and Col. Richard Gridley, an engineer and artillery officer, met for an informal conference. Putnam had an added reason to be present, as Prescott's party included approximately two hundred men from Connecticut, many of them from his own regiment. When the conference ended, it was decided to fortify Breed's Hill and not Bunker Hill. Although it was lower than Bunker Hill, it was closer to Boston and in full view of the British, something sure to get their attention, which, after all, was the point. A brief time later, the trio gathered on Breed's Hill where, under Putnam's direction, Gridley laid out the lines for the redoubt approximately 125 feet on each side, and on the following morning, he laid out an adjoining breastwork that extended north another three hundred feet.[37]

A Busy Morning

For his part, as the ranking officer, Putnam believed that he was in command, and he acted as such. He was not idle, in part due to his nature, but also because he lacked an experienced staff, and there was no official chain of command. However, since Putnam could not be everywhere at once during the battle and the lead-up to it, some critical decisions would later be made by the individual commanders on their own initiative.

After spending the night between the redoubt and Bunker Hill, Putnam rode back to his headquarters in Cambridge sometime before first light. No doubt he had set out to confer with General Ward about reinforcements, as well as replacements for the men who had labored all night on the redoubt. He would also need men to dig entrenchments on Bunker Hill as a fallback position. At this time, however, he had neither the men nor any picks and shovels to do so. His stay at Cambridge was cut short when, sometime after dawn, he heard firing from British warships and the batteries on Copps Hill, and he galloped back to the front line, satisfied that provision would be made to send over additional troops.[38]

Later that morning, General Ward did send word to Col. John Stark and Col. James Reed, then camped in Medford, to bring their New Hampshire regiments to Charlestown. Stark received the order between 10:00 and 11:00 a.m., assembled his men, and drew ammunition. It was about this time that an anxious Putnam rode back to Cambridge to find out why no reinforcements had been sent. He was informed that Ward had alerted Stark's regiment, but to his great annoyance, it was the only substantial relief force dispatched by Ward that day. Putnam then rode back to Bunker Hill.[39]

At 10:00 a.m., Lieutenant Colonel Storrs reported to Putnam at his post on Bunker Hill. He noted in his diary that "[Putnam] has the command." By that time, the British fire had become heavier, and, in his words, "some shot whistled around us." When their conference ended, Storrs returned to his company to make it ready to provide relief if needed and to await further orders.[40]

By late morning, work on the redoubt and breastwork was completed, and the tools were set aside. Shortly after 11:00 a.m. Putnam returned to the redoubt, and he commandeered the picks and shovels, along with a few men to carry them. In a curt exchange, Putnam told Prescott that the tools would otherwise be lost. Prescott retorted that if he did what he ordered, the men would never return. Putnam vigorously disputed this, citing his belief in the innate valor of the American soldier. In the end, Prescott was proven right, as many of those troops simply melted away after leaving a pile of picks and shovels on Bunker Hill. Thus, Putnam continued to be frustrated in his plan to entrench on Bunker Hill to cover any withdrawal.[41]

Sometime after his exchange with Prescott, as it became clear that the British were preparing to land troops, Putnam again rode up to the redoubt. He realized that the earthen fort and breastwork could be easily outflanked. Pointing to a rail fence running north from the base of Breed's Hill toward the Mystic River, and apparently unaware of Colonel Prescott's prior orders, he directed Capt. Thomas Knowlton to lead 120 men off Breed's Hill and to take up a position behind that slim barrier. This was a critical decision, since it would block the British from flanking the redoubt and breastwork.[42]

Lieutenant Thomas Grosvenor, of Pomfret, and his company were part of Knowlton's detail. They had spent the night atop Breed's Hill. Many others in Knowlton's party were from his native Ashford, Connecticut, including fifty-seven-year-old William Cheney, who had left his farm and large family to take up the fight. Whether at Putnam's direction or on his own initiative, Knowlton had his men construct three small fleches at an oblique angle to provide fire on the flanks of the enemy, and, at the same time, to fill the gap between the redoubt and breastwork and the south end of the rail fence line. With the Connecticut men was Capt. Samuel R. Trevett and his small battery consisting of two field pieces. Knowlton's men hurriedly piled hay bales behind and additional fence rails atop the existing fence and bravely awaited the enemy. Despite their efforts, in truth, there were simply not enough of them to defend the entire rail fence line.[43]

Between 1:00 and 2:00 p.m., the British had begun to load boats and land troops at Morton's Point, and with a separate detachment, began to burn Charlestown. It became apparent to Putnam that Ward was not sending any further reinforcements, at least not any time soon, and he ordered his son and aide, Capt. Israel Putnam Jr., to ride to Cambridge to find Chester's and Coit's companies, and any others under his direct command, to tell them make haste to the scene of the battle. Captain Putnam also brought orders for Storrs to lead the balance of the Third Connecticut Regiment to Fort Number 1, one of three small redoubts in Cambridge, and await further orders.[44]

Earlier that morning, Putnam had issued orders for a further draft from among those companies that had remained behind to stand in readiness to provide a relief force. One of these was Capt. William Coit's company. Coit had been ordered to pick ten men, fully dressed, and supplied with two days' rations, to assemble on the parade ground in Cambridge at 6:00 p.m. and to await orders. The situation at Breed's Hill altered that timetable. Instead, at the younger Putnam's direction, Coit started his men toward the Charlestown Neck. Anxiously awaiting reinforcement, Putnam had periodically returned to Bunker Hill and the Charlestown Neck to spur on arriving relief companies, some leaderless, and others reluctant to brave the British cannonade.[45]

HELP IN THE NICK OF TIME

Stark, and his contingent of New Hampshire men, got under way from Medford about 1:00 p.m. and arrived at Putnam's post atop Bunker Hill an hour later, as the British continued their landing of troops near Morton's Point. Reed and his regiment had also caught up by then. Although Putnam and Stark were not personally on the best of terms, the former must have been pleased to see another experienced soldier. Riding up to him, Putnam exhorted him to join Knowlton's troops at the rail fence: "Push on Colonel Stark, the enemy have landed and formed!" Colonel Stark assumed command at the rail fence, and, on his own initiative, prudently extended the left of the line all the way to the Mystic River, piling stone upon stone to form a rude barrier across the small shingle of exposed shoreline beyond the north end of the rail fence.[46]

TWO EARNEST PATRIOTS

In the meantime, as soon as Putnam had heard the plan to seize Bunker Hill, he sent an express to Seth Pomeroy to bring him up to date. "We have determined to draw our forces nearer the city, and to take possession of the heights of Charlestown," he told the old soldier. The message reached Pomeroy within hours of the time he had returned to Northampton for a respite. Not wishing to be left out of what was likely to be a sharp fight, at noon on June 16, he had his horse saddled and back he rode all night to Cambridge, which, after two changes of mounts, he reached at approximately 2:00 p.m. on July 17. Pomeroy left his horse at the Charlestown Neck and headed toward the redoubt.[47]

No one was more surprised than Putnam to see Pomeroy standing there in front of him. As the two old soldiers approached each other, Putnam grabbed Pomeroy's hand and said in a loud voice: "You here, Pomeroy? God! I believe a cannon would wake you if you slept in a grave." Warmly received by Putnam's small contingent of Connecticut troops, Pomeroy took his place with them. By then, the British had already been lobbing shells at the men in the redoubt. With one gruesome exception, when a man was decapitated by a cannon ball, the casualties at that stage were, for the most part, minor.[48]

While making his rounds that afternoon, Putnam also met Maj. Gen. Joseph Warren rushing toward the scene, carrying his own musket. Putnam suggested to Warren that, as his superior, he should take command. True to his word, as he had done earlier at Chelsea Creek, Warren declined. He would fight as an ordinary soldier. "I came not here for command," Putnam recalled the doctor saying, and "I know nothing of your dispositions for defense, but what I can do, by example and encouragement to others, shall be done." Seeing that Warren was determined, Putnam told him to take a place in the redoubt, while he returned to his command post on Bunker Hill.[49]

The Attack

At 3:00 p.m. the British dressed ranks and began their attack. On the British right flank, General Howe led his grenadiers and light infantry against Stark and Knowlton at the now fortified rail fence, hoping to turn the American flank and expose the redoubt to a simultaneous attack. Certain that these elite soldiers would quickly overcome any resistance, he was shocked to see the effectiveness of the Patriots' fire. On the left, Gen. Sir Robert Pigot sent his soldiers forward up Breed's Hill toward the redoubt and breastwork, who experienced the same withering fire. Particularly vulnerable were the officers with their gleaming gorgets, easy targets for Prescott's sharpshooters. Lieutenant John Waller, adjutant of the 1st Battalion, Royal Marines, found it "astonishing what a number of officers were hit . . . but the officers were particularly aimed at." The

British fell back to regroup, and then they marched back up the hill, over the bodies of their fallen comrades, only to be again repulsed.[50]

WHERE WAS PUTNAM

For more than three hours from 2:00 to 5:30 p.m., Putnam was clearly a man in constant motion. While there is no concrete evidence that he entered the redoubt again at any time after he issued orders to Knowlton to take his detail to the rail fence, there are ample firsthand accounts of his activity during this period. From time to time, he even dismounted to load and sight a field piece.[51]

Abner Allen was in Lieutenant Grosvenor's company, and he recalled seeing Putnam "on horseback urging men to fight with great earnestness," and observed that he was "exposed as any man engaged." Philip Bagley in Frye's regiment told the same story, adding that, "the shot were very thick where he was; [and] he had a very calm, encouraging look." Reuben Kemp, of Stark's regiment, saw Putnam "constantly passing backward and forward from right to left." Simeon Noyes of Salem confirmed that Putnam was not in the redoubt when the British attacked; on the contrary, he was "riding to and fro in all parts of the line, encouraging the men, pressing them forward, and giving orders to the officers." Noyes added that Putnam "did not stop long in any one place." Major General Dearborn's later claim that there was "no officer on horseback," a clear symbol of high authority and command, was simply untrue. In fact, of all the senior officers present, it was Putnam alone on horseback.[52]

Shirkers and skulkers were particular objects of Putnam's wrath, threatening most with some choice oaths and imprecations, and, for others, the tip or flat of his sword. Isaac Barrett's father was helping a wounded man off the field when Putnam "pricked his arm with his sword," telling his father to get back in the line. John Holden watched as Putnam rode up to a man cowering behind a haystack and "gave him one or two blows with his sword," and at the same time crying, "God curse him! Run him through if he won't fight."[53]

TOO LITTLE, TOO LATE

Captain John Chester and his company had also answered Putnam's call. As his company began to cross Charlestown Neck, fire from British warships in the Charles River had become heavy. "Bombs, Chain shot, Ring shot, and Double-headed shot flew as thick as Hail Stones," Samuel Webb recalled. In addition to the British fire, the scene at the Charlestown Neck had become chaotic, as the retreating wounded and others mingled with the relief forces. Webb wrote that there they, "met many of our worthy friends wounded, sweltering in their blood, carried on the shoulders of their fellow soldiers," no doubt fleeing the carnage at the redoubt. Webb noticed that some of the wounded were being attended by as many as twenty men, where in his words, three could make do.

The heavy shelling and the sight of so many wounded must have shocked the men in some of the other relief companies as they approached the fighting, and, to Webb's disgust, many refused to proceed any farther, and "lay skulking" behind Bunker Hill. One company appeared leaderless, as their captain had told them to "go ahead" and that he would "catch up with them later." As they walked on, it had become obvious to the men that he had no intention of doing so, and, at Captain Chester's urging, the men fell in behind his company.[54]

Putnam was able to round up a few brave men like Webb and his comrades, who "pressed on," up and over Bunker Hill and down into the small valley below, with "no more tho't of ever rising the Hill [Bunker Hill] again."[55]

THE REDOUBT FALLS

From his vantage point atop Bunker Hill, Putnam could see and hear the battle, and he watched the flow of wounded leaving the redoubt. While Stark and Knowlton were holding firm at the rail fence, it was an entirely different story at the redoubt and the breastwork. What first began as a trickle soon turned into a steadier flow of wounded men aided by their friends, as well as skulkers fleeing Prescott's position.

Unknown to the British below, there was grave concern in the redoubt, as powder and ball were now in short supply. The defenders watched and waited as the British troops went forward once again, with

Figure 7. Sketch of General Israel Putnam, circa 1780, by John Trumbull
COURTESY OF THE WADSWORTH ATHENEUM MUSEUM OF ART (ALLEN PHILLIPS PHOTO)

grim determination, bayonets fixed, the ground more littered than before. This time, though, they reached their objective. Their blood was up, and they began the work they had first set out to do, only now with a vengeance. At first, the defenders resisted the final onslaught with musket butts, rocks, and fists, however, they soon knew that the end was upon them. Prescott estimated that the fight lasted an hour and twenty minutes, although it probably lasted longer. It was likely as late as 5:30 p.m. when Prescott ordered a retreat. What had been a steady flow soon became a flight pell-mell toward Bunker Hill and the safety of Cambridge beyond.[56]

The British soldiers followed close on their heels, killing without quarter—bayonetting the wounded and smashing skulls with their musket butts. Lieutenant Waller described the grim scene: "I was with those two companies who drove their bayonets into all that opposed them. Nothing could be more shocking than the carnage that followed the storming this work. We tumbled over the dead to get to the living, who were crowding out of the gorge of the redoubt." One of the lucky ones was Amos Farnsworth. He was twice wounded during the retreat from the redoubt, a flesh wound in the back and another, more seriously, in the arm. Nevertheless, he thanked God for his deliverance, "althoe thay fell on my Right hand and on my left."[57]

At the rail fence, the story was much the same. Wave after wave of British soldiers were repulsed by the accurate fire of the defenders. The Americans never broke. However, looking to the right, Stark could see that the redoubt had been overwhelmed, which left his men in danger of being cut off. Accordingly, Stark, along with Reed and Knowlton, formed up their men and staged a fighting withdrawal, all the way to the Charlestown Neck, although they lost one of their field pieces in the process.[58]

Putnam also tried to rally the men to make a stand. Anderson Miner recalled seeing Putnam "riding through the ranks amidst showers of ball, undaunted, with his sword drawn exhorting the troops: 'In the Name of God, give them one more shot, and then retreat.'" Another heard him call out to fleeing soldiers to help entrench on Bunker Hill: "Make a halt here, my lads, and we can stop them yet." Captain Frances Green of Gardner's regiment had just reached the rail fence when the retreat began. Putnam was on Bunker Hill, "in danger from balls flying there," Green recalled, and "he tried to stop us and to make us take up intrenching tools . . . [and] to throw up a breastwork there." Putnam only gave up on his plan to entrench on Bunker Hill when the overwhelming tide of men streaming toward Cambridge made clear the futility of that objective.[59]

In the end, Putnam was able to cobble together a small aggregation of troops behind a rough stone wall in the valley at the base of Bunker Hill to make a stand to help cover the retreat. Captain James Clark of Lebanon, Connecticut, along with his 6th Company, which was part of Putnam's Third Connecticut Regiment, was one of these units. Clark and his company had reached the rail fence sometime after the fight had commenced, when the order was given to retreat. He recalled Putnam "actively managing the retreat, as he and his company quickly fell back to the rough stone wall and commenced firing. Chester's fresh company joined them there and began to shoot at the advancing British."[60]

Samuel Webb later expressed admiration for the "red coats," as he could see their disciplined ranks take withering fire. Even after they "fell in great plenty," he noted, they continued to advance, right up to the stone wall. Lieutenant Waller told his brother that during the pursuit, the light infantry "suffered exceedingly." As the fighting raged, Webb watched as "four men were shot dead within five feet" of him, but by then, he said that he had "no other feeling but that of Revenge." He wrote that he and his comrades kept up "a brisk fire from our small arms," until the British began to overrun their position. The intensity of the short fight, which, for Webb, lasted about "six minutes," must have seemed like an eternity to the young soldier, who soon fell back with the rest, leaving the dead and wounded behind.[61]

One of Sam Webb's companions shot two British regulars dead, and when the fighting became hand to hand, he "wrenched the gun out of the hands of another [regular] and shot him dead and brought off the gun." In all, Captain Chester's company would suffer four dead and five wounded in that fight, including Roger Fox and Gershom Smith.[62]

Captain Coit and his company also reached the valley at the base of Bunker Hill in time to help slow the British tide. During that short, intense fight, Sgt. Robert Hallum stood his ground, firing twenty-eight times, eight of them after he was wounded. Before retreating, Coit's company would suffer ten wounded, two of them seriously.[63]

The British pursued the Patriots to Bunker Hill and would have gone farther, but they were recalled. By most accounts, Putnam was one of the last to cross the Charlestown Neck to the relative safety of Cambridge. Once across, Putnam raced to nearby Prospect Hill, gathering all the men he could find along the way, and, with a handful of salvaged picks and shovels, he ordered the men to entrench there. For their part, the British began to entrench on the now abandoned Bunker Hill, expanding on the modest works that Captain Montresor had dug there following the British retreat from Concord on April 19, to stem the tide of the rebel Militias.[64]

ARTISTIC LICENSE

Amid all the chaos of the withdrawal, there were a few random acts of gallantry, most notably, Maj. John Small's gesture preventing a soldier from bayonetting the mortally wounded Joseph Warren, who, face still toward the enemy during the retreat, had received a shot below his left eye that blew out the back of the head. Dr. Warren and the amiable Scotsman had established a warm friendship during the British occupation of Boston. Small's act was romantically, if not inaccurately, portrayed by John Trumbull in his famous painting of the scene, in which Small is seen pushing away the bayonet of a British soldier.

The story as told years later to John Trumbull by Small, if less dramatic, was certainly more poignant. After the redoubt was taken, as Howe and Small followed the pursuit, the former pointed to a young, wounded American, who looked familiar, and asked Small if he knew him. "Good God, Sir!" Small exclaimed, "I believe it is my friend Warren." Howe told Small to immediately go to him and "keep off the troops." Small quickly reached the wounded man. "My dear friend," he said, "I hope you are not badly hurt." Warren, he said, "looked up, seemed to recollect me, smiled and died."[65]

As for Putnam's gallant gesture, in later years, Small himself would recall that at the height of the second attack on the redoubt, he had clearly heard Putnam's voice cry out above the din, to spare his [Small's] own life, "for he is dear to me as a brother!" Small would later bring this up to Putnam, as well as to Trumbull. So, it certainly happened at some point during the intense fighting that day, though more than likely in the valley between the two hills, during the retreat. At that time, Putnam and Small would have been near each other.[66]

THE BUTCHER'S BILL

The American losses were high, 115 killed and 305 wounded, but nowhere near those of the British. The dead would include the prominent, like Dr. Joseph Warren, as well as the ordinary, like William Cheney, a simple farmer from Ashford, Connecticut, who died at the rail fence. Both would be hastily and unceremoniously buried in common graves along with other casualties.[67]

Putnam proved correct in his earlier prediction that the Americans would exact a heavy price on the British. When they toted up their losses, the British were shocked to find that nearly 50 percent of their attacking force of 2,300 had been either killed or wounded. The losses were particularly severe among the officers. One of those was Maj. John Pitcairn, mortally wounded as he mounted the redoubt shouting: "The day is ours!" Looking back at the events of the day, Putnam was heard to remark that he had "never seen such a carnage of the human race."[68]

No one should have been surprised by what occurred that day, from the deadly effect of the Patriots' muskets and their steadiness under fire, to the feral ferocity of the British soldiers in pursuit of the retreating rebels, bayonetting the wounded and crushing the skulls of the dead and dying. From their early boyhoods, the Americans were hunters of small game and became deadly shots. Moreover, by the time of the Revolution, about a quarter of the Militiamen from Massachusetts alone had served during the French and Indian War, as did most of their officers, and they were fighting to defend their home turf. Because of that joint service with British soldiers, they knew that their enemies were men just like themselves, and not formidable, larger-than-life figures. From the standpoint of the British, the carnage of the day, as well as the humiliation of April 19, still fresh in their minds, easily caused them to descend into a state of rage and bloodlust.[69]

A tense exchange between Prescott and Putnam took place at some point during the retreat when they came face-to-face. "Why did you not support me, General, with your men, as I had reason to expect according to our agreement," Prescott heatedly charged. His frustration evident, Putnam stammered, "I could not drive the dogs up!" "If you could not drive them up," Prescott snapped sarcastically, "you might have led them up." The upshot of this brief exchange sounds simple enough; blame Putnam for the loss. However, it ignores the fact that, except for the mixed force in the redoubt, each regiment at Boston fought as a separate unit under their chosen officers. As a result, they were "unwilling to obey Israel Putnam as he attempted to move units from Bunker Hill to Breed's Hill," observed historian Seanegan Sculley. He attributes this "in large part to a lack of political coordination between the four New England governments and their forces in the field." In other words, it was still "early days."[70]

Finally, if any blame for the outcome is to be assigned, it should lie with the Committee of Safety and General Ward, who had overall command of the forces, and who failed to anticipate the need to reinforce and resupply the troops on the Charlestown Peninsular in a timely manner. More men should have been committed on the night of June 16, with a portion of them entrenched on Bunker Hill, where they would function as a ready reserve just as Putnam had intended. In daylight, to reach the field of battle, any relief force had to endure the murderous fire from *Glasgow* while crossing Charlestown Neck, when they could have crossed over unseen the night before. Understandably, for many skittish, untested men, it was a bridge too far. As it was, the bulk of the available troops remained in Cambridge, prepared to defend the town should the attack on Breed's Hill be a feint, and when it was learned that it was not, any relief was dispatched far too late.[71]

All that said, it lends support to the argument that the battle itself was initially intended to be a limited engagement. Only after the near victory did it take on more importance and the "what ifs" begin.

THE DAY AFTER

On Sunday, June 18, the day following the battle, Abigail Adams picked up her pen to write to her husband. "Dearest Friend," she began. "The day; perhaps the decisive Day is come on which the fate of America depends." With "bursting heart," she relayed the sad news that their family physician and friend, Dr. Joseph Warren, had been killed. In those troubled times, the minister's daughter fell back upon her strong faith, with a firm belief that, in the end, with God's help, things would work out. "The race is not to the swift, nor the battle to the strong," she recited, "but the God of Israel is he that giveth strength and power unto his people."[72]

PROMOTIONS AND PIQUE

Artemas Ward, along with Putnam and his other subordinate generals, had worked hard to instill some semblance of order in the multitude of anywhere from fourteen thousand to twenty thousand men living in rude encampments with little or no sanitary discipline. There were shortages of tents, gunpowder, and armorers to repair weapons. In addition, so many soldiers were sick, one officer lamented that, "our medicine chests will soon be exhausted." At the end of the day, however, the army remained a loose aggregation of various Provincial regiments. Requests for complete troop returns went uncomplied with, and a true state of readiness could not be determined. Moreover, many units had only signed on for a limited period of service, and the clock was ticking.[73]

The Continental Congress did eventually act on a plan for a more permanent structure, and one of the first orders of business was to select a commander in chief, as well as the senior command structure. At the suggestion of John Adams, to promote a sense of unity among the colonies, by a unanimous vote on June 15, they selected George Washington as commander in chief. The move was not unexpected, as Washington had shown up in Philadelphia as a delegate from Virginia dressed in his uniform as a colonel in the state Militia. Nevertheless, his was a popular selection.[74]

Four days later, four major generals were appointed, and on June 22, eight brigadiers. In order of seniority, the major generals were Artemas

Ward, Charles Lee, Philip Schuyler, and Israel Putnam. As a testament to his reputation, other than Washington, Putnam's was the only other unanimous appointment. One delegate waxed enthusiastic at the selection, writing that Putnam's "fame as a warrior had been so far extended thro the Continent that it would be vain to urge any of our gen'll officers in competition with him."[75]

The eight brigadier generals, appointed in order of seniority, were: Seth Pomeroy, Richard Montgomery, David Wooster, William Heath, Joseph Spencer, John Thomas, John Sullivan, and Nathanael Greene. At the same time, at Washington's suggestion, Horatio Gates was appointed as the adjutant general of the army with the rank of brigadier general. Washington was handed the commissions to give to each of the general officers when he met them in Cambridge, but word had already leaked out as to the selections.[76]

Washington and his small entourage arrived in Cambridge on Monday, July 3, in his words, "after a journey attended with a good deal of fatigue, and retarded by necessary attentions to the successive civilities, which accompanied me in my whole route." One of the first officers to greet him was Israel Putnam. The initial selection of the general officers was intended to recognize the contribution of New York and the various New England colonies, and to help create a unified chain of command. Sadly, for Washington, that was not the case when he arrived at Cambridge, as there was already some grumbling and ill-feeling among some Provincial officers, who had wound up in what each believed to be a more subordinate role than he warranted. Governor Jonathan Trumbull of Connecticut, a steady friend of Washington, promptly weighed in. While he recognized Putnam's "singular merit and services," at the same time, he anticipated trouble: "I have to observe to your Excellency that the Honorable Congress have altered the arrangement of the Generals appointed by our Assembly. Wish the order we adopted had been pursued."[77]

Washington wisely withheld nearly all of the commissions and appealed to Congress: "I am sorry to observe, that the appointment of general officers, in the provinces of Massachusetts and Connecticut, has not corresponded with the wishes and judgment of either the civil or military," he told John Hancock, adding that, "the great dis-satisfaction expressed on this subject, and the apparent danger of throwing the whole army into the utmost disorder, together with the strong representations made by the Provincial Congress, have induced me to retain the commissions in my hands until the pleasure of the Continental Congress should be further known." Complicating matters was the fact that he had already given Putnam his commission on the day he arrived at Cambridge, "before I was apprized of these disgusts." In the interim, among the soldiers themselves, Sam Webb told Silas Deane that the selection of Putnam "gave universal satisfaction." He added for his stepfather's eyes only, that it would be "better for us to lose four Spencers than half a Putnam."[78]

David Wooster and Joseph Spencer from Connecticut were a case in point. Both, it will be recalled, had seniority over Putnam within the Connecticut forces. The latter already had left camp for home, without even consulting Washington. The arrogant and crusty sixty-four-year-old Wooster remained on duty, but he complained bitterly. Roger Sherman, a representative to the Continental Congress in Philadelphia, wrote to Wooster, informing him that preference for the fourth major generalcy was given to Putnam on the strength of his actions at Noddle's Island. The situation with Putnam was further complicated by the fact that Washington had already delivered his commission to him before he caught the full measure of the upset feelings.[79]

Washington anticipated a comparable situation involving Massachusetts' generals John Thomas, Seth Pomeroy, and William Heath. Pomeroy partially settled that situation when he declined his commission, and he also left camp. Spencer eventually returned to camp.[80]

The issue of seniority in making promotions would continue to plague Washington for most of his time as commander in chief, as he tried, and sometimes succeeded, in advancing the careers of younger men in whom he saw promise like Nathanael Greene and John Sullivan. As a case in point, he issued General Orders on August 9, 1775, in which he sought to fill the vacancies of officers in certain regiments. Specifically, he sought: "any particular *gentlemen*, who signalized themselves in the action on Bunkers Hill, by their spirited behaviour and good conduct, and, of which, sufficient proof is adduced to the General; he will, in filling up the commissions, use his endeavors to have them appointed (if not already commissioned) to some office, or promoted if they are; *as it will give him infinite pleasure at all times to reward merit, wherever it is to be found*" (emphasis added). Washington would be frequently frustrated in achieving this goal for, as the war wore on, the ranks became filled predominantly with young men with less education and fewer means.[81]

Dealing with Fame

In the aftermath of the battle, the participants told the tale of the fight and their role in it, starting around every campfire, until it reverberated far and wide, to Philadelphia and beyond. Each colony vied with the others in praising the exploits of their native sons. Among those that played a part, no one's reputation stood higher than Putnam's. A contemporary letter printed in the New London papers lauded several Connecticut officers, including Putnam, Knowlton, and Coit, for their recent conduct at Bunker Hill. Putnam, it said, with messianic hyperbole, "seems to be inspired by God Almighty with a military genius and formed to work wonders in the fight of those uncircumcised Philistines at Boston and Bunker's Hill, who attempt to ravage this country, and defy the armies of the living God."[82]

Brigadier General William Heath, who was offended by the glaring omission in the letter of any mention of the role played by Massachusetts, observed that "it is not surprising that jealousies do subsist, and that misrepresentations have been made respecting our Colony." However, he was realistic about the situation. "Men who judge wisely," he observed, "will not expect suddenly that Regularity in an army (may I not say) raised almost from chaos, which is to be found in an army of veterans."[83]

On July 11, Silas Deane, then a delegate to the Continental Congress from Connecticut, told his wife how proud he was of Putnam's selection as a major general by a unanimous vote. "Putnam's merit rung through this Continent," he wrote, "his fame still increases, and every day justifies the unanimous applause ... [and] his health has been the second or third at almost all our tables in this city."[84]

The voluble Putnam, no doubt was not shy about talking about his own role at Bunker Hill. Captain Chester told a friend just that. "A certain big bellied General, will make the most of his great doing, I very well know," he wrote. Major General Charles Lee, noted for his caustic criticism and explosive temper (the Iroquois referred to him as "Boiling Water"), took advantage of the situation to poke a little fun at Putnam. The two had remained friends since their service together in the last war. When a Reverend Page sought an introduction to Putnam, Lee obliged him. "Dear General," he wrote, "the bearer of this . . . has the laudable ambition of seeing the great General Putnam." Lee continued: "I therefore desire that you would array yourself in all your majesty and terrors for his reception. Your blue and gold must be mounted, your pistols stuck in your girdle; and it would not be amiss if you should black one half of your face." He ended the letter with: "I am, dear General, with fear and trembling, your humble servant, Charles Lee." No doubt, Putnam had a good laugh at his own expense.[85]

PUTNAM PICKS HIS STAFF
Silas Deane wrote to his stepson from Philadelphia referring to Putnam's recent promotion to major general and strongly suggesting the young man apply to Putnam for the position of aide-de-camp. In fact, Deane wrote to Putnam himself just to make sure. Sam followed the advice, and on July 22, 1775, he and Putnam's son Daniel were appointed as Putnam's aides. Webb would not serve long on Putnam's staff, as he soon caught the eye of the commander in chief, and he would join his staff as an aide-de-camp in June 1776.[86]

PUTNAM RECEIVES AN OFFER
In early July 1775, shortly after the Battle of Bunker Hill, Maj. John Small requested a meeting with Putnam, without stating its purpose. Washington approved the meeting, which took place somewhere in Cambridge between Prospect Hill and Bunker Hill. Considering his "services in Canada [during] the last war," Small told him, "I am authorized by General Gage to say to you, if you will leave that Rebel service . . . and will join us . . . you shall have the same rank in the British Army as you now hold in the American." He also assured him that Putnam's sons would be similarly treated. Finally, appealing to their long-standing

friendship, and not wishing to see him hanged as a traitor, Small told him: "Putnam, you saved my life but yesterday, as it were. I have a grateful heart, and wish henceforth to hail you as my friend, and never more meet you as an enemy." Putnam's response to Small was a firm refusal, which, at the same time, acknowledged their strong bond of friendship. "Having embarked in the contest from a full conviction of the justice of the cause," he replied, I shall "stand or fall with [my] Country." He added: "It is only in defense of that Country, that [I] could ever meet [you] as an enemy." Not wishing to be seen in a bad light by his fellow officers at that time, aside from confiding in General Washington, Putnam kept the offer to himself and his family.[87]

DECLARATION OF CAUSES AND NECESSITIES

The Second Continental Congress, meeting in Philadelphia on July 6, 1775, adopted a *Declaration of Causes and Necessities of Taking up Arms*. It was a lengthy document that outlined the reasons for the current conflict; yet it held out a hope that the breach was still reparable. Two days later, as a follow-up, Congress published an open letter, explaining their arguments at greater length. On Saturday, July 15, General Washington assembled the regiments quartered in Cambridge for a ceremony, at which the congressional declaration was read aloud to the troops by the Rev. Dr. Samuel Langdon, president of Harvard College. The men answered with "three huzzahs" and were dismissed.

Whether or not Putnam was one of the five other general officers present that day is not known; however, he opted to hold a more elaborate, separate ceremony for the "Continental troops under his immediate command" atop Prospect Hill, the following Tuesday morning, where he had erected the mast from the sloop *Diana* as a flagpole. The reading of the declaration was followed by an "animated and pathetic address" by his regimental chaplain, the Rev. Abiel Leonard of Woodstock, Connecticut. The chaplain then finished with a "pertinent prayer." At Putnam's signal, the troops yelled a loud amen followed by three cheers. A cannon was fired from the redoubt that he had built there, and his new flag was raised for the first time. It bore on one side the Connecticut motto, "*Qui Transtulit Sustinet*," in gold letters on a red field, and on the other, the words,

"An Appeal to Heaven." Hearing the shouts, the British troops stationed on Bunker Hill became alarmed and turned out ready for battle! Putnam had achieved a small psychological victory.[88]

REORGANIZING THE ARMY

One of Washington's first tasks was to organize the mass of men he had inherited into a more efficient, functioning army with clear lines of command. By way of General Orders issued on July 22, he took the first steps toward that goal. He divided the army into three large divisions, each commanded by a major general. Each division had two brigades commanded by a brigadier general. The First Division, or right wing, was under the command of General Ward, and it was centered on Roxbury and the area south of Boston. The Second Division, or left wing, was commanded by General Lee, and it was centered on Prospect and Winter Hills. The Third Division, or reserve, was commanded by General Putnam. In another change, general officers would no longer hold the simultaneous command of their regiments, and field officers would no longer command their respective companies.[89]

It was a good start, however, the issue of enlistments remained unresolved and would soon surface. In addition, some other conditions remained problematic. A chaplain expressed his frustration at the "wickedness" he saw on display every day. "The Prophanety in our Camps is very great; the stupidity of our sick amazing," he wrote, "and I could wish that those of us who officiate as Chaplains were not lacking in Faithfulness." He added that, "We have a large field for Action."[90]

A CASE OF COLLECTIVE INDISCIPLINE

By the middle of October, one of Washington's great concerns came to pass, as the terms of enlistment for most regiments would soon expire. As of then, recruiting had been slow, and he did not yet have the manpower to replace the departing units. The majority of three Connecticut regiments, the 3rd (Putnam's own), 6th, and 7th, indicated that they planned to leave despite Washington's request that they remain through December, which was beyond the term of their original enlistments. Lieutenant Joshua Huntington from Norwich, a member of John Durkee's Third

Company in the 3rd Connecticut Regiment, expressed the feelings of many of his comrades. "I can't say when I shall be at home . . .," he told his father. "I am Afraid that our Soldiers will not Stay any longer than they first Engaged for, So [I] Shall Stay as Long as our Company will Tarry and then Return."[91]

Washington asked the commanding officers to poll the ranks. All three reported that there was some sentiment to extending, but only if a short furlough was granted to allow the men to go home to retrieve their winter clothing. However, on December 1, several days prior to the expiration of their enlistments, the Connecticut troops, both officers and enlisted, left camp en masse. Most were persuaded to return to camp. In a letter to John Hancock, Washington referred to their conduct as "scandalous," and he called on the Militia of Massachusetts, New Hampshire, and Rhode Island to fill the gap. Meanwhile, he feared similar incidents with those as well.[92]

On November 22, Putnam bought a large bay horse from four men from his regiment who had earlier captured the animal on Charlestown Neck. No doubt it belonged to a British officer and had strayed from the lines. Putnam paid each of them £20.[93]

"CONGRESS"

The siege dragged on for months, right through the fall and winter, and as a result, there were shortages of foodstuffs, wood, and forage that plagued both the citizens of Boston and their occupiers. In addition, scurvy was increasing among the soldiers and inhabitants, and there was an outbreak of smallpox. While some British shipping reached Boston safely, American privateers were becoming increasingly successful. One notable incident occurred on November 28, 1775, when British-born captain John Manly, sailing the converted merchantman *Lee*, captured the British ordnance brigantine *Nancy* as she was inbound to Boston. The prize ship was taken to Gloucester, where Washington, immediately after learning of its seizure, ordered four companies of Militia to guard the vessel, as well as wagons and teams to haul the cargo away. Colonel John Glover and his local Militiamen were ordered to unload and transport the cargo to secure locations.[94]

Not only were there muskets, bayonets, and lead on board, but also found among her cargo was a large, brass 13-inch mortar. When Putnam found out that the gun was in Gloucester where the prize ship had been taken, he had it transported by wagon to his redoubt atop Cobble Hill. There, in an informal ceremony, he christened it with good New England rum and named it "Congress."[95]

Putnam's contributions to the Cause were not always obvious and were often attributable to his many connections throughout New England. Joseph Reed, Washington's secretary, credited Putnam, in part, with Manly's success, as he had initially enlisted the captain in the Cause. "Is it not very strange that he [Manly] should monopolize all the Honour of the Sea?" he wrote, then adding, "Manly excepted, we have not shone in that Way as yet." Captain Manly went on to become one of the most successful privateers, and he was appointed a commodore by Washington in January 1776.[96]

TIGHTENING THE RING

At ten o'clock in the morning on December 17, Putnam led a detail of four hundred men to Lechemere Point to commence work on a new earthwork and bridge over the small creek separating the point from the mainland. At first, a heavy fog concealed the effort, however, when it lifted around midday, the work party was exposed to fire from the *Scarborough*, which wounded one man. Putnam quickly dispersed the men to safety and at the same time sent orders to the battery at Cobble Hill to fire on the British warship. The counterbattery fire was so effective that the *Scarborough* weighed anchor and sought safety at Charlestown. The working party gave a hearty cheer as the ship got under way. Putnam recommenced the work that evening, undeterred by fire from another British battery at Barton's Point, which continued until midnight. Despite the shelling, the work was finished the following night.[97]

TUGGING ON THE LION'S TAIL

On January 8, 1776, General Putnam ordered Maj. Knowlton to lead a contingent of about 130 men across the mill dam to Charlestown to burn the fifteen remaining houses there that had survived the conflagration caused by the British bombardment on the previous June 17. Since then, the British had fortified Bunker Hill and stationed a small guard detail in Charlestown, consisting of a sergeant and five privates, that used the buildings for shelter. Once on the peninsular, between 8:00 and 9:00 p.m., Knowlton divided his force, some under Major Henly to burn the houses closer to Bunker Hill, and the latter, under Major Cary, to torch the houses farthest away. The plan called for Cary's detail to start the first fire, which would serve as a signal to the other detail to start their fires. As it turned out, in his eagerness, one of Henly's men prematurely lit his torch, thus alerting the British in the defensive works on Bunker Hill, who thought that they were under general attack and began to fire wildly in all directions. Luckily, none of the raiders was hit.

In Charlestown, one British soldier offered some resistance and was killed, but the remainder of the guard, along with a woman camp follower, were taken captive. Although some homes remained undamaged, Knowlton and his detail accomplished the basic task, and the raiders beat a hasty retreat without loss. Another casualty of the affair was the abrupt end to an evening of theater for British officers at Faneuil Hall when the alarm was sounded during an intermission between plays. Observing the raid from the mainland from their post at Fort Putnam on Cobble Hill were Generals Washington and Putnam, as well as other assorted officers of rank. The mood there, observed Chaplain Ebenezer David of Rhode Island, "was as merry as you please."[98]

Putnam rode out to meet the returning detail, and upon seeing that the woman was "something fatigued," he ordered two soldiers to carry her. That proved awkward, and the gallant general reached his hand out and yelled, "Here, hand her up to me!" Putnam hauled her up on the rump of his horse, and the grateful lady put her arms tightly around his waist. As they rode off toward headquarters, she exclaimed, "Jesus bless you sweet general! May you live forever!" The following day, Washington commended Knowlton and his men for their "spirit, conduct and secrecy" in carrying out their mission.[99]

"IN THE NAME OF THE GREAT JEHOVAH"

Benedict Arnold, along with Ethan Allen and his company of "Green Mountain Boys," seized Fort Ticonderoga in a bloodless raid on the night of May 10, 1775. Crown Point was taken the following day in a similar effort. That following November, it was a corpulent bookseller from Boston by the name of Henry Knox who convinced Washington that he could transport Ticonderoga's now silent guns to Boston to aid in the siege. Knox left Cambridge on November 15 and arrived at Ticonderoga on December 5; at which time he began to choose an assortment of guns of assorted sizes that he thought would prove most effective. In an amazing feat of mechanics and endurance, over the course of forty days, he oversaw the transport of fifty-eight guns weighing sixty tons up Lake George and then on sleds and sledges more than 250 miles through deep snow and over the rugged Berkshires in mid-winter. Knox and his party made good time. In Albany, Maj. Gen. Philip Schuyler watched the first of the sleds cross the Hudson River on Sunday, January 7. "Should there be Snow all the way to Cambridge," he predicted to Washington, "they will probably arrive there about this Day [in a] Week." On January 18, 1776, Knox appeared at Washington's headquarters, pleased to announce that the guns were safely parked in Framingham, just twenty miles to the west.[100]

DORCHESTER HEIGHTS

As early as January 11, 1776, Washington was certain that Boston would be abandoned. It was just a matter of when. The more important question was where would the British army go next? His best guess was that they would go to New York City, and in anticipation thereof, he dispatched Maj. Gen. Charles Lee to begin the process of setting up defensive works there.[101]

However, the British were not ready to leave, and the fact that the Dorchester Heights left them vulnerable gnawed at them. At some point, General Howe drew up a plan to storm the Heights before the Americans could occupy them in force. At the same time, Washington had some plans of his own. He called upon Israel Putnam's cousin, now

Lt. Col. Rufus Putnam, a farmer, as well as a self-taught surveyor and engineer, to undertake the fortification of the Heights.[102]

Knowing that time was of the essence, like a prefabricated home, Rufus Putnam created the defensive position in portable pieces so that they could be easily carried to the site and assembled quickly. Samuel Webb wrote that for several days starting March 1, the men were put to work "erecting great numbers of Facines, Gabions, pressing hay, etc." After which, during the evening of March 4, two thousand men under the command of Brig. Gen. John Thomas began to install the fortifications, which included two small forts and as many small redoubts. Thomas' troops were relieved at 3:00 a.m. on March 5 by a contingent of three thousand men, including Captain Chester's company, who finished the job and occupied the works that morning to the "utmost consternation" of the British, who quickly tested them with an artillery barrage.[103]

While the fortifications were being assembled, Putnam staged a nightly artillery barrage as a diversion, hoping the British would anticipate an attack from that quarter. In the process, either through metal fatigue or the inexperience of the gun crews, several mortars, including "Congress," cracked and became unusable.[104]

Howe assembled his forces in preparation for an all-out attack on the heights that day, but he postponed it until the next morning. At the same time, Washington, anticipating such a move, had assembled four thousand troops and sixty flat-bottomed boats at Cambridge for a counterattack, in the form of a two-pronged amphibious assault on Boston, to be commanded by Israel Putnam. As fate would have it, a large wind and rainstorm blew up, and the British attack was cancelled. Lieutenant Eben Huntington of Captain Chester's company was disappointed. "Had an action taken place," he speculated, "we went in so well Prepar'd . . . the town [Boston] would have been in the hands of our great and brave Gen'l Putnam in a little time after they [the British] had come out." The garrison's fate, however, was sealed.[105]

The final act in the drama was played out and evacuation orders were issued on March 7. Between then and Sunday, March 17, when the last of the troops sailed away, there was a considerable amount of work to do, from disposing of excess stores and property, for both soldiers and civilians leaving for other parts of the British Empire, cargoes loaded, and manifests prepared. According to Lt. Ebenezer Huntington, while the British soldiers evacuated in obvious haste, they did stop to plunder "everything they wanted without respect to persons," and that the damage to Boston, though relatively minor, was greater "at the North and at the South End than anywhere else." As he wandered through the streets, one Connecticut soldier witnessed "the general dilapidation of the houses, [and] several churches emptied of all the inside work and turned into riding schools for their [British] cavalry."[106]

The first stop for the evacuees would be Halifax, Nova Scotia. As a parting shot, on March 20, Howe removed the few remaining troops and essentials from Castle William in the outer harbor and blew the fortress to pieces, along with such munitions that could not be carried away. George Washington and his staff entered a free Boston on Monday, March 18. Putnam did so two days later.[107]

CHAPTER TEN

The American Revolution

The Trying of Souls

PUTNAM HEADS TO NEW YORK

WASHINGTON HAD DISPATCHED MAJ. GEN. CHARLES LEE TO NEW York even before Howe had made his exit from Boston. Lee was charged with formulating a plan for the defense of Manhattan and the surrounding area from an anticipated attack. While Howe was regrouping, he sent a portion of his army under Maj. Gen. Henry Clinton to Charleston, South Carolina, to secure that important city. Washington then redeployed Lee to meet that threat. As he still had matters to attend to in Boston, Washington turned to Putnam, relying upon his "long service and experience," as well as his "perseverance, activity and zeal." Rather than issuing specific instructions, he ordered Putnam to take charge of the forces in New York City to complete Lee's plan of defense, and, after consultation with other senior officers, to improve upon them if he saw fit, until such time as he [Washington] could get there himself.[1]

Putnam was preceded first by Brig. Gen. John Sullivan, who was accompanied by the Pennsylvania Rifle Regiment, followed by five additional regiments under the command of Brig. Gen. William Heath. Washington wanted these troops to arrive fresh and able to get to work right away preparing the defenses at New York. Time was of the essence, and because of the likelihood of muddy New England roads in spring, he arranged for the troops to leave Boston at staggered intervals and to assemble first at Norwich, Connecticut, where waiting ships would transport them and their baggage to New London, and then, if the way were clear, to New York City. If not, the troops would march the rest of the way.[2]

The remaining units of the nascent Continental Army began to make their way to New York slowly on foot. For many the trek was over the same, familiar roads through Massachusetts, Connecticut, and Rhode Island that they had traveled to Boston a year ago. No doubt, many soldiers fell out of line to say farewell to friends and family as they passed through their own hometowns, catching up with the column later.

Typical of the new recruits was young Joseph Plumb Martin, who was then living on his maternal grandfather's farm outside of New Haven, Connecticut, when he enlisted as a private to fill the ranks of Col. William Douglas's battalion of Connecticut levies, which, with six other battalions, formed Brig. Gen. James Wadsworth's brigade in Maj. Gen. Joseph Spencer's division. Douglas had served under Putnam in 1759 during the invasion of Canada. He was a prosperous farmer and merchant from Northford (now North Branford) near New Haven, who had also served in the later stages of Montgomery's failed attack on Canada. Upon his return home, he raised a regiment. Martin arrived in Manhattan by sloop, passing through the Hell Gate. Until barracks could be built, Douglas's battalion was quartered in Lower Manhattan at or near Broadway, in empty homes of residents who had fled the city at the start of the troubles.[3]

Israel Putnam and his aide Samuel Webb stopped first at Brooklyn for a brief visit and then went on to Wethersfield, where they spent the night of April 1 at the Webb family home. Putnam arrived in New York City during the evening of Wednesday, April 3, and he established his headquarters in the Kennedy House at One Broadway. Two days later, he instituted a curfew for soldiers and residents alike. No one was permitted out and about between tattoo and reveille without a pass. Putnam soon realized the magnitude of his responsibilities, and he asked the Continental Congress for a large appropriation of funds. President John Hancock promptly replied in the affirmative, with a commitment of $300,000. As was the case in Boston, Putnam was soon joined by his wife, Deborah, and two of his daughters, Mary ("Molly") and Eunice.

The ladies spent much of their time spinning flax to be made into cloth for shirts for the soldiers.[4]

Putnam went about his duties with his usual high energy and zeal. Earlier, Governor Tryon and various Loyalist officials had taken refuge aboard the British warship *Duchess of Gordon*, lying in the harbor. Putnam found that not only were there regular communications by members of the large Tory element with the governor taking place, but also many merchants were supplying him and his entourage with provisions. He put a stop to the practice with the issuance of an order dated April 8. Henceforth, any persons having any such interaction without authorization would be "considered as enemies and treated accordingly."[5]

Among his other duties, Putnam acted as a quartermaster, from expediting the delivery of stores and ammunition to General Schuyler's forces fighting in the north, to locating sufficient lead to make bullets. To that end, he made a request of General Ward in Massachusetts. In addition, at the suggestion of his aide-de-camp, Samuel Webb, he authorized the use a small fleet of armed schooners under his overall command to ply the waters off New Jersey and Long Island to intercept British supply ships.[6]

KEEPING THE PEACE

Both Washington and Putnam deplored looting. They recognized that it was a sure way to lose the support of the local citizenry, and New York had a large Tory population. Private Joseph Plumb Martin's quarters were on Stone Street, about fifty feet away from Putnam's headquarters, and, as it turned out, just across from a wine cellar. The temptation of those large pipes of Madeira so close by was simply too great for him and his fellow soldiers. One day, Martin watched one of his comrades push open the cellar window and crawl through. As one by one his fellow soldiers joined in, drinking, and filling empty oil flasks to take away, Martin finally succumbed, and he joined in.

When the owner of the shop realized what was happening, the angry merchant ran down the street to Putnam's headquarters, and the general quickly arrived on the scene. Mounting the steps of Martin's quarters, a visibly angry Putnam "harangued the multitude" and ordered the men to disburse or he would hang every one of them. The soldiers quickly obeyed. Later in his room, still shaken by the general's threat, the young man took one sip of the pilfered wine and, through guilt or fear, threw the rest away, container and all.[7]

On a more serious note, during Putnam's tenure, there were tensions between Tories and Patriots, and on May 21, Washington gave a direct order to Putnam to "afford every aid" to the New York Provincial Congress to seize "principal Tories and disaffected Persons on Long Island," if requested. On rare occasions these tensions erupted into violence, as happened on June 10, and again on June 12. At those times, many Tories were dragged from their homes and shops and publicly subjected to ridicule and physical abuse. Putnam and his troops had difficulty controlling the crowds of rowdy onlookers. However, to Putnam's credit the city was remarkably calm and quiet. Many people had expected an increase in violence and crime with the large influx of troops. One observer noted, however, that, "I do believe there are very few instances of so great a number of men together, with so little mischief done by them."[8]

Not everyone agreed with that assessment. While the city itself may have remained calm, William Tudor, Washington's judge advocate, was appalled by the behavior of some of the American soldiers. Calling for stricter punishments, he told John Adams that, "almost every Villainy and Rascality that can disgrace the Man, the Soldier or the Citizen, is daily practiced without meeting the Punishment they merit." Tudor went on: "The infamous and cruel Ravages which have been made on the wretched, distress'd Inhabitants of this unfortunate Island by many of our Soldiers, must disgrace, and expose our Army to Detestation. I have heard some Tales of Woe, occasioned by the Robberies of our Army, which would extort Sighs from the Hearts of Tygers."[9]

Colonel Jedediah Huntington told his brother Joshua, also serving in the New York area, that on April 24, after a group of soldiers found one of their comrades dead in a local whorehouse, they "riotously undertook to avenge his death by pulling down the House" where he was found. When they also began to do the same to other whorehouses on the street, they were stopped through the efforts of Brig. Gen. Thomas Mifflin. Not to be deterred, the men came back the next day with the intention of doing the same, despite the presence of senior officers at the scene, until they were finally "dispersed or confined." Other than this incident, Jed matter-of-factly told Joshua, "there has scarcely been the least Disorder in the City since the Troops came here."[10]

FORTIFYING NEW YORK

Notwithstanding his efforts to keep the peace, Putnam's primary focus was on the construction of artillery batteries and other fortifications along the waterfront in Lower Manhattan, on Governor's Island, and at Red Hook, on Long Island. To that end, during the evening of Monday, April 8, Putnam led a thousand men over to Governor's Island and set them to work digging trenches and erecting a breastwork. Ordnance was then installed to keep British warships at bay. To assist Putnam's efforts, Washington ordered that the quartermaster general deliver to Putnam, "all the Sandbags in his possession," as well "as many sound empty Hogs-heads as he can."[11]

On May 2, while inspecting a battery in Lower Manhattan, Putnam had a friendly exchange with Lt. Samuel Shaw, a young artillery officer from Boston, then on guard duty. After the general had asked Shaw several questions, the officer felt emboldened to ask one of his own. "General, what do you think about the enemy?" he asked. "They will endeavor [to] give us a brushing here," replied Putnam. "Then we will have a little business, General." To which Putnam said, "Not a little, neither, for when they come up with their ships, you'll have your hands full, I warrant you." Shaw pushed back: "A smart fire from eight or ten ships of the line, well returned by our batteries, would give a young person some idea of a cannonade." Walking away, the old warrior laughed and told Shaw, "Ay it would, and of a pretty hot one, too!"[12]

"MAGGIE LAUDER"

Israel Putnam was naturally gregarious with an engaging personality, and he was a welcome guest at any gathering large or small. He had made many loyal friends over the course of his life, particularly among the soldiers with whom he had served, many of whom were now on the opposite side. Colonel Joseph Reed from Pennsylvania was typical. "I perfectly long to see the old General," he told Samuel Webb, "we toast him every

Day, which I assure you is doing a great Deal for a Connecticut Man," as there had been some lingering antipathy between the two colonies over the Susquehanna dispute. Putnam had a good singing voice, and two decades before he was right at home with the officers in the Highland regiments then serving at Forts Edward and Ticonderoga. It must have been there that he learned the words (in dialect) to a lively, traditional Scottish song called "The Ballad of Maggie Lauder," reputedly written by Francis Semphill about one hundred years before.[13]

The song became a staple for Putnam, and ever since, at dinners and other gatherings of soldiers, he was frequently called upon to sing the song and to lead the refrain. On June 18, sometime after Washington had returned from Philadelphia, Congress hosted a dinner for him at the Queen's Head Tavern (later Fraunces Tavern). During the evening, there was, as could be expected, considerable drinking of toasts and singing. The call went out for Putnam to sing "Maggie Lauder." To the disappointment of all, he was feeling ill and had left the dinner early. Captain Caleb Gibbs told his wife that "we missed him a marvel, as there is not a chap in the camp who can lead him in the *Maggie Lauder* song."[14]

Staff Changes

On June 21 Lt. Samuel B. Webb left Putnam's staff to join General Washington. Along with that appointment came a promotion to the grade of lieutenant colonel. The following day, at the recommendation of John Hancock, Putnam appointed twenty-year-old Aaron Burr as his new aide-de-camp. Major Burr had returned from the failed Canadian expedition led by Benedict Arnold and Richard Montgomery the previous year, and he was staying as a guest at Washington's headquarters awaiting reassignment. His mother, Esther, was the daughter of the great evangelist Jonathan Edwards. Burr's parents had both died when he was a young boy, and he and his sister, Sarah, were raised by his uncle Timothy Edwards. A graduate of Princeton at age seventeen, Burr went on to study law at what would become known as the Litchfield Law School under the tutelage of his future brother-in-law, Tapping Reeve. Burr and his sister had been tutored by Reeve as children, and Reeve would later marry Sarah.[15]

"Hickey's Plot"

In March 1776, while still at Cambridge, Washington set about to form an elite guard for himself and his baggage. The colonel of each regiment (except artillery and rifle units) was ordered to send four men to Washington's headquarters at noon on March 12, from which pool he would select his guard. The men were not to be armed or in uniform. It was not just any men he was seeking, and he relied upon the colonel of each regiment to choose men who were known for their "sobriety, honesty, and good behavior," as well as being "neat and spruce." In addition, he wanted the candidates to be "from five feet eight inches high to five feet ten inches, handsomely and well made," and above all clean, "as there is nothing in his eyes more desirable than cleanliness." Finally, each man had to have been drilled and "perfectly willing and desirous" of serving in his guard. Washington chose Caleb Gibbs to lead a contingent of fifty-eight men, including four sergeants and an equal number of corporals.[16]

It must have come as a shock to Washington, and those close to him, when a plot to kill him and other senior officers was uncovered by chance in June 1776, when a prisoner in jail in City Hall overheard other prisoners talking about the plot. It was even more so, when it was learned that one of those named plotters was Thomas Hickey, a member of Washington's personal guard, then in the jail on counterfeiting charges. After a brief investigation, and a court-martial hearing on June 26, presided over by Col. Samuel H. Parsons, Hickey was convicted and sentenced to hang, which he did two days later with a large crowd watching.[17]

Although several other persons were rounded up and incarcerated, including the mayor, David Mathews, but for want of sufficient evidence, no one other than the hapless Private Hickey was ever put to death. William Tudor, Washington's judge advocate, was particularly incensed over the failure to hang the mayor, telling John Adams: "If political institutions are insufficient, those of Nature are not. The laws of Self Preservation point out the Criminality of Mr. Matthews's Conduct and prescribe the Punishment of his Villainy." Nevertheless, Washington took the opportunity to use his public execution as a warning and an object lesson. That same day, he issued a blunt statement. "The unhappy fate of Thomas Hickey, executed this day for mutiny, sedition, and treachery," he began, "the General hopes will be a warning to every soldier in the Army to avoid those crimes, and all others, so disgraceful and pernicious to his country, whose pay he receives and bread he eats."[18]

THE RETURN OF ROBERT ROGERS

In December of 1775, while he was still in Boston, Washington received a letter from Putnam's old comrade in arms Robert Rogers, who, at that time was staying at a tavern in Medford, Massachusetts. Rogers had returned from England in June, where he had served a term in Debtor's Prison. Currently a major in the British army on half pay, he had given his parole to the Congress, and since then, he had been roaming the Northeast. He sought a meeting with Washington to obtain his permission to freely go about his business. He was, Rogers assured him, attempting to settle with his creditors and he "never expected to be called into service again."[19]

Several days before, Washington had been forewarned of Rogers' presence by Eleazar Wheelock, who had met with Rogers. Wheelock reported that there were unsubstantiated rumors of suspicious activity by the former Ranger and that he had skipped out on a thirteen-shilling tavern bill. Washington was unsure of Rogers' bona fides, and he asked a fellow New Hampshire man, Brigadier General Sullivan, to meet with Rogers and find out just what he was up to. He also sounded out Maj. Gen. Philip Schuyler, who was unable to confirm the truth of any of Wheelock's rumors. Rogers recounted his travels throughout New York and New England to Sullivan, but he denied that he had been to Canada. He was, Rogers told Sullivan, as a courtesy, seeking Washington's "license to travel unmolested." Although Rogers was not detained, Sullivan remained suspicious of him, and he urged the commander in chief not to have anything official to do with him. Washington took that advice.[20]

Six months later, Rogers turned up in South Amboy, New Jersey, still "travelling through the country under suspicious circumstances" and without any visible means of support. Washington's concerns were fully aroused, and he ordered Rogers detained on the suspicion that he was acting as a spy for the British. The former Ranger was arrested and brought to New York for interrogation by Washington himself. It is likely that Rogers renewed his acquaintance with Putnam at this time. Impoverished and still in debt, Rogers had given a different explanation for his activities, depending upon who was asking. His stories had just enough plausibility about them so that he was able to move about freely, but they were not sufficiently credible to allay all suspicions. His meeting with Washington was no exception. Afterwards, Washington ordered that Rogers be taken to Philadelphia with an officer as escort. He escaped from custody on July 9 and made his way back to Staten Island and General Howe. Thereafter, all suspicions were confirmed when, during the next month, he formed a Loyalist regiment called the Queen's American Rangers.[21]

A SPATE OF GRAND IDEAS

Of serious concern was the fact that British warships sailed up and down the Hudson River with impunity. There were fears that a vital link to New England would be severed or that Tories outside New York City would be given support and encouragement. Putnam was full of ideas about how to strike at the British, from the launching of attacks by fire rafts against the British fleet anchored off Staten Island, to a blockade of the North [Hudson] River. The construction of a blockade was discussed at a conference of Washington and his officers on July 8 and unanimously approved. The plan was to sink two ships stern to stern, seventy feet apart and linked together with large logs, to form a cheval de frise of sorts, some 280 feet wide.[22]

Putnam shared these details with his friend Maj. Gen. Horatio Gates, then serving at Fort Ticonderoga, New York. In a letter dated July 26, he also told Gates that he was anxious to, in his words, "pay them a visit on their island [Staten Island]." Gates responded in a letter dated August 11, which he addressed to "Dear Put." At first, he teased his good-natured friend about Putnam's earlier efforts helping to build the log stockade at Crown Point during the French and Indian War, which was now crumbling to dust, and compared them with his own present imperfect efforts to improve Ticonderoga. Anxious to hear how things were going in New York City, Gates asked Putnam: "Joking apart: Have you blown up Staten Island? Have you burnt the enemy's fleet . . . What have you and what have you not done?" He could have saved the paper.[23]

In early August, six row galleys attacked the *Phoenix* and *Rose*, then swinging at anchor in the Hudson. After a two-hour battle, only minimal damage was inflicted, at a cost of eleven American casualties, including two dead. Approximately two weeks later, on August 16, two fireships once again attempted to burn the warships *Phoenix* and *Rose* but only managed to burn one of the three tenders moored nearby.[24]

In the end, all of Putnam's stratagems to block passage on the Hudson River proved ineffective, as British warships continued to sail up and down the river with relative impunity. On October 9, three British warships, the *Phoenix*, *Rose*, and *Tartar*, and their tenders, sailed past the barrier with apparent ease, despite a fierce barrage from the guns of Forts Washington and Lee, as well as that of a small American flotilla, and continued upriver to the Tappan Zee. All, however, was not as it seemed, as it turned out, both the *Phoenix* and *Tartar* had suffered considerable damage from the shelling, not to mention the loss of nine dead and twenty-seven wounded sailors.[25]

On November 5, once again, three British warships made the dangerous passage upriver, more than likely just to make the point. Though damaged, they passed through the gauntlet of Forts Washington and Lee. When Washington was informed of the passage of the ships, he told General Greene that it was "so plain a proof of the inefficacy of all the Obstructions we have thrown into it." Greene agreed. When all was said and done, however, it was the depth of the river itself, and not the British fleet, that stymied Putnam's efforts.[26]

THE "CHILD INDEPENDENCE"—FIRST STEPS

On July 9, 1776, General Washington ordered the troops to assemble for a reading of the Declaration of Independence. From that point on there would be no ambiguity as to what the fight was all about. Echoing Julius Caesar, Brig. Gen. Thomas Mifflin told the assembly that, "the Rubicon has been crossed." The army would now fight to defend that independence.[27]

That evening during the celebrations, a mob of soldiers and citizens swarmed the park at Bowling Green and tore down the lead statute of King George III and smashed it to pieces. Some clearheaded persons gathered up the pieces that had not been carried away as souvenirs (one of which was the king's head) and loaded them on a sloop bound for Norwalk, Connecticut, where the cargo was transferred to several ox-drawn wagons to be taken to Litchfield, Connecticut, there to be made into musket balls.[28]

A DAMSEL IN DISTRESS

Thirteen-year-old Margaret Moncrieffe was a charming, vivacious, and strikingly pretty young lady, who was also physically mature for her age. She was the daughter of Putnam's former colleague Maj. Thomas Moncrieffe, an engineer officer in the British army. He had seen extended service in Canada and America, beginning with the French and Indian War, where he became friends with Israel Putnam. While on active duty, the thrice-widowed Moncrieffe sent his children to stay with friends and relatives, most of whom were ardent Patriots, one of whom was the governor of New Jersey. At this time, Margaret was boarding with the family of a Colonel Banks, ten miles outside Elizabethtown, New Jersey, when she learned that her father had arrived at Staten Island as part of General Howe's invasion force. Her relatives were particularly ungracious in their treatment of the girl, based on her father's choice to remain in the British army. It became so uncomfortable for her that, one day while Colonel Banks' family was at church services, she sought refuge with Sarah DeHart's family back in Elizabethtown.[29]

Anxious to see his daughter again, shortly after his arrival at Staten Island, Moncrieffe wrote a letter or sent a message to Putnam and asked him, as a friend, to help reunite him with his daughter. Following Howe's lead, Moncrieffe neglected to follow basic military courtesy and addressed Putnam as a private citizen. For whatever reason, Putnam did not answer the letter right away. This may have prompted Margaret herself to write. Having seen a copy of her father's letter, or hearing about it, she asked Putnam if that unfortunate omission had made a difference.[30]

Putnam sent the young lady a gracious reply on July 26, brushing aside any suggestion of ill will, pleading instead the press of business. "The omission of my title in Major Moncrieffe's letter, is a matter I regard not in the least," he assured her, "nor does it, in any way, influence my conduct in this affair, as you seem to imagine." Putnam continued: "Any political difference alters him not to me in a private capacity. As an officer, he is my enemy, and obliged to act as such, be his private sentiments be his private sentiments what they will. As a man, I owe him no enmity; but far from it, will, with pleasure, do any kind office in my power for him or any of his connections." Putnam went on to explain that such matters were within the purview of Congress, and that he had already spoken to General Washington about it, who sounded optimistic. In the interim, he offered to bring her to his home in New York City as the guest of he and his wife and two daughters until the matter could be sorted out.[31]

Putnam asked Lt. Col. Sam Webb, now one of Washington's aides, if he would go over to New Jersey and bring the young girl to New York. The following day, Webb appeared at her doorstep. Once at One Broadway, Margaret described being "received with the greatest tenderness by both Mrs. Putnam and her daughters." Her days were mostly spent spinning flax with the ladies or visiting with General and Mrs. Washington, who also showed her "every mark of regard." She became very fond of General Putnam and performed little tasks for him. In doing so, she observed that the portly soldier was no dandy in dress or manner but was rather "one of the best characters in the world; his heart being composed of those noble materials, which equally command respect and admiration." During those days, the closest she came to seeing her father were those rare moments when she was able to view Howe's fleet and the British encampment on Staten Island through the lens of a telescope, from the gallery atop the house.[32]

One night General and Mrs. Putnam hosted a dinner attended by General and Mrs. Washington and others, at which Putnam's good nature was put to the test. At the conclusion of the dinner, Washington proposed a toast to the Continental Congress. All present but Margaret raised their glass. Washington gave her a stern look and said to her sarcastically, "Miss Moncrieffe, you don't drink your wine?" Embarrassed and flustered, she was momentarily silenced by his steely look. Quickly composing herself, she looked straight at him and said, "General Howe is the toast." Some of the guests, including Washington, were aghast and chided her for her brashness in talking back to an adult. Not so Putnam. He was quick to assure his guests that Margaret, "did not mean to offend." In fact, no doubt with a smile, he said, "Everything she said or [is] done by such a child ought rather to amuse than affront you." Mildly irritated by Putnam's defense, but not wishing to exhibit any bad manners and confront his host, Washington smoothly put the matter to rest. "Well, Miss," he said, "I will overlook your indiscretion, on condition that you drink my health, or General Putnam's, the first time you dine at Sir William Howe's table, on the other side of the water."[33]

Some days later, with an exchange of correspondence between the two armies, came a another from Major Moncrieffe, this one to the commander in chief "demanding" the return of his daughter. Sensing perhaps that Washington had changed his mind, Putnam asked if he intended to meet the major's demand. "Absolutely not," Washington replied, the girl "should remain a hostage for her father's good behavior." Once again, Putnam challenged his superior. Hitting the hilt of his sword for emphasis, he swore one of his many creative oaths, stating firmly, "Moncrieffe's request should be granted!" Washington conceded the point and agreed to press Congress to allow the girl to return to her father.[34]

While awaiting word from Congress, Margaret was moved north to Kingsbridge, to the quarters of Brig. Gen. Thomas Mifflin and his wife, both of whom treated her with kindness. While there, the precocious, if not impressionable, teen accepted a marriage proposal from a dashing "colonel," who, as it turned out, was Putnam's aide-de-camp, Maj. Aaron Burr. She asked Putnam what he thought, expecting that he would be supportive. On the contrary, in his typical direct manner, he emphatically poured cold water on the scheme. While such a match was otherwise "unexceptionable," he told her, it would be unwise, given the different politics and the ardor that Burr and her father each brought to the current conflict. As a result of their conversation, Putnam's concern for her increased. From that point on, he kept a close eye on her, and at the same time he continued to press the Congress for her release. In that he was successful.[35]

Finally, the day of Margaret's release arrived. She rode across the Upper Bay in a twelve-oar barge, with none other than Col. Henry Knox as her escort. Soaked to the skin following a rough crossing, the exchange took place, and Margaret was delivered safe and sound aboard Adm. Richard Howe's warship, *Eagle*. Later that night at a dinner hosted by General Howe, with forty or fifty guests in attendance, she kept her word to Washington, and to the astonishment of all, offered a toast to General Putnam. Howe made light of it, saying "Oh! By all means, if he be the lady's sweetheart, I can have no objection to drink his health." Whereupon she handed Howe a letter from Putnam addressed to her father, written in his own rough hand, complete with his teasing sense of humor and creative spelling. "Ginrole Putnam's compliments to Major Moncrieffe. [He] has made him a present of a fine daughter. If he don't lick [like] her, he must send her back again, and he will provide her with a fine good Twig [Whig] husband." That provided the evening with a good laugh. The next day, accompanied by Maj. John Small, she was taken to Lord Percy's headquarters, where she had a tearful reunion with her father.[36]

Too Many Cooks

General Sir William Howe had arrived in the Lower Bay on June 25 with little or no fanfare. During the morning of July 2, the first of his fleet sailed into the Lower Bay, and by evening, all had disembarked at Staten Island. Some three weeks and four days later, his brother, Adm. Lord Richard Howe, aboard the flagship, *Eagle*, arrived on July 25, followed by dozens of warships and transports four days later, at which time defensive preparations continued in earnest. By then, Howe had more than thirty thousand troops on hand.[37]

In addition to the fortification of Manhattan, Washington knew that the likely first strike by General Howe would be on Long Island, particularly the high ground near Brooklyn. He had sized up many of his generals, and he liked the look of Brig. Gen. Nathanael Greene of Rhode Island. To him and his brigade he entrusted the preparations for the defense of Long Island, building upon those initially contemplated by Maj. Gen. Charles Lee. Greene and his brigade (composed of two Rhode Island regiments, a Massachusetts regiment, and a regiment of Pennsylvania riflemen led by Col. Edward Hand) crossed over to Brooklyn on May 1 and made camp about a mile from the ferry.[38]

Matters hit a snag on August 15, when Greene reported that he was confined to his bed with a high fever. By then Greene's defensive plans were well along, but he would not be there to implement them. Of necessity, on August 20, Washington turned to Brig. Gen. John Sullivan to "take command upon Long Island," and at the same time turn over the command of his division to Brig. Gen. Lord Stirling (William Alexander). That arrangement would be short-lived, as on August 24, Washington assigned the overall command to Israel Putnam, the most senior major general, who had been heard to complain that he was being left out of the action. That day, Col. Joseph Reed told his wife that Putnam, "was made happy by obtaining leave to go over; the brave old man was quite miserable at being kept here [Manhattan]."[39]

Meanwhile, on August 22, on Staten Island, Howe embarked his army in boats and landed it on Long Island, which should have eliminated any speculation on Washington's part as to where the attack would be made. By coincidence, Putnam was at Washington's headquarters when that news of Howe's landing was received. He was certain that an attack at Brooklyn was imminent and told Washington so. The following day, however, the latter was still unsure if the movement were a feint, telling General Heath that it was possible that the real attack would be on Manhattan.[40]

In an attempt to manage what was a very awkward situation, Washington worked out an arrangement whereby Putnam would be in overall command, but that he would remain at the works on Brooklyn Heights, which was the main line of defense. To deal diplomatically with any bruised egos, Putnam was told to "soothe and soften as much as possible." At the same time, Sullivan was given command of the forward line and, contrary to Greene's original thinking, began to heavily fortify most of it.[41]

Sullivan's line ran east to west along a heavily wooded, four-mile-long ridge called the Heights of Guana. It should have been well-suited to the American style of fighting, as noted by Col. Joseph Trumbull. "We have a fine ridge of hills and woods to meet them in on Long Island before they come near our lines," he told his brother. Along with the

Shore Road near Gowanus Marsh, four passes crossed over and through the heights, the first two, Martense Pass and Flatbush Pass ("Battle Pass"), in the west, Bedford Pass in the middle, and Jamaica Pass on the east. The main attack was expected in the west, and the first two passes were well-defended. At Bedford Pass, General Sullivan stationed about four hundred soldiers. Finally, inexplicably, instead of fortifying Jamaica Pass, the easternmost one, he used his own money to pay five mounted militia officers to function as a trip wire, to provide a timely alert should the British come that way.[42]

Washington, however, was not content to leave it at that. The following day, he issued lengthy and quite specific orders to Putnam. He told him to put a halt to the indiscriminate firing up and down the line since it wasted precious ammunition and could well mask the actual start of hostilities. Moreover, he said, it deters any defections from the British side. He added that guards should be alert, and officers must be prepared to quickly issue appropriate orders. He did, however, encourage patrols and, if necessary, related skirmishes, although he said to respect property and refrain from burning down houses, as "good order and discipline" are what separate a "well-regulated army and a mob." Finally, he told Putnam to secure the woods in front of the main position with the best men and use Militia behind the breastworks.[43]

The major flaw with the plan was the fact that the various defensive positions in the forward line were isolated from one another, thus limiting the ability to mutually support one another, leaving each open to being rolled up one at a time. More important, should the enemy get in behind that line, the defenders would be unable to retreat to the safety of the main line as planned. On August 26, Washington rode along the line with Generals Putnam and Sullivan and, despite some reservations, approved the plan. Perhaps because of those concerns, at the very last minute, Washington did send the regiments from Maryland and Delaware over to strengthen the western part of the first line. However, their senior officers, Col. William Smallwood and Col. John Haslet, remained behind in Manhattan on court-martial duty. Earlier in the day, Col. Samuel Miles, who had been observing the British movements for several days, had informed Sullivan that he believed that, given Howe's present position in the encampment, he was poised to use Jamaica Pass. Sullivan ignored the advice, and on the night of August 26/27, Sullivan's fivesome settled comfortably into a local inn on the Jamaica Road and waited.[44]

A Missed Opportunity

Governor Jonathan Trumbull of Connecticut was a staunch supporter of General Washington. When recruitment of a new batch of levies was going slower than planned, on July 5, he dispatched Lt. Col. Thomas Seymour and three regiments of light horse, nearly five hundred men, to New York as a stopgap. Washington had made no plans to use cavalry in his defense of Long Island. Moreover, he did not have the wherewithal to support the cavalry horses with feed and forage, which was needed for his artillery horses. Upon their arrival on July 8, he explained that to Lieutenant Colonel Seymour, who promptly pastured the horses near Kingsbridge and agreed to fight the troop as infantry, if needed, while waiting for more Connecticut Militia to arrive. However, when asked to mount a guard or to perform fatigue duty, Seymour and his officers balked, stating that such duty was, in effect, beneath their dignity as they were, by law, exempt.[45]

Notwithstanding assurances by his friend Trumbull that the horsemen would do whatever Washington ordered "for the good of the service," they still refused and asked to be relieved. What to do with the Connecticut Troop of Light Horse was the subject of a conference of general officers on July 8. Finally, on July 17, Washington discharged them and sent them packing. He made it clear to a group of officers dining with him that he was "displeased" with the affair. As a serious challenge to his authority, he really had no choice. In one of history's many "what ifs," it is interesting to speculate what an additional mounted troop of five hundred men might have done to slow Clinton down at Jamaica Pass, or at the very least deliver a timely warning.[46]

"A Severe Flogging"

Howe had learned a hard lesson at Breed's Hill the previous year, and he was not about to repeat the experience. His savvy but haughty deputy, Maj. Gen. Sir Henry Clinton, had a solution. Clinton's plan was to feint with an attack in the west with his Hessians and others, while he and Howe, along with Gen. Charles Cornwallis, conducted a forced march through rural Long Island, aided by Tory guides, to Jamaica Pass to flank the Americans. His strike was to be timed with a diversionary attack by Maj. Gen. James Grant and his Highland regiments on the morning of August 27, and another by Lt. Gen. Leopold Philip de Heister and his Hessians.[47]

The fighting began virtually by accident between 10:00 p.m. and midnight on the night of August 26 when American pickets noted movement in and around a watermelon patch near the Red Lion Inn on the Shore Road (sometimes referred to as the Gowanus Road), and both sides started shooting. It looked like it would be another typical night, where each side fired at each other for a brief period after which things settled down. This apparently indiscriminate firing was precisely what Washington had ordered Putnam to put a stop to. On the picket line that night was Col. Jedediah Huntington's 17th Continental Regiment, part of Brig. Gen. Samuel H. Parson's brigade. Huntington, who had been sick for days with a persistent fever was still in New York City recuperating and hoped to be given a furlough. However, as it happened, this was not an ordinary night, and, as it fit within his orders, Grant began to feed more men into the fight. When it became apparent to Parsons that this could well be the start of the attack, he sent word back to Putnam's headquarters.[48]

With Washington's orders fresh in his mind, at 3:00 a.m. on August 27, Putnam summoned Lord Stirling to his headquarters. By then he had received word from Parsons of the exchange of fire and the fact that the British had been sighted moving in force from Flatbush along the Shore Road toward the Red Lion Inn. "Take your two closest regiments," he told him, "and meet them!" By dawn, Stirling was in motion with the cream of his brigade, John Haslet's Delaware, and William Smallwood's Maryland regiments (both colonels were still in New York on court-martial duty).[49]

By the time Stirling had come within half a mile of the Red Lion Inn, he encountered Col. Samuel Atlee and his Pennsylvania Rifle Regiment. Atlee's unit was also part of Stirling's brigade, and they, too, were now in the firefight. A short time later, Stirling found that Huntington's regiment was also still actively engaged, and he quickly deployed his regiments and Huntington's in a defensive perimeter. Seizing whatever advantageous ground he could find, he aggressively resisted the onslaught. Opposing Stirling was General Grant's wing, which consisted of two full brigades, with four regiments in each, together with the 42nd Foot and two companies of Tories led by Governor Tryon. Initially, Grant was supposed to deliver a blow sufficient to divert attention away from the main thrust at Jamaica Pass. While Grant was successful in getting and holding the attention of the Americans, in the process, Stirling had inflicted heavy casualties on his troops.[50]

Meanwhile, Putnam rode to Sullivan's command post near the Flatbush Pass, and he arrived there about 4:30 a.m. He told him about Grant's movements and his orders to Stirling. Both men were still of the belief that the point of the main attack had occurred just where it had been expected. Sullivan immediately sent a detachment of four hundred men to aid Stirling, stripping his forces at Flatbush Pass of much-needed troop strength. Then Putnam returned to his headquarters. Clinton's plan was unfolding just as he had envisioned, and Sullivan, at Flatbush Pass, would soon experience an attack by Lt. Gen. de Heister and his Hessians, who were then awaiting a signal that Clinton and Cornwallis were in place at Jamaica Pass.[51]

Washington arrived at Brooklyn Heights about 8:00 a.m. and assumed command. Among other things, he ordered reinforcements from Manhattan, including Joseph Plumb Martin's unit. He walked the line encouraging the men and exhorting them to do their duty, even at one point threatening death to any man who left his post.[52]

Earlier, General Clinton and the leading elements of Howe's force halted about half a mile from Jamaica Pass, two hours before dawn, after what had to have been a fatiguing all-night march. One of his patrols discovered that the pass was unguarded, a fact confirmed when they captured the five horsemen Sullivan had paid to keep a watch. He quickly dispatched a battalion of light infantry to secure the pass. Clinton waited for General Cornwallis and the balance of the force, including artillery, to catch up, and to allow the men to take a short rest, before proceeding through the pass.

Finally moving forward, Clinton arrived at Bedford around 8:30 a.m. and commenced the main attack. He was now behind the left of the American line. Meanwhile, on his own initiative that morning, Col. Samuel Miles and his Pennsylvania riflemen patrolled the area between Bedford and Jamaica Pass and discovered, too late, the British vanguard. His small force was soon overwhelmed and in no position to stop the attack. Those not killed or captured managed to make their way back to the main American line, some of them by a circuitous route over Hell Gate, and alerted General Putnam.[53]

Soon, Howe's wing led by Clinton and Cornwallis began to roll up Sullivan's line, and by 10:00 a.m. Stirling quickly found himself caught between two powerful forces, as Grant and de Heister stepped up their attacks. Clinton's forces got behind the Americans at Bedford and Flatbush Passes and blocked their line of retreat. Many who surrendered, expecting quarter, would be summarily bayonetted. One British officer gloated when recounting his actions: "The Hessians and our brave Highlanders gave no quarters; and it was a fine sight to see with what alacrity they despatched the Rebels with their bayonets after we had surrounded them so that they could not resist." He went on to justify his actions, arguing that "all stratagems are lawful against such vile enemies to their King and country." Those who were not killed and managed to evade capture fled back to the trenches on Brooklyn Heights, as individuals or in small groups, all that day and well into the night and early the following morning.[54]

That is, all but Lord Stirling and the Delaware and Maryland troops, who were locked in a bitter contest, where the casualties were high on both sides. For their part, the British had brought to bear a force five times the size of the defenders. Stirling turned the tables when he and four hundred selected Marylanders went on the attack six times, twice driving the British from an old stone house (Vechte-Cortelyou House) where Cornwallis had placed his guns. His aggressiveness gave the bulk of his and Parson's men a chance to retreat to the main line. "Our troops" wrote Colonel Reed, "lost everything but honor." The ultimate sacrifice made by 256 Marylanders during their heroic stand near the Stone House earned them the name "Immortals."[55]

What remained of Parson's forces, particularly Huntington's regiment, which had suffered heavily, were ordered to retreat, covered in part by the Connecticut State Troops that Washington had ordered forward to assist. General Parsons became separated from his brigade, and he and seven of his troops barely eluded capture. In the end, both Generals Sullivan and Lord Stirling were captured, while the survivors retreated across Gowanus Creek and through the adjacent marshy area to the safety of the American lines at Brooklyn Heights. Tragically, many would drown making the effort, as related by an officer from a Maryland battalion: "We retreated through a very heavy fire, and escaped by swimming over a river, or creek rather. My height was of use to me, as I touched almost all the way. A number of men got drowned." In position on the near side of the Gowanus Marsh, Private Martin called it a "truly pitiful sight" as the surviving Marylanders "came out of the water and mud to us, looking like water rats."[56]

In the aftermath, Col. William Douglas, who commanded the Fifth Battalion of Brig. Gen. James Wadsworth's Connecticut State Troops, summed it up best. In a letter to his wife, he wrote: "Tuesday last we got a Sevear Floging on Long Island. The enemy Surrounded a Large Detachment of our Army, Took many, Kil'd Some and the Rest got off."[57]

THE SIEGE

Howe did not immediately follow up on his initial success and allowed a considerable number of Americans to reach the safety of Putnam's second line on Brooklyn Heights. Instead, he prepared for a siege, and there the opposing forces sat, six hundred yards apart, taking potshots at each other. Colonel Gold Selleck Silliman commanded the First Battalion of Connecticut State Troops holding a position in the front line. He described the stress of the daily skirmishes. "We are in a constant expectation of a general battle," he wrote, "no one can be here long without getting pretty well-acquainted with the whistling of cannon and musket shot." The weather turned cold and rainy, adding to the misery of the troops. Colonel Joseph Reed wrote that, "when the heavy rains came only half of the men had tents; they lay out in the lines, their arms, ammunition, etc., all got wet; they began to sink under the fatigues and hardships."[58]

Throughout the siege, Putnam frequently inspected the front line. Many years later, veteran Samuel Greene from Bernardston, Massachusetts, recalled one such visit by Putnam during an artillery barrage. At that moment, a shell slammed into the rude log breastwork, dislodging a large piece of sod that served as chinking, with such force that it struck Putnam and knocked him down. Quickly rising to his feet and dusting himself off, he exclaimed in a loud voice: "God take it all! They mean to kill folk, don't they!"[59]

BOLD MOVE

Washington knew that Howe would not hold off his attack forever, and if the weather cleared, his warships would slip in behind to pound them from the rear, making the position untenable. Washington's solution was bold; transport his army across to Manhattan at night, right under the noses of the British navy. The plan to withdraw from Long Island was unanimously approved at a council of general officers, including Putnam, held on August 29.[60]

Washington's luck had held for the time being, and, under the cover of inclement weather, Col. John Glover's oarsmen had delivered the bulk of his army to the relative safety of Manhattan during the night and early morning hours of August 29/30. To be successful, the plan had called for a ruse. Campfires were lit all up and down the line, tended by the brave men, like Col. John Chester and Benjamin Tallmadge, who would be the last to leave, and who also made enough noise to convince the British that the Americans were still manning their lines. A thick morning fog also helped. Finally, after he was assured that the last of his men were safely across, Washington stepped into a boat and crossed over to Manhattan.[61]

Nevertheless, thousands of American soldiers remained behind as prisoners of war. They had been taken to noisome prison hulks offshore, where disease and malnutrition would soon kill hundreds.[62]

NEXT MOVES

In the aftermath, as Washington gathered his senior officers together in Manhattan, everyone expressed their relief at their safe deliverance, though some, no doubt, like Putnam were surprised by the lack of British effort. "General Howe is either our friend or no general," he pronounced, "He had our whole army in his power . . . and yet he suffered us to escape without the least interruption." Putnam added what must have been obvious to all present: "Had he instantly followed up his victory, the consequence to the cause of liberty must have been dreadful."[63]

In a letter dated September 5, General Greene, freshly recovered from his fever, was the first of Washington's generals, and the most junior major general to boot, who first raised concerns about the inability of the American army to hold Manhattan. He called for a "general and speedy retreat." In addition, he strongly recommended that the "city and suburbs" be burned. It caused Washington to pause long enough to call a general council of his senior officers on September 7, at which time, a vote to hold on to the city passed by a large majority. Greene doubled down, and on September 11, calling the situation "critical and dangerous," he drafted a petition signed by himself and some junior commanders requesting another officer's council. Greene assured Washington that they were not proceeding "from fear of personal danger, nor the expectation of deriving . . . any honor and reputation . . . [but] from a love of our country and a determined resolution to urge the best and wisest measures." Washington reconvened the council the following day at Brig. Gen. Alexander McDougall's headquarters. This time Greene was more persuasive, and it was the consensus of the officers to take steps to move the bulk of the army north to Kingsbridge and to fortify Fort Washington.[64]

In the meantime, given Howe's cautious nature, and calculating that the army had more time, Washington ordered Putnam's division to stay behind. Silliman's battalion and Knox's artillery would remain in Lower Manhattan, in part to gradually remove artillery and stores. The balance of his division would spread out along the East River from Corlear's Hook in Lower Manhattan, north to modern-day 15th Street, fortifying or barricading possible British landing sites. North of that point was the responsibility of Spencer's division.[65]

THE AMERICAN TURTLE

In the interim, during the night of September 6/7, while standing on the dock at Whitehall Battery, Putnam oversaw the groundbreaking launch of David Bushnell's submarine, aptly named the *Turtle*, piloted by Sgt. Ezra Lee. Towed part of the way across the Upper Bay by a whaleboat, the vessel submerged and slowly made its way toward the man-of-war *Eagle*. About dawn, once beneath Howe's ship, Sergeant Lee intended to drill a hole through the copper bottom; however, a minor miscalculation had brought him just below the rudder and the iron plate that held the rudder in place. Unable to drill through the iron, and not wishing to be caught in broad daylight, Lee headed back to the shore. To be safe, he detonated the explosive device in open water. There was a loud roar as a huge column of water rose high in the sky, and the force of the blast was felt both on the *Eagle* and on shore. In the excitement of that moment, Putnam was heard to utter one of his colorful oaths. "God curse 'em," he shouted, "that'll do it for 'em!"[66]

"A MISERABLE, DISORDERLY RETREAT"

Putnam had five brigades with which to defend Manhattan. Colonel Gold Selleck Silliman's battalion, along with Col. Henry Knox's artillery, occupied the fort and battery in Lower Manhattan. Consistent with the vote in the officer's council and anticipating a landing by Howe's forces somewhere on Manhattan, Putnam had his men erect barricades or dig ditches on cross streets ending at the water's edge all along the East River. The remaining brigades, including Samuel Holden Parsons's Connecticut Continentals, along with the brigades of John Fellows, John Morin Scott, and James Clinton, lined the East River north from Corlear's Neck.[67]

Behind the defenses near Kip's Bay were stationed various Connecticut State troops. One of those was Pvt. Joseph Plumb Martin's company, part of Col. William Douglas's battalion in Wadsworth's brigade, Spencer's division. They had dug a ditch at Kip's Bay (between present-day East 32nd and East 38th Streets) to block any such attempt to land. When Martin awoke at dawn on Sunday, September 15, he noted in his memoir that the sight of British warships "saluted our eyes." So close were the vessels that Martin could make out the voices and read the ships' names. The British took their time making their preparations, but when the bombardment began, Martin "made a frog's leap for the ditch." Inexplicably, the defenders did not fire upon the approaching Hessians, when suddenly, deeming resistance futile, and there being no senior officer on the scene, their own officers gave the command to retreat, and they ran "as if the Devil was in them." Martin described what came next: "In retreating we had to cross a level clear spot of ground, forty or fifty rods wide, exposed to the whole of the enemy's fire; and they gave it in prime order, the grape shot and language flew merrily, which served to quicken our motions." The young man finally made it to the clear.[68]

Colonel Douglas was one of the last to leave his position, doing so only after it was clear that the left side of his line had broken and the rest were soon in full retreat. He told the ten men remaining with him to make their own way to safety, while he himself, "made the best of [the] way out," running "a mile to retreat through as hot a fire as could well be made." Fortunately, he wrote, "they mostly shot over us." Exhausted and unable to go any farther, he stopped, resigned to his being captured. Once again, his luck held, as several platoons of regulars paused their own retreat to cover him with their fire. More important, he found a horse abandoned by its owner, who had been unable to get it across a fence. That was not a problem for Douglas, who mounted, jumped the fence, and rode to safety in the new American lines at Harlem Heights.[69]

Some of Wadsworth's brigade was in position just below Colonel Douglas's battalion. Such was the case with Capt. Joshua Huntington's company, a part of Col. Samuel Selden's battalion. Like his brother Jedediah, Joshua was back in northern Manhattan recovering from a fever and dysentery. In danger of being trapped, his company briefly skirmished with the British as they retreated toward the main road north and safety. Huntington told his father that "in this Skirmish we Lost Some men Though I think not many." Among those lost was Colonel Selden, who was taken prisoner and later died in British custody.[70]

The sound of the naval gunfire reached Washington at his headquarters at the Mortier Mansion, and he knew immediately that the British were landing somewhere along the East River. He and his aides rode south toward the scene to find General Greene already there, hoping that his men had made a stand. When partway there, to his "great surprize and Mortification," Washington found that the soldiers had broken and were running helter-skelter to the rear. Washington weighed into the mob and attempted to stop them, shouting a flood of curses and imprecations, and at some point using the flat of his sword. During this incident, he was heard to exclaim, "Are these the men with whom I am to defend America?" Washington was so frustrated and angry that he threw his hat to the ground and refused to budge in the face of the advancing Hessian Grenadiers, only to be pulled back to safety by one of his aides, who grabbed the bridle of the general's horse and led him away. Washington established his new headquarters at the home of Roger Morris (Morris-Jumel Mansion) in what is now Washington Heights.[71]

At the same time, the sound of the guns reached Putnam's headquarters in Lower Manhattan. Never one to fret over his personal appearance, Putnam rode to the scene wearing a dirty shirt and a sleeveless vest, and at the same time, dispatched Parsons' and Fellows' brigades to assist Wadsworth. However, by the time they had reached the crossroads linking the Post Road to the Bloomingdale Road, these units had lost some cohesion, as their officers seemed confused as to what their orders were and, worse, began to lose control. Neither Washington and Greene, nor Putnam and Parsons were able to form up the panicked soldiers in the face of the precipitous flight, and to Putnam's dismay, his own troops, too, soon joined the retrograde movement. Greene would later refer to it as a "miserable, disorderly, retreat." Recognizing the danger to the remainder of his command, General Putnam galloped headlong back to his headquarters.[72]

Fortunately, Putnam's aide, Major Burr, anticipating the need, began to move the remaining soldiers stationed in Lower Manhattan northward to avoid being cut off as the British pushed inland. Using his knowledge of the area, Burr started the soldiers along the heavily wooded Bloomingdale Road and off onto back roads, although in the process they had to leave many of their cannons and much of their equipment behind. After rounding up his guard mounts that were scattered throughout Lower Manhattan, Putnam caught up with Burr's column and rode from company to company along the route, urging his soldiers to pick up the pace. David Humphreys, a company commander in Col. Silliman's battalion, had frequent opportunities to observe Putnam's actions firsthand, "issuing orders and encouraging the troops, flying, on his horse covered with foam, wherever his presence was most necessary." He went on to assert: "Without his [Putnam's] extraordinary exertions the guards must have been inevitably lost, and it is probable the entire Corps would have been cut in pieces."[73]

As the last to leave Lower Manhattan, Silliman's battalion was, in his words, in danger of being "hedged up," and he had fought rearguard actions all afternoon. Earlier, Putnam had ordered the brigade to occupy the fort at Bayard's Hill north of the city limits in hopes of stemming the general flight. From there, Silliman saw the British "land above me and spread across the island from one river to the other river until my retreat seemed to be entirely cut off." He soon received the order from Putnam to retreat, "if he could." Silliman told his wife that, "I attempted it along up through the woods by the North River, where I came in sight of the enemy several times." He kept the battalion moving until the last of the British appeared, "who pursued and fired on" his rear units. At that, Silliman formed a detail of three hundred men on a small hill to make a stand, at which sight, the British fled.[74]

Putnam's troops, including Silliman's battalion, reached Harlem Heights late that evening, exhausted by the effort, soaked by a sudden shower, and chilled by plunging temperatures, as they lay without cover on the ground that night. During the previous week, Putnam had sent Deborah and his daughters to safety, first to Kingsbridge, and from there, home.[75]

Earlier that day, Lt. Samuel Shaw was with Col. Henry Knox at Fort Washington when the sounds of the British cannons at Kip's Bay first reached them. As both men rode closer to the action, it became clear that the British had overcome any American opposition. Knox ordered Shaw to ride back to Lower Manhattan and see to it that the artillery companies were prepared to take a stand. However, when the lieutenant reached there, it was apparent that any effective opposition to the British would be futile. As with Putnam's infantry, the various artillery companies made their way north through the more wooded west side, frequently dodging

British patrols. Shaw and the others escaped the impending trap with just the clothes on their back. The experience taught him a valuable lesson. "A soldier," he concluded, "has no business with more than he can, on a pinch, carry off on his back." In all the hubbub, Henry Knox, who had been thought by some to have been lost, found a small boat and escaped across the Hudson River to New Jersey.[76]

TEA AND TREASON

As the British columns approached Murray Hill, the mistress of the house, Mary Lindley Murray, invited Generals Howe and Tryon in for cakes and Madeira, and as the story goes, delayed the march long enough to allow the American forces, principally Putnam's, to escape the impending trap. While the hospitality was no doubt real and enjoyed by the generals, the delay can be attributed to Clinton, who awaited Howe's further orders, and to Howe, a cautious commander, who had, in fact, waited until the balance of his troops had landed late that afternoon before closing the trap. Manhattan had been effectively sliced in two, and, except for Burr's anticipatory actions, Putnam's division would have been trapped. While it is interesting to think of Howe being bested by a woman, the truth is that it is simply a charming tale, with little or no significance to the overall result that day.[77]

INTO THE FIRE

As Washington's army retreated up Manhattan Island and assumed new defensive positions, the commander in chief never lost his inherent aggressive instincts. On September 16, he ordered Knowlton and his troop to reconnoiter the advancing British forces. Thomas Knowlton had shown steady courage and poise under fire both at the rail fence below the redoubt at Breeds Hill as well as during the retreat to Cambridge. Afterwards, he was entrusted with other duties, including the nighttime raid on Charlestown. He soon caught the attention of General Washington, who saw in the younger man much promise as a leader. Now a lieutenant colonel, he led a troop of Rangers, reminiscent of his service in the French and Indian War.

Coincidently, that same day, Howe had also sent out a reconnaissance force of light infantry ahead of a much larger body of troops, and the inevitable collision occurred at Harlem Heights, where a vigorous firefight with Knowlton's Rangers ensued. Soon, however, Knowlton, seeing that he was seriously outnumbered, withdrew a short distance to a wooded area where they had more cover and continued to fight. The impetuous British commander thought that the Americans were in full flight, and his buglers taunted them with a call associated with a fox hunt. The Redcoats dashed after Knowlton's men, who by now had been reinforced by three companies of a Virginia regiment led by Maj. Andrew Leitch.

Sensing an opportunity, Washington directed Putnam to person-ally order Knowlton and Leitch to circle to the left behind the enemy, while a smaller force remained behind and feinted a counterattack, with the hope of trapping the British in an area called the "Hollow Way." The British advance halted unexpectedly and took shelter behind a rail fence. Unaware that the British had stopped short, Knowlton and Leitch turned too soon. Instead of attacking the enemy from behind as planned, his force struck the British on their right flank. Both sides poured reinforcements into the fight, which was fierce. One soldier later counted nineteen bullet holes in one fence rail alone. Putnam, Greene, and other senior officers, including Joseph Reed, were in the thick of the fighting, issuing orders and encouraging the men. Reed told his wife their presence was needed to "animate the troops." Greene himself praised the "spirited conduct" of both Reed and Putnam. Some of the American reinforcements were companies from the selfsame battalion of Connecti-cut State Troops under Colonel Douglas that had run away at Kip's Bay. This day they stuck.[78]

The British retreated with the now augmented force of Americans close on their heels, until they reached the safety of their main army and the protective fire from their warships anchored in the Hudson River. Then, on Washington's orders, the Americans gave a loud shout of "Hur-rah!" and withdrew. It was a costly little victory, in which Knowlton and Major Leitch were both mortally wounded in the effort. Knowlton died within hours at Cross Keys Tavern, his brother and sixteen-year-old son at his bedside. His death was a personal blow to Putnam, who had long known the fellow Windham County native and served with him during the French and Indian War. Washington also lamented the loss of such fine men. Of Knowlton he wrote: "He would have been an honor to any country." Knowlton was buried with honors in a grave by the roadside, as was Major Leitch two weeks later. Although it was, all things considered, a small action, nevertheless, it gave the Americans a much-needed morale boost. General Silliman told his wife that, "when we meet them on equal ground we are not a set of people that will run from them, but that they now have had a good drubbing."[79]

That night, Washington placed Putnam in charge of the important right side of the line, just in case the British staged a counterattack. General Spencer was to remain ready to support Putnam should the need arise. However, the British had had enough, and the night was otherwise quiet.[80]

MINOR ACTIVITIES

Within days afterward, Putnam led a large foraging party of between sixteen hundred and eighteen hundred men and several wagons into the no-man's-land between the lines for the purpose of removing a large quantity of hay and grain stored there. At dawn, as the Americans continued to gather up the grain, the British pickets discovered their presence and began to raise the alarm. Soon a large body of British soldiers was spotted advancing toward them. As his detachment was half that size, and rather than bring on a major engagement, Putnam prudently withdrew with the grain his troops had already loaded on the wagons.[81]

After a while, the troops settled into the dull routine of soldiering. Young private Martin was returning to his company after a long night on picket duty. The rest of the guard had gone ahead, and he was ambling along a narrow lane deep in thought. At some point, he heard the unmistakable sounds of a horse coming up behind him. Ahead was a stone wall and a gate made up of several large logs piled one on top of the other. As he approached the gate, Martin turned to see General Putnam riding alone, some distance behind. The general was no doubt out inspecting the lines early that morning. Martin heard Putnam yell, "Soldier, let down those bars!" Martin appeared to obey as he removed the top bar, and then he quickly climbed over and disappeared off to the side and out of the general's line of sight. Putnam pulled a pistol from his belt and shouted, "Curse ye!" By then Martin was well out of range, and Putnam had to remove the remaining bars by himself to pass through the gate. If Putnam was incensed by the breach, surely, he appreciated the young man's independent spirit and had a good laugh at his own expense.[82]

LEAP FROG

General Howe was doggedly determined to flank Washington, who for the moment seemed content to occupy the Harlem Heights. In fact, the latter had begun work on two fortifications on the high ground on each side of the Hudson, and he placed Israel Putnam's cousin, Col. Rufus Putnam, the army's chief engineering officer, in charge of the work.

On October 12, Howe landed a force at Throg's Neck that was vigorously opposed by Gen. William Heath. After a sharp fight Howe was forced to withdraw. Six days later, he forced the issue once again, this time farther east at Pell's Point. The peninsular was defended by Col. John Glover's 750-man brigade. Glover was seriously outnumbered, but he made strategic use of stone walls and the topography, contesting every inch, before withdrawing to another vantage point. Eventually, superior numbers won out, and Glover yielded the field, but not before large casualties had been inflicted on the British. Although Howe did not pursue the rebels, his way to White Plains in Westchester County was now clear.[83]

At this time, Maj. Gen. Charles Lee had just returned from New Jersey and immediately recognized Howe's plan and the danger it posed to Washington's forces. Lee convinced him to withdraw to the vicinity of White Plains. On October 27, word reached Washington that Howe was on the move, and he dispatched Brigadier General Spencer's brigade to slow the British down, so that a proper defensive position could be established. Spencer placed his force directly in the path of the enemy with the Bronx River at his back, although fordable at that place. At dawn the following morning, a column of Hessian troops appeared, and a hot firefight ensued. When it became apparent that the enemy had overwhelming force and was about to flank them, Spencer ordered a retreat. Taking advantage of numerous stone walls, the Americans paused repeatedly to fire, and after fording the river, gained the summit of Chatterton Hill.[84]

By the time Spencer's men had reached the summit, Washington had reinforced what had been a small contingent of Militia on Chatterton Hill with troops from Delaware led by John Haslet, and later with a brigade led by Gen. Alexander McDougall, along with Alexander Hamilton and two field pieces, some two thousand defenders in all. In addition, Washington had directed Col. Rufus Putnam to Chatterton Hill to oversee the construction of earthworks. He arrived at about 10:00 a.m. just as the British began to shell the hill. The stubborn fight lasted all day, the defenders turning back two determined assaults, until the Militia finally gave way as the position was in danger of being flanked. Reinforcements led by General Putnam were unable to reach the defenders prior to the retreat, while once again, the Marylanders conducted a valiant fighting withdrawal. Howe had planned to renew his attack, but he postponed it because of heavy rains. The dead were hastily interred in shallow graves, and Washington slipped quietly away.[85]

As he retreated, Washington divided his forces, sending Greene to New Jersey, Heath to the vital Highlands, and Lee to Westchester. The latter was the gateway to Connecticut, a primary source of men and supplies, so vital, in fact, that it would come to be called the "Provision State." In time, the situation in Westchester County devolved into a bitter partisan contest, and it would be a constant source of concern to the Highlands as well.[86]

Certain that Howe would press his advantage, on November 9, Washington told Putnam that, "not a moments time should be lost in throwing your men over upon the Jersey shore" and to take a position opposite Dobbs Ferry. That very day, Putnam began to cross his brigades over, starting with that of Lord Stirling, followed by Col. Edward Hand and General Bell, four thousand men in all. As for the troops themselves, they were tired but not disheartened. Samuel Shaw said as much to his parents. "This [continuous movement] greatly fatigues our army, but by no means discourages them," he wrote, "as they pretty generally believe we shall beat them at last, though a few cross incidents and hard knocks may probably intervene."[87]

Tragedy at Washington Heights

After White Plains, Howe turned his attention to Fort Washington. On the surface, the post looked impregnable. However, looks were deceiving; the fort was, in fact, vulnerable. For one thing, it was built on solid rock, and efforts to dig a well failed miserably. Second, there were large gaps in its outlying defenses, and not enough men to fill them. On the other hand, during a siege, there was not enough space within the main fortification to support all the troops under Col. Robert Magaw's command. Lastly, Howe controlled access by land and water, and, in short, there could be no escape as originally contemplated.[88]

Shortly after 1:00 p.m. on November 15, Colonel Magaw summarily rejected General Howe's demand for surrender, vowing to defend it to the last extremity. At the same time, Magaw sent word to Greene of the surrender demand. Later that day, Greene and Putnam crossed over from New Jersey to assess the situation and returned about 9:00 p.m., when they met Washington getting into a boat to do the same. Given the lateness of the hour, they convinced him to wait until the next day. Early the following morning, Washington, accompanied by General Putnam, General Greene, and Gen. Hugh Mercer, returned to Fort Washington to further assess things. Their arrival was coincident with the start of the British attack on the outer works. They determined that nothing further could be done. Greene, Mercer, and Putnam each offered to remain with the defenders, but they were ordered to return to the New Jersey side with Washington. Despite some reinforcements previously sent by General Greene, and considerable casualties inflicted on the Hessian forces under Gen. Wilhelm von Knyphausen by Magaw's riflemen, the siege was over within a matter of hours. Magaw was forced to surrender his 2,800-man command, most of whom would languish and die with other prisoners in the hulks in New York Harbor.[89]

Washington would later write that he had not wanted to hold the fort, but this was disingenuous at best. Admittedly, he had expressed some concerns, particularly, the fact that the British continued to have free passage up and down the Hudson River, but these were allayed after he had heard from both Putnam and Greene. More important, as commander in chief, he never overruled them. For his part, Nathanael Greene later agonized over the inevitable "what ifs." He told Henry Knox that he "felt mad, vexed, sick, and sorry" over the whole matter.[90]

"WE SHALL BE OLD IN TIME"

George Washington learned much from the events in and around New York City, not only about himself, but also about the men who would continue to serve the Cause, and more important, about the men who would lead them. He came to rely upon his Continentals as the reliable core of the new American army, and, at the same time, he learned that there was a time and place to use the less reliable Militia. Even though he did not have all the answers, Nathanael Greene's place was secure, as a loyal young officer who could think strategically. His single-handed insistence that New York City be abandoned and burned no doubt saved all, if not a good part, of the army to fight another day.

As for Israel Putnam, while he was not a strategic thinker, his boundless energy and reliable courage under fire were just what Washington needed at a critical time. "Old Put's" rough edges may have rankled some of his colleagues, but he always moved to the sound of the guns and willingly shared the experiences of his troops. Putnam acted quickly and decisively in meeting threat posed by General Grant during the early morning of August 27. If he was mistaken in his belief that this was the main point of the British attack, he was not alone, and he should not be faulted for his actions. On September 15, he could well have abandoned Silliman's battalion to its fate, but he rode back to Lower Manhattan when everyone else was rushing north toward Harlem. At Harlem Heights, he was right in the thick of the fight, giving orders and encouraging his men. Small wonder that Washington continued to call upon him.

On the negative side, the battle exposed some disturbing rifts within the army itself, based upon intersectional rivalry, as the usual postmortem blame game played out. Colonel William Douglas expressed his concerns in a letter to his wife, Hannah. "One thing more prevails in the army, which I fear the consequence," he told her, "[that is] there is some officers that are pleased to stigmatize New England troops and set up the Southern troops, and if a division should take place it will be unhappy for

America." As an example, General Parsons accused the "southern" troops, that is those outside of New England, of cowardice, particularly Colonel Miles' Pennsylvania riflemen. They were in his estimation at fault for the defeat. Lieutenant Colonel Daniel Brodhead, who served with Colonel Miles, in turn, wrote that "no troops could behave better than the Southern." He went on to accuse part of a regiment of Continentals from Connecticut for causing a panic, and in a bitterly sarcastic postscript, blamed "The Great Putnam" [who] could not, "tho' requested, send out one Reg't to cover our retreat." However, since neither Washington nor Putnam knew Howe's full intent, they could not be sure if it would be a mistake to weaken the main defense position should Howe continue his attacks. Hence the decision not to dispatch more troops.[91]

More than a year after the battle, during an inquiry into his conduct at the Battle of Brandywine, Brig. Gen. John Sullivan, another favorite of Washington, tried to escape any blame for the failure to robustly defend the Jamaica Pass. Although given the sheer size of Howe's main force, it is unlikely that, unless well-entrenched and supported with artillery, any defensive force could have held that juggernaut at bay for long. At best, sufficient time could have been bought for more frontline troops to have safely retreated to the line at Brooklyn. Nevertheless, still smarting from his being superseded by Putnam, he sought to shift the blame with several out-and-out lies.

First, he falsely claimed that he was designated as second-in-command to Putnam "within the lines," and that Lord Stirling commanded "the main body without the lines." Washington's order regarding the respective command responsibilities was clear. Second, and perhaps more egregious, Sullivan claimed that he had always believed that the main attack would come through Jamaica Pass, "but could not persuade others of my opinion" (presumably referring to Putnam and Washington). In point of fact, it was Col. Samuel Miles who led a five-hundred-man regiment of Pennsylvania riflemen, and who had been watching the enemy movements for four days, who suggested that very course. Sullivan ignored it, when, according to Miles, "he [Sullivan] might have obtained [the information] by his own observation," on August 26, when the two of them stood together on the heights viewing the size and position of Howe's army.

Next, Sullivan claims to have led a four-hundred-man party to reconnoiter, when he was surrounded by the force "who had advanced by the very road I had foretold." It is true that he was captured. However, at that time, he was, in fact, leading another body of men toward the sound of the fighting near Bedford. In the event, that decision alone was ill-timed and stripped still more much-needed troops from the Flatbush Pass at the critical moment of de Heister's thrust.

Finally, Sullivan carped about the fact that he had never been reimbursed for the fifty dollars he had advanced to the five horsemen to watch Jamaica Pass. For all the good they did, he could have saved the money![92]

For men like Col. William Douglas, the recent defeats were simply a question of a lack of experience compared with that of the British. "I hope the Country will not be discouraged at our making some missteps," he told his wife, "at first we are new, but shall be old in time as well as they."[93]

CHAPTER ELEVEN

The American Revolution

Cowboys and Skinners

NEW JERSEY

FOLLOWING THE FALL OF FORT WASHINGTON AND THE ABANDONMENT of Fort Lee, along with the loss of much-needed tents and other equipment, Putnam crossed the Hudson River and joined General Greene in New Jersey. Washington and this much-diminished force made their way south. Hanging over Washington's head was the upcoming winter and the imminent expiration of enlistments. These were matters of grave concern. Yet, Howe continued to cautiously press his advantage. "[It is] a sacred truth they never yet have ventured to attack us but with great advantages," wrote Samuel Webb, "[and] they pursue no faster than their heavy artillery can be brought up." Webb added that, "with this they scout every piece of wood, stone walls, etc., before they approach." As a result, Washington was given some much-needed breathing room.[1]

More troubles came in the form of General Lee's embarrassing capture in his nightshirt by Coronet Banastre Tarleton on the night of December 12/13, thus depriving Washington of experienced counsel until sometime later when Lee was exchanged. Washington led his forces across the Delaware, and afterwards, prudently made sure that all the watercraft for miles up and down the river were rowed over to the west bank or sunk. Putnam played a role in this effort, reporting to Washington that he had sent a party to the New Jersey side of the Delaware River "to bring off all the Craft out of the Creeks" feeding into it. Howe went into winter quarters, leaving behind several garrisons in New Jersey, including one at Trenton, manned by a troop of Hessians under Col. Johann Rall.[2]

THE CITY OF BROTHERLY LOVE

Washington dispatched Putnam with several thousand troops to secure the peace in Philadelphia and to supervise its defense. By the time Putnam reached the city, the situation was chaotic to say the least. Many citizens had expected an attack by the British as Howe's forces marched south through New Jersey. Consequently, the wealthier element hired wagons to evacuate their valuables and other belongings. Militia companies pressed young men into their ranks. Those inhabitants, known to be loyal to the Crown, and there were a fair number of them, were harassed. Even some members of Congress were seen leaving the city, despite adamant protests to the contrary. On top of it all, there was an outbreak of typhus and smallpox.[3]

On December 12, three days after his arrival, Putnam imposed martial law, including a 10:00 p.m. curfew. That day he also sent a report to Washington. "All Things in this City remain in Confusion, for Want of Men to put them into Order," he began pessimistically. He quickly added that, "the Citizens are generally with you." Putnam's duties kept him busy, and he went on to list all his actions taken to date and the situation in general. He had, he reported, inspected the lines with Brig. Gen. Thomas Mifflin, Washington's quartermaster general, as well as some French engineering officers who were helping to lay out the lines. The small contingent of Continental recruits, he told him, had been set to work on "fatigue and guard duty," however, there were not enough of them to mount more than a single watch. In addition, he had critical supplies moved to "Christeen Bridge" (Christiana, Delaware), on orders from Congress. As to the latter, Washington expressed some concern that the supplies there could be "easily seized" and should be moved to Lancaster, Pennsylvania. This matter should be "enquired into," he told him.[4]

As with any fluid situation, rumors abounded. One such warned that Philadelphia was about to be burned down by the Continental Army. Putnam was outraged by the suggestion and issued a general order on December 13. "The General has been informed," he began, "that some weak or wicked men have maliciously reported that it is the design and wish of the officers and men in the Continental Army to burn and destroy the city of Philadelphia." He continued with an assurance to the inhabitants that he was under orders to protect the city from "all invaders and enemies." He finished with a threat to punish with summary execution any such attempt: "The General will consider every attempt to burn the city of Philadelphia as a crime of the blackest dye, and without ceremony, punish capitally any incendiary who shall have the hardiness and cruelty to attempt it."[5]

In late December, as Washington was retreating through New Jersey, Putnam was having problems of his own. He wrote Washington two letters (both now lost) outlining the difficulties he was experiencing, particularly, the lack of cooperation among the citizenry to help build the necessary defensive works around Philadelphia. Washington was appalled at the short-sighted lack of patriotism, let alone the refusal of Philadelphians to act in their own best interest. "Intreat, exhort and use every exertion, to induce the people to act for their own preservation," he urged, "strain every Nerve for carrying on the necessary Works, [for] without them, we shall have but little to hope for." Use the Militia to build the works, he told Putnam, and do not send them to him. Putnam also had trouble with the rowdiness and lack of discipline among the new recruits. Washington found the behavior to be "highly reprehensible," and once again, he urged Putnam to encourage his officers to use the "utmost care and vigilance" to prevent it. Ever the practical man, Washington conceded that while "the abuse cannot fully be totally suppressed, but it may perhaps be checked in some degree."[6]

Putnam believed that it was the duty of all citizens to come to the defense of their city and the seat of government. Although he would refer to the Quakers as "Drones of Society," many of them were leading citizens, and he resignedly honored their "conscientious scruples" and exemption from military service. However, he ordered those persons who would not bear arms on behalf of the city to turn in their weapons and receive compensation for them. Those who failed to do so and hid their weapons would be punished, he warned. In some cases, the merchant class needed a little nudge. Such was the case with Tench Coxe, a prominent merchant, when "a considerable quantity of bar iron" was found at his store on Arch Street. Putnam issued an order for its seizure.[7]

A man of action, Putnam as administrator must have chafed with the daily round of problems large and small that were brought to his attention. When he found that certain merchants were not accepting Continental currency, he not only questioned their patriotism but also threatened to arrest them and confiscate their goods. Perhaps stating the obvious, he urged all citizens to assist the local fire brigades with "engines and buckets" in the event of an alarm. On the other hand, he was clearly within his element in seeing to the training of the troops and the building of fortifications. At this time, Putnam rounded up all able-bodied men and set them to work digging the entrenchments that he had laid out, particularly on the northern reaches of the city, "from the Delaware to the Schuylkill," as Washington had suggested to John Hancock, the president of Congress, and no doubt, to him.[8]

Putnam was also under enormous added pressure. Congress had moved to Baltimore on his and General Mifflin's recommendation. Several delegates were unhappy with the move and decried the crime and high cost of living they found in Baltimore. John Hancock's quarters had been robbed within two days of his arrival, and another delegate referred to the town as a "dirty infamous extravagant hole." At the same time, Congress had ordered Putnam to defend Philadelphia "to the last extremity."[9]

Putnam took his responsibilities seriously, so seriously that his health suffered for it. At some point he became so physically exhausted that he was confined to his quarters for several days. In any event, his younger son Daniel, who was serving as an aide-de-camp, reported to Washington that his father was "much improved" by Christmas Day. Washington told Putnam that he was "glad to hear . . . you are getting better."[10]

What neither Putnam nor Washington grasped at that time was the fact that, given his age and experience, with the Philadelphia assignment, Israel Putnam had been given a task beyond his capabilities. Although Putnam did not lack drive, he obviously had difficulty dealing with myriad day-to-day problems of managing the most populous city in the colonies, and he would have benefitted from having a capable subordinate to lift the more mundane administrative burdens from his shoulders. He was driven to succeed, and he had simply worn himself out, physically and mentally, grappling with his assignment. Putnam was at his best when focused on one task, large or small, like leading men in battle, from a company to a brigade, or building a fort. He was at once the beneficiary of the seniority system, as well as its victim, something that would become clearer with a later assignment in the Hudson Highlands.[11]

"A Diversion or Something"

On December 22, Col. Joseph Reed gave Washington some unsolicited advice. Something urgently needed to be done before the army melted away as enlistments expired and the Continental currency became worthless. Even a loss was better than doing nothing. "Delay with us," he reasoned, "is now equal to a total defeat." He suggested: "Will it not be possible my dear Gen'l for your Troops or such part of them as can act with Advantage to make a Diversion or something more at or about Trenton.... Our Affairs are hasting fast to ruin if we do not retrieve them by some happy event."[12]

Washington was at his best when his back was to the wall. Naturally aggressive, the dire circumstances called out the best in him. "Give me one more effort," he asked the tired, dispirited men he had brought to Pennsylvania. They responded to his bold plan to attack the Hessian garrison at Trenton when least expected. Although Colonel Rall had had some advance warning that the Americans were planning an imminent attack, he believed that they could successfully defend Trenton. On Christmas Day, he was lulled into a false sense of security when a heavy snowstorm developed late that day. Moreover, the Delaware River was laced with large chunks of floating ice that would make a winter crossing more difficult.

Washington needed a diversion to aid his plan. He hoped to tie up Col. Carl von Donop's garrison of Hessians at Bordentown, New Jersey, just six miles south of Trenton. As a result, he ordered Col. John Cadwalader and his Pennsylvania Militia to cross the Delaware near Bristol, Pennsylvania, simultaneously with his crossing farther north. Although a small contingent of the Militia was able to work their way across the ice, the state of the river that night made it impossible for Cadwalader to cross his entire force. He recalled the advance party.[13]

Colonel Reed came to Putnam's headquarters on Christmas Eve and asked him if he would send what troops he could spare across the river to New Jersey to assist in the effort to harass von Donop. Putnam indicated that he could send about five hundred men and possibly an artillery battery. However, as he was in the process of mustering this force, yet another rumor circulated the city to the effect that if he were to leave the city, the Tory element would cause trouble. Accordingly, he cancelled the plans. In any event, it is likely that he would have had the same difficulty as had Cadwalader if he had attempted the crossing.[14]

As things turned out, however, it was von Donop himself who inadvertently aided Washington. Following the American retreat from New York, Col. Samuel Griffin, who had cobbled together a substantial force of some eight hundred to a thousand Militia and Continentals from Pennsylvania, was conducting operations in that area with some success. At 10:00 a.m. on December 21, as Griffin approached Mount Holly, New Jersey, the British contingent, being forewarned, "abandoned it . . . to all appearances in great confusion." Griffin's presence in the area was reported to von Donop, and two days later, the Hessian marched his brigade to Mount Holly to pick a fight with Griffin, after which the numerically inferior American force withdrew. Von Donop decided to remain at Mount Holly through Christmas, simply sending out some foraging parties. That decision placed him twenty miles from Trenton, thus rendering any possible coordination with Rall much more difficult.[15]

TRENTON

Once again, on the evening of December 25, Washington called upon the dependable Col. John Glover and his men to row the rugged Durham boats through the ice flows and land his party on the eastern shore of the Delaware. Given the weather and the thickness of the ice, much time was lost. By the time his entire force was assembled there, it was early morning. The attackers were behind schedule and in danger of losing the element of surprise. Luckily for them, the snow persisted. Although it was a complicated plan that depended upon a coordinated attack, somehow it worked, and the victory was complete. That same day, Washington crossed back over the Delaware into Pennsylvania with his troops and their prisoners.[16]

In addition to the weapons and other gear, the patriots captured 896 officers and men. The Hessian prisoners were rounded up together and marched south to Philadelphia, where they were paraded through the streets to the delight of some, and, no doubt, to the astonishment of others. Washington had ordered that the prisoners be treated well, in contrast to the British treatment of those Americans captured at New York. Putnam ordered that a barracks be cleared for their confinement. On New Year's Day, an unabashedly convivial Putnam entertained a group of Hessian officers, where he shook their hands, and they all shared a glass of Madeira. Later, one of them would describe the evening and their host. "This old gray-beard may be a good, honest man," he wrote, then adding uncharitably, "but nobody but the rebels would have made him a general."[17]

PRINCETON

Washington received the morale boost he and his soldiers needed. However, he was not idle. Crossing back yet again, he reoccupied Trenton on December 30. When word reached Washington that Cornwallis was approaching with a large force, he established a camp on the high ground on the other side of Assunpink Creek, near a solid stone bridge. Upon his arrival, Cornwallis had tried to force his way across, and the Americans had stubbornly denied him, but at a high cost to both sides. It was then that Washington conceived another bold plan.

On the night of January 2/3, Washington started his army northward over what had been a muddy back road, now hardened by the deep freeze. As a ruse, he left behind a small force to make noise and stoke the campfires. General Cornwallis was completely fooled and continued to occupy Trenton. The Americans arrived at Princeton that morning, just as a mixed column of Dragoons, Grenadiers, along with the 17th and 55th Foot, led by Lt. Col. Charles Mawhood, was traveling south to join Cornwallis. At first, the Patriots completely surprised Mawhood; however, after the initial shock, the British regrouped and charged, causing the American line to waiver. Although there were many acts of individual bravery, the British onslaught began to overwhelm the Americans. General Hugh Mercer was surrounded but refused to surrender. For his act of bravery, he was bayonetted repeatedly as he lay on the ground, mortally wounded. Colonel John Haslet of Delaware quickly stepped in. Away on other duty in Manhattan, he had missed the fight at Gowanus. As he had done at White Plains, Haslet was determined to show his mettle. He died with a bullet to the head. The timely arrival of Colonel Cadwalader's regiment helped to briefly steady the line, but it, too, began to give way.[18]

Nearby, Washington watched the unfolding fight and seized the moment. He quickly rode forward to personally steady his faltering line. Astride his horse, he weighed into the melee as the bullets flew all around, and he called to the men in a loud voice: "Parade with us, my brave fellows!" The troops rallied, and a defeated Mawhood retreated south to Trenton. On another part of the field, General Sullivan overwhelmed the remaining opposition in and around the village of Princeton, particularly at Nassau Hall, and Washington was assured of yet another victory. Within days, Cornwallis retreated to the relative safety of Brunswick and Amboy, and, in doing so, conceded most of New Jersey to Washington.[19]

THE AFTERMATH OF VICTORY

At midnight on January 2, Col. Joseph Reed returned to Putnam's headquarters, this time to deliver Washington's orders in person, by way of a letter requesting that Putnam send along as many men as he could spare to help guard the army's "entire baggage" train that had been sent to the safety of Burlington. Washington's men had set out for Princeton with a bare minimum, and only a "few" even had their blankets. In addition, Putnam himself was ordered to move to Crosswicks, a village several miles south of Trenton.[20]

Putnam cobbled together a force of between 700 and 800 men, and by January 5, he was in Bristol, Pennsylvania. From there the next day, he crossed the river to Burlington and moved north to Bordentown, where he found an additional 500 Militia and a small number of Continental troops that had become separated from Washington. For whatever reason, Putnam marched his now augmented force to Trenton and not to

Crosswicks, arriving there on January 7; the British having abandoned it. In a letter dated January 5, the commander in chief told Putnam about the victory at Princeton and repeated his order for him to move to Crosswicks. While Putnam did not receive this letter until he had already reached Trenton, Colonel Reed had clearly told him Crosswicks.[21]

Putnam moved to Crosswicks on January 8, where yet another letter from Washington reached him. This time, he was ordered to march immediately for Princeton to secure precious supplies seized from the British, which were in danger of being appropriated by the local Militia. To Washington's great frustration, Putnam still had not arrived in Princeton on January 15. "What in the name of heaven he can be doing at Crosswicks I know not," wrote a frustrated Washington to Colonel Reed. Unknown to Washington was the fact that Putnam was losing his Pennsylvania Militia through desertions, despite his pleas to them to wait until new levies had arrived. He pleaded with the Council of Safety to "continue to forward the militia as fast as they come into town."[22]

Putnam finally arrived at Princeton four days later. With the British in winter quarters in New Brunswick and Perth Amboy, but within easy striking distance, Putnam was warned to keep his guard up and to give appearances that the number of men under his command was double the actual figure. He was also ordered to forward any remaining baggage and stragglers on to Washington at Morristown. Putnam continued to have problems retaining the Pennsylvania Militia. "No arguments can prevail upon them to stay beyond their six weeks," he wrote.[23]

THE MILK OF HUMAN KINDNESS

Putnam was a compassionate man, especially when it came to his wounded adversaries. While at Princeton, he was summoned to the bedside of a seriously wounded British officer, a Captain McPherson of the 17th Foot, part of Lt. Col. Charles Mawhood's command that had clashed with troops led by Hugh Mercer and John Cadwalader south of town. His care had been neglected until Putnam had moved among the prisoners and directed that he be attended to. The man wished to dictate his Last Will and Testament and had asked for permission for a fellow officer to pass through the American lines. Putnam was then faced with a dilemma. He wanted to honor the man's wish, but in doing so he did not want to reveal just how small his detachment was. He granted the man's wish and at the same time resorted to a ruse—lighting candles in the windows of all the surrounding homes and marching his men up and down the main street all night in front of the wounded officer's quarters. It worked, as the visiting officer returned to his superiors with the news that Putnam had four thousand to five thousand men! The grateful officer thanked Putnam and found it hard to believe that an American would show him such kindness.[24]

On February 8, after all the wounded prisoners who were well enough had been transported to Philadelphia, Putnam once again demonstrated his consideration for his defeated enemy. The British had left behind a small contingent, consisting of a corporal and three privates, to care for their wounded at Princeton. Putnam had the opportunity to observe firsthand the care they rendered their fellow soldiers. He praised their behavior to the Council of Safety as "orderly and sober." They were the last to be sent to Philadelphia, and based upon their actions, he recommended that they "may have their liberty and not be kept in close confinement."[25]

"MEN NOT MONEY"

If the situation with the Militia in Pennsylvania was problematic for Putnam, it did not get any better for him in New Jersey, as desertions were up and enlistments were down. Everyone agreed, including Putnam, Washington, and Gov. William Livingston, that the law needed to be changed to eliminate the option to pay a fine in lieu of service. Putnam suggested that the new law should "render it [in] no man's interest to be conscientious against bearing arms." Washington urged Livingston to ask the legislature to make the change. Without it, however, Putnam was forced to deal with the situation as best he could.[26]

To that end, Putnam ordered the Militia colonels to collect the fines, which he suggested should be applied to the purchase of war material for the state. Some officers had collected the fine and distributed the monies among the troops, something Putnam strictly forbade, as he felt that it was "unjust and attended with many evil consequences." Putnam advised Governor Livingston of his orders.[27]

When Governor Livingston read Putnam's letter telling him what he had done, he quickly countermanded the order to his Militia. Although Livingston agreed that the law was "absurd," he rightly pointed out that, "we want men and not money." Besides, he reasoned, since only the more affluent could pay the fine, it would leave the poorer men to serve and, worse, introduce "the invidious distinction between rich and poor." Finally, he told Putnam that, by law, the fines were the property of the company to which the "delinquent belongs," and not that of the state. In his reply, Putnam conceded the point. "At a time like this," he wrote, "no sum can be really equivalent." Nevertheless, drawing a distinction between a forced payment and a voluntary one, Putnam correctly pointed out that unless it had been amended, he understood the current law to give any eligible male the option to pay a fine in lieu of service, and he questioned whether he even had the authority to deny anyone the exercise of that right. Thus, he recognized a core republican principle that the military should be subservient to the civil authority.[28]

That having been said, Putnam, who was well-acquainted with the Quakers, having dealt with that sect during his tenure in Philadelphia, placed the blame for the situation squarely at their feet. Not only would they not serve as soldiers, but they also refused to provide useful labor for the army in lieu of service. He continued to refer to them as "Drones of Society." Despite his strong feelings, Putnam exhibited his practical side. I could have "detained them their month," he told Livingston, by "keeping them under constant guard, but this would have been gratifying spleen to very little purpose." Instead, he collected the fine as permitted by law and released them. Nevertheless, he told the governor that the legislature should be able to compel their [Quakers] service. Livingston adamantly disagreed, and earlier he had told Putnam that he objected to the implementation of such a proposal as a violation of their [Quakers'] consciences.[29]

Governor Livingston passed copies of Putnam's letters on to General Washington, who reacted quickly. "I desire therefore that this practice [imposing fines] may have an immediate end put to it," Washington told him, and that "no steps of this nature be taken without the countenance of the civil power of this state."[30]

Recruitment was not Putnam's only problem with the Militia. It had come to his attention that some men with Loyalist sympathies had recently enlisted "with a view to assist the enemy in behaving ill." Putnam's solution was to move those companies away from their more familiar area and replace them with those "who can be more relied on." Washington approved the move.[31]

HARASSING THE ENEMY

The next several months would become known as the "Forage War." On February 7, 1777, Putnam led a four-hundred-man contingent north from Princeton to a stretch of the Raritan River near New Brunswick known as the "Roundabouts." There, pursuant to Washington's orders, they rounded up "all the horses, waggons, and fat Cattle" in a wide radius of the British positions. He left a fifty-man detail to harass the boat traffic sailing up and down the river to and from the British garrison wintering there. Putnam made his report to the commander in chief the following day.[32]

Putnam and his men engaged in similar raids, and at one point during the night of February 17/18, they captured Richard Stockton, a prominent Tory, during a fight at Lawrence Island in the Raritan River. Putnam had the captives transported under heavy guard to Philadelphia. Along with Stockton's party were "sixty-three excellent muskets." Putnam suggested to the governor that they be purchased and given to the Militia. The legislature approved the purchase on the governor's recommendation. The legislature did eventually amend the Militia law.[33]

In early April, Putnam's scouts noticed considerable activity among the British forces from New Brunswick to Amboy. For one thing, there were many ships in the harbor at Amboy, some loaded with Hessian troops, while others had set sail for New York. In addition, several parties of the enemy were seen cutting timber and stripping the siding off houses in the vicinity and setting them on fire. Putnam speculated that it had something to do with modifying the troop transports. In any event, the massive movement meant that Howe was on the move. Putnam sent a warning to Congress to be prepared, as he "had the greatest reason to think that Philadelphia is their greatest object at present." This guessing game of where General Howe would strike next played out over the next several months, ultimately affecting Putnam's command.[34]

The Passing of a Patriot

February 1777 found Gen. Seth Pomeroy at the head of a regiment of Massachusetts Militia serving under Gen. Alexander McDougall in the Highlands north of New York City. He would turn seventy-one years of age in May, and Washington had requested that he join him with his regiment in Morristown, New Jersey. Pomeroy was tired, and his family had advised against it, but the call of duty was strong. From Peekskill, on February 11, he wrote to one of his sons, sad to be leaving General McDougall, whom he liked. Apprehensive and hoping to find a like-minded superior in New Jersey, he wrote: "I go cheerfully, for I am sure the cause we are engaged in is just, and the call I have to it is clear, and the call of God." He added: "With that assurance, who would not go on cheerfully, and confront every danger?" The old soldier died of pleurisy six days later, before he could join Washington.[35]

The Hudson Highlands

Citing the "importance" of the post, on May 8 Washington assigned Benedict Arnold, recently appointed a major general, to command the Hudson Highlands. Still smarting from his perceived slights, Arnold, thin-skinned as ever, declined the command and instead went to Phila-delphia to sort things out. Washington then turned to Putnam, and on May 12, he ordered him to vacate his current command at Princeton immediately upon the arrival of his successor. John Sullivan arrived there on May 15, and as directed, Putnam reported to Washington's headquar-ters at Morristown, before going on to Peekskill. No doubt Washington and Putnam had a frank discussion about what was expected of him, but just in case, Washington reinforced his position in a letter to General McDougall, whom he trusted would prove to be a steady hand. "You are well acquainted with the old Gentleman's temper," he wrote, "he is active, disinterested and open to conviction, and I therefore hope, that by affording him the advice and Assistance, that your knowledge of the post enables [you] to do, you will be very happy in your command under him." Washington knew his man.[36]

Putnam established his headquarters at John Mandeville's farm in Peekskill, New York, which lay on the east bank of the Hudson River, forty miles north of New York City. On the grounds was a large farmhouse, along with a carriage house, barn, and several outbuildings. Mandeville sometimes let rooms to travelers. Putnam, along with Generals McDougall and Huntington, and his staff were also quartered there. Huntington, a young man from a prominent family from Norwich, Connecticut, described the scene: "I am in a comfortable House, incorporated with the Family consisting of an honest Farmer, his Wife, and a number . . . of pretty Children. The Fare is homely but wholesome, and there is a Tidyness . . . about them that you seldom meet with among the Class I am speaking of." Putnam must have felt right at home.[37]

Not only did the Highlands sit astride the route north to Albany, but they also provided a vital link to New England. Putnam set about improving or erecting a series of three forts near the narrows: Clinton and Montgomery on the west bank and Fort Constitution on the east bank above Peekskill and opposite West Point. His assignment became more critical when word was received in late June that General Burgoyne had started an army south from Canada, the objective being to split New England off from the rest of the states.[38]

General Howe had withdrawn most of his forces from New Jersey by early January, leaving smaller garrisons at New Brunswick and Perth Amboy to winter over. However, by April, as we have seen, Putnam had reported that the latter were also being withdrawn. It then became a guessing game as to where General Howe would take his army next. From the very start, Putnam was at odds with Washington over the issue of necessary troop strength. Washington was certain that Philadelphia was the objective, but when Howe's fleet bypassed the mouth of the Delaware River, it created even more uncertainty. Howe played the game masterfully, and until he sailed up the Chesapeake and landed at Head of Elk (present-day Elkton, Maryland) on August 25, it was anybody's guess.

Washington remained convinced that Philadelphia was the objective, and he repeatedly demanded that Putnam send most of his Continentals to him to bolster his army. Putnam had complied, but not without some pushback. Putnam was equally convinced that the Highlands were in jeopardy, from both a northern and a southern strike, and more important, he felt that he would not have a sufficient force to defend them. He was aware that the British had previously staged successful raids on American supply depots at Peekskill on March 23, and at Danbury, Connecticut, on April 26. The knowledge of both had to weigh heavily on Putnam's mind.

"The Ragged, Lousey, Naked Regiment"

Part of Putnam's responsibilities included the care and clothing of all the Continental troops under his command. The Militias were the responsibility of the various states, but they came and went with the season or terms of their muster or enlistment. Soon after Putnam assumed command of the Highlands, he wrote to Washington about serious deficiencies, particularly the lack of shoes. On June 2, Hamilton responded that Washington was "astonished at that extraordinary want of clothing you mention." He could not account for the lack, unless, he speculated, that shoes allocated to Putnam had been misdirected to Gates. In that instance, he recommended that Putnam investigate, and if that was the case, to "redirect" them as originally intended. This suggestion was impractical at best, since if that were true, Putnam would have to take the shoes off the feet of Gates' soldiers! Just for emphasis, Hamilton told Putnam that any shoes currently in his warehouse were not to be distributed and were reserved for Washington's soldiers, adding enigmatically, "unless it shall prove to have been so misapplied as to render it impossible to make it answer the end." Hamilton followed up a week later, reaffirming the order and adding that Putnam was, in any event, to wait for the arrival of a "Deputy Clothier." Notwithstanding this exchange, the situation became increasingly problematic for Putnam's command during the summer of 1777.[39]

Typical were the men of the 2nd Rhode Island Regiment, part of Brig. Gen. James Varnum's brigade. In August of 1777, Col. Israel

Angell found the situation in his regiment so desperate that he sat down and wrote to Gov. Nicholas Cooke. First, he reminded the governor of his past pleas. He then related that after Angell returned from a recent furlough, he found his men worse off than he expected. "Not one half of them can not be termed fit for duty on any emergency," he reported, and of those "who went with me on a late expedition near Kings Bridge many were barefoot." Angell called the situation "scandalous" and said that it left the men open to mockery from other regiments, as well as the inhabitants of the villages through which they frequently passed, often being referred to as the "Ragged, Lousey, Naked Regiment." In sum, he said, "Such treatment . . . is discouraging, dispiriting in its tendency; [and] it does effectively unman ye men and render them almost useless in the Army." He told the governor that his plea was not one of "Empertinence but of Importance."[40]

Brigadier General Huntington pleaded with his brother Andrew for help clothing the men of his brigade. "The Troops are bare footed, bare leg'd and almost bare [assed]," he wrote, "do procure all the Shoes, Stockings and breeches possible; Linnen Overalls, even for Winter, will be serviceable as they hide Rags, and, in Addition to them, afford sufficient Warmth."[41]

"Four Legs Good; Two Legs Better"

There was a wide gulf between the conduct and expectations of officers and the rank and file, and nowhere was that more evident in the punishment for breaches of discipline. For the latter, corporal punishment was the rule, from flogging for minor offenses to death for major ones, like mutiny. On the other hand, officers were looked upon as gentlemen, and the usual punishment ranged from reprimand to dismissal from the service. A good example of this disparity can be found in the court-martial of Col. Henry B. Livingston in June 1777. Livingston was charged with, among other things, "traducing the conduct" of his superior, Brigadier General McDougall, and failure to obey his orders regarding the movement of his regiment and the delay in the preparation of a return detailing his troop strength. The court convicted him of failure to follow his orders. As to the other charges, although his language pushed the bounds of "imprudence and indiscretion," he was acquitted of those charges as they were not "such as will warrant the appellation of being unbecoming a gentleman and officer." He was, however, cautioned about using such words in the future.

Putnam approved the judgment of the court, stating that he "nevertheless laments there should ever be a necessity of publickly reproving any gentleman, particularly of so respectable a rank as Colonel." In a presciently ironic rebuke, he continued: "The consequences of the smallest delay in the execution of any order are evidently most dangerous, and the least wilful neglect of this nature too serious to be passed in silence. . . . In the formation of an army, rigorous subordination cannot be too strictly adhered to." Livingston was released to duty, and Putnam used this example "to warn all ranks against similar offenses."[42]

THE "NEUTRAL GROUND"

As was the case with all of Westchester County, inaptly, if not ironically, called the "Neutral Ground," the Highlands was an active region, with Rebels and Tories embedded within the populace, along with a brutally lawless element. The active participants were divided into so-called "Cowboys" (Tories), led principally by Col. James De Lancey and his Light Horse Battalion, and "Skinners" (Patriots). Information about troop movements was a commodity, and spying, though dangerous, was commonplace. When caught, the typical punishment was hanging. That said, the customary practice was to try the accused before a military panel, but that was sometimes observed in the breach, when a nearby oak served the same purpose.[43]

One such instance occurred near Peekskill on July 15, 1777, when Putnam's men apprehended a Tory named Edmund Palmer. The miscreant stood accused of robbing a home at gunpoint, taking the rings from a woman in bed, and beating her elderly husband nearly to death. Palmer was well-known for cattle stealing and, worse, spying for the British. Putnam's dilemma was whether to try him as a Loyalist spy or to hold him as a prisoner of war to be exchanged later. While he believed that hanging was appropriate, he was also concerned that there be a modicum of due process, and he ordered the fellow held in irons and scheduled a trial for Tuesday, July 22.[44]

In the interim, Putnam wrote to General Washington seeking his input. "A question is made," he began, "whether he may be Tried by a Gen'l Court martial by the articles of war—because he belonged to this state & owed allegiance to it." There was also a question, in fact, as to whether the accused held a commission in a Loyalist regiment, and Putnam alluded to an earlier incident where a captive was summarily executed upon capture without benefit of a trial. He offered the commander in chief his opinion that while, "a speedy Execution of Spies is agreeable to the laws of Nature & nations & absolutely necessary to the preservation of the Army & without such power in the Army, it must be incompetent for its own safety." There is no record of Washington's response if any.[45]

Putnam decided to try Palmer as a spy in a military tribunal and to ignore the charges of "robbery or burglary, which are crimes cognizable by the civil power." Accordingly, four witnesses to Palmer's conduct testified at the hearing.

Palmer pled not guilty and offered for his defense the fact that he was a commissioned officer. This was confirmed by a letter from Brig. Gen. Montfort Browne, introduced at trial. If anything, the letter served to confirm Palmer's guilt. The "letter clears every doubt of Palmer's being an Enemy," wrote Putnam, "and contains a striking specimen of the idea our enemies have of the character of a gentleman and of the conduct that corresponds therewith." Palmer was found guilty of spying and ordered hanged on August 1. In pronouncing sentence, Putnam observed that, "spies are the most detestable of all enemies, and ought to be speedily executed, though not without a trial and legal conviction . . . and for this . . . do I sentence him."

Upon hearing about the anticipated fate of the prisoner, Governor Tryon threatened retaliation if Putnam went through with the execution of Palmer. British warships sailed virtually unimpeded up the Hudson River, and Clinton's message was delivered to Putnam by an officer from one of those vessels under a flag of truce. Putnam's response to Tryon was brief and to the point: "He was tried as a spy; he was condemned as a spy; and you may rest assured, sir, he shall be hanged as a spy." Putnam added a succinct postscript to his letter: "P.S. Afternoon. He is hanged." The officer returned to Tryon, his mission a failure.[46]

Notwithstanding Putnam's blunt message, Palmer's execution was delayed a couple of times due to the intercession of members of his wife's family, who were sympathetic to the American Cause. The pause, however, was temporary, and the execution by hanging finally took place at Gallows Hill near Peekskill at dawn on August 8, with the regiments of Col. Israel Angell and Col. Samuel B. Webb in attendance.[47]

Putnam's patriotism and humanity, as well as his firm belief in the subordinate role of the military in a just society, were eloquently expressed in his written statement at the time of the sentencing, and they should serve as a model for all citizen-soldiers: "Considering that the sweets of liberty, the rights and emoluments of civil society, are the most important and sublime of all earthly enjoyments; and that they derive their perfection and security (under God) from the regular and uninterrupted administration, of a rational system of civil government; and to preserve and perpetuate the felicities of society, to support the rights of civil government against foreign force and invasion; the military power was originally erected. . . . The military, I consider subservient to and attendant upon the civil: invested with competent powers for its own executive government, and to preserve its own existence against all open and secret enemies, of the latter denomination are all spies, and thereby answer the end [purpose] of its institution [, and] by guarding its own safety, [it] is enabled to defend the community against hostile invaders."[48]

THE CHAPLAIN FIGHTS A LOSING BATTLE (SEPTEMBER 1777)
The Rev. Abiel Leonard was popular and influential in the eyes of both the officer corps and the common soldiers as a man who could deliver an effective sermon, full of passion and patriotism, and one who was willing to serve alongside them. Hailing from Woodstock, Connecticut, just twelve miles north of Brooklyn, in May 1775 he was chosen by Putnam as chaplain of the Third Connecticut Regiment, and he had served in the Continental Army continuously ever since its beginning. As with most men of the cloth, Chaplain Leonard was not a wealthy man, and his

congregation back home needed a minister. As a result, he had to pay a substitute to perform his duties there in his stead, something he could ill afford. When pressure mounted for him to return to Woodstock toward the end of 1775, he asked Washington to write a letter to Gov. Jonathan Trumbull on his behalf.[49]

On December 15, 1775, Washington wrote to Gov. Jonathan Trumbull of Connecticut and expressed his concerns. Calling Leonard's anticipated departure from the army a "loss," he went on to say that the chaplain's conduct had been "exemplary and praiseworthy" and that he was "active and industrious" in discharging his duties. "He has discovered himself a warm and steady friend of his Country," Washington wrote, "and taken great pains to animate the Soldiery and impress them with the knowledge of the important Rights we are contending for." Three months later, with added pressure on Leonard to return to his flock, Putnam and Washington signed a joint letter. It was a plea to the congregation of the First Church of Woodstock, with the hope that, after "knowing how nobly he is employed . . . will cheerfully give up to the public, a gentleman so very useful." The letter had the desired effect, as Leonard remained in service.[50]

Along the way, he caught the attention of other prominent officers, such as Nathanael Greene, who told John Adams, then serving in Congress, that Leonard had "engaged early in the army and has been indefatigable in the duties of his Station," adding that, "he has done every thing in his power both in and out of his line of duty to promote the good of the service." In time, Leonard was appointed as chaplain for an artillery brigade within Putnam's command.[51]

At Putnam's request, Chaplain Leonard conducted religious services for his troops on Sunday, July 13, 1777, and all appeared normal. However, on July 28, while visiting a friend at nearby Kakiat (now Ramapo, New Jersey), Leonard became despondent and attempted to take his own life by slitting his throat with a straight razor. Other than a bout of smallpox the previous winter, Leonard had enjoyed good health. When he heard the news, Putnam, accompanied by Dr. Philip Turner, rode "post haste to the scene of the horror." Leonard lingered on, barely alive, for several days, before he finally succumbed on September 14. As the first and only man appointed as a brigade chaplain, his death was another casualty of war.[52]

AN AMBIGUOUS TURN OF PHRASE

Washington was not idle during Howe's occupation of Philadelphia, and despite his loss at Brandywine and a check at Germantown, he actively sought to harass his opposite number at every turn. All the while, he was conscious of the often-ephemeral nature of his command, as enlistments for the various units expired. For those units he was unable to cajole into re-enlisting, he needed replacements. It was a continuing issue. Part of the problem was Washington's manner of expression, which could well come across to some subordinate commanders, in the words of a noted historian, as a mere "deferential request," as opposed to a firm command. Although the commander in chief had the title, he was also never quite sure that he had the unwavering support from the Continental Congress.[53]

On August 26, Maj. Thomas Yates joined Putnam's military family as an aide-de-camp.[54]

APPEAL TO VIRTUE

On September 9, 1777, John Hancock sent Putnam a letter directing that he immediately prepare to send a detachment of fifteen hundred men under the command of a brigadier general to join Washington upon receipt of orders. Congress was anticipating a British attack somewhere in New Jersey on the strength of a letter from the governor two days earlier. Putnam would be shocked by Washington's directive five days later, as it served to fuel his growing concerns for his ability to defend the Highlands.[55]

The signs were all there as to just how vulnerable the Highlands were to attack, as Putnam told the New York Council of Safety: "A single galley of the enemy is constantly cruising up and down the river at pleasure, [and] has been as far as Fort Independence [Verplank's Point] and can stop the ferry [King's Ferry] at any time. We have nothing on the water that can oppose her. The crew land and plunder the inhabitants for more than fifty miles without molestation. I have desired Gen'l Clinton to write you on this subject and beg leave to inform [you of] the urgency of it in the strongest manner."[56]

Washington continued to downplay Putnam's concerns in a letter dated September 14. Based upon his review of Putnam's current troop returns, which showed an effective strength of 3,608 men, including Militia, Washington reminded him of his outstanding troop request and then added an additional one. "Besides the detachment of 1,500 already ordered," Washington told him, "a further detachment will be necessary to reinforce the first." That amounted to another 1,000 men and would leave Putnam with just over 1,100 Continentals and a small number of Militia to defend both sides of the river, including the three forts. "Ask Governor Trumbull in 'the most pressing terms' for 2,000 militia to bolster your force," Washington ordered. For Putnam, the consequences of Washington's order would prove catastrophic.[57]

The following day, Putnam wrote to Governor Trumbull from Peekskill requesting three thousand Connecticut Militia for a three-month tour. Other than the soldiers who were defending the forts, he told the governor that he had approximately seven hundred men that he could "call into the field in case of an attack," and those were scattered about the area. He also asked Trumbull if he had any ship guns available, preferably 18- to 24-pounders. Ever the optimist, he wrote: "I hope we shall be waked up to virtue and to mighty exertions in this great contest. Should that ever be the case, I am certain we should soon put a period to these troubles."[58]

Two days later, on September 17, Putnam followed up with another letter to the governor, emphasizing the need for troops. He also indicated that he had received intelligence that Henry Clinton had had an unexpected influx to troops at New York, and that, based upon Washington's orders, he had no choice but to try to find reinforcements in other quarters. Putnam had also given orders to General Parsons to create a diversion at Kingsbridge ("the Bridge"). Despite the dire prospects, once more, Putnam ended on an optimistic note: "I doubt not but that with the assistance that will be afforded us from the militia, through the smiles of heaven accompanying our exertions, we shall be able yet to call out soon to our fellows and friends with joyful hearts."[59]

On September 28, at Pennypacker's Mills, thirty-five miles north of Philadelphia, Washington called his senior officers together for a council of war. General McDougall's contingent of Continentals had arrived from Putnam, as had various Militia units from Maryland, Pennsylvania, and Virginia. In total, that day his force amounted to 8,000 Continentals and 3,000 Militia. In addition, he had requested that Putnam send an additional 1,500 or so troops from Peekskill. The question he posed to his officers in council was simple: Should he attack the British with his present force or wait for reinforcements? The clear majority recommended that no attack be made, but that Washington move "to some grounds proper for an encampment within about twelve miles of the enemy and there wait for further reinforcement, or be in readiness to take advantage of any favourable opportunity that may offer for making an attack."[60]

At the same time, Putnam's sources confirmed what had been suspected, that is, that General Clinton was ready to stage an attack in the Highlands. Writing to Governor Clinton on September 29 that he only had eleven hundred Continentals and four hundred Militia on hand, Putnam sent a blunt warning to him, stating that, "you cannot have the least expectation the posts in the Highlands can be maintained with our present force, against the strength the enemy may, or probably will send." He urged him to call up more Militia so that he could defend the critical post [Fort Montgomery]. "Unless a greater force than at present is here, or appears probable to be here, is applied for the defense of the post," he further warned, "you must be sensible that I cannot be answerable for the defense of it."[61]

On October 2, Putnam told Washington he was having trouble getting the New York Militia to turn out and that he had asked Connecticut to provide some "small assistance" with a fresh levy. At the same time, he reminded him that "at present this post is very weak."[62]

A TUG OF WAR

During the late summer and fall of 1777, General Burgoyne cautiously made his way south from Canada with a large army, including Loyalist and Indian allies, with the objective to split New England from the rest of the colonies. He had hopes of some relief in the form of a thrust north from New York City, but William Howe was more intent on pursuing his efforts near Philadelphia, and each passing day made such an effort less likely. Meanwhile, a third prong of the British strategy was stymied by Gen. Nicholas Herkimer at Oriskany on August 6, and later by a stubborn defense of Fort Stanwix in western New York, buoyed by the arrival of a relief column led by Maj. Gen. Benedict Arnold.[63]

Major General Sir Henry Clinton, feeling unsupported and unappreciated, was in a bit of a funk. Although he was given command of the forces in New York City, they were stretched thin. Like Putnam, he had been under pressure not only to defend the city, but also to provide troops from his limited number to assist General Howe. At the same time, he was expected to strike north to "make any diversion" and draw off some of the rebel forces opposing Burgoyne. And so, he sat idle until September 24, when, with the receipt of a windfall in the form of an unexpected contingent of 1,700 British and German troops from England, he could justify his inertia no longer.[64]

Finally, on October 4, 1777, Henry Clinton with approximately four thousand soldiers sailed north up the Hudson River. That evening, the fleet anchored in the Tappan Zee opposite Haverstraw. When Putnam's scouts had reported this movement, he sent General Parsons that same day to reconnoiter. At first, it was thought it might be a cattle raid, but the size of Clinton's force told them otherwise. Although Putnam could not be sure that Clinton's initial objective was the capture of Forts Clinton and Montgomery, even before Parsons had returned, that evening he dashed off a quick warning to Governor Clinton to be prepared.[65]

On October 5, hoping to hold Putnam in place, Henry Clinton landed fifteen hundred men on the east bank at Verplank's Point near the King's Ferry to Stony Point on the west bank, where the Militia contingent on guard there fled without a fight. Sir James Wallace led this force north along the east bank, where they destroyed some military stores, burned several homes in Peekskill, including the Mandeville farm, and then re-embarked. This action had the desired effect, as Putnam, who had not yet received any reinforcement, scrambled to find a suitable defensive position. The following day, Putnam personally went south to Fort Independence at Verplank's Point to have a look for himself. When he returned to his headquarters, he wrote to Clinton again, this time confirming that the enemy had landed on the west bank between King's Ferry and Dunderberg, with the objective of attacking Forts Clinton and Montgomery, and that he would send reinforcements.[66]

That same day while Putnam was at Verplank's Point, an early morning fog masked Clinton's effort to land 2,500 men on the west bank, with the object of capturing Forts Clinton and Montgomery. By 10:00 a.m. Clinton's advance parties clashed with Governor Clinton's pickets, bringing on a running fight, as the latter retreated to the fortifications. However, after British artillery commenced firing around 1:00 p.m., the situation became abundantly clear. By then, Putnam had returned and had cobbled together a small relief force of 400 to 500 picked men under Col. Return Jonathan Meigs, and he ordered them to cross the river, but just as they were boarding the flat-bottomed boats, it was apparent that they were too late to help the beleaguered garrisons, and they returned to camp. For five hours, the gallant defenders had turned back assault wave after assault wave, but by dusk, the Americans bowed to the inevitable. Casualties were high on both sides. Brigadier General James Clinton, though wounded in the thigh by a bayonet, managed to escape, as did his brother, Brig. Gen. George Clinton, who had recently been elected governor of New York. The victors destroyed Fort Montgomery, and they chose to rebuild and occupy Fort Clinton.[67]

On October 7, Putnam ordered Brigadier General Parsons to Danbury to meet and hurry along the levies from Connecticut. The following day, he sent Colonel Webb's regiment of four hundred Continentals to Governor Clinton to help bolster his force. Finally, he ordered his remaining forces to Fishkill to await reinforcement. Along the way, Putnam stopped at the Beverly Robinson House, in what is now the hamlet of Garrison, on the east bank, just across the Hudson from West Point. It was an odd, but convenient choice of temporary headquarters. The owner, Col. Beverly Robinson, a prominent Tory, was away with his Loyalist regiment, and, according to General Gates, his wife, Susanna, was anything but discreet and liable to pass along vital information. "That consummate, artful woman, Mrs. Robinson," he warned Putnam, "will do all in her power to be acquainted with your secrets." However, it is likely that Putnam had had an urgent need to find a comfortable place for Deborah Putnam to rest. Still grieving over the recent loss of her son, Septimus, to a sudden illness, she herself was gravely ill with a long-term illness, most likely cancer. Assured of Deborah's comfort, Putnam left her there, and by nightfall on October 7, he had joined his troops at Fishkill twelve miles to the north.[68]

After Washington had heard the first reports of Clinton's expedition, and prior to any word from Putnam, while ostensibly offering some encouragement, he was still downplaying the threat. "I am fully satisfied that every thing in your power will be done in calling in reinforcements and making a vigorous defense," he wrote, "assuring you that the number of the enemy cannot possibly be great even should they leave New York, Staten Island, and Long Island quite bare." He reinforced his thinking the same day with another letter in the same vein, alluding to Putnam's estimated troop strength. Washington was wrong. Before the arrival of the Connecticut Militia, Putnam's force was only about one-third the size of Clinton's, and he was obviously upset with that assessment. Understandably, his rejoinder was, if anything, impolitic, as he could not resist telling the commander in chief "I told you so." "I have repeatedly informed your Excellency of the enemy's design against this post," he wrote, "but from some motive or other, you always differed with me in opinion [as] this conjecture of mine has for once proved right." He went on to advise Washington that he was certain Clinton's objective was to join Burgoyne.[69]

At first, Henry Clinton held the advantage of numbers, and he deployed his troops well. Utilizing the mobility and safe harbor afforded by his fleet, he was able to land virtually at will on either bank and then re-embark as he worked his way north. On October 9, Clinton's force destroyed Fort Constitution, which by that time had been abandoned, and, at the same time, they also attacked and destroyed the barracks and supply depot at Continental Village, three or four miles above Peekskill. Anticipating such a move by Clinton, Washington had ordered Putnam to "remove your supernumerary arms and stores of all kinds" to Fishkill. Putnam had complied with this order, as he managed to save virtually all the ammunition and stores at Continental Village. The loss, he reported to Washington, amounted to only "a few barrels of flour and bread."[70]

Between October 7 and 8, the Connecticut Militia had finally begun to arrive, bringing Putnam's total command to about 6,000 men. However, almost immediately, many of them began to desert. Putnam ordered Parsons to Peekskill with 2,000 men to retake the town. Anticipating Henry Clinton's push to the north, after holding an officer's conference, Putnam held the remainder of his now augmented force, approximately 4,000 mostly Militia, at Fishkill, and he suggested that Governor Clinton remain on his side with his troops. Putnam correctly reasoned that since Henry Clinton had the advantage of landing on either side of the Hudson, if he and the governor consolidated forces on the wrong side, it could prove catastrophic, particularly to their principal stores.[71]

George Clinton was initially optimistic about the expected turnout of the New York Militia in response to his call, only to be sorely disappointed. He was told that many Militiamen who resided along both sides of the Hudson River, after viewing the destruction by the British, were reluctant to leave their farms and families. Under the circumstances, Clinton believed that it was unrealistic to expect them to do so. Accordingly, after Putnam ordered two regiments of Dutchess County Militia under Col. John Freer and Col. Dirk Brinkerhoff to join Clinton, the governor promptly overruled the order. At the same time, he also expressed disappointment with Putnam for sending Militia to him instead of additional Continentals.[72]

Death of Deborah Putnam

All during the period of Henry Clinton's attacks, Putnam was also engaged on another front. His wife, Deborah, finally succumbed to the disease after her lengthy battle on Tuesday, October 14. She was buried in a nearby churchyard in the Beverly Robinson family vault. From his headquarters at Fishkill, two days after Deborah's death, soldier first, Putnam reported on the situation in the Highlands. At the end of his report, as a postscript, he told Washington the sad news. "I have the unhappiness to inform you," he wrote, "that Mrs. Putnam after a long and tedious illness departed this life last Tuesday night." The brevity and lack of emotion in Putnam's announcement was consistent with the "social convention" of the times, as it was not a gentleman's place to "make others feel uncomfortable." Putnam knew his place, and Washington's response was consistent with his.[73]

The commander in chief was prompt with his reply, writing soon after receiving Putnam's sad tidings. "I am extremely sorry for the death of Mrs. Putnam & sympathise with you upon the occasion," he wrote. Washington added some encouraging words for his subordinate: "Remembering that All must die, and that she had lived to an honorable age, I hope you will bear the misfortune, with that fortitude and complacency of mind, that become a man and a Christian."[74]

BACK TO BUSINESS

Clinton's fleet continued to sail farther north toward Kingston and closer to Burgoyne. On October 15, Clinton landed a force commanded by Maj. Gen. John Vaughn near the mouth of Esopus Creek, where Vaughn brushed aside token resistance by a 150-man contingent of local Militia and then moved inland and burned the town of Kingston. George Clinton advised Putnam of the loss. "For want of a proper number of troops," he charged, "no effectual resistance could be made." In any event, the governor's small relief force was unable to reach Kingston in time, and he withdrew to Hurley, just west of Kingston, to guard the military stores there.[75]

Impatient, Clinton had written to both the governor of New Jersey and to General Gates for reinforcements. Foreshadowing trouble for Putnam, Clinton expressly told Gates that he would not be the scapegoat for the loss of Fort Montgomery, and later, the town of Kingston. He shifted the blame, implying that he could have done more if only Putnam had sent him the three thousand troops that he had promised. A day earlier, in a letter to Washington, he made the same assertion. This claim was both self-serving and disingenuous, as Putnam had only asked Governor Trumbull for three thousand men in total. Moreover, Putnam had twice reinforced Clinton from the limited number of men he had on hand.[76]

General Clinton's convoy sailed as far north as the Saugerties, more than one hundred miles from New York City, carrying out further destruction along the way, potentially placing Fishkill and Poughkeepsie in danger. However, by that time, word had reached Henry Clinton of

Burgoyne's surrender. More important, General Vaughn advised Clinton that with Putnam's move north with an estimated five thousand men, together with an additional fifteen hundred with Parsons, his "situation was desperate." As a result, in Henry Clinton's words, he was now "under the mortifying necessity of relinquishing the Highlands." Following that news, Cdre. William Hotham told Adm. Richard Howe that as, "the object of their going up the river seeming to be now over," he had turned the fleet around and sailed back to New York, transporting the various units in separate convoys, thus bringing an end to the threat to the Highlands.[77]

Meantime, Putnam, his headquarters at Staatsburg, stationed his forces at Fishkill and Poughkeepsie and moved cautiously north as he awaited word from General Gates about the current situation with Burgoyne. Putnam also wrote to Governor Clinton about possible next moves. He reasoned, if Henry Clinton continued north and Gates could hold him, an attack at Kingsbridge would be in order, with the idea of drawing the British back to New York City. Governor Clinton dismissed the idea out of hand. He then informed Putnam of the burning of Kingston, adding a dig, saying that it was "because I had not troops to defend it." More important, Clinton petulantly declined to act in concert with Putnam in the future, preferring instead to act alone, telling him, "having once settled our plan and afterwards deviated from it." Clinton was clearly pointing the finger at Putnam. Moreover, he reminded Putnam that Gates had approved the idea of them proceeding north separately along both sides of the river.[78]

Putnam ignored Clinton's pique and continued to suggest that they keep in touch so that, "we may act in conjunction as much as circumstances will permit." He also gave Clinton an order to retrieve the guns from the row galley that had been scuttled in Esopus Creek, as they could be put to good use, adding diplomatically, if not with a slight note of sarcasm, "if your Excellency has no capital objection to the measure."[79]

In the end, Henry Clinton recognized the futility of his effort, and he decided to withdraw to New York. Putnam reported to Washington that the British fleet had passed south of Fishkill on October 26 and had been spotted in the vicinity of the ruins of Forts Clinton and

Montgomery. Just in case Clinton's movement was a ruse, Putnam prudently directed Parsons to send scouts south through Westchester County, as far as Kingsbridge, and he ordered a second detail under Colonel Meigs to shadow the retreating British along the west bank. In addition, he detained the Militia for a couple of days, at least until he received some expected reinforcements from Gates. Some of the Militia had already deserted, and Putnam took the time to appeal to the patriotism and sense of duty of those remaining, assuring them that they would soon be released.[80]

On October 27, Putnam released the Militia on the strength of news that Enoch Poor's New Hampshire Regiment was only a two-days' march away. He also asked Governor Clinton to join him for a conference at his headquarters at Fishkill, "with all convenient dispatch," as he wanted his "advice and counsel." Clinton replied a week later, blaming illness and bad weather for the delay, indicating that he would soon join Putnam. Interestingly, he added that he now considered a change of focus to New York to be important, to prevent any troops there from joining Howe, as it was unlikely that there would be any further major British activity in the Highlands this season.[81]

The Aftermath

Washington recognized the fact that his emphasis on the Philadelphia campaign could well have caused the loss of the vital Highlands and proven helpful to Burgoyne. He said so in a letter to Gov. William Livingston of New Jersey, dated October 8, 1777, in which, belatedly, he sought help for Putnam: "The situation of our affairs in this way has obliged us to draw off so large a part of our force from Peekskill, that what now remains there may perhaps prove inadequate to the defense of it." Later, the Council of Safety of New York arrived at the same conclusion and placed no blame on Putnam for the loss of Fort Montgomery, but on the "want of a proper and seasonable reinforcement."[82]

It was also common knowledge among the troops. Lieutenant Samuel Shaw, then serving with his artillery unit near Philadelphia, told his parents about his participation in the recent battles at Brandywine and Germantown. His father had commented about the loss of Forts Clinton and Montgomery, and the young man offered his opinion that it "might have been attended with fatal consequences, had it happened early in the year." Moreover, he wrote, "the drawing of troops for reinforcing this army so weakened our posts in that quarter, that it was a great temptation to the enemy to risk a little." He had not yet heard of Burgoyne's surrender, which would happen four days later, but he felt that Clinton would be smart to exercise caution, as the "hazard the enemy would run by leaving General Putnam in their rear must make them extremely cautious how they venture to his [Burgoyne's] assistance."[83]

TROUBLE BREWING

Meanwhile, now that the threat to the Highlands had subsided, the next steps needed to be worked out. Washington told Putnam he agreed with his suggestion to send a small detail toward Kingsbridge, which, hopefully, would force Clinton to withhold sending any more troops to Howe. However, he said "I had rather it should be principally with Militia." This limitation must have been a disappointment to Putnam, since he had long wanted to attack New York now that the British forces were scattered thin there. Although the same thought had crossed Washington's mind more than once, and it would continue to linger there, at present, Washington was focused solely on General Howe. When Putnam consulted Gates about his plans, the latter "strongly disapproved" of any general attack on New York City. Gates rightly reasoned that there would be no advantage gained in such an attack, since all military stores would likely have been removed, and, more important, he could never hold the city so long as the British fleet could operate freely in the East and Hudson Rivers. "I see no good in taking an empty town we cannot hold," he told him.[84]

After Henry Clinton's precipitate withdrawal to New York, Putnam called a council of war at his Fishkill headquarters on October 31. Among those present were the Clinton brothers, Col. Samuel Webb, and Col. Daniel Morgan. The events of the past three weeks were reviewed, as well as options for future action. It was decided to maintain a minimum force of a thousand men to man and repair the Highland forts, while the balance of the available troops, amounting to four thousand men, would march toward New York as a diversion. Along the way, Col. Daniel Morgan's riflemen would be detached to join Washington, as requested. Several days later, after he was apprised of the conclusions of Putnam's council of war, Washington told him that it gave him, "pleasure to find that the opinion of your Council coincided exactly with ours here." That would be the high point.[85]

A SERIES OF UNFORTUNATE EVENTS

Putnam's problems began several days earlier and slowly gained momentum. On October 25, without specifying which, Putnam advised Washington that "some heavy artillery and a reinforcement of Continental troops, I am informed by General Gates are on their way to join me." Without receipt of Putnam's letter, Washington had independently heard, incorrectly, that General Gates was sending two brigades, Nixon's, and Glover's, to reinforce Putnam. In that case, Washington told Putnam, on October 26, send me the detached New England regiments, specifically Huntington's and Varnum's, that you are holding so that they can reunite with their assigned brigades. The following day, not having received Washington's letter, Putnam informed the commander in chief that he was, in fact, expecting Enoch Poor's brigade within two days. That being the case, he told Washington that he had already dismissed the Connecticut Militia, after repeated requests that he do so, as they had been agitating to go home. These letters obviously crossed in transit.[86]

Things became more complicated on October 30 after Washington sent Alexander Hamilton to Albany to meet with General Gates to determine just what was going on there. Although Putnam was in frequent contact with Washington, since his victory at Saratoga, Gates was not. In fact, it was Putnam, not Gates, who informed Washington about the victory at Saratoga. Washington was obviously peeved. "As I have not received a single line from General Gates, I do not know what steps he is taking with the army under his command," he told Putnam. Specifically, he wanted Hamilton to find out if, in fact, Nixon's and Glover's brigades were being sent to Putnam. In addition, if he ran into Daniel Morgan's corps of riflemen, Hamilton was to hurry them along south to Washington.[87]

That same day, October 30, Washington sent Putnam a letter advising him that Hamilton was on the way. He then amended his previous order, telling Putnam that, in addition to the detached Connecticut regiments, if Glover's and Nixon's brigades arrive, he is to send them along too. This must have confused Putnam. He had clearly told Washington that it was Poor's brigade that was expected. From Putnam's standpoint, where Washington got the erroneous information was anybody's guess. Finally, on October 31, when in receipt of Putnam's letter of October 25, Washington amplified his order. "I am glad to hear that General Gates is sending down a reinforcement to you," he wrote, [and] "*as they will not now be wanted by you, they will be so far upon their way towards this army, and I beg they may be sent forward with as much expedition as possible for the reasons given you in mine of yesterday*" (emphasis added). Putnam must have been beside himself. Did Washington not see his previous letter? Besides, he had sent the Connecticut Militia home on the strength of the promise of Poor's brigade. Surely Washington would not take that from him![88]

Intelligent, ambitious, and self-assured to the point of arrogance, as Washington's aide-de-camp, young Alexander Hamilton lacked some of the diplomatic skills of his chief. However, he enjoyed Washington's confidence and was intimately aware of the immediate need for troops to meet the challenge that Howe presented at Philadelphia. Hamilton stopped at Putnam's headquarters in Fishkill on November 2 on his way to Albany, where he would meet with Gates as well as Governor Clinton. He informed Washington that Poor's brigade had just arrived at Fishkill, but that Patterson, Glover and Nixon's Continentals, as well as Warner's Massachusetts Militia, were still at Albany, some ninety-five miles away.[89]

When Hamilton met with Putnam, there was no hint of trouble at first. In fact, in a letter dated November 3, Putnam outlined, in detail, the specific units, including Poor's brigade, that he had directed south to join Washington, "in consequence of your orders." He also reminded Washington that the transfer of troops only left him with Parson's brigade, which was operating near White Plains in Westchester County, along with three regiments of New York Continentals. In a letter dated November 4, which obviously crossed with Putnam's the day before, Washington emphasized that "to crush General Howe effectually is the real and great object." To that end, he told Putnam, once again, to forward all troops coming from Gates, including Poor's brigade, except those from New York, to him. "I therefore beg," he repeated for emphasis, "*no more Continental troops may be retained than are absolutely necessary* with the assistance of the Militia to repair the works in the Highlands" (emphasis added). Putnam could logically conclude that Washington would leave him with at least a minimum, albeit unspecified, number of Continentals.[90]

On November 7, Putnam took the time to explain to Washington, in some detail, his status. First, he reported that term of enlistment for Jonathan Warner's brigade of Massachusetts Militia would expire in December. Putnam felt that, as a practical matter, it would be unfair to have them march all the way to Pennsylvania only to have to turn around and march back. As a result, he retained them, at Warner's request, to build obstructions in the Hudson. Second, he informed Washington that General Poor's brigade had mutinied for want of pay and the men refused to cross the Hudson. An officer shot and killed an enlisted man, and he was, in turn, killed by a fellow soldier. Putnam was working on the problem, even to the point of personally borrowing enough money to give them a month's pay. To top things off, the entire brigade was being treated for the "Itch" (Hookworm). For those who had deserted, he sent the light horse after them. Finally, he told the commander in chief that, in the interim, he had received a letter from Hamilton ordering that he forward an additional thousand Continentals, more than when they had met on November 2. That would, he told Washington, leave him with just three hundred Continentals and some Militia, whose enlistments expired in three weeks, to cover what he called "this distressed country." He asked to be heard before he acted. "I don't think I can justify myself in this, without first acquainting you [with the facts]," he respectfully pleaded, "and if I then have your Excellency's orders, *I will with pleasure immediately, and punctually comply with them*" (emphasis added).[91]

While awaiting a reply, Putnam received another letter from Washington, this one dated November 9. Once again, their letters had crossed in transit. Putnam must have been encouraged to learn that Washington had himself come to the same conclusion about Warner's brigade and that he added the same thinking should be applied to the New Jersey Militia, both of which had a short time to run on their enlistments. Not willing to leave the decision to Putnam as to which Continentals to retain, Washington designated several specific regiments, which with the Militia, "will fully answer your present purposes." Once again, he stressed the need for haste and the need for Putnam to request additional levies from the states.[92]

In the meantime, Hamilton had arrived at Albany at noon on November 5, and he "immediately" went to meet with General Gates. Their first meeting did not go as well as Hamilton had hoped. Hamilton told Washington that he "was sorry to find that his [Gates'] ideas did not correspond with yours for drawing off the number of troops you directed." Moreover, he reported, "I used every argument in my power to convince him of the propriety of the measure, but he was inflexible." Gates insisted that he retain two brigades of Continentals just in case Henry Clinton would return upriver and attack the arsenal at Albany, or if he needed them in case he decided to retake Fort Ticonderoga. Besides that, he argued, the roads were too bad to move artillery and supplies in any event. Despite all his logic and argument, Hamilton was unable to shake Gates from his position.

After some thought, and seeing that Gates would not budge, Hamilton did an about-face, explaining his thinking to the commander in chief in practical, political terms. He reasoned that it was "dangerous to insist on sending more troops," given Gates' refusal to do so, considering his recent popularity in New England due to his victory at Saratoga. Washington, he argued, was risking Gates' overt criticism, as well as "censure" if "any accident or inconvenience happen in consequence of it." In other words, play it safe. His answer was to take more troops away from Putnam, including a thousand Continentals and Warner's Massachusetts Militia, whose enlistments were expiring, even though Washington had agreed they should remain with Putnam. Hamilton rationalized that Putnam would not need them now that the valuable military stores had been moved and the threat of any attack was diminished. On the strength of that change of thinking, he had sent Putnam the peremptory letter that the latter had received on November 6.[93]

Although Hamilton could not have known it at the time, Thomas Mifflin's efforts had borne fruit with the Congress, which, coincidently, while he was meeting with Gates in Albany, enacted a sweeping set of orders on November 5 lodging significant control of the northern army with Gates and limiting Washington's power to use those troops. In brief, among other things, Putnam was ordered to join the main army with a contingent of no more than 2,500 men drawn from Gates' troops. More important, given the critical military value of the Highlands, no other troops could be taken from Gates without first consulting him and Governor Clinton, and only then "with their concurrence." Although the order was never complied with, still this must have concerned Washington, as it bolstered Gates' position.[94]

In a letter to General Gates dated November 5, Delegate James Lovell of Massachusetts, no friend of Washington, heaped praise on Gates and explained the order as it related to Putnam. "I wish good Old Putt may not think hard of the proposals of Congress," he began. "He is really wanted in the neighborhood of Philadelphia." Lovell continued with an obvious dig at Washington: "He is a brave man and will not rest long without enterprise, though he cannot maintain posts and fight battles without soldiers. He was stripped almost to the skin."[95]

At the same time, Israel Putnam had the misfortune to be in the sights of another ambitious man, Gov. George Clinton. He was the first elected governor of New York State and, in time, became its longest-serving one (twenty-one years, eighteen of them consecutively). He saw Putnam as an impediment to his plans. Despite ostensibly being of a like mind with Putnam, Clinton took pains to curry favor with Congress, with Generals Gates and Washington, and more immediately with Alexander Hamilton, while at the same time taking every opportunity to undermine Putnam. "Had I been reinforced from General Putnam's army in the manner I had reason to expect," Clinton told Washington in hindsight, "I should have thrown a force into Kingston sufficient to have preserved it."[96]

Hamilton had also met with George Clinton while in Albany, where he found that his "ideas coincide with mine." After leaving Albany, Hamilton traveled south to New Windsor, New York, on the west bank of the Hudson, ten miles south of Fishkill. He arrived there on the evening of

November 9 and immediately drafted a new order to Putnam based upon the advice of the governor and, more important, without first consulting Washington. He was able to report to Washington that before he left Albany, he was, however, able to pry loose another brigade from Gates.[97]

The tone and tenor of the letter to Putnam was haughty and insulting, and the situation much exaggerated. To give him his due, Putnam was awaiting a response from Washington and had already taken some steps to comply, while other matters were completely out of his control. As a prime example, Glover's and Patterson's brigades had not even reached Fishkill. In brief, Hamilton peremptorily ordered Putnam to immediately send *all* his Continentals to King's Ferry, and to "hasten" them to join with Washington. Putnam could, he said, furnish his needs for Continentals from the brigades of Glover and Patterson after they arrived. This was clearly at variance with Washington's explicit permission to retain some of the existing Continentals. In addition, as the terms of the Massachusetts and New Hampshire Militia were about to expire, he was directed to ask for reinforcements from New York and Connecticut. Finally, Hamilton reiterated Washington's directive that there should be no general attack on New York, only a "diversion" if Putnam could find enough troops. The latter was unnecessary since at his officer's council on October 31, Putnam had already abandoned the idea of a general attack in favor of a diversion.[98]

Putnam was leery of stripping the Highlands of troops, particularly the Continentals, but for the most part, he had complied with Washington's earlier orders to dispatch specific New England regiments after Gates released them. Where he had not complied, he felt that he had given Washington a satisfactory reason. Moreover, Hamilton confirmed Putnam's assertion that Poor's brigade mutinied for lack of pay, and that Learned's had also. From Putnam's standpoint, he had just recently experienced a loss at the hands of Henry Clinton, and, once burned, he was wary of a repetition. Putnam clearly believed that the recent losses were caused by the reduction in the size of his command, resulting from his compliance with previous troop requests. Whether or not he pushed back with Hamilton is unknown. He was not outright defiant of Washington's order, but he felt Washington would understand if he explained his situation directly and not through Hamilton. In fact, Putnam believed that he had the selfsame need for troops that Washington did, which he had explained in his letter to the commander in chief on November 7.[99]

While Putnam was awaiting a reply from Washington to his report on the situation at Fishkill, Hamilton was either still in Albany or in New Windsor, and without knowledge of the exchange of letters between Putnam and Washington. Putnam's apparent continued dilatory behavior struck a raw nerve with Alexander Hamilton, who, no doubt, took the challenge to his authority as a personal slight, which, in fact it was. The tone of his letter to Putnam on November 9 clearly showed that he was overwrought. "I cannot forbear Confessing that I am astonished and Alarm'd beyond measure," Hamilton claimed erroneously, "to find that his Excellency's views have been hitherto frustrated, and that *no single step* of those I mention'd to you has been taken to afford him the aid he absolutely stands in Need" (emphasis added). In an appeal to Putnam's patriotism, he added, with some supercilious hyperbole, that any delay would put the "Cause of America" to the "utmost conceivable Hazard."[100]

In a letter to Washington the following day explaining his actions, Hamilton erroneously claimed that Governor Clinton was the only one doing anything about the problem with Poor's brigade, when Putnam was personally trying to borrow sufficient money to pay them for one month. He also claimed that Putnam was planning to attack New York City, when he had given up that plan on October 31 at a council of war, at which Clinton himself was present. "Everything is sacrificed to the whim of taking New York," he lied. Hamilton urged Washington to replace Putnam with Governor Clinton, if he would accept it, as "the blunders and caprices of [Putnam] are endless." Hamilton had a long memory, and he would continue his pointed criticism of Putnam.[101]

Putnam was incensed by the tone and the message of Hamilton's letter. He felt he was working things out with Washington until this unwanted and unwarranted intrusion by Hamilton. He promptly wrote a letter to Washington, enclosing a copy of Hamilton's letter. "This letter contains some most unjust and ungenerous reflections," he wrote, "for I am conscious of having done every thing in my power to succor you as speedily as possible." He told Washington that he would go and meet with Hamilton in person, and at the same time, he made his second fatal mistake, he failed to respect Hamilton's status. "[However,] until I have your orders, I cannot think of continuing at this post myself and send all the troops away," he wrote sarcastically. It would be an open invitation to Howe.[102]

Putnam had already written to the governors of Connecticut and Rhode Island, and, for a variety of reasons, he expected no timely cooperation. Elsewhere in the same letter he told Washington about some practical changes he hoped would suit Washington. For one, he was forwarding General Poor's brigade along with the attached New York regiments, and that Col. Charles Webb's regiment had marched the day before. On the other hand, he had detained Wyllys's and Meigs's regiments from Parson's brigade for the simple reason that half of them had no shoes or stockings, until a supply, which he expected shortly, arrived. Hamilton dismissed Putnam's claims out of hand, and he told Washington that the delay was simply due to his wanting to retain Parson's brigade. Once again, Hamilton was wrong. At this time, Parsons himself had written directly to Governor Trumbull for help: "Clothing for the troops is now much wanted, especially shoes, stockings, and breeches, and will very soon be much more wanted." He added that, "our men are almost all barefoot."[103]

Hamilton had arrived at New Windsor suffering from a painful rheumatic condition, which certainly did not help his mood, and he was still resting there on November 12. In a letter to Washington, he reiterated his reasons for not challenging Gates, and he sought the former's approval for his actions. More important, without realizing it, he validated Putnam's claims, as he himself was experiencing difficulties forwarding the troops to Washington. Specifically referring to Parson's, Poor's, Glover's, and Learned's brigades: "[T]he disposition for marching in the officers and men in general of these troops, does not keep pace with my wishes or the exigency of the occasion. They have unfortunately imbibed an idea that they have done their part of the business of the campaign and are now intitled to repose. This and the want of pay make them averse to a long march at this advanced season." Those problems could hardly be laid at Putnam's feet![104]

THE CONWAY CABAL

In the middle of this back-and-forth, Putnam's position was further complicated after Washington received a letter from Lord Stirling dated November 3, informing him of some "wicked duplicity of conduct." For some time, Washington and his close aides had become aware of discontent brewing in Congress and among some officers, including friends, at the lack of his battlefield success. This now was concrete evidence. Earlier, General Gates had sent his aide, Col. James Wilkinson, to York, Pennsylvania, where Congress was meeting, to deliver the news about the victory at Saratoga. On October 28, Wilkinson stopped at a tavern in Reading along the way, where, in his cups, he told Stirling's aide, Maj. William McWilliams, that one of Stirling's brigade commanders, Brig. Gen. Thomas Conway, had written a letter to Gates in which he alluded to Gates' victory and observed, with an obvious reference to Washington, that, "Heaven has been determined to save your country; or a weak general and bad counselors would have ruined it."[105]

Upon receipt of Stirling's letter, Washington and his aides reacted swiftly and forcefully to what was perceived to be a challenge to his position as commander in chief. On November 5, Washington sent a brief note to Conway, simply repeating the quote attributed to him. Conway got the message and issued a prompt but unconvincing denial. If anything, he argued, the quotation was taken out of context. As to Conway, Congress promoted him to major general and appointed him inspector general of the army over Washington's objections.[106]

In October, Congress had established a new Board of War, naming Maj. Gen. Thomas Mifflin, the recently retired quartermaster general, as a member. At a meeting of the board on November 21, Mifflin proposed that Gates be appointed president of the board, "from a conviction that his military skill would suggest reformations in the different departments of the Army essential to good discipline, order and economy, and that his character and popularity in the Army would facilitate the execution of such reformations when adopted by Congress."[107]

Although, a decision was briefly postponed, Congress did make the appointment. When Washington learned that Mifflin had made the motion to appoint Gates, in his mind Mifflin became part of the "conspiracy." Washington was already sensitive to Gates' reluctance to send him troops, as well as to the slight to his authority in not directly informing him of the victory at Saratoga; Washington had to hear that from Putnam.

In the end, Washington's position became more secure than ever, as friends and supporters rallied around, and, according to historian Stephen Taaffe, the cabal turned out to be "more imagined than real," fomented by men with large ambitions and little discretion, expressing the frustrations of many regarding a war that was dragging on without any seeming end. On the other hand, Prof. Mark Edward Lender makes a compelling argument that the so-called "Conway Cabal" was more than just a letter, and was, in fact, an attempt by prominent delegates to Congress to limit Washington's authority as commander in chief and to lodge control over the war effort in the Board of War, coincidently headed by Horatio Gates. He referred to it as an "administrative coup" that very nearly worked. Nevertheless, for Putnam, who no doubt knew nothing of Conway's letter, or for that matter, any conspiracy, the timing was most unfortunate, as Washington was more sensitive to any challenges to his authority at that precise moment.[108]

Putnam Proposes, Washington Disposes

The problem for Putnam was that, under all the circumstances, he was wrong to persist in his challenge to Washington and his aide, Hamilton. While it may have been reasonable for Putnam to rely upon his exchange of correspondence with Washington, in the end, Washington's perceived needs were greater, and, more important, he was Putnam's superior. This was especially so now that the immediate threat to the Highlands was over. Moreover, Hamilton had the authority to speak for the commander in chief. Putnam should have complied, wherever possible, without complaint. Sadly, for him, he leaned right into the one-two punch that Clinton and Hamilton had delivered.

In the end, Washington supported Hamilton. In a short letter to Putnam dated November 19, he firmly made his point: "The urgency of Colonel Hamilton's letter was owing to his knowledge of our wants in this quarter, and *to a certainty there was no danger to be apprehended from New York if you sent away all the Continental troops that were with you* and would replace them by those expected down the river. I cannot but say that there has been more delay in the march of the troops than I think necessary, and *I could wish that in the future my orders may be immediately complied with without arguing upon the propriety of them. If any accident ensues from obeying them the fault will be upon me and not upon you"* (emphasis added). Given the previous circumstances, the last sentence must have stung bitterly. One thing was clear: Hamilton was "family," and Putnam was not.[109]

FROM MILITIA TO A STANDING ARMY

In July 1775, Washington inherited a loose aggregation of twenty thousand mostly New England Militiamen. Over time, as participation gradually became more broadly based, he came to rely upon a steady core, his Continentals, as the numbers of Militia waxed and waned. In one of history's ironies, it became a standing army of sorts, something anathema to most Americans. Moreover, as time passed, Washington came to the realization that the spirit of the Revolution lay, like hot embers, in the hearts and minds of this stalwart band; that it was, in fact, more important that the army remain intact and cohesive, than the retention of any patch of ground. So long as the army, his army, stayed in being, the British would never achieve victory.

So, Washington can be forgiven if his focus was somewhat narrow and he failed to fully appreciate the fact that subordinate commanders, like Putnam and Gates, were experiencing the same stresses that he was, and that they might view as unfair or unreasonable his peremptory demands for them to send him their Continentals at the expense of their own assigned missions, leaving them to be carried on by often unreliable Militia. Given Putnam's limitations, it is unlikely that he fully appreciated Washington's strategic vision.

As a result, while not overtly insubordinate, in some limited instances, he may have slow-walked his compliance. This disconnect came to the fore in the Highlands, where a challenging task to simultaneously defend positions on both sides of the Hudson with an inadequate force became that much harder, if not impossible. In the end, Washington's broader vision proved correct, and Putnam's reputation has suffered.

CHAPTER TWELVE

The American Revolution

Farewell to Arms

WESTCHESTER AND LONG ISLAND

As it turned out, now that the British threat in the Highlands had ended, Washington may have had second thoughts about maintaining a presence in Connecticut and Westchester County. Howe was still in Philadelphia, and Washington was looking for the means to increase his troop strength, either to match Howe's forces man for man, or, better yet, exceed them. As he had emphasized to Putnam, "to crush General Howe effectually is the real and great object." Accordingly, forcing the British to keep as many British troops as possible in Manhattan was essential.[1]

To that end, on November 1, 1777, in the middle of his contretemps with Putnam, Washington received a letter from Maj. Gen. Philemon Dickinson, commander of the New Jersey Militia. Dickinson was concerned with the present situation, as his sources had informed him that, "the enemy are embarking troops from New York and Staten Island to reinforce Mr. Howe." He suggested a bold plan: Give an order "to Generals Gates and Putnam, to raise a number of Militia and make an attack upon Long Island and New York, and myself with what Militia I could collect from this part of the state, to make a descent upon Staten Island, all at the same time." Dickinson continued: "Although we should not all succeed," he argued, "it would answer a valuable good purpose."[2]

Washington agreed in principle, but he had some concerns about the consequences of a failed attack, particularly on Long Island, where the attackers could potentially be trapped. "Your idea of counteracting the intended reinforcements for Mr. Howe's army by a demonstration of designs upon New York I think an exceeding good one," he wrote on November 4, "and [I] am very desirous that you should improve and mature it for immediate execution." However, instead of a simultaneous attack by Putnam, he suggested spreading some disinformation, by letting it be known in New York City, as if it was a secret being divulged by an informant, that Putnam was going to stage an imminent attack there. That same day, he authorized Putnam, who was at Sawpits (then a part of Rye, New York, and now Port Chester) with General Parsons, to stage a feint toward New York, adding that he preferred that it be with Militia. Putnam was still in that area six days later.[3]

Dickinson assembled a force of fourteen hundred Militiamen, and he finally launched his attack at dawn on November 27. Unfortunately, despite careful precautions, word leaked, and aside from some brisk skirmishes, the enemy fled to the safety of their works. Dickinson returned to New Jersey eight hours later, having incurred no casualties. Washington told him that he was glad that all had returned safely, because the plan had been divulged. "Experience shews us," he observed, "that the most trifling incidents will frustrate the best concerted schemes."[4]

Washington's concerns came to fruition during the evening of December 9/10 when a raid on Long Island led by General Parsons partially failed through a series of mishaps, including the failure of one contingent to make it across the Sound due to rough water and the sinking of another boat within sight of a British warship, resulting in the capture of Putnam's former aide, Lt. Col. Samuel B. Webb, and others. The objectives of the raid upon eastern Long Island included the destruction of ships loaded with timber and boards bound for New York to be used to construct barracks, as well as the capture and destruction of various sites with military stores. Parsons, whose part of the raid was successful, concluded that the other officers participating in the raid "were more unfortunate than guilty of any criminal neglect."[5]

On December 16, while still at his headquarters at Sawpits, Putnam advised Washington of Webb's capture, and, anticipating censure, at the same time, he quickly assured Washington that he would remove his troops to Fishkill "as speedily as possible" and that "nothing in my power shall be wanting to secure the river." However, he could not help adding a slight dig, telling Washington that, "works without men will answer but little purpose." Putnam promptly passed on his orders to Parsons, who was nearby at Horseneck (Greenwich), and he ordered him to join him in Fishkill. Just to make sure that Parsons understood the urgency, on December 20, he reiterated his order to bring all his Continentals to Fishkill as "soon as possible," but that he could leave behind a small party of fifty or a hundred men under a good officer to keep abreast of the situation there.[6]

Surprisingly, Washington did not castigate Putnam for the raid itself, as he was likely aware of it beforehand and as he had sanctioned such an action. Putnam had already moved his headquarters to Westchester County some time before, with the same objectives as the unsuccessful raid carried out by Major General Dickinson. In fact, the day of Dickinson's raid, he had ordered Parsons to create a diversion near Kingsbridge. Moreover, Washington told Putnam that he was "exceedingly sorry" to hear of Webb's capture. However, he did take the time to suggest to Putnam that "these small excursions" on Long Island and in lower Westchester County were not particularly productive, and "divert our attention from more material objects" (i.e., the defense of the Highlands). While he considered the "works upon the River" as having "more solid advantages" than the attempts to destroy "part of the enemy's stores," nevertheless, Putnam could, he said, assign such troops "as are necessary to patrol towards the plains and keep small parties from ravaging." As if to validate the importance of his efforts, a month later, Putnam described for Washington a raid on Fort Independence near Verplank's Point by a body of Hessians and the successful pursuit and capture of prisoners by alert Militia units.[7]

WHOSE OX

Washington had received a complaint from Col. Samuel Drake in November 1777 to the effect that Putnam's men, in particular, those from Parson's brigade, "frequently take property which they pretend is going to, or is within reach of the enemy and make sale of it for their own benefit," citing Washington's General Order dated June 10, 1777. Colonel Drake and James Hunt were commissioners (sometimes referred to as sequestrators) appointed by the state of New York to dispose of lost or stolen property, with some profit to themselves. Washington clarified his order, stating that he had meant it to limit the application of the order to property seized by the enemy, and not simply threatened with seizure. The order was meant to incentivize his soldiers, he explained, by allowing them to retain the profits from the sale of such seized property, and not to provide carte blanche to help themselves to any animals they came across.[8]

Putnam vigorously denied any violation of the order, and, at the same time, he defended Parsons, implying that Drake's character was less than admirable. In fact, Humphreys relates that Putnam had developed "an unconquerable aversion" to Drake and others charged with the disposition of Tory property, in that he believed that they were "guilty of peculation and other infamous practices." Putnam went on to relate that, "Parsons and the Sequestrators [Drake and Hunt] have had some dispute respecting cattle that was taken from the enemy at Verplanks Point and up the river," and he suggested that event was the cause of the present claim. Washington told Putnam that he was "glad to find that matters are not as represented in Colonel Drake's memorial." He stressed that it was "his wish that the people may be protected as far as circumstances will permit without detriment to the public cause."[9]

General Parsons returned to camp in mid-February, at which time Putnam showed him Colonel Drake's charge. A lawyer in civilian life, Parsons offered a vigorous and detailed defense. "[S]ome parts thereof particularly [with] respect [to] me and represent facts in a most false and injurious light," he wrote. The truth of the matter, he went on to say, is that, during the past September, Colonel Drake failed to do his duty and round up the loose stock in the Hudson River Valley to keep it from the enemy. When Clinton attacked the Highlands in October, Drake fled to the mountains, leaving the stock to roam. Putnam had then ordered Parsons to round up the stock. He continued. Although it was impossible to maintain a detailed list of the animals taken, given the emergency, the inhabitants were notified that they could claim their animals. In the end, Parsons turned the unclaimed animals over to the quartermaster for sale, thus depriving Drake and Hunt of the proceeds from the sale. Nothing untoward had occurred. The inhabitants, he said, could take their claims to the quartermaster. Parsons argued that he was simply following his orders, and that he was not accountable to either Drake or Governor Clinton. Washington replied that it would appear that "Colonel Drake and his colleague had been guilty of neglect of duty," and he suggested to Parsons that he bring those facts to the attention of Governor Clinton.[10]

Washington's General Order of June 10, 1777, was not exactly a model of clarity, and it left considerable leeway for interpretation. It was enacted as a direct response to numerous complaints by New Jersey residents to soldiers under his command. As a result, Washington had ordered that "no officer, or soldier, is to judge for himself, and appropriate their [inhabitants'] property to their own use, or to seize it *without proper orders.*" Just to clarify matters, Washington told Putnam that, in the future, any animals or forage seized by his soldiers were to be turned over to the commissioners for sale. In addition, if his troops needed beef or forage, his commissary or quartermaster could purchase it from the commissioners.[11]

It would appear from the record that the incident referred to in Drake's memorial was a one-time dispute that he had with General Parsons. A selective review of general orders reveals that Putnam made a genuine effort to abide by the spirit, if not the letter of Washington's order. For instance, on September 2, 1777, in his general orders Putnam gave notice that "five oxen, seven cows and seven horses, which were taken from the enemy by Major [Lt. Col. Samuel] Blagden's Light Dragoons," were to be sold the following day at a public auction by Colonel Drake at his house. Likewise, after a stray horse was brought to headquarters, a detailed description of the animal was posted, and Putnam ordered that "any person that can evince his title to him, may have him."[12]

To his credit, Putnam consistently issued orders protecting the property of noncombatants. After a calf was stolen from a poor local family, he called upon "his officers of every rank, and soldiers . . . in the strictest positive terms to exert themselves in detecting the offenders that justice may be done to the injured inhabitants and the camp cleansed from the imputation of robbery and theft." When "thirty-two yards of cotton linen, three and one-half yards of coarse linen, and one-half yard of blue velvet" went missing from the Widow Warren's home, he offered a $3.00 reward for its return. In another instance, he forbade "all plundering of private property, robbing gardens, [and] burning rails or fences."[13]

However, if Putnam thought that the matter had been put to rest, he was mistaken, as it would come up again as part of the campaign to relieve him. Unfortunately, he had been made the target of one man's ego and ambition, and his lack of sophistication left him vulnerable.

On December 16, 1777, Putnam asked for leave to return home to Connecticut to take care of some business related to his late wife's death. Washington approved the request on the condition that either General Gates take charge at Fishkill or upon the return of General Parsons from his leave, with the further condition that Putnam conduct a recruiting drive while in Connecticut. As neither was likely to happen soon, Putnam would remain in the Highlands for the time being.[14]

MUCH WORK TO BE DONE

Although Gen. Henry Clinton's foray into the Highlands in October was short, his troops had wreaked severe damage to the fortifications and armament there. Putnam reported on the damage, as well as his efforts to repair same. Washington was obsessed with the need to prepare adequate defenses in the vital Hudson River Valley, both within the river itself as well as its strong points on shore. He pressed Putnam on his efforts to rebuild the forts destroyed by Clinton, and to lay obstructions in the river. "I request you in the most urgent terms," he wrote, "to turn your most serious and active attention to this very infinitely important object." He continued: "Seize the present opportunity, and employ your whole force and all the means in your power for erecting and completing, as far as possible, such works and obstructions as may be necessary to defend and secure the river against any future attempts by the enemy."[15]

In early October, Washington had ordered Lt. Col. Louis-Guillaume-Servais des Hayes de la Radière, a French engineering officer, to report to Fort Montgomery, where his assignment would be to direct work upon the forts and other works "deemed necessary by the commanding officer in that Department." Later, Washington directed Putnam to "consult with Governor Clinton, and General Parsons, and the French engineer, Lieutenant Colonel Radière," in formulating a plan for the defenses of the Highlands. In fact, in early November, Putnam and Governor Clinton had already conducted an inspection tour to determine the state of the several forts. Putnam reported that many of the guns had been rendered useless, although some could be made serviceable again. He also told Washington that he and the governor felt that a new chain placed across the river at Fort Constitution, combined with batteries, would be more effective than the present location at Fort Montgomery, and he would begin the construction immediately.[16]

In connection with the placement of another chain to obstruct the river, some consideration was given to the construction of a new fort on the high west bank, or "west point," opposite Fort Constitution. To that end, in accordance with Washington's instructions, Putnam assembled a group of officers, including Governor Clinton, his brother Brig. Gen. James Clinton, and Lieutenant Colonel La Radière, to inspect the grounds for the proposed new fort. Except for the latter, all of them concluded that West Point was the ideal location. La Radière was unconvinced and stalled for nearly a month before he offered his opinion, which, as it turned out, was that he favored the site of Fort Clinton. Meanwhile, Putnam turned to the Provincial Convention of New York State to confer on the selection. Since there was a split of opinion between West Point and Fort Clinton, on January 8, they, in turn, appointed a smaller select committee who inspected both locations and six days later, in a detailed report, unanimously concluded that West Point was the better location.[17]

Given the decision of the committee, Putnam ordered Parson's brigade to the site, and he directed La Radière to immediately lay out the works. Governor Clinton concurred with Putnam's decision to move forward. By that time, the weather had turned bitterly cold, and the area was blanketed with a two-foot snowpack. Parsons' troops cleared the snow from the site and commenced work on January 20. At first, the men had no shelter and lacked the proper tools. Despite his orders, a "petulant" La Radière, still fussing and fuming, continued to stall, and a frustrated Putnam told Washington: "[H]e seems greatly disgusted, that every thing does not go as he thinks proper, even if contrary to the judgment of every other person. In short, he is an excellent paper engineer, and I think it would be as well for us if he was employed wholly in that way. I am confident if Congress could have found business for him with them, our works would have been as well constructed and much more forward than they now are."[18]

In the meantime, Putnam sent Col. Hugh Hughes, the deputy quartermaster general, to the Stirling Iron Works to arrange construction of a new iron chain to stretch across the river. After a successful negotiation, a contract was signed on February 2. By March 13, the day before he left for Connecticut, Putnam was able to report substantial progress all around. In addition to the chain, he found that part of the boom originally intended for Fort Montgomery was reusable and the chevaux-de-frise would be ready to sink as soon as the ice in the river would permit. He had also constructed a barracks for artificers and huts for three hundred men. In addition, barracks for an additional three hundred were nearly completed. He had also built a road down to the river. Finally, he told Washington, that timber was being cut to build the fort and batteries.[19]

On the negative side, Putnam was hampered in his efforts by harsh weather and ice in the Hudson. Of greater concern was a lack of sufficient funds, and the deputy quartermaster had already bought a substantial amount of supplies and labor on credit and was overextended. In addition, many of his soldiers were ill-clothed and unpaid. To top things off, there was a shortage of forage and teams, and the wages of the artificers were seven months in arrears, and some of them were deserting.[20]

Putnam still smarted from the loss of the Highland forts, which, in his opinion, was due to the lack of an adequate force to defend them. When the select committee appointed by the Provincial Convention in New York also recommended substantial force levels necessary to defend West Point, Putnam asked Washington if he agreed. He emphasized his concern in very personal terms: "[T]he mortification of being left to defend an important post without a sufficient force your Excellency can better conceive than I can express, although it is what I have once experienced."[21]

PUTNAM TAKES HIS LEAVE
Due to the press of his duties in the Highlands, Putnam was unable to leave right away. Finally, on February 14, 1778, Putnam left his command

at West Point and traveled to Connecticut. Once again, Washington appointed Alexander McDougall to assume command of the Highlands in March, however, in the interim, the command devolved upon Parsons. For weeks, Putnam had been anxious to leave, and he must have done so in a hurry without fully briefing his successor. As a result, on February 15, Parsons told Governor Clinton, that he had, "come to this command in most disagreeable circumstances, nothing done, everything expected and wished for, and everything in confusion."[22]

Four days after Putnam had left West Point, after getting a clearer picture of the situation there, Parsons took the time to lend support to Putnam's efforts to fortify the Highlands despite the challenges. In a letter to Washington, he wrote that: "Almost every obstacle with the circle of possibility has happened to retard the progress of the obstructions in and fortifications on the banks of the Hudson River. Preparations for completing them are now in a state which affords a good prospect of completing them in April, and unless some difficulties yet unforeseen should prevent, I think we cannot fail by the forepart of that month to have them in a good degree of forwardness." One of those so-called "obstacles" was La Radière, who "found it impossible to complete the fort and other defenses" at West Point to "effectually withstand" a British attempt to pass up the Hudson. Concerned for his reputation, the troublesome engineer asked for and was granted permission to bring the matter before Washington and Congress. He would not return. Even Washington had to concede that, "from last accounts, [the works] are in more forwardness than I expected."[23]

BAD NEWS TIMES TWO

Unknown to Putnam, while assembled at York, Pennsylvania, on November 28, 1777, the Second Continental Congress had passed a resolution calling for General Washington to convene a Court of Enquiry to investigate the loss of Forts Clinton and Montgomery in New York and Fort Mifflin in Pennsylvania, as well as "the conduct of the principal officers commanding" there. According to Washington, he neglected to attend to this duty until March 16 due to Putnam's absence on personal business. However, this was a hollow excuse, and it ignores the fact that Putnam had been available for more than three months after Congress had acted. The truth is that, at the time, Washington had no recourse but to turn to Putnam to oversee the operations in the Hudson Highlands, and, moreover, the whole thing was an annoyance that could reflect badly upon his own role in the affair. Now, he felt that he could no longer delay it, and he appointed a panel composed of Maj. Gen. Alexander McDougall, Brig. Gen. Jedediah Huntington, and Col. Edward Wigglesworth. McDougall would be the presiding officer for the hearing scheduled for March 30. As an indication that he may have already prejudged the outcome, he advised McDougall to be wary of the claims of Putnam and the others in their defense, as they will, "of course make it appear [otherwise] by the evidence produced in their own justification." Washington wanted it finished quickly. He sent a letter to Putnam that same day, with orders to immediately ride to Fishkill to participate in the hearing. Putnam raced back to Fishkill, arriving there on March 29. When the hearing was concluded, he rode back to Connecticut to, "endeavor to forward on the new levies, with the utmost expedition."[24]

If the last-minute notice for the hearing caused Putnam any anxiety, which no doubt it did, what Washington told him next was cause for humiliation. In the same letter, Washington told Putnam that he had been relieved of his command in the Highlands. "Whether well or ill grounded," he wrote, there had been a groundswell of public sentiment against him, that "must be indulged." As an example, in February, Washington had heard from Col. Ann Hawkes Hay, who commanded a small regiment of Militia near Haverstraw. Hay complained that Putnam had refused to send over a detail to guard a large amount of forage stored there. As a result, he wrote that, "the inhabitants have lost all confidence in General Putnam." In fairness, Putnam could not be everywhere at once with his limited forces, and the local Militia would simply have to do the job themselves. Nevertheless, without more, Washington sided with Colonel Hay and later, "given General Putnam's inattention to this matter," he ordered General Parsons to "see to it."[25]

Of more concern was an exchange of letters that Washington had with Chancellor Robert R. Livingston of New York. In December, Washington had solicited Governor Clinton's thoughts on the "present management" (meaning Putnam) and the defense of the Highlands, and at the same time had openly recruited him to take over the command. Clinton had responded to Washington and Livingston at the same time. While the chancellor praised Putnam's "capacity and diligence" to do the job, on the other hand, echoing Clinton, he said that those qualities had been undermined by "his imprudent lenity to the disaffected, and too great intercourse with the enemy." He went on to say that the "current popular opinions" of him among the local citizens and his troops "runs strongly against him." Livingston left the verdict on the loss of Forts Clinton and Montgomery to the Court of Enquiry, and at the same time, he offered the following observation: "I respect his bravery, and former services, and sincerely lament that his patriotism, will not suffer him to take that repose to which his advanced age and past services justly entitle him." Washington, he was sure, needed a younger man with more "spirit and activity," one with a "fertile genius."[26]

Washington's reply to Livingston was very telling. "It has not been an easy matter to find a just pretense for removing an officer from his command, where his misconduct rather appears to result from want of capacity, than from any real intention of doing wrong," he wrote, "and it is therefore, as you observe, to be lamented that he cannot see his own defects, and make an honorable retreat from a station, in which he only exposes his own weakness." Washington then stretched the truth. "Proper measures are taking to carry on the inquiry into the loss of Fort Montgomery, agreeable to the direction of Congress," he wrote, four days before he had appointed a panel, and more than three months after Congress had first ordered the hearing. Finally, what he told Livingston demonstrated that Washington had already made up his mind, and that the seeds planted by Hamilton and Clinton had taken root. "It is more than probable, *from what I have heard*," he wrote, "that the issue of that enquiry will afford just grounds for a removal of General P[utnam], but whether it does or not, the prejudices of all ranks in that quarter against him are so great, that it would be impolitic to suffer him to return" (emphasis added).[27]

The source of the so-called "groundswell" of public opinion against Putnam was clearly Gov. George Clinton. In December, the ambitious

Clinton had declined Washington's suggestion that he assume active management of the Highlands, pursuant to the earlier suggestion of Congress. His excuse was the press of his duties as governor of New York. That, however, did not prevent him from frequently offering detailed suggestions as to how to do the job, while at the same time taking some subtle, and not so subtle, jabs at Putnam. In a letter to Washington on March 5, he used his duties as governor as an excuse to, once again, decline the post and offered up yet another veiled attack on Putnam. Calling for a change, he predicted that it will not be "easy to persuade the Militia to repair to the standard of an officer [Putnam] in whom they have no confidence," he wrote, "and to whom they ascribe no little share of their misfortunes." The latter claim is puzzling, since Putnam always enjoyed a good reputation with the troops under his command. With Clinton's continued declination, and Gates now serving on the Board of War, Washington was in a bind. He could not afford to lose the goodwill of Governor Clinton, however, he had little choice but to leave Putnam in command of the post until sufficient progress could be made with the fortifications in the Highlands.[28]

THE FOURTH ESTATE
One of the more puzzling charges leveled against Putnam by Clinton was that, in his behavior, he demonstrated a "want of common prudence." He was, Clinton claimed, too liberal with flags of truce, allowing the enemy to see for themselves the state of the American defenses due to the "constant intercourse . . . between country and city." Moreover, he claimed that Putnam showed "complaisance and indulgence to the disaffected" citizenry, regardless of their side in the conflict. Although he freely admitted that Putnam's motives were based upon "benevolence and humanity," nevertheless, he said they raised suspicions among the "common people," and even in the ranks of his soldiers. Finally, he charged that Putnam regularly exchanged newspapers with Governor Tryon.[29]

Common courtesy and decency were traits that Putnam constantly demonstrated throughout his life. Friends and enemies alike would say the same. If he saw suffering, and there was much of it among the common folks in the Highlands and Westchester County, Putnam would try to relieve it if it were in his power to do so. If it meant returning a milk cow or a horse to its rightful owner, often a small subsistence farmer or a widow with children, he would do so without regard to politics. That is simply who he was, and it is clearly not grounds to support a so-called groundswell for his relief as claimed by Governor Clinton.[30]

One situation that may have rankled Governor Clinton involved Lt. Col. Beverly Robinson, a prominent landowner and Tory Militia captain, who was frequently absent, serving with his unit. He and his family had been the subject of frequent harassment from both soldiers and neighbors because of his politics. After Putnam took command in 1777, he saw to it that Robinson's wife and family, as well as his property, were protected. It will be recalled that Putnam's wife died at the Robinson home. Later, the large grounds, with its outbuildings, served both as a headquarters and military hospital. Robinson was so grateful that he asked for a meeting, and with Henry Clinton's approval, he offered Putnam a commission if he would change sides. Not surprisingly, Putnam flatly refused. While he understood Robinson's feelings, nevertheless, he told him that the offer was an "indignity offered [my] character and as such, should never be repeated by one professing respect and gratitude."[31]

His communication with British officers, such as Major Small, many of whom he had known for two decades, all done in the open, was hardly the stuff of Benedict Arnold's duplicitous deceit. In fact, New York newspapers were a source of information, particularly about British shipping, and they were used by Washington himself to glean intelligence about the enemy. Putnam had even sent a copy of a New York paper to Washington without receiving any complaint. As was the case in Boston, prior to the start of hostilities, Putnam took delight in tweaking his former comrades. In one instance, his sense of humor was on full display when Putnam sent several newspapers to his friend Gen. James Robertson in New York City, "with his compliments." The newspapers were accompanied by a brief note, which read in part that, "when General Robertson shall have done with them, it is requested that they be given to Rivington in order that he may print some truth." James Rivington was the publisher of the *New York Loyal Gazette*, a Tory newspaper.[32]

IMPATIENT RECRUITER

By the middle of April, Putnam reported from Hartford that the recruiting drive was going well, and he asked leave to return to his troops. Washington told him to stay in Hartford for a while longer, as no firm plans had been made yet for a new campaign. During this time, Putnam advised Governor Trumbull by letter that he would shortly be forwarding the new recruits from Connecticut that he had raised, and he sought assurances that they would be provided with clothing. He followed this up with a personal visit to the governor in Lebanon. Putnam also ordered all soldiers whose furloughs had expired to immediately rejoin their regiments.[33]

The commander in chief articulated his ongoing dilemma in a letter to Gouverneur Morris in May 1778: "What am I to do with Putnam? If Congress mean to lay him aside, *decently* I wish they would devise the mode. He wanted some time ago to visit his family; I gave him leave and requested him to superintend the forwarding of Connecticut recruits. This service he says, is at an end, and is now applying for Orders. If he comes to this Army, he must be in high command (being next in rank to Lee). If he goes to the North River, he must command Gates, or serve under a junior Officer. The sooner these embarrassments could be removed the better. If they are not to be removed, I wish to know it, that I may govern myself accordingly; indecision and suspense in the Military line, are hurtful in the extreme" (emphasis in the original). For the time being, Washington continued to ignore the congressional resolution of the previous November 5, which, among other things had ordered that Putnam join the main army with 2,500 troops culled from General Gates' force.[34]

In the meantime, the Court of Enquiry had reached its conclusions, but for some reason, their report was not made public. Putnam only found out in June that, in fact, a report had been made, after he had asked his friend Col. Jeremiah Wadsworth to ask General Huntington what, if anything, had been done. He learned that the report had never been sent to Washington or to the Congress. It is also likely that Wadsworth told him that the report was favorable, but for Putnam, that was not enough. Meanwhile, some tongues had undoubtedly wagged months after the fact, and Putnam was concerned for his reputation, especially since he was between assignments. As he waited in Hartford, in his words, "with the utmost impatience for orders," he concluded that the lack of a final report was holding up his reassignment.[35]

Putnam was incensed and wanted the report of the Court of Enquiry sent to Washington or Congress. "I have just learnt that the proceeding of the Court, and the papers relating thereto, have never been laid before His Excellency," he told President Henry Laurens. He was incredulous that General McDougall would have held on to something that was important to both "the United States as well as to my character." He was also exasperated. "[I]f I had been reported guilty of any *Capital Crime* I might have the benefit of a court martial, and have been condemned or acquitt'd so that my character might stand in a clearer light in the world," he complained (emphasis in the original). He told Laurens that he was frustrated "to be posted here [Hartford] as a publick spectator for every ill minded person to make their remarks upon," and that as such, it "is very poor encouragement for any person to venture their lives and fortunes in the Service." Finally, he pleaded with Laurens to have Congress take the matter up and either acquit him "with Honor," or try him by general court-martial. Laurens replied that he had just received a copy of the report from General McDougall, and he assured Putnam that he would send him a copy and see to it that appropriate steps would be taken.[36]

Laurens ordered that Putnam's letter be read at the session held on July 8, and it was referred to the Board of War. In the meantime, on June 18, Washington had sent the report from the Court of Enquiry to Congress, but no action appears to have been taken as to either. Putnam then sent Congress a letter from Washington, which was then referred to a committee on August 4, which reported back with its conclusions on August 17. After considering the evidence, the committee found that, "it appears that those posts were lost not from any fault, misconduct or negligence of the commanding officers, but solely through the want of adequate force under their command to maintain and defend them." Congress agreed with the findings, and Putnam finally had his official vindication.[37]

By the time Congress had passed its resolution, Putnam was finally back in command of troops. The favorable conclusions notwithstanding, the old soldier was not going to simply "fade away." Notwithstanding the fact that Washington had returned him to the fold, if only reluctantly, Putnam's reputation was far too important to him to simply leave things at that. His vindication had to be made public, particularly to the citizens of Connecticut.

A sense of honor was an essential element of the character of an officer. According to historian Caroline Cox, all officers were, "exhorted to serve with honor that they might receive the thanks and recognition of posterity." Putnam was no exception. Accordingly, on August 22, from his camp at White Plains, he wrote to the *Connecticut Courant* and asked that the paper print a copy of the resolution, "for the vindication of my character," despite the passage of time since the loss of the Highland posts. As to the congressional inquiry, Putnam wrote: "This my reputation demanded. This my country had a right to expect." He remained convinced of the "rectitude" of his conduct despite the "detraction of a contemptable number of designing men" who worked to "prejudice the reputation of an old soldier and an honest servant to the public, who while he assumes no merit for his long services, nor will put his experience or military knowledge in competition with those of others, yet dares contend with the foremost in the faithful performances of his duty, the patriotic love of his country, and the hazard of his own person in defense of its rights and independence."[38]

Another person concerned for his honor and reputation was George Clinton. With a guilty conscience or a sense of frustration with his attempts to shift the onus to Putnam, when word of Putnam's exoneration reached him, he worried that the report had impliedly criticized his conduct regarding the loss of Forts Clinton and Montgomery, as he was the commanding officer that day. He expressed those concerns in a letter to Henry Laurens dated September 9. Laurens reassured him that the report "signifies the entire approbation of Congress" for his conduct. If he was at all mollified by Laurens' words, he did not say.[39]

BACK IN THE SADDLE

Following the withdrawal of the British from Philadelphia and the Battle of Monmouth in June 1778, Maj. Gen. Charles Lee sought vindication for his actions and demanded that Washington grant him a court-martial.

He was thereafter tried and convicted by the court for his failure to follow orders, and he was relieved from duty for one year. Putnam was, once again, the beneficiary of seniority. He was ordered to join Washington at White Plains, New York, where he was given command of the Virginia Line. His command included the brigades of Peter Muhlenberg, William Woodford, and Charles Scott.[40]

At this time, no doubt harking back to Putnam's previous tenure in the Highlands, Lt. Col. Robert Troup, then aide-de-camp to General Gates, convinced Washington to order the limitation of flags of truce to "public purposes," lest the army become "Putnamized" by persons freely coming and going into New York. Troup made that point clear to John Jay when he denied Jay's request on behalf of Rebecca Bayard, the daughter of a prominent Loyalist, to travel to New York City to tend to her ailing brother.[41]

In late August or early September, Washington called a council of war, at which he solicited the written opinion of his commanders as what the next move for the army should be. Putnam replied on September 2. In his opinion, the army should keep the pressure up on New York City, which he believed would force the British to hold troops there as opposed to attacking elsewhere in New England. Washington agreed, and the army was repositioned primarily in the Hudson Valley. For their part, the British seemed in no hurry to venture from New York, other than through foraging parties throughout the immediate region. For the next couple of months, Putnam would frequently move his troops to counter British foraging parties and any threats to West Point.[42]

Putnam's stay near White Plains was brief. On September 15 he was ordered to move his division the next day to reinforce the garrison at West Point and to help complete the works there that he had begun last winter. In addition, he was to collect and store forage for the upcoming winter. Along the line of march, Washington reminded him to maintain "strict discipline" to protect the person and property of the inhabitants. Four days later, Washington had second thoughts, and he ordered Putnam to encamp on the east bank of the Hudson and, among other things, to provide fatigue parties to help with the construction of the fort at West

Point. Putnam established his camp on familiar ground near the Beverly Robinson House.[43]

It had been almost a year since Deborah Putnam had died at the Robinson House, and, no doubt, it still must have dredged up some unpleasant memories, as the general chose to sleep "under canvas." Currently, the outbuildings were being used as a field hospital by Dr. James Thatcher, while the house itself was used as their quarters by Brigadier Generals Woodford and Muhlenberg. Shortly after his arrival in the vicinity, Putnam visited the hospital accompanied by Thatcher, who was meeting him for the first time. Thatcher described the sixty-year-old general: "In person he is corpulent and clumsy, but carries a bold, undaunted front. He exhibits little of the refinement of the well-educated gentleman, but much the character of the veteran soldier." Walking from soldier to soldier, it was apparent to Thatcher that their welfare was important to Putnam. Many of his men were suffering from hookworm, popularly referred to as "ground itch," without any apparent treatment being administered. "Why aren't these men cured?" Putnam asked. To which Thatcher answered that, "we have no hog's lard to make an ointment." The old soldier looked puzzled. "Did you never cure the itch with tar and brimstone [sulfur]?" "No, sir," said Thatcher. The general laughed, and at the same time said, "then you are not fit for a doctor!"[44]

Throughout that summer and fall, Putnam was energetic and vigilant, and he actively resisted various British raids and foraging parties. In addition, he continued to send fatigue parties to West Point. On September 24, 1778, he notified Washington that three large columns of British soldiers had ventured out of New York City, one on the New Jersey side of the Hudson near Hackensack, and two others, one at Mamaroneck and the other at Tarrytown. The apparent purpose was to forage for "cattle, sheep, and hogs." Washington replied quickly, ordering Putnam to continue his readiness and, if necessary, to oppose the enemy if they got closer. At Washington's order, Putnam moved Woodford's brigade to the west bank of the Hudson with orders to march south to counter a British foraging party near Clarkstown, New York. One large foraging party, led by Gen. Charles Grey, surprised and badly mauled Col. George Baylor's 3rd Continental Dragoon Regiment in an attack at dawn on September 28.[45]

On November 3, Brigadier General Muhlenberg, an ordained minister in civilian life, staged an elaborate dinner at the Robinson House, attended by more than forty invited officers, where fourteen separate dishes were served. After the tables were cleared and the Madeira poured, Muhlenberg asked Putnam to preside over the evening's entertainment. Doctor Thatcher wrote that Putnam, "displayed no less urbanity at the head of the table, than bravery at the head of his division." The doctor went on to describe the festivities: "A number of toasts were pronounced, accompanied with humorous and merry songs. . . . [W]e were cheered with military music and dancing, which continued till a late hour in the night." Surely, at some point during the evening Putnam led the group in the singing of "Maggie Lauder."[46]

Redding Encampment

As winter approached and the threat of British incursions diminished, Washington divided his force, taking part of the army to Middlebrook, New Jersey. On November 20, Putnam was ordered to take immediate command of the brigades of Brig. Gen. Jedediah Huntington and Brig. Gen. Samuel H. Parsons from Connecticut, and Brig. Gen. Enoch Poor of New Hampshire, all of whom had been ordered to winter in the vicinity of Danbury, Connecticut. In addition, there were some attached cavalry and unaffiliated infantry. The brigades were separated into three different camps in Redding, located in the upper Saugatuck River Valley near the present-day Bethel town line. Putnam selected a nearby farmhouse on Umpawaug Hill for his headquarters.[47]

As ordered by Washington, Putnam utilized the plan developed in Pennsylvania the previous winter. As such, the Redding encampment was referred to by many as "Connecticut's Valley Forge," given the similar living arrangements, including rows of wooden huts built on stone foundations. However, constant rains slowed the work and added to the misery. Jedediah Huntington told his brother Andrew: "We are huting [hutting] (that is my brigade) at a place called Umpowaugh [Umpawaug] on the line between Danbury and Reading. General Parsons is about two miles east of me, and General Poor less than two miles east of Parsons."

With Putnam were his sons Israel and Daniel, as well as a new aide-de-camp, David Humphreys, who had been appointed on December 17.[48]

An Active Winter

After four years as commander in chief, Washington was able to assess the strengths and weaknesses of most of his generals. For example, he appears to have put aside some of his previous reservations about Putnam's age and competency, as he had come to realize that Israel Putnam worked best when given a general framework, coupled with specific directions, which Washington laid out in some detail in a letter dated November 27. "You will keep a succession of small parties down towards the enemy's lines mostly towards the [Long Island] Sound," he wrote, "[in order to] prevent small parties from penetrating too great a distance into the country, and to gain any intelligence which may be collected." Putnam suggested that it might be more efficient if a larger force of two hundred men went out under a field officer, who would, in turn, be in a better position to break his party into smaller details, as the situation demanded. Washington approved, calling the plan "a good one."[49]

Washington was primarily concerned with the cross-border raids by Loyalist units led by Governor Tryon and Col. James De Lancey, seeking cattle, hogs, and forage. Complicating matters was the fact, according to Putnam and Brigadier General Parsons, that it was common knowledge that some residents, eager to accept the hard currency offered by British agents, drove their cattle and hogs right up to the border and left them to be "stolen." It was a delicate situation and called upon Putnam's soldiers to exercise their utmost discretion, so as not to injure local inhabitants of southwestern Connecticut that were loyal to the Cause. In short, all cattle and hogs, if found near the border or in the hands of Loyalist raiders, were to be driven back by Putnam's men to be auctioned off by the commissary, with the proceeds from the sale of animals that had actually been stolen paid to their rightful owners.[50]

In addition, "particular attention is to be paid to keeping a stock of fire wood [at camp]," Washington wrote, "which will take [away] every pretense for consuming fences or out houses." Thus the order was not to burn excess forage, as Putnam had suggested to deprive the British in New York of its use, but to simply leave it. In other words, Washington strenuously objected to any plundering or marauding under any circumstances.[51]

Finally, Washington stressed the importance of the Highlands and the need to work closely with General McDougall, and that Putnam should be prepared to support him with one or two brigades if needed. Any raids on Long Island should be done only where there was a high degree of success. Hoping to avoid any similar complaints about his previous accommodating practices in the Highlands, Washington told Putnam to scrupulously restrict travel across the state line to those having passes issued by the highest authority and to limit the use of flags of truce to those requested by the governor of the state. Also, Putnam was to limit furloughs, particularly for senior officers. Any other such requests were to be referred directly to Washington himself. A month later, after an apparent alarm, Washington complimented Putnam for his initiative in removing stores of ammunition inland and for forbidding his quartermasters from storing such materials in towns along the shoreline.[52]

THE ROUTE TO REDDING

As if the winter weather was not bad enough, a much more serious challenge confronted the army. A chronic lack of shoes and clothing had plagued the troops, as well as a dearth of proper rations. This was attributable, in part, to an inefficient supply system, and, in part, to strict orders regarding looting and otherwise preying upon the local populace. Each state was expected to provide for their own Militia, and some were better than others in meeting their obligation. The Continentals, however, were to be supplied through a centralized quartermaster, commissary, and clothier. In addition, a lack of regular pay, and worse, rampant inflation, even when they were paid, left the soldiers and their families unable to pay the bills and caused local merchants and farmers to hoard food and other essentials. The situation was ripe for trouble.[53]

Brigadier General Samuel Holden Parsons was frustrated. His pleas for sufficient clothing for his men went back to the fall of 1777. Since that time, the promises made remained largely unkept. He wrote to Washington from the Redding encampment, indicating that, "I believe I have eight hundred men who are totally destitute and many of them have never had a blanket since their enlistment." He told Washington that other brigades had received clothing and, without directly saying it, implied that Washington was playing favorites. "I have not the least doubt of your Excellency's intentions to do equal justice among the troops; this justice we have not yet had, when other troops have received blankets nearly sufficient for them; we have not yet had one third part." Parsons begged Washington to order the release of five hundred blankets, along with their allotted shirts and stockings, and at the very least, direct the quartermaster to place an order for blankets, so that "we may at least have some distant prospect of receiving some benefit from the public promises so often made to us." Putnam had made a similar point the same day.[54]

Parsons's letter did not sit well with Washington, and he brought the matter to Putnam's attention, telling him that it contained "some insinuations not of the most delicate nature." In making his response to the commander in chief, Putnam had to thread the needle between his respect for a superior and his duty to support a subordinate, so he shaded the truth a bit when he replied that he had never seen the letter "or heard the contents, except in the most general terms." Putnam attempted to assuage Washington's pique. "I am fully convinced, all the troops of these states have ever experienced an equal share of your attention," he wrote, however, "I am as well persuaded, those of Connecticut have fared worse in the late distribution of clothing to the Army than any other." He added diplomatically that, "I am conscious, I have been very far from attributing, in my own mind, to the partiality of anyone." He suggested that given the press of business Washington had to deal with, somehow the Connecticut troops had been inadvertently overlooked. By way of example, he pointed out that a supply of uniforms had recently arrived at Hartford, and before they could be allotted, they were all distributed to Massachusetts troops, who were now in the Hudson Highlands. Putnam boldly made his point with a touch of humor, if not sarcasm. He was sure that none of those uniforms were destined for his troops, "as it was well known, that the route from Hartford to Reading was not usually through Fishkill; and that the expense of transportation must, in that case be vastly augmented."[55]

COLLECTIVE INDISCIPLINE

The American soldier, particularly one from New England, had a long tradition of service based upon an implied contract that, beyond supplying his own musket and kit, he would otherwise be equipped and paid a set wage, and, in most instances, for a fixed term or the end of the emergency, whichever happened first. Brief work stoppages, or whole units simply marching home, with or without their officers, were commonplace during the French and Indian War. It was a relationship built upon trust and mutual respect. Provincial officers, for the most part, came from the same county or community. They were, in essence, "one of them," and not some elite gentlemen who maintained their distance. Officers were expected to listen to and look out for their troops. The soldiers from New England responded better to an appeal to duty rather than to the fear of punishment.

However, if Washington had his way, that tradition would dramatically change, as the core of the army shifted to an army of regulars, enlisted for multiple years or the duration, led by "socially distant gentlemen," and all guided by a rigid code of conduct. As the war wore on, Washington came to rely increasingly upon the regular "Continental" regiments raised from each state. However, that concept rubbed up against reality, as, by far, the bulk of Washington's Continentals came from the New England states, led by farmers and shopkeepers, and old habits die hard.[56]

On more than one occasion, particularly later in the war, Washington was faced with mutinous conduct, both on a small scale and by whole regiments. His response was usually swift and harsh. He expressed his philosophy regarding capital punishment, which combined "humanity and policy," in a letter to Putnam: "The conduct which a commanding officer is to observe . . . is to use every means for discovering the authors of the mischief; to inflict instant punishment on them; and reclaim the rest by clemency. The impression made on the minds of the multitude by the terror of the example, and their inability to take any resolution when deprived of the ring leaders, are a sufficient security against further attempts." Washington's philosophy was put to the test in May 1780 at Morristown, when two Connecticut regiments threatened to march home in a dispute involving pay and rations. It was resolved peacefully.

In New Jersey, in January 1781, separate mutinies erupted involving the Pennsylvania Line at Morristown and the New Jersey Line at Pompton over the same issues. Washington again negotiated a peaceful resolution of the first, but he exercised swift justice with the latter, when he summarily executed two of the ringleaders.[57]

On December 30, while in camp at Redding, Putnam successfully quelled a mutiny in Brig. Gen. Jedediah Huntington's brigade. The soldiers were unhappy with the lack of adequate clothing and no pay, and the assurances of their officers were wearing thin. Captain Nathaniel Webb noted in his orderly book that the men "are naked in a severe Winter; they are hungry and have no Money." These Connecticut troops, including their non-commissioned officers, threatened a march, under arms, to Hartford, where the General Assembly was then in session, to deliver a petition and force it to act upon their grievances.[58]

When word reached Putnam about the disturbance, he raced to address each of Huntington's regiments in turn. With "drums beating," the men were called to attention, and Putnam exhorted them to stack arms and return to their regimental areas. "My brave lads, whither are you going?" he asked. "You have behaved like men so far . . . and posterity will stand astonished at your deeds," he continued, "but not if you spoil it all last." He told them that their officers had also not been paid, and that he firmly believed that, in time, the country "will do us ample justice." He ended by appealing to their sense of duty and comradeship: "Let us all stand by one another, then, and fight it out like brave soldiers, think what a shame it would be for Connecticut men to run away from their officers." As a testament to the respect that his soldiers held for him, each regiment that Putnam spoke to complied, and the only casualty was a particularly obstreperous soldier out of the several ringleaders who had been taken to the guardhouse to cool off, and he was shot and killed in an attempted escape. After drafting a petition to Putnam acknowledging their mistake as "a want of serious consideration and for not having a right understanding of things," the others were soon released.[59]

Although Parsons forcefully denied it in a letter to Washington, his brigade was not immune from the grumblings of his men. Little wonder, given the chronic shortages of clothing and food. Shortly after the mutiny in Huntington's brigade, a similar incident occurred among Parson's men. One night after roll call, the hungry men turned out and assembled in formation in front of their quarters, without arms, in hopes of gaining the attention of their officers. They succeeded; however, the regimental officers were able to restore order with promise of relief, and the men went back to their quarters. Still hungry and unsatisfied, some men played a trick on the officers by secretly and repeatedly discharging a musket in an unfinished hut, against standing orders prohibiting the discharge of weapons in camp, thus disturbing their officers' sleep all through the night. Although the situation improved somewhat, it was clear that nothing of substance would be done, and, like the men from Huntington's brigade, they talked of going home en masse, and once again, on the following day they assembled without officers, but this time under arms. With some difficulty, order was finally restored, and the men went back to their quarters, "muttering over [their] forlorn condition."[60]

Putnam did not ignore the underlying discontent among his soldiers once the indiscipline was quelled. He recognized that the men were frustrated by what they perceived to be a lack of support from Hartford, and they simply wanted their grievances heard, and not by Putnam, who already knew them all too well. Instead of imposing capital punishment on the ringleaders, he permitted the brigade officers to bring the petition to the General Assembly outlining their grievances. As a result, a delegation composed of Generals Huntington and Parsons, along with Col. Philip Burr Bradley and Col. Return Jonathan Meigs, as well as Capt. William Judd, carried the petition directly to Hartford and presented it to the current session of the General Assembly.[61]

When Putnam found out that the General Assembly had been briefly adjourned, he wrote a letter to Governor Trumbull in support of the petition, stressing the importance of it being heard and suggesting that any debate on the subject should happen in the presence of the delegation. "These gentlemen, or such of them who shall attend, will lay before the Assembly an estimate of the loss sustained by the troops of this State," he wrote, "in consequence of the inhanced price of all the necessary articles of life, and the unequal value of their pay to what it was at the time of their engaging in the service." Putnam went on to advocate for his men: "[It is] my sincere wish that justice may be done to the troops, in which case I do not entertain the least doubt but that they will fulfill the engagement on their part with fidelity, will continue to do their duty as brave and faithful soldiers, in defense of their injured country, with reputation to themselves and honor to the State."[62]

Washington complimented Putnam for his prompt actions, and, while he left the punishment to Putnam's discretion, he suggested that it be applied with "wholesome severity." Washington's letter, however, had arrived well after the fact. Putnam and the brigade officers were able to restore order so quickly that by the time he had heard from Washington, he had already released the two ringleaders back to their company. More important, in response to the petition, in February the General Assembly voted to grant an initial sum of £45,000 to be paid to the officers and enlisted soldiers in Parson's and Huntington's brigades by April 1, 1779. In addition, legislators pledged to raise a "sufficient sum" to do justice to the "officers and soldiers of this State," as soon as circumstances permitted.[63]

On the other hand, not so fortunate were two young deserters who had been found spying for the enemy. The first one, Edward Jones, had deserted and served as a guide for the enemy. He was tried and convicted on February 4. The court pronounced a sentence of death by hanging to take place on February 11. The second soldier was John Smith, who was tried and convicted on February 6. He was sentenced to be shot on Tuesday, February 16. The execution of Jones was postponed to February 16. Both young men were brought under guard to the Redding Meeting House on Sunday, February 14, to hear the sermon. On the day appointed for the execution, Putnam issued an order that "the brigade parade . . . at nine o'clock, well dressed and neat, to attend the execution of the prisoners under sentence of death," at which time both were executed, although one of them strenuously protested his innocence right up to the end.[64]

DEFENDING THE CONNECTICUT COAST

The fact that Putnam's troops were settled into winter quarters should not be thought of as a period of idleness—quite the contrary. Putnam's area of responsibility ran from the border with Westchester County east beyond the Connecticut River, as well as parts of Long Island across the

Sound. At this time, both sides conducted raids and foraging expeditions. A question arose as to the scope of Putnam's authority pursuant to Washington's explicit orders, giving rise to a difference of opinion between Parsons and Putnam on that score. After Parsons raised the issue with Washington, the latter seemed surprised that there would be any such question. In a letter to Putnam dated January 8, 1779, Washington wrote: "In executing the measures necessary to prevent this commerce [looting and foraging by the enemy], I cannot but think that my instructions, and in addition to them my letter of the 26th of December, allow ample latitude for the most effectual measures."[65]

To that end, Putnam had dispatched Parsons and about three hundred Continentals to help defend the important port of New London, as well as sending smaller contingents to Horseneck, Stamford, Norwalk, and Fairfield. These men provided a core force to be supplemented by local Militia in the case of a raid. All were expected to meet the enemy before any serious loss occurred, as had happened during Tryon's raid on the supply depot at Danbury, Connecticut, in 1777. Washington approved of Putnam's deployments, but, given the importance of New London, he suggested that in addition, a large Militia contingent be called up there and other local units be alerted to respond in the event of an attack. The commander in chief then demonstrated that he, too, had learned some valuable lessons over the past four years: "I can devise no better plan at present for the general security of the Coast than the foregoing. To cover every place effectually is impossible, and to attend particularly to any one, except it be of the utmost importance, would be giving the enemy the advantage which they would always gain by making diversions in favor of their real object."[66]

The British chose this period to stage hit-and-run raids all up and down the Connecticut coast. Stymied in his effort to advance farther up the Hudson River than Stony Point, Henry Clinton timed this effort in hopes that Washington would shift substantial forces away from the Highlands. The signs had been there for months, particularly given the movement of various portions of the British fleet near Rhode Island and in Long Island Sound. Parsons had raised the alarm in late March, fully expecting an attack on New London, serious enough that he chose to remain there despite Putnam's order to return to Redding. The anticipated raid was postponed by the British after a portion of their fleet was driven ashore during a storm. Putnam sought guidance from Washington as to the disposition of his forces, especially since he had been given orders to begin to send his brigades to the Highlands to be closer to Washington. Without waiting for a reply, Putnam sent an additional three hundred men to New Haven to be ready to assist Parsons, if necessary.[67]

A NARROW ESCAPE

On the evening of February 25, following dinner, General Putnam, who was a guest at the home of Gen. Ebenezer Mead, retired for the night. He had come to Horseneck to inspect his small contingent of troops there. That same evening about 11:00 p.m., Major General Tryon set out from Kingsbridge with a fifteen-hundred-man force composed of British regulars, Hessians, and some new recruits. His primary objective was the saltworks located at Horseneck. Not long after, a thirty-man American patrol, led by Capt. Titus Watson of the 7th Connecticut Regiment, operating in Westchester County, discovered the raiders at New Rochelle and followed them at a safe distance.

As the sun rose the next day, Watson's small force was discovered near Rye Neck, where it soon came under attack. After a sharp exchange of fire, Watson and his men, clearly overmatched, withdrew to some high ground near Sawpits, where another brief firefight took place. Once again, Watson was forced to withdraw. As they retreated across the bridge over the Byrum River, his men removed much of the planking to slow the pursuit. Once across, they quickly spread the alarm.

Following the alert, Putnam quickly assembled roughly one hundred troops on a nearby hill adjacent to a Congregational meetinghouse. While Tryon advanced down the main road with the main body, Putnam saw that he had also sent out flankers to cut off the American line of retreat. He ordered some men to secure the flanks, while about sixty men remained to meet the British. After a brief exchange of fire, including the discharge of "some old field pieces," the Americans were able only to slow the attackers by just a step. The general told Lt. Col. Hezekiah Holdridge to take what troops that remained, withdraw to a nearby hill, and prepare to resist a further attack. In the meantime, he told Holdridge that he would ride to Stamford, five miles away, where there was a larger "body of Militia and a few Continental troops."

As he neared the Episcopal church, Putnam saw that he was pursued by some of Tryon's troopers. With the British close behind him, at the brow of the steep hill there, he made a daring decision. Without hesitation, he rode headlong down seventy stone steps. The British fired a parting shot and declined further pursuit.

Putnam returned to Horseneck with a large mixed troop of Militia and Continentals. In his absence, Lieutenant Colonel Holdridge "mistook" Putnam's orders and withdrew altogether, leaving the British free to plunder the town unmolested. Although the saltworks had been destroyed, along with a sloop and some houses, Putnam's reinforcements were able to secure more than fifty British stragglers, lingering behind to loot, as well as an ammunition wagon and a wagon full of plundered property, "which he had the satisfaction of returning to the inhabitants from whom it was taken." Inexplicably, upon his return to Redding, in his official report to General Washington dated March 2, 1779, he omitted the details of his hairbreadth escape, which is strange since the tale has become such an integral part of his life story.[68]

SHRINKING COMMAND

Washington was not pleased. In April 1779, he granted Putnam another short leave to attend to family business. However, the commander in chief felt that such leaves, particularly for Generals Huntington and Parsons, were too freely granted, particularly at a time when it was important for senior officers to be present, and he told Putnam so. Putnam took the time to travel to New London on his way to Pomfret. In the meantime, Washington had requested that Putnam send most of his command, including Parsons' brigade, to the Highlands, anticipating activity there by the British. Putnam returned briefly to Redding before traveling to Hartford to meet with the governor and the General Assembly, which was in session, to encourage them to meet their new quota of troops.[69]

Putnam returned to Redding on or about May 7 to a much-reduced command. Moreover, he had received no new orders. In fact, Washington

Figure 8. "Putnam's Escape at Horseneck" by Anna Hyatt Huntington, Putnam Memorial State Park, Redding, Connecticut

told him that his services were needed in Connecticut "to arrange and forward the Militia." Putnam tactfully addressed both points in a letter to Washington that day. "Although I do not in the least doubt the necessity and propriety of these measures, or wish to be inform'd of the secrets of the ensuing campaign," he wrote, "yet it is exceedingly natural for me to have some little curiosity of my future destination." He wanted to know if he would retain command of the troops he had wintered with in Redding, or, he added plaintively, if not sarcastically, "whether I am to remain to guard the Huts at this place." He repeated the fact that, "nothing is said concerning the part which I am to act." In a knowing nod to Washington's dilemma regarding Putnam's standing, the old soldier appealed to the commander in chief's better nature: "However disagreeable the situation may be, I know there is a *delicacy* in thinking and treating on a subject where one's self is so intimately concerned beyond the limits of which, I hope I shall not be accused of passing" (emphasis in the original).[70]

Putnam maintained strong friendships within the officer corps, particularly with Samuel Parsons and Nathanael Greene. At this time both officers were discouraged with their situations and contemplating resigning their commissions. Both men had a genuine affection for Putnam. On April 11, 1779, during an exchange of letters with Greene, Parsons wrote: "I believe General Putnam has been abused. I have the same sentiments of the man which I believe you entertain, and however, well it might be for him to retire from his public station at this time, it must affect in the most sensible manner a feeling mind to see the measures taken to remove from office one who has been a faithful servant and has grown old in honest endeavors to do his country good; and the means used to induce him to relinquish his place are such as renders it impossible for him to retire with honor, and who can wish disgrace to attend him in his last days." What was happening to Putnam, he felt could one day apply to anyone. "I confess I think when the public have no longer occasion for the exertion of any of their servants," he added, "it requires no great skill to dismiss them in a manner which would not wound the feelings of a good man."[71]

Washington's Dilemma

As time passed, Washington continued to get a better feel for the strengths and weaknesses of his various senior commanders. He could only recommend, but Congress held the power of appointment. What seemed right at the time of the siege of Boston no longer held true in all cases. Younger officers, like Benedict Arnold and Nathanael Greene, had emerged and showed considerable promise, while older officers, many more senior but less capable, blocked their way upward. Petty jealousy and stubborn arrogance were often complicating factors.

A case in point was Horatio Gates, the "hero" of Saratoga. If anyone cared to listen, Daniel Morgan and Benedict Arnold could well point to Gates' inertia and lack of initiative. Still, he received the credit for the victory, and, worse, he very nearly parlayed that into a successful coup against Washington. Moreover, Gates had his supporters in Congress, and Washington had to proceed carefully. Gates' disgraceful and incompetent performance at Camden, South Carolina, in 1780, followed by his cowardly flight from the field, would prove them right and ultimately open the door for Greene. Yet, Washington could not afford to hold on to the premise that time and fate would always get things right.

George Washington continued to fret regarding Putnam, who was one of his most senior major generals, as well as one of the oldest. His concerns about him seem to have softened. He liked Putnam personally, and he trusted him within limits. Moreover, an army board of review had cleared Putnam of any wrongdoing in the loss of Forts Clinton and Montgomery, but Washington wanted to utilize some less-senior general officers whom he saw as more capable overall, and he worried that the old soldier would not want to serve in a subordinate role to one less senior. Now, Putnam had just returned from winter quarters in Redding, Connecticut, and he had asked for a new command.[72]

Back with Washington

Finally, in late May, Washington made up his mind and sent for Putnam. Washington intended to leave Middlebrook, New Jersey, and establish a new headquarters in the Highlands. He ordered Putnam to send Parsons's brigade to join McDougall immediately and for Putnam to follow as soon as possible. Prior to leaving Redding, Putnam addressed his remaining troops, who would fall under the command of William Heath. An obviously upbeat Putnam issued a final general order dated May 27, 1779: "Maj. General Putnam being about to take command of one of the Wings of the Grand Army, before he leaves the Troops who have served under him the winter past, thinks it his duty to Signify to them his entire approbation of their Regular and Soldier-like conduct, and wishes them (wherever they may happen to be out) a Successful and Glorious Campaign."[73]

By June 1779, Putnam was back with the main army. He established his headquarters at Smith's Clove, a long cleft through the mountains on the west side of the Hudson River terminating near the present village of Monroe, New York. Pursuant to Washington's orders, Putnam would lead the right wing of the army, having under his command troops from Virginia, Maryland, and Pennsylvania, all of whom had just left their winter encampment in Middlebrook, New Jersey. It was the important assignment that he had hoped for. Washington stopped over at West Point for a brief visit, and he asked Putnam to join him there for a conference, as he wanted his "opinion on several matters of importance." On June 21, Washington established his headquarters at New Windsor, New York, and Putnam returned to his camp at Smith's Clove, where he remained in command.[74]

All this was happening at the same time as the British renewed active operations in the Hudson Valley, with the obvious intent to capture the forts at King's Ferry and to seize or threaten West Point. To that end, on May 31, Henry Clinton divided his forces, landing simultaneously on each bank of the Hudson, on the east below Verplank's Point and on the west below Stony Point. The latter fell without a fight, the defenders having abandoned it upon the approach of the British. The former surrendered the following day after a bombardment. The enemy remained active in the area, which called for an aggressive response. On the night of July 15/16, Brig. Gen. Anthony Wayne recaptured Stony Point in a bold surprise attack. Putnam was ordered to send Brig. Gen. William Smallwood's brigade to the Forest of Dean, and Brigadier General Woodford's brigade to June's Tavern, on July 19 to block any countermove by the

British. By the time his orders had reached him, Putnam had established his headquarters at Buttermilk Falls (now Highland Falls) just south of West Point.[75]

HIT AND RUN

In July, Norwalk, Westport, Fairfield, and New Haven all suffered to one degree or another, as Major General Tryon was able to land with virtual impunity and burn homes and shops, including two church buildings. Washington's warning to Governor Trumbull came too late; however, he later praised the New Haven Militia, saying that their conduct "does them the highest honor." He also ordered William Heath to send his two Connecticut brigades south to assist. In some cases, the Militia responded quickly and forcefully enough that Tryon's stay was short. It was a strong reminder that the British navy gave the army a decided advantage.[76]

A STROKE OF ILL LUCK

Putnam maintained his headquarters at Buttermilk Falls for the next several months, and he was tasked with finishing the fortifications at West Point. According to Humphreys, who along with Putnam's son Daniel composed his military family, the general was, "happy in possessing the friendship of the officers of that line, and living on terms of hospitality with them." He added that, "there was no family in the army that lived better than his own."[77]

In the fall of 1779, Putnam requested and received another short leave to return to his home in Pomfret to attend to some family business, accompanied by his two aides-de-camp, his son Daniel and David Humphreys. His business done, sometime during the week of Monday, December 20, Putnam and his entourage set out from Pomfret on the way back to his waiting command at Morristown, New Jersey. He was, no doubt, pleased and looked forward to being with troops once again.

After a night or two on the road, they resumed the journey early on the morning of December 24. It was the general's intention to spend that night at the home of his friend Jeremiah Wadsworth in Hartford, although at the time, Colonel Wadsworth was away with the Continental Army. As the party neared Hartford later that morning, Putnam felt the first hint of a stroke. It began with some numbness in his right hand. By the time he had arrived at the Wadsworth home, his right arm had also become numb, and an hour later, so had his right shoulder. In a state of denial, the old warrior tried to work through it, but by that afternoon, his whole right side had become paralyzed. His son Daniel and David Humphreys carried him to an upstairs chamber, where he would spend the next ten days recuperating sufficiently to where he could be moved back home to Brooklyn. At that time, he informed Washington of his situation and acknowledged the fact that he would not be able to resume his duties, at least not anytime soon. For Israel Putnam, the war was over.[78]

THE ROAD TO RECOVERY

Back home in Brooklyn, Connecticut, Putnam struggled with his disability. Yet, with his typical determination, he gradually regained limited use of his right leg, such that, he walked with a cane and, with assistance, he was able to ride a horse. Still, his dominant right arm never really recovered, although he worked hard to be able to write his initials, "IP." His speech may have also remained slurred, which, if so, had to be frustrating for an such an avid storyteller. Pleased with his progress after nearly six months, on May 29, 1780, he wrote a letter to George Washington and asked David Humphreys, who was returning to the army, to deliver it in person. "I have been gradually growing better," he told Washington. "I have now so far gained the use of my limbs, especially of my leg, as to be able to walk with very little impediment, and to ride horseback tolerably well. In other respects, I am in perfect health, and enjoy the comforts and pleasures of life with as good a relish as most of my neighbors."[79]

Putnam valued his friendships, old and new. Since the war began, he had grown particularly close to Nathanael Greene, and he was delighted to hear that the latter had inquired about the state of his health and offered his wishes for a full recovery. "I beg you will do me the justice to believe that the recollection and kindness of so good a friend is almost a sovereign remedy against every disorder," he wrote, "and will (if anything in nature can) set me upon my legs again." He then related his progress in regaining some activities like riding. Putnam longed to be back in active service. "I would like to be near at hand, where I can see for myself and know the certainty of matters without being obliged to doubt of every-thing," he told Greene, then adding with a flash of his old sense of humor, "or on the other hand, to swallow every lie a News Paper is pleased to impose upon me, although it should be as big as a mountain."[80]

Putnam missed his comrades and longed to see them again. David Humphreys returned to duty with Washington in May 1780, and at Putnam's request delivered a letter to the commander in chief. "Altho I should not be able to resume a command in the Army, I propose to myself the happiness of making a visit and seeing my friends there sometime in the course of the Campaign," Putnam wrote. Washington's response was gracious. "I am very happy to learn . . . that the present state of your health is so flattering," he wrote, "and that it promises you the prospect of being in a condition to make a visit to your old associates sometime this cam-paign." He added: "I wish it were in my power to congratulate you on a complete recovery. I should feel a sincere satisfaction in such an event, and I hope for it heartily, with the rest of your friends in this quarter."[81]

That September, no doubt to the amazement of all, Putnam made the journey to Tappan, New York, quite literally at the same moment that Benedict Arnold's perfidy had been exposed with the capture of Maj. John Andre. Notwithstanding that situation, Putnam's visit provided a welcome diversion, and he was the toast of Washington's mess. Nathanael Greene told his wife that, "General Putnam is here talking as usual, and telling his old stories, which prevents my writing more." Greene added that, "the old gentleman, notwithstanding the late paralytical shock, is very cheerful and social." It would be nice to think that he led them all in the "Ballad of Maggie Lauder" one last time.[82]

Fading Away

On February 25, 1782, Israel Putnam took the time to execute his Last Will and Testament. He divided the land and buildings nearly equally in value among his three sons. To Israel, in addition to slightly more than 100 acres previously given to him, he left 193 acres that were a part of his original purchase. Daniel was currently occupying the former inn near the Brooklyn Meeting, which Putnam had purchased from Deborah's heirs. This was part of Daniel's legacy, along with 20 acres of woodland in Canterbury. Finally, to Peter Schuyler, he left 120 acres and his homestead, including all livestock and husbandry tools, as well as two slaves, a Negro named "Kitt" and an Indian named Charles Pease. To his four daughters, Hanna, Mehitable, Molly, and Eunice, and his grandson Elisha Avery, he made cash bequests of between £150 and £400. Four years later, he added a short codicil, adjusting the bequests to Eunice and her son.[83]

Putnam retained his commission as a major general through 1783, even though his active service had ended with his stroke, and he continued to maintain a keen interest in the progress of the war. When the fighting had stopped, and the treaty signed, he was quick to write to Washington. "I take this opportunity to congratulate your Excellency on the Establishment of peace after a long tedious & Glorious Struggle," he wrote, "conducted under your Excellency's auspicious command, against the whole power of Britain." He then took the time to wish Washington "the peaceful Injoyments of civil life" after the "tumults of war," as well as the "Love, Esteem & Veneration of the free people of these States." Finally, he asked Washington to remember the sacrifice of "those who have contributed their mite towards the Salvation of their Country," including himself. Specifically, he asked that he also receive his back pay and in retirement, the half-pay that the other officers were entitled to due to their long service.[84]

Washington's response was prompt and full of encomiums for his old comrade at arms: "Your favor of the 20th of May I received with much pleasure. For I can assure you, that among the many worthy & meritorious Officers, with whom I have had the happiness to be connected in Service, through the Course of this War, and for whose chearfull Assistance & Advice I have received much support & Confidence in the various & trying Vicissitudes of a Complicated Contest, the name of Putnam is not forgotten." The general went on to acknowledge Putnam's sacrifices in service of his country, where "you have exhausted your Bodily Health, & expended the Vigor of youthful Constitution." Finally, he assured Putnam that he would be treated as would be the other officers, with pay through the end of the war, and half-pay thereafter.[85]

FINAL FAREWELLS

Israel Putnam reintegrated himself into the local community, attending church services and social gatherings. When the town of Brooklyn considered licensing two more public houses, the former publican urged that only one be approved. "Being an enemy to Idleness, Dissipation, and Intemperance," he argued, since the one existing public house did not have enough traveling patrons to begin with, the new ones would have a "direct tendency to ruin the morals of youth and promote idleness and intemperance among all ranks of people." When the Connecticut General Assembly granted Brooklyn its charter at its May Session in 1786, the first town meeting was held on June 26, with Israel Putnam as chair.[86]

Later that same year, the old general, accompanied by Dick, journeyed back to Danvers, Massachusetts, to visit family and friends. It would be his final long trip. Remarkably, he rode on horseback the entire way. Before returning to his home, he stopped at Harvard College and visited with Samuel Putnam, a student there.[87]

In 1788, Putnam was faced with another imminent farewell. His eldest son, Israel, told him that he had decided to join his distant cousin Rufus in the new "Territory Northwest of the Ohio River," which had been recently opened to settlement by members of the Ohio Company. The area chosen for the settlement, the first legal one in the territory, was situated at the junction of the Muskingum and Ohio Rivers and would soon be called Marietta in honor of Queen Marie Antionette. As the old man received the news, it must have been with sadness, knowing that he would likely never see his son again, but also with a sense of pride that his firstborn retained a spirit of adventure.

That summer, Putnam said good-bye to Israel Jr. for the final time, as he, accompanied by his own son Aaron and the slave Kitt, set out for Ohio. The colonel's small party traveled with two yoke of his prize oxen, pulling a wagon, heavily loaded with "a few household goods, with agricultural implements and mechanical tools." He left behind his wife and other children, until such time as he could get settled on his homestead.[88]

A NEAR MISS

President George Washington toured New England during the fall of 1789, visiting in all about sixty towns throughout, except Rhode Island, which had not yet joined the Union. The crowds of well-wishers enthusiastically cheered as his coach passed by. Washington was hopeful that the situation in Rhode Island would soon change with the newly elected state legislature, as up to that point, he opined, that the majority had "bid adieu, long since to every principle of honor, common sense, and honesty." Overall, however, he was pleased with his trip to New England, where he found that it had "in a great degree, recovered from the ravages of War—the Towns flourishing, [and the] people delighted with a government instituted by themselves and for their own good."[89]

On the return leg of his journey to New York, Washington's route took him along the Middle Road from Boston, through Thompson and Woodstock on the way to Pomfret, where he planned to stay the night at an inn there run by Col. Thomas Grosvenor. He had purposely taken the road so that he could stop and see his old companion in arms Israel Putnam. As he passed the crossroads leading to the old soldier's home, he was told that it would be a ten-mile round-trip. Already behind schedule, Washington reluctantly chose to pass on. It would be a missed opportunity for both men.[90]

DEATH COMES FOR THE OLD GENERAL

Israel Putnam contracted a fever, and he died at his home a couple of days later, on Saturday, May 29, 1790. His funeral took place on the following Tuesday, and it was well-attended as befitted a genuine hero. The Rev. Josiah Whitney delivered the sermon. Putnam was buried in the yard of the Second Church.[91]

Dr. Albigence Waldo, surgeon and diarist of the sufferings of Washington's soldiers at Valley Forge, delivered a short but eloquent graveside eulogy: "Born a hero, whom nature taught, and cherished in the lap of innumerable toils and dangers—he was terrible in battle, but from the amiableness of his heart, when carnage ceased, his humanity spread over the field like the refreshing zephyrs of a summer's evening. The prisoners; the wounded; the sick; and the forlorn experienced the delicate sympathy of this soldier's pillar." Waldo called Putnam a "Christian soldier" who "pitied littleness, loved goodness, admired greatness, and ever aspired to its glorious summit."[92]

At the time of his death, Putnam was living in the same homestead as his youngest son, Peter Schuyler. An inventory of Putnam's estate compiled on June 12, shortly after his death, lists his various real properties, but it does not list any cash or slaves. However, the U.S. Census for 1790, the year of his death, lists Israel as head of a household that had one slave, perhaps belonging to Peter Schuyler. It is clear that he had given Kitt to Israel Jr. to accompany him to Ohio. The identity of that other slave is not known, whether he was Charles Pease, mentioned in his will, or his longtime slave, Dick. In any event, without evidence to the contrary, it is apparent that despite the changing law and attitudes toward slavery in Connecticut, the old man still clung to that "peculiar institution."[93]

In the decades following his death, hundreds of visitors came to see his grave, many of whom left with a chipping from the stone; so many, in fact that the stone was in danger of considerable damage. Accordingly, in 1888, his body was moved nearby in town, and, with much ceremony, a fitting memorial was erected to mark the spot. On a large base atop a sarcophagus bearing his mortal remains was placed a larger-than-life statue

Figure 9.   Putnam Grave, Brooklyn, Connecticut
COURTESY OF THE LIBRARY OF CONGRESS

of Putnam astride a horse, leading his troops forward. A wolf's head is attached to two sides of the base, reminders of his youthful exploit.

Happy Endings

Israel Putnam Jr. traveled back to Connecticut in the fall of 1790 to retrieve his family, and they all returned to Ohio in 1796 following the end of the Indian hostilities. The year before, he had sent two relatives to Ohio accompanied by two large saddlebags packed with grafted apple seedlings that he had carefully wrapped in beeswax for their protection. His son Aaron, who had remained in Ohio throughout the period of the Indian attacks, planted an orchard with them on the family lands staked out by his father near Belpre in 1790. It would be the start of a major industry along the southern tier of Ohio. Some, if not most, of the plants were taken from the old general's orchard, including his Roxbury Russet trees, sometimes called "Putnam Russet." Had he known about the plan, he would have enjoyed a hearty laugh to signify his immense pleasure.[94]

CHAPTER THIRTEEN

Afterward

THE MAN

The answer to the "Riddle of the Sphinx" is, of course, man, from infancy, to middle age, and finally, to decrepit old age. And Israel Putnam was, after all, a man with all his virtues and faults. A defining feature of this man is that he recognized the humanity in all free men, even his enemies, and he rarely, if ever, demonized them. Yet, like many of his generation, he failed to see the contradiction in the ownership of other men and women of color. Putnam had the rare ability to perform his duty as a soldier to the fullest and then to detach when the fighting was done. He could fight to kill without reservation, but in victory, he was able to show kindness to his vanquished adversary. This was in sharp contrast with the cruelty of his comrade in arms Robert Rogers. Putnam was horrified as he watched Rogers methodically kill, one by one, every seriously wounded French prisoner before withdrawing from the camp near Fort Carillon in 1758. What made it worse was that these were the same men Putnam had tended to the night before, and, in fact, to whom he had given his solemn assurances for their safety. It is another of life's ironies that, weeks later, Putnam would experience this same kindness from the Canadian Partisan leader, Marin, to whom he owed his life, after his capture and torture, and from the "savage" Caughnawaga chief, who oversaw his trek into captivity at Montreal.

During his decade-long service as a Provincial officer, Putnam had proven his leadership and fighting skills repeatedly. As a result, he had developed relationships, if not friendships, with many British officers.

During the Revolutionary War, he maintained cordial, but professional, relations with many of them, against whom he was now fighting. This was true at the siege of Boston, when he sent small gifts of provisions to Maj. Thomas Moncrieffe, and later at New York by facilitating the return of the major's daughter Margaret. It is easy to see why he would extend a courtesy to a gravely wounded British officer near Princeton to help him draft his will, or to share New Year's cheer with captured Hessian officers. This continued cordiality was something that many of Putnam's colleagues did not fully understand or appreciate. Certainly, Gov. George Clinton did not. It was simply part of Putnam's nature.

Putnam also had an innate sense of fairness and justice. In the case of the spy Edmund Palmer, or the two young men in Redding, he had no problem in enforcing the death penalty. With the mutiny of the Connecticut Line at Umpawaug, he meted out proportional justice, knowing full well that the men and their families had sacrificed much, were at their wits' end, and merely wanted to be heard by the General Assembly. Despite Washington's order to the contrary, he sent them all back to their huts, briefly incarcerated the ringleaders, and sanctioned a meeting in Hartford, rather than summoning a firing squad. In keeping with the New England tradition, he appealed to their patriotism and sense of duty, and his troops responded well.

Putnam's spelling notwithstanding, his later correspondence, mostly dictated to an aide, demonstrates that he was intelligent and articulate, able to express his thoughts well, if sometimes ungrammatically. This would be a source of much adverse comment by historians and others, who would quickly point to this trait as evidence of a lack of intelligence. In truth, he was more of a doer than a thinker, which may also have contributed to this false impression. One historian has narrowly opined that Putnam was good for one thing, fighting. It is true that he had a certain simplicity and lack of sophistication about him that has often been misread as ignorance by others, and if he suffered the verbal slights from the likes of Clinton, Dearborn, Hamilton, and Stark, he had many more loyal friends and admirers.

Putnam also had good sense of humor, even if it was at his expense. If he became a little full of himself at times, he was able to accept the good-natured ribbing from fellow officers like Horatio Gates and Charles Lee.

THE DEARBORN CONTROVERSY

Putnam's role and his whereabouts on June 17, 1775, were never an issue at all until some forty years after his death, when his reputation became the focal point of a lengthy political fight. Amid that controversy, Daniel Putnam asked John Adams if he was aware if "any dissatisfaction existed in the public mind against General Putnam" regarding his conduct at Bunker Hill. The old founder's reply would have been typical. "[I] do say without reserve that I never heard the least insinuation of dissatisfaction with the conduct of General Putnam through his whole life."[1]

During the first two decades of the nineteenth century, the Federalist Party still held sway in New England, but the Republican Party was making inroads. The contest for governor of Massachusetts in 1817 pitted the incumbent John Brooks, a Federalist, against Maj. Gen. Henry Dearborn, a Republican, and former secretary of war in the Jefferson administration. Both men were Revolutionary War veterans, each of whom served honorably throughout. Dearborn lost that contest and chose not to run against Brooks the following year.

Unable to challenge Brooks' courage, which was unassailable, he chose instead to attack the reputation of Israel Putnam, as the embodiment of Federalist ideals, when Dearborn wrote a short article in *Port-Folio Magazine* in 1818, detailing his own part in the Battle of Bunker Hill, on June 17, 1775, some forty-three years before. Dearborn called Putnam's popularity "ephemeral and unaccountable," and, among other things, he cited Putnam's overall lack of leadership and failure to cover the retreat.

No doubt there was a touch of envy and wounded pride in Dearborn's action. The bold Putnam's star still shone brightly after all these years, while the cautious and corpulent Dearborn, a senior major general, was forced to resign by President Madison after a lackluster performance during the late war. "[I]t was a duty I owe to posterity," Dearborn solemnly declared, "and [to] the character of those brave officers who bore a share in the hardships of the revolution."[2]

On June 17, 1775, Captain Dearborn had led a company in Stark's regiment, and he fought at the rail fence and not the redoubt. His claim that Putnam had absented himself from the front and, worse, that he failed to cover the retreat simply does not square with the reality as told by numerous eyewitnesses. For one thing, Dearborn did not reach the battlefield until around two o'clock that afternoon, when Stark reported to Putnam atop Bunker Hill, just as the British troops were landing at Morton's Point and forming up. Accordingly, he could not have known firsthand what Putnam's actions were earlier in the day. Second, at Putnam's direction, Captain Chester's company and others did make a short stand to cover the retreat, but like everyone else, in the end they joined the general retreat in the face of the overwhelming tide of British troops. Perhaps caught up in that movement, Dearborn failed to see the stand.

Nevertheless, the verbal cut and thrust quickly became a proxy war between Federalists and Republicans, involving family and friends in both camps. To paraphrase historian Robert Cray Jr., it created a "collision between past memories and present politics." For years, the debate generated dozens of pamphlets and other writings. It ran the gamut from who commanded at Bunker Hill, to the meaning of the "Spirit of '76," as each party appropriated the myths of the Revolution.[3]

The war of words finally ended in 1825 with a truce of sorts when both sides came together for the dedication of the Bunker Hill Monument on the fiftieth anniversary of the battle. Calling for "a true spirit of union and harmony," Daniel Webster's eloquent address on that occasion praised all the participants in the battle, both living and dead, harking back to their united sacrifice, when they were united in "one cause, one country, [and] one heart." The controversy reared its head, if only briefly, in 1843, with John Fellows' publication of *The Veil Removed*, a wholesale, baseless attack on Humphreys' essay on Putnam's life. The echoes of the Dearborn controversy, however, still reverberate to this day.[4]

CIVIC VIRTUE

Putnam was a natural leader, and he brought a passion to his work, whether farming or soldiering. He was as dependable as he was engaging, and he never lost that sense of duty. Time and again, throughout his long life, Israel Putnam demonstrated his commitment to the community, from his foray into the wolf's den, to his terms as a delegate to the General Assembly, or his service as a soldier. As the community prospered, so did he. Putnam would be the first to acknowledge the common wisdom of the saying that, "a rising tide lifts all boats."

In 1767, during the Stamp Act crisis, John Dickinson referred to the "decay of virtue." He told his readers in Letter XII that: "A people is traveling fast to destruction, when individuals consider their interests as distinct from those of the public. Such notions are fatal to their country, and to themselves." He went on to say that we should be on our guard against men who would lure us down that path. "Our vigilance and our union are success and safety," he observed, "and our division are distress and death."[5]

THE ENDURING LEGACY

Too often, Putnam was judged by his appearance and not by his honest heart. To many observers, he did not fit the image of a high-ranking officer; not one of the "gentlemen" Washington had in mind to fill his officer ranks. Dr. Thatcher described him as corpulent, with a booming voice. The captive Hessian officers in Philadelphia could hardly believe that he was a general officer. Putnam was not a grand strategist. He was a fighter, a blunt instrument, who lived in the moment and more than likely failed to grasp Washington's grand strategy. He was at his best when the assigned task was well-defined and he could focus all his energy on it. He would, therefore, have been a better regimental or brigade commander, as opposed to having an independent command. Historian Robert Middlekauff called Putnam a "natural force," and that "at the head of a regiment in assault he had few equals; in a staff meeting, few inferiors." As a result, he was out of his depth to a great degree in some situations.[6]

Israel Putnam was a man of the people, a farmer, a son of the soil, as were most of the men who served with him. It should, therefore, come as no surprise that John Dickinson chose the persona of a farmer to get his message across. Putnam was not one of the elites. He did not have a college degree, but a minimal formal education, if any. He was older and stout, and he bore the scars of battle during most of his adult life; he was not bewigged, but left his unruly curls, now white, for all to see. In short, he did not fit the stereotype. Silas Deane summed Putnam up best in a letter to his wife: "[It] seems he does not wear a large wig, nor screw his countenance into a form that belies the sentiments of his generous soul; he is no adept either at political or religious canting and cozening; he is no shake-hand body; he therefore is totally unfit for everything but fighting; [and] that department I never heard that these intriguing gentry wanted to interfere with him in."[7]

Putnam understood men and their everyday troubles and those of their families. When Washington urged firmness in quelling the mutiny at Redding, Putnam instinctively acted with compassion and exercised common sense. He had no pretenses. While George Washington was aloof, Putnam was approachable. He was beloved, while Washington was revered.

In February 1777, the often-acerbic John Adams remarked on the dearth of great generals, Washington excepted: "Many persons are extremely dissatisfied with numbers of the general officers of the highest rank. . . . Schuyler, Putnam, Spencer, Heath, are thought by very few to be capable of the great commands they hold. We hear of none of their heroic deeds of arms." He then bluntly concluded: "I wish they would all resign." Stephen Taaffe summed it up best when he observed that Putnam, and most of Washington's other generals, often, "displayed more courage than skill."[8]

Why is it important to preserve the heroic reputation of men like Israel Putnam? In the decades following the American Revolution, the concept of heroism became "democratized." No longer was it limited by race, gender, social status, or, for that matter, military service alone. The common threads running through it are service and sacrifice. Each succeeding generation is entitled to add to that continuum. This notion became frayed when caught up in the partisan politics during the first two decades of the nineteenth century, when Putnam's reputation came under attack. Daniel Webster issued a blunt warning to future generations of Americans. "The public . . . has an interest in the reputation of its distinguished men," Webster cautioned, "which, when it ceases to preserve or protect, it will cease to deserve distinguished services from any of its citizens."[9]

Is Israel Putnam relevant in the modern era? He should be, as his virtues transcend time. When each of us acts for the common good, the republic itself becomes that much stronger, and, in turn, the rights of all individuals within it flourish. As Michael Connolly's detective, Harry Bosch, frequently says: "Everybody counts, or nobody counts." Israel Putnam was flawed like every one of us, but we should overlook those flaws and celebrate, if not emulate, his virtues, such as his energy, passion, and willingness to sacrifice for the common good, as well as his humanity and deep love of country.

Notes

Preface

1. John S. Pancake, *1777: The Year of the Hangman* (Tuscaloosa: University of Alabama Press, 1992), 13.

2. George Washington to John Hancock, June 17, 1776, *Founders Online*, National Archives, https://founders.archives.gov/documents/Washington/03-05-02-0012; Stephen R. Taaffe, *Washington's Revolutionary War Generals* (Norman: Oklahoma University Press, 2019), 266.

Chapter 1

1. In 1787, David Humphreys returned from a diplomatic assignment in Europe and interviewed Putnam at his home in Brooklyn, Connecticut, to gather material for a monograph about his life. Humphreys also relied upon the writings of the Dr. Albigence Waldo, a friend of Putnam and his graveside eulogist, who had interviewed the old general about his early years and experiences during the French and Indian War. Much of the work was written at Mount Vernon while a guest of George Washington. The monograph, which went through several editions, was first published in the fall of 1788. Putnam died a little more than a year later. William Farrand Livingston, *Israel Putnam: Pioneer, Ranger, and Major General, 1718–1790* (New York: G. P. Putnam's Sons, 1901), 410; David Humphreys, *An Essay on the Life of the Honorable Major General Israel Putnam* (Indianapolis, IN: Liberty Fund, 2000), 8.

2. This date is expressed in the so-called New Style ("NS") Calendar that came about as a result of the adoption of the Gregorian Calendar in England and the Colonies in 1752. Prior to that time, the Julian Calendar was in effect, according to which, among other things, the New Year began on March 25. In order to make the adjustment, eleven days were removed from the calendar in 1752. Thus, if in fact, in Putnam's case the new calendar had been followed (i.e., eleven days had been added), according to the Julian Calendar, the so-called Old Style Calendar ("OS"), Israel Putnam was born on December 27, 1717. However, the transition did not occur uniformly, and many persons continued to hold on to their OS birthdate. Robert Middlekauff, *The Glorious Cause: The American Revolution, 1763–1789* (New York: Oxford University Press, 1982), 14–15.

3. Salem Village would later change its name to Danvers in 1752.

4. While many biographers hold that Putnam was born in an upstairs chamber, the evidence would not appear to support this. For one thing, according to a survey of the

dwelling found at the Library of Congress, the core of the existing structure, or "hall" as it was called, was a story and a half tall, possibly a "Cape Cod box" built by Israel's grandfather Thomas about 1641. The front of the house faced south along the highway, and it did not take on its present appearance until a major renovation in 1744, well after Putnam's birth. More than likely, the first floor of the hall consisted of two rooms, one behind the other, with a sleeping or storage loft above, and at most, the home had no more than four or five rooms. The inner room was sometimes referred to as the "buttery," and it was often used as an all-purpose room. By the turn of the eighteenth century, it would have been common for the home to have a brick chimney. L. Rowell, "General Notes on General Plan, Gen. Israel Putnam Birthplace, Danvers, Essex Co., Mass.," Works Progress Administration, Project No. 267-6907 (1936), Historic American Buildings Survey, Prints and Photographs Division, Library of Congress; Increase N. Tarbox, *Life of Israel Putnam ("Old Put") Major-General in the Continental Army* (Boston, MA: Lockwood, Brooks, 1876), 20–22 (description of home); David Hackett Fischer, *Albion's Seed: Four British Folkways in America* (New York: Oxford University Press, 1989), 62–68 ("Cape Cod box"); John Demos, *A Little Commonwealth: Family Life in Plymouth Colony* (New York: Oxford University Press, 2000), 29–31; James Deetz and Patricia Scott Deetz, *The Times of Their Lives: Life, Love, and Death in Plymouth Colony* (New York: W. H. Freeman, 2000), 173–74.

5. Livingston, *Israel Putnam*, 13; Barbour Collection, "Pomfret," CSLA ("Israel, Jr."); Henry Wheatland, *Baptisms at Church in Salem Village, Now North Parish, Danvers* (Salem, MA: Salem Press, 1880), 18–19; Robert Ernest Hubbard, *Major General Israel Putnam: Hero of the American Revolution* (Jefferson, NC: McFarland, 2017), 9–10.

6. I am aware of no contemporary descriptions of Putnam as a young man. Major Christopher French of the 22nd Regiment had been captured in August 1775, paroled, and taken to Wethersfield, Connecticut. On Monday, April 1, 1776, French dined with Putnam at Samuel Webb's family home and described Putnam as "about five feet six inches high, well set, and about 63 years old, and seems a good natured, merry man." By that time, Putnam (actually age fifty-eight) had gained considerable weight, but his height would have remained the same. Christopher French, "Major French's Journal, no. 2," April 1, 1776, *Collections of the Connecticut Historical Society*, vol. 1 (Hartford, CT: Connecticut Historical Society, 1860), 197.

7. At this time, it is estimated that one-third of New England brides were pregnant at the time of marriage. Mary Beth Norton, *Liberty's Daughters: The Revolutionary Experience of American Women, 1750–1800* (Boston: Little, Brown, 1980), 55.

8. The main routes from Boston to Hartford followed ancient Indian trails scattered throughout New England. One of the principal paths was called the "Great Trail" or the "Connecticut Path." With a wife and an infant in tow, Putnam would more than likely have used such a well-traveled route between established settlements, possibly with inns, taking them to the northeast corner of Connecticut. The area had been rapidly settling since the late 1600s. An early route from Boston passed through the towns of Medfield, Mendon, and Uxbridge in Massachusetts, and on through Killingly to Pomfret. Harral Ayres, *The Great Trail of New England: The Old Connecticut Path* (Boston: Meador Press, 1940), 298. This same route would later become an improved road called the "Middle

Road," which would pass through Hartford and on to New York City. George Francis Marlowe, *Coaching Roads of Old New England: Their Inns and Taverns and Their Stories* (New York: Macmillan, 1945), 52–72.

9. Livingston, *Israel Putnam*, 10–11.

10. Humphreys, *An Essay*, 15–16. Author's Note: The "servant" was undoubtedly a slave. See note no. 15.

11. Livingston, *Israel Putnam*, 13.

12. Humphreys, *An Essay*, 16–17; Farrand Livingston, *Israel Putnam*, 13–14. The cave has been preserved and is part of Mashamoquet Brook State Park in Pomfret.

13. The Roxbury Russet apple is considered the oldest cultivar grown in the United States. It traces its origins to Roxbury, Massachusetts, in about 1650. It is also sometimes alternately called "Putnam Russet," "Boston Russet," and "Sylvan Russet."

14. After the birth of Israel Jr. in 1740, the following children were born: Daniel (1742, died young), Hannah (1744), Elizabeth (1747, died young), Mehitable (1749), Mary ("Molly") (1753), Eunice (1756), Daniel (1759), David (1761, died young), and Peter Schuyler (1764), Barbour Collection, "Pomfret," CSLA; Mark Allen Baker, *Connecticut Families of the Revolution: American Forbears from Burr to Wolcott* (Charleston, SC: History Press, 2014), 109.

15. While the evidence is limited, it is irrefutable that Putnam had been a slave owner for decades. Other than Humphreys' reference to Putnam's unnamed servant at the wolf den, in the earliest recorded example, church records for Pomfret list the death of Putnam's "negro servant Pegge" [Peggy] on November 29, 1761. Barbour Collection, "Pomfret," CSLA; and in 1782, according to his Last Will and Testament, Putnam bequeathed two slaves, a Black and an Indian, to his youngest son, Peter Schuyler. Estate of Israel Putnam, Court of Probate, District of Pomfret, June 15, 1790, CSLA. While an early biographer acknowledges the prevalence of slavery in Massachusetts, and, in fact, throughout all the farming districts in New England, he pointedly neglects to make any mention of the fact that Putnam was a slaveholder. Rather, he chose to recite an apocryphal tale about Putnam's intervention in a dispute between his neighbor and the neighbor's unruly slave named "Cudge" to demonstrate Putnam's practical and humane solution to the problem. William Cutter, *The Life of Israel Putnam, Major-General in the Army of the American Revolution* (New York: George F. Cooledge & Brother, 1850), 29–30.

16. David Menschel, "Abolition Without Deliverance: The Law of Connecticut Slavery 1784–1848," *The Yale Law Journal* 111 (September 2001): 183–222; Jill Lepore, *The Name of War: King Philip's War and the Origins of American Identity* (New York: Knopf, 1998), 150–58 ("Indian captives"); Joel Lang, "Chapter One: The Plantation Next Door," *Hartford Courant* (September 29, 2002). Available at www.courant.com/news/special -reports/hc-plantation.artsept29-story.html. Accessed March 2021; David Prior, "Slavery in Revolutionary-Era Connecticut (Topical Guide)," *H-Net: Humanities & Social Sciences Online* (10-25-2017), available at https://networks,h-net.org/node/11465/pages/671377 /slavery-revolutionar-era-connecticut-topical-guide. Accessed March 2021.

CHAPTER 2

1. Charles J. Hoadly, ed., *The Public Records of the Colony of Connecticut, From May, 1751, to February, 1757, Inclusive*, vol. 10 (Hartford, CT: Case, Lockwood, 1877), 336–38 and 344–45 (hereafter PRCC 10); Thomas Fitch, "A Short Narrative of the General Conduct of Connecticut Relating to the War and Since the Year 1755," *The Fitch Papers: Correspondence and Documents During Thomas Fitch's Governorship of the Colony of Connecticut, 1754–1766*, vol. 1, May 1754–December 1758, Albert C. Bates, ed. (Hartford, CT: Hartford Printing Co., 1918), 345 (hereafter FP 1); Caroline Cox, *A Proper Sense of Honor: Service and Sacrifice in George Washington's Army* (Chapel Hill: University of North Carolina Press, 2004), 5 ("Provincials").

2. John R. Galvin, *The Minute Men: The First Fight: Myths and Realities of the American Revolution* (Washington, DC: Potomac, 2006), 6–7 and 10 ("Militia tradition"); Parkman, "Montcalm and Wolfe," in *France and England in North America*, vol. 2 (New York: Library of America, 1983), 1045 ("under penalty of a fine"); Hoadly, PRCC 10:344 ("fire-lock, sword, or hatchet").

3. Delphina L. H. Clark, *Phineas Lyman, Connecticut's General* (Springfield, MA: Connecticut Valley Historical Museum, 1964), 3–5; Livingston, *Israel Putnam*, 18–19 ("new home"); Suffield Library, "Phineas Lyman (1716–1774)." http://www.suffield-library.org/local history/lyman.htm. Accessed 2/28/2019.

4. Parkman, "Montcalm and Wolfe," 1041–46. Author's Note: During the fall of 1755, Dr. Richard Shuckburgh, a British army surgeon, was a guest at "Fort Crailo," the substantial home of John van Rensselaer in Green Bush. There, he was able to observe the passing of numerous Provincial troops going to and from their hometowns in Connecticut. The appearance of these unsoldierly appearing Provincials in their homespun, perhaps one or two young men with a feather in their hats, struck him as humorous. At night, Shuckburgh, who fancied himself a poet of sorts, entertained his hosts with a bit of doggerel set to a popular tune from *The Beggar's Opera*, a well-known staple of colonial entertainment. In time, it would be called simply, "Yankee Doodle." The obvious butt of his song was these Connecticut troops, as the term "Yankee," a corruption to the epithet "English Johnnies" (*Englese Jankes*), stemmed from its common usage by their early Dutch neighbors. A "Doodle" was Dutch for a fool. The term "macaroni" was clearly mocking, and a reference to the outrageously foppish fashion worn by some young men in England at the time. The song became enormously popular and was repeated in many versions with different verses by both the British and later, the Americans. Stuart Murray, *America's Song: The Story of "Yankee Doodle"* (Bennington, VT: Images from the Past, 1999), 10–11, 74–87, and 167–69.

5. John F. Ross, *War on the Run: The Epic Story of Robert Rogers and the Conquest of America's First Frontier* (New York: Bantam, 2011), 73–74 ("chokepoints"); Livingston, *Israel Putnam*, 17–18; Mary Pomeroy to Seth Pomeroy, August 9, 1755, Seth Pomeroy, Louis Effingham De Forest, ed., *The Journals and Papers of Seth Pomeroy: Sometime General in the Colonial Service* (New Haven, CT: Tuttle, Morehouse, 1926), 133–34 ("Braddock's defeat").

6. Parkman, "Montcalm and Wolfe," 1046–47 ("Fort Lyman"); Livingston, *Israel Putnam*, 147–48; Pomeroy, journal, July 17 through August 20, 1755, 103–109 and 130; Ian

K. Steele, *Betrayals: Fort William Henry and the "Massacre"* (New York: Oxford University Press, 1993), 38–39 ("eight miles"); Clark, *Phineas Lyman*, 15 ("Wood Creek road"); Livingston, *Israel Putnam*, 18–19 ("new home"); David R. Starbuck, "British Forts in Northern New York State," Christopher R. DeCorse and Zachary J. M. Beier, eds., *British Forts and Their Communities: Archaeological and Historical Perspectives* (Gainesville: University Press of Florida, 2018), 33 ("Fort Edward"). Author's Note: The so called "Great Carrying Place" was also the terminus of an alternate overland route to Lake Champlain, eleven miles to the site of Fort Anne on Wood Creek, which flows north and empties into the lake just beyond the present town of Whitehall (formerly Skenesboro). In 1755, it was not frequently used. However, it is likely that there were still traces of the old route that were used by raiding parties. Lyman and his troops began to build a road from Fort Edward to Fort Anne, perhaps along the old trace, but ultimately abandoned the project after seven or eight miles.

7. Parkman, "Montcalm and Wolfe," 1046–47.

8. Hoadly, PRCC 10:397–98; Fitch, "A Short Narrative of the General Conduct of Connecticut Relating to the War and Since the Year 1755," FP 1:344–45.

9. Hoadly, PRCC 10:398–400; Albert C. Bates, ed., *Rolls of Connecticut Men in the French and Indian War, 1755–1762*, vol. 1, 1755–1757 (Hartford, CT: Case, Lockwood, 1903), 41; Edmund S. Morgan, *The Genuine Article: A Historian Looks at Early America* (New York: Norton, 2004), 242 ("selection of officers"); Caroline Cox, *A Proper Sense of Honor: Service and Sacrifice in George Washington's Army* (Chapel Hill: University of North Carolina Press, 2004), 21–26 ("good discipline"); Richard M. Bayles, ed. *History of Windham County Connecticut* (New York: W. W. Preston, 1889), 53–54 ("enlisted in August"). Livingston incorrectly assumes that Putnam initially enlisted as a private in one of the Militia companies and was later commissioned. He also places Putnam at the Battle of Lake George. A review of the existing muster rolls does not support this, as he does not appear on any roll until September. Moreover, the muster rolls show that payments to Captain Putnam and his company commenced in September, which would be consistent with a later enlistment. Most telling is Humphrey's account, which describes the Battle of Lake George as a high point for the Provincial troops after Braddock's disastrous defeat. Humphreys wrote that he took the "liberty to swell this essay with reflections on events, in which Putnam was not directly concerned." Livingston, *Israel Putnam*, 17 ("volunteer"); Humphreys, *An Essay*, 20 and 41.

10. Phineas Lyman to Eleanor Lyman, September 10, 1755, and September 11, 1755, quoted in William Chauncey Fowler, *History of Durham, Connecticut* (Hartford, CT: Wiley, Waterman, 1866), 133–39; Steele, *Betrayals*, 44–47; William Johnson to Charles Hardy, September 16, 1755, FP 1:150–53; Parkman, "Montcalm and Wolfe," 1051–52.

11. Pomeroy, journal, September 8, 1755, 114–15; Parkman, "Montcalm and Wolfe," 1052–53 ("Bloody Morning Scout"); Ross, *War on the Run*, 75–76; Ephraim Williams made his Last Will & Testament in Albany at the start of the expedition. In it he made a bequest that became the foundation for the beginning of Williams College. Parkman, "Montcalm and Wolfe," 1044 ("Ephraim Williams").

12. Phineas Lyman to Eleanor Lyman, September 10, 1755, and September 11, 1755, Fowler, *History of Durham*, 133–39; Pomeroy, journal, September 8, 1755, 114–15; Parkman, "Montcalm and Wolfe," 1053–54.

13. Pomeroy, journal, September 8, 1755, 114–15; Parkman, "Montcalm and Wolfe," 1054 ("hailstones") and 1057 ("like devils"); Seth Pomeroy to Israel Williams, September 9, 1755, Pomeroy, 137–39 ("steadiness and resolution"); Ross, *War on the Run*, 74. The question of whether Johnson or Lyman should get the credit for the victory at Lake George has been an issue among some historians, while at the same time, ignoring Whiting's "handsome retreat." Milton W. Hamilton, "Hero of Lake George: Johnson or Lyman," *The New England Quarterly* 36, vol. 3 (September 1963): 371–82.

14. Parkman, "Montcalm and Wolfe," 1056; Ross, *War on the Run*, 76.

15. Pomeroy, journal, September 9–10, and October 9, 1755, 115 and 123; Steele, *Betrayals*, 61–62; Clark, *Phineas Lyman*, 20 ("votes to continue the expedition").

16. Fitch, "A Short Narrative of the General Conduct of Connecticut Relating to the War and Since the Year 1755," FP 1:345–46; Humphreys, *An Essay*, 18 ("command of a company"); Livingston, *Israel Putnam*, 20 ("second lieutenant"); Pomeroy, journal, October 9, 1755, 123 ("arrival of Connecticut troops").

17. Livingston, *Israel Putnam*, 26 and 29 ("endurance and bravery"); Humphreys, *An Essay*, 19.

18. Ross, *War on the Run*, 113–14; Fred Anderson, *Crucible of War: The Seven Year's War and the Fate of Empire in British North America, 1754–1766* (New York: Knopf, 2000), 180–81.

19. Ross, *War on the Run*, 17–23 ("early life") and 64–68 ("counterfeit currency"); Robert Rogers, *Journals of Major Robert Rogers* (Reprinted from the original edition of 1765) (New York: Corinth, 1961), iv–v; Parkman, "Montcalm and Wolfe," 1137 ("counterfeit currency").

20. Starbuck, "British Forts," 33–36; Jabez Fitch Jr., *The Diary of Jabez Fitch, Jr., in the French and Indian War 1757*, September 23, 1757 (Fort Edward, NY: New York State French & Indian War 250th Anniversary Commemoration Commission, 2007), 26 ("new bridge to island"). One historian described the pontoon bridge built on "cabled bateaux." Ross, *War on the Run*, 145 and 152. Ross also states at pages 146–47 that, "Rogers had been camping on the island ever since the late summer of 1757." I have used Starbuck's earlier date.

21. David Hackett Fischer, *Champlain's Dream* (New York: Simon & Schuster, 2008), 266–70.

22. Robert Rogers to William Johnson, *Report*, October 12, 1755, "Journals of Sir Wm. Johnson's Scouts, 1755, 1756," E. B. O'Callaghan, ed., *The Documentary History of the State of New York*, vol. 4 (Albany, NY: Charles Van Benthuysen, 1851), 262–63 (hereafter DCHNY).

23. Israel Putnam to Robert Rogers, *Report*, October 12, 1755; and Samuel Hunt to Robert Rogers, *Report*, October 12, 1757, DCHNY 4:264–65.

24. Robert Rogers to William Johnson, *Report*, October 12, 1755, DCHNY 4:262–63; Rogers, *Journals*, 2–3; Livingston, *Israel Putnam*, 30–33 ("first scout"); Pomeroy, journal, October 7 and 11, 1755, 122 and 124 ("Rogers returns"). Rogers' journal for the period

October 7 through 10 describes a similar mission carried out by Rogers and five men and is clearly at variance with his own contemporaneous report, and that of three others, including Putnam. Since it was published nearly a decade later, I have discounted it.

25. Robert Rogers, Jonathan Butterfield, and Israel Putnam to William Johnson, Report, October 22, 1755, DCHNY 4:269–70; Pomeroy, journal, October 15, 1755, 125 ("Rogers leaves on October 14"); Livingston, *Israel Putnam*, 33–36; Humphreys, *An Essay*, 19–20. Humphreys' account of the incident is out of sequence, as it occurred more than six weeks after the "Bloody Scout" that took place on September 8. Curiously, in the report Rogers makes no mention of Putnam by name, only that "I with another man ran up to him" (the lone French soldier). In his journal, Rogers describes this same incident as having taken place between October 21 and October 30. This is clearly an error as indicated by his contemporaneous report to Johnson, which I have relied upon. Rogers, journal, October 21, 1755, 4.

26. Robert Rogers, Israel Putnam, and Noah Grant to William Johnson, Report, November 3, 1755, DCHNY 4:272–73; Rogers, journal, November 4, 1755, 4–6; Livingston, *Israel Putnam*, 36–40; Rogers' journal states that the scout took place between November 4 and November 8. Once again, I have relied upon the contemporaneous report for the dates. The facts are at some variance, but he is describing the same incident.

27. Humphreys, *An Essay,* 20–21; Robert Rogers, Israel Putnam, and Noah Grant to William Johnson, Report, November 3, 1755, DCHNY 4:272–73; Livingston, *Israel Putnam*, 36–40. Humphreys' account places Putnam's scout near the "ovens," which are on the east side of the La Chute River near the portage itself. However, there is no indication in the official report that any party crossed over the lake or the river. Rather, the activity in question would appear to be near the French camp on the west side of Lake George near its outlet.

28. Robert Rogers, Israel Putnam, and Noah Grant to William Johnson, Report, November 3, 1755, DCHNY 4:272–73; Rogers, journal, November 4, 1755, 4–6; Livingston, *Israel Putnam*, 38–40.

29. Robert Rogers, Israel Putnam, and Noah Grant to William Johnson, Report, November 3, 1755, and Roger Billing to William Johnson, Report, November 2, 1755, DCHNY 4:272–74; Rogers, journal, November 4, 1755, 4–6; Livingston, *Israel Putnam*, 40.

30. Livingston, *Israel Putnam*, 41; Pomeroy, journal, October 11, 1755, 124 ("lack of blankets and proper clothing"); Parkman, "Montcalm and Wolfe," 1060 ("close to mutiny").

31. Bates, *Rolls of Connecticut Men*, 1:76 ("Col. Bagley") and 1:79 ("Putnam's Company"); Parkman, "Montcalm and Wolfe," 1060 ("composite regiment").

32. Livingston, *Israel Putnam*, 42 ("Ebenezer Dyer"); Israel Putnam, Certification, May 19, 1760, CSLA #973.26 P98.

33. Hoadly, PRCC 10:469–474 ("Fourth Company"); Fitch, "A Short Narrative," FP 1:347 ("2,500 men").

34. Barbour Collection, "Pomfret," CSLA; Livingston, *Israel Putnam*, 42 ("daughter Eunice born") and 43 ("Spanish dollars"); Hoadly, PRCC 10:538–39 ("fifty Spanish-milled dollars").

CHAPTER 3

1. Fitch, "A Short Narrative," FP 1:347. Author's Note: The British commanding general's name has been spelled two ways, "Abercromby" and "Abercrombie." I have used the former, as that is the spelling used by Fred Anderson.

2. Rogers, *Journals*, 16–17.

3. Anderson, *Crucible of War*, 180–81; Luke Gridley, diary, May 25, 1757, *Luke Gridley's Diary of 1757: While in Service in the French and Indian War* (Hartford, CT: Hartford Press, 1907), 30–31 ("wooden horse"); Rufus Putnam, journal, June 27, 1757, E. C. Dawes, ed., *Journal of Gen. Rufus Putnam: Kept in Northern New York During Four Campaigns in the Old French and Indian War, 1757–1760* (Albany, NY: Joel Munsell's Sons, 1886), 32 ("first time").

4. Gridley, diary, May 25, 1757, 30 ("gauntlet").

5. Livingston, *Israel Putnam*, 45–46.

6. Humphreys, *An Essay*, 23–24; Livingston, *Israel Putnam*, 46–47.

7. Humphreys, *An Essay*, 21–23; Livingston, *Israel Putnam*, 48–50. This incident along with the scout of November 4, 1755, are described in detail by Humphreys, who erroneously lumps them together into the same summer. Curiously, this action is not mentioned by Rogers in his journal, while the other is described in detail. Since Putnam did not arrive at Fort Edward until sometime after September 8, 1755, I have placed the incident as occurring sometime during the summer of 1756, that is, after the November 1755 scout. Rogers did recount several other scouts during the summer of 1756 in his journal written a decade after the event described, while Humphreys' account is based on a more than thirty-year gap. Livingston's account is very detailed.

8. Anderson, *Crucible of War*, 151–55; Parkman, "Montcalm and Wolfe," 1123–27; Steele, *Betrayals*, 79 and 133.

9. Parkman, "Montcalm and Wolfe," 1135; Livingston, *Israel Putnam*, 51. Parkman observed that of all the other Provincial officers, "blunt and sturdy" Putnam stood out from among all the rest.

10. Livingston, *Israel Putnam*, 52; Fitch, "A Short Narrative," FP 1:348; Anderson, *Crucible of War*, 181–82 ("quartering").

11. Hoadly, PRCC 10:598–602; Bates, *Rolls of Connecticut Men*, 1:176; Fitch, "A Short Narrative," FP 1:348; Ashbel Woodward, *Memoir of Col. Thomas Knowlton of Ashford, Connecticut* (Boston, MA: Henry W. Dutton, 1861), 3 and 15.

12. Robert Rogers, journal, 36 and 38 ("illness"); Ross, *War on the Run*, 136–39.

13. Gridley, diary, May 19, 1757, 28–29.

14. Jabez Fitch, diary, May 29, 1757, 2–3; Ross, *War on the Run*, 137 ("Richard Rogers"); Robert Rogers, journal, 36–37 and 55–56 ("Loudoun's order"); Bates, *Rolls of Connecticut Men*, 1:176 ("Lt. Porter and Ensign Hayward").

15. Gridley, diary, June 6 and 10, 1757, 33–35; Samuel Porter to wife, June 1757, cited in Livingston, *Israel Putnam*, 54–55. Author's Note: The area commonly referred to as "the Narrows" is halfway down Lake George where a peninsular formed by Tongue Mountain juts into the lake from the west, along with a scattering of small islands close by. There are other narrow places in the wider area, one being the outlet of the lake where it enters the La Chute River (sometimes called the "French Narrows"), as well as the place where that

river enters Lake Champlain. Also, on old maps, Wood Creek meets Lake Champlain near Ticonderoga, however, in more recent times, that portion of Wood Creek south to South Bay is considered part of Lake Champlain. There is a narrowing north of White-hall, referred to in an old source as the "Elbow." All these locations, in one account or another, have been referred to as narrows.

16. Gridley, diary, June 6 and 10, 1757, 35.

17. James L. Kochan, ed., Introduction, "Joseph Frye's Journal and Map of the Siege of Fort William Henry, 1757," *Bulletin of the Fort Ticonderoga Museum* 15, no. 5 (1993): 340–41; Rufus Putnam, journal, June 15 and June 16, 1757, 23 and 29.

18. Gridley, diary, June 6 and 10, 1757, 35–36; Rufus Putnam, journal, June 15 and June 16, 1757, 29; Samuel Porter to wife, June 1757, cited in Livingston, *Israel Putnam*, 54–55.

19. Jabez Fitch, diary, June 25–26, 1757, 7; Livingston, *Israel Putnam*, 56–57; Hum-phreys, *An Essay*, 31–32.

20. Steele, *Betrayals*, 84. When Putnam was held a prisoner in Montreal in 1759, he was told that the leader of the raiding party on June 30, 1757, was the partisan Marin. Livingston, *Israel Putnam*, 59.

21. Jabez Fitch, diary, July 1 to 4, 1757, 8–10; Livingston, *Israel Putnam*, 58–59; Hum-phreys, *An Essay*, 32–33.

22. Jabez Fitch, diary, July 1, 1757, 9; Humphreys, *An Essay*, 34 ("all friends"); Living-ston, *Israel Putnam*, 60.

23. Jabez Fitch, diary, July 1 to 4, 1757, 8–10; Rufus Putnam, journal, July 1 and July 4, 1757, 33 ("South Bay") and 34–35 ("horribly mutilated"); Livingston, *Israel Putnam*, 56–60; Humphreys, *An Essay*, 31–35; James Montresor, journal, July 1, 1757, G. D. Scull, ed., *The Montresor Journals* (New York: New York Historical Society, 1882), 18; Gridley, diary, June 29 ("East Bay") and July 1, 1757, 39; Benjamin Hayward, diary, July [1], 1757 ("General Lyman"), Robert O. Bascom, ed., "Diary of Ensign Hayward of Woodstock, Conn., Kept Principally at Fort Edward in 1757," *The Fort Edward Book: Containing Some Historical Sketches with Illustrations and Family Records* (Fort Edward, NY: James D. Keating, 1903), 95.

Author's Note: (1) Humphrey's account is more expansive and differs from Putnam's journal in minor details. He incorrectly wrote that the fight took place after the fall of Fort William Henry, which actually occurred the following month. Since the Rufus Put-nam, Montresor, and Gridley journals were written contemporaneously with the events, they should be relied upon as to the date they took place; (2) The area of the fight is fairly inaccessible by land given the terrain and the changes to Wood Creek, with the later construction of a lock and dam at Whitehall. Wood Creek commences about five miles east of Fort Edward and flows north and east through the towns of Fort Ann (site of the then-abandoned Fort Anne) and Whitehall, where today it forms Lake Champlain. At that time, the waterway flowed freely through woods and later through a valley flanked by steep granite walls. There was a falls at what is now Whitehall, New York, that later powered grist and sawmills, and it is more than likely the falls mentioned in Fitch's diary. Its principal tributary is Halfway Brook, so called, as it is crossed halfway along the road from Fort Edward to Lake George. Halfway Brook also begins east of the Hudson and flows north and east into Wood Creek near Fort Ann. Shortly before it enters Wood Creek, it drops sixty feet at a place called Kane Falls. Putnam's Ledge or Rock was a shelf of rock at water's edge. According to Jabez Fitch, the bay or creek at that point was about fifteen rods wide. It was a good place for an ambush.

24. Rufus Putnam, journal, July 5 and July 27, 1757, 35 ("six companies") and 39 ("rum ration"); Bates, *Rolls of Connecticut Men*, 1:262–63; Rogers, *Journals*, 51 ("camp on island").

25. James Montresor, journal, July 13, 1757, 20.

26. Gridley, diary, July 23, 1757, 43–44; Rufus Putnam, journal, July 23 and 24, 1757, 37–38; Rowena Buell, ed., *The Memoirs of Rufus Putnam and Certain Official Papers and Correspondence* (Boston, MA: Houghton, Mifflin, 1903), 13 ("such scenes" and "cautious"); James Montresor, journal, July 23, 1757, 22; Humphreys, *An Essay*, 28–30; Livingston, *Israel Putnam*, 61–65.

27. Anderson, *Crucible of War*, 185–89; Parkman, "Montcalm and Wolfe," 1182.

28. Anderson, *Crucible of War*, 193; Parkman, "Montcalm and Wolfe," 1182 ("log rampart"); Buell, *Memoirs of Rufus Putnam*, 14. At a council of war on July 27, several questions were discussed, including the number of men needed to defend the fort, and more important, whether to defend both sites or one, and if one, which one. Colonel James Montresor, a Royal engineer, noted in his diary that he felt two thousand men would be needed, and that they should only defend one site, the Retrenched Camp on Titcomb's Mount. As it turned out, General Webb and Lieutenant Colonel Monro thought otherwise. James Montresor, journal, July 27, 1757, 24; Benjamin Hayward, "Diary of Ensign Hayward," Robert O. Bascom, ed., *The Fort Edward Book: Containing Some Historical Sketches with Illustrations and Family Records* (Fort Edward, NY: James D. Keating, 1903), 95n6 ("Upper Fort").

29. James Montresor, journal, July 24, 1757, 22; Gridley, diary, July 26, 1757, 45; Ross, *War on the Run*, 139–40 ("Sabbath Day Point"); Anderson, *Crucible of War*, 189–90; Parkman, "Montcalm and Wolfe," 1174–75.

30. Humphreys, *An Essay*, 25–26 ("What do you think"); Rufus Putnam, journal, July 25 and 30, 1757, 38–39; James Montresor, journal, July 25 and 29, 1757, 22–23; Gridley, diary, July 25 and 29, 1757, 44–46 ("all the carpenters"); Montresor's journal entry for July 29 states that they "set out from" Fort William Henry that day, while Rufus Putnam's journal entry for July 30 notes that "General Webb came down from the lake."

31. Joseph Frye, journal, August 1–2, 1757, James L. Kochan, ed., "Joseph Frye's Journal and Map of the Siege of Fort William Henry, 1757," *The Bulletin of the Fort Ticonderoga Museum* 15 , no. 5 (1993): 339–61; Jabez Fitch, diary, August 2, 1757, 16–17; James Montresor, journal, August 2, 1757, 23; Rufus Putnam, journal, August 1 and 2, 1757, 39; Humphreys, *An Essay*, 26; Steele, *Betrayals*, 98; Humphreys incorrectly states that Webb sent Monro to Fort William Henry to reinforce it. Lieutenant Colonel Monro had replaced Maj. William Eyre and was already there. Webb sent Col. Joseph Frye with part of his Massachusetts Regiment, along with some regulars under a Lt. Col. John Young. Several field pieces and crews had been sent earlier.

32. James Montresor, journal, August 3, 1757, 23 ("flotilla"); Frye, journal, August 3, 1757, 348–49 ("surrender demand"); Jabez Fitch, diary, August 3, 1757, 17 ("cannon fire"); Ross, *War on the Run*, 139 ("Rogers in Nova Scotia").

33. Gridley, diary, August 5, 1757, 47 ("two of Putnam's men"); Ross, *War on the Run*, 140–41; Steele, *Betrayals*, 102 and 105 ("letter").

34. Jabez Fitch, diary, August 10, 19; Anderson, *Crucible of War*, 191–96; Parkman, "Montcalm and Wolfe," 1181–88; Fitch, "A Short Narrative," FP 1:348–49 ("Webb's emergency request"); Parkman, "Montcalm and Wolfe," 1183 ("patently hypocritical").

35. James Montresor, journal, August 6, 1757, 26–27; Ross, *War on the Run*, 191–92 ("Lord Howe").

36. Rufus Putnam, *Memoirs*, 14–15 ("coward"); James Montresor, journal, August 8, 1757, 27 ("surveyed high ground").

37. Frye, journal, August 3–9, 1757, 347–53; Steele, *Betrayals*, 99–108.

38. Frye, journal, August 10, 1757, 356–57; Steele, *Betrayals*, 112–24.

39. Frye, journal, August 10, 1757, 356–57 and 359 ("tore to pieces"); Anderson, *Crucible of War*, 195–98; Parkman, "Montcalm and Wolfe," 1188–93.

40. James Montresor, journal, August 14, 1757, 29 ("Montcalm's letter").

41. Jabez Fitch, diary, August 21, 1757, 21; Rufus Putnam, journal, August 21 and 30, and September 1 to 3, 1757, 43; Humphreys, *An Essay*, 28; Rufus Putnam, *Memoir*, 15 ("lacking in humanity").

42. Jabez Fitch, diary, August 30, 1757, 22; Rufus Putnam, journal, August 30 and September 1 to 3, 1757 ("Black soldier"), and September 20, 1757 ("Rogers returns"), 44; Gridley, diary, August 26, 27, and 30, 1757, 51. Putnam had two Black men in the 4th Company that had been enlisted as privates in Connecticut by Gallup and Creary, to wit: Cato and Cesar (Caesar), possibly free men, but just as easily slaves serving as substitutes. It is likely that Putnam had recruited one or both for his Ranger Company.

43. Gridley, diary, October 13 and 17, 1757, 57.

44. Charles J. Hoadly, ed., *The Public Records of the Colony of Connecticut, From May, 1757, to March, 1762, inclusive*, vol. 11 (Hartford, CT: Case, Lockwood, 1880), 61–62; Livingston, *Israel Putnam*, 71; Bates, *Rolls of Connecticut Men*, 1:262 (reference to Putnam at Fort Edward on November 10); Fitch, "A Short Narrative," FP 1:349 ("contingent of 280 Rangers"). Although their one-year enlistments ran until March 1, 1758, the men expected to be sent home at the close of the 1757 campaign. Connecticut was by no means alone. Loudoun also demanded that Massachusetts leave behind a contingent of 360 men to man the forts that winter. Rufus Putnam was one of those "drafted" to remain. Rufus Putnam, *Memoirs*, 13; Rufus Putnam, journal, November 18, 1757, 49–50; William Seward, ed., *General Orders of 1757: Issued by the Earl of Loudoun and Phineas Lyman in the Campaign Against the French* (New York: Dodd, Mead, 1899), 134 ("twelve men").

45. Ross, *War on the Run*, 150–52; Seward, *General Orders of 1757*, 135 ("firewood and vegetables").

46. Jabez Fitch, diary, December 25, 1757, 38–39 ("fire"); Rufus Putnam, journal (longer), April 6, 1773, 168; Humphreys, *An Essay*, 35–36 ("fire"); Livingston, *Israel Putnam*, 71–72 ("fire"). Author's Note: Throughout the years, Putnam has had his share of naysayers and skeptics, none more so than John Fellows, who by casting doubt on the incident

at Fort Edward applies that skepticism across the board to Humphreys' biographical essay. However, facts are stubborn things, and history does, in fact, back Humphreys up. John Fellows, *The Veil Removed; or Reflections on David Humphreys' Essay on the Life of Israel Putnam* (New York: J. D. Lockwood, 1843), 55–56.

47. Jabez Fitch, diary, January 3–6, 1758, 41; Ross, *War on the Run*, 143–44 and 161–62 ("flood").

48. Jabez Fitch, diary, January 10 and 12, 1758, and February 21, 1758, 42 and 49–50.

49. Jabez Fitch, diary, February 28, 1758, 50–51; Rogers, *Journals*, 57–58.

50. Livingston, *Israel Putnam*, 73.

CHAPTER 4

1. Anderson, *Crucible of War*, 371–72 ("contract of service") and 410–14 ("contributions of Provincial soldiers"); John Whiteclay Chambers II, *To Raise an Army: The Draft Comes to Modern America* (New York: Free Press, 1987), 14–17 ("contract" and "substitution").

2. Rufus Putnam, journal, June 27 and September 5, 1757, and February 2, 1758, 33 and 45 ("flogging"), and 50–52 ("headed for home"); Ross, *War on the Run*, 149–50 ("corporal punishment"); Theodore Draper, *A Struggle for Power: The American Revolution* (New York: Times Books, 1996), 177 ("Connecticut and Massachusetts").

3. Anderson, *Crucible of War*, 139–40, 214, 226, and 229.

4. Hoadly, PRCC 11:92–99 ("major"); Fitch, "A Short Narrative," FP 1:349–50; Albert C. Bates, *Rolls of Connecticut Men in the French and Indian War, 1755–1762*, vol. 2, 1758–1762 (Hartford, CT: Case, Lockwood, 1905), 58 ("3rd Company"), and 92 ("Ranger Company").

5. James Abercromby to William Pitt, July 12, 1758, Gertrude Selwyn Kimball, ed., *Correspondence of William Pitt When Secretary of State with Colonial Governors and Military and Naval Commissioners in America*, vol. 1 (New York: Macmillan, 1906), 297–302 (hereafter CWP); Anderson, *Crucible of War*, 241.

6. Rufus Putnam, journal, July 1–5, 1758, 63–66; Rufus Putnam, *Memoirs*, 23; Hayden, journal, July 1–5, 1758, Augustin Hayden, *The French and Indian War Journals of Augustin Hayden, 1758–1759* (Windsor, CT: Windsor Historical Society, 1984).

7. Anderson, *Crucible of War*, 259–60 ("Bradstreet"); Francis Parkman, *The Oregon Trail and the Conspiracy of Pontiac* (New York: Library of America, 1991), 735 ("more activity than judgment"); Rufus Putnam, *Memoirs*, 23.

8. Abercromby to Pitt, July 12, 1758, CWP 1:297–302; Rufus Putnam, journal, July 5–6, 1758, 66–67; Rufus Putnam, *Memoirs*, 23; Hayden, journal, July 5–6, 1758; Livingston, *Israel Putnam*, 75–76.

9. Parkman, "Montcalm and Wolfe," 1265–66 ("abatis"); Livingston, *Israel Putnam*, 80–81; Anderson, *Crucible of War*, 241–42 ("abatis"); Ross, *War on the Run*, 201–202 ("abatis"); Ian Macpherson McCulloch, "'A blanket of inconsistencies. . .' The Battle of Fort Ticonderoga," *Journal of Military History* 72, no. 3 (July 2008): 895–96 ("living trees" and "picket posts").

10. Robert Rogers, journal, 82; Humphreys, *An Essay*, 36–37 ("your life"); Livingston, 76–78. Captain Charles Lee of the 44th Foot would later write that Howe's "only fault

was not knowing his own value." Charles Lee, "The Lee Papers, vol. 1, 1754–1776," *Collections of the New York Historical Society for the Year 1871* (New York: Printed for the Society, 1872), 9–15.

11. Abercromby to Pitt, July 12, 1758, CWP 1:298; Parkman, "Montcalm and Wolfe," 1263–65 ("death of Howe"); Humphreys, *An Essay*, 37–38; Livingston, *Israel Putnam*, 78–80; Charles Lee, "Narrative-enclosed in letter of September 16, 1758," Lee Papers 1:9–15 ("Indian war cry"); Hayden, journal, July 6, 1757. Author's Note: There is some difference of opinion among historians as to the spelling of Captain Dalyell's surname, some referring to him as "D'Ell" (Humphreys), "Dalyell" (Anderson and Ross), and Dalzell (Parkman). The spellings are variants of a Scottish surname found in the Clyde Valley in Scotland, as well as Counties Down and Louth in Ireland. Rogers uses "Dalyell" in his journal, and Humphreys uses what is undoubtedly a phonetic spelling, no doubt passed on to him by Putnam. Accordingly, I have used Dalyell.

12. Humphreys, *An Essay*, 38; Robert Rogers, journal, 9. Not surprisingly, Rogers does not mention the execution of the French wounded.

13. Abercromby to Pitt, July 12, 1758; McCulloch, "'A blanket of inconsistencies,'" 894–95; Robert Rogers, journal, 83; Parkman, "Montcalm and Wolfe," 1264.

14. Robert Rogers, journal, 83; McCulloch, "'A blanket of inconsistencies,'" 895 and 897–98.

15. McCulloch, "'A blanket of inconsistencies,'" 895–97; Rufus Putnam, journal, July 8, 1758, 69 ("floating batteries").

16. McCulloch, "'A blanket of inconsistencies,'" 896; Anderson, *Crucible of War*, 242–43 ("without artillery"); Livingston, *Israel Putnam*, 81 ("warnings").

17. Rufus Putnam, journal, July 8, 1758, 69–70 ("breastwork"); Robert Rogers, journal, 83–84; Ross, *War on the Run*, 201–204.

18. Anderson, *Crucible of War*, 243–46; Parkman, "Montcalm and Wolfe," 1268–72; Rufus Putnam, journal, July 8, 1758, 70 ("Lyman's regiment"); Livingston, *Israel Putnam*, 83.

19. Charles Lee, "Narrative-enclosed in letter of September 16, 1758," Lee Papers 1:9–15.

20. Parkman, "Montcalm and Wolfe," 1272 ("1,944 killed, wounded, and missing"); Humphreys, *An Essay*, 39 ("two thousand"); Livingston, *Israel Putnam*, 83 ("covers retreat").

21. Charles Lee to Sister, September 16, 1758, Lee Papers 1:6–9.

22. Abercromby to Pitt, July 12, 1758 CWP; McCulloch, "'A blanket of inconsistencies,'" 895–96; Ross, *War on the Run*, 199–200 ("Bradstreet and foreign engineer"); Parkman, "Montcalm and Wolfe," 1267; Anderson, *Crucible of War*, 242–43; Livingston, *Israel Putnam*, 81–83; Humphreys, *An Essay*, 38–39; Rufus Putnam, *Memoirs*, 24–25; Charles Lee, "Narrative" enclosed in Letter of September 16, 1758, Lee Papers 1:9–15 ("stripling").

23. Rufus Putnam, journal, July 9, 1758, 72; Phineas Lyman to Jonathan Trumbull, August 1, 1758, FP 1:350–51; Clark, *Phineas Lyman*, 41–42.

24. Humphreys, *An Essay*, 39–41; Livingston, *Israel Putnam*, 85–86.

25. Rogers, journal, July 27 to August 8, 1758, 85–86; Abercromby to Pitt, August 19. 1758, CWP 1:316–27; Humphreys, *An Essay*, 41; Ross, *War on the Run*, 207–208.

26. Rogers, journal, August 8, 1758, 85–86; Abercromby to Pitt, August 19, 1758, CWP 1:316–27; Humphreys, *An Essay*, 41–42; Ross, *War on the Run*, 209–211. Author's Note: After the passage of more than thirty years, in relating his story to Humphreys, Putnam referred to the partisan leader as "Molang." Close, but he more than likely confused the name with Paul Marin. Perhaps Humphreys misheard him.

27. Hayden, journal, August 8, 1758 ("Putnam captured"); Bates, *Rolls of Connecticut Men*, 2:57; Rogers, journal, August 8, 1758, 85–86; Abercromby to Pitt, August 19, 1758, CWP 1:316–27; Humphreys, *An Essay*, 42–44; Parkman, "Montcalm and Wolfe," 1280–82; Ross, *War on the Run*, 209–211.

28. Rogers, journal, August 8, 1758, 85–86; Abercromby to Pitt, August 19, 1758, CWP 1:316–27; Bates, *Rolls of Connecticut Men*, 2:57 and 92 ("casualties").

29. Daniel Putnam to Henry Dearborn, May 4, 1818, *Account of the Battle of Bunker's Hill by H. Dearborn, with a Letter to Maj. Gen. Dearborn, Repelling His Unprovoked Attack on the Character of the Late Maj. Gen. Israel Putnam by Daniel Putnam, Esq.* (Boston, MA: Munroe & Francis, 1818); Humphreys quoted a different version of the saying in connection with that incident: "Rogers always sent, but Putnam led his men to action." Humphreys, *An Essay*, 42 ("Putnam leads").

30. Barbour Collection, "Pomfret," CSLA ("Daniel"). Author's Note: In 1922, the Daughters of the American Revolution erected a bronze tablet on a rough granite stone, marking the spot approximately 182 feet away where the tree stood that Putnam was tied to and nearly burned alive. The marker is on the east side of Lake Road in Essex County, New York, approximately five miles south of the remains of the fort at Crown Point. Assuming that the placement of the marker is correct, the escaping French raiding party would likely have already passed Fort Carillon, since the location of the tree is closer to Crown Point. However, Putnam is clear that after his brush with death while tied to the tree, he was brought before General Montcalm at Ticonderoga before being taken to Montreal. French records indicate that Montcalm remained at Fort Carillon until early November 1758, when he left for winter quarters in Canada. The most logical explanation is that Marin feared that at some point his Indian allies would find a way to kill Putnam before they reached Montreal, and that Montcalm was the only person with sufficient stature to keep them in check, so he doubled back to Fort Carillon.

31. Humphreys, *An Essay*, 44–47.

32. Humphreys, *An Essay*, 47–48.

33. Pitt to Abercromby, September 18, 1758, CWP 1:353–54; Pitt to Colony of Connecticut, September 18, 1758, Thomas Fitch, "A Short Narrative," FP 1:353–54.

34. Abercromby to Pitt, November 25, 1758, CWP 1:399–406; Anderson, *Crucible of War*, 259–65.

35. Anderson, *Crucible of War*, 283.

36. Abercromby to Vaudreuil, October 1, 1758, and Abercromby to Schuyler, October 1, 1758, DCHNY 10:878–79 ("authorize Schuyler"); Humphreys, *An Essay*, 48.

37. James Prevost to Captain de Becourt, November 13, 1758, DCHNY 10:897 ("arrived November 11"); Abercromby to Pitt, November 25, 1758, CWP 1:399–406; Humphreys, *An Essay*, 48–53.

38. Thomas Fitch to William Pitt, April 16, 1759, CWP 2:84–87.

39. Hoadly, PRCC 11:221–26.

40. Hoadly, PRCC 11:251–57; Anderson, *Crucible of War*, 317–21 ("recruiting difficulties").

41. Parkman, "Montcalm and Wolfe," 1139; Hoadly, PRCC 11:226–28 ("lt. col."); Bates, *Rolls of Connecticut Men*, 2:163 ("2nd Company").

42. Henry Skinner, journal, June 3 to July 20, 1759, Gary S. Zaboly, ed., "A Royal Artillery Officer with Amherst: The Journal of Captain-Lieutenant Henry Skinner, 1 May–28 July 1759," *The Bulletin of the Fort Ticonderoga Museum* 15, no. 5 (1993): 363–81.

43. Jeffery Amherst, journal, July 21, 1759, J. Clarence Webster, ed., *The Journal of Jeffery Amherst: Recording the Military Career of General Amherst in America from 1758 to 1763* (Toronto, Canada: Ryerson Press, 1931), 141–42; Skinner, journal, July 21, 1759, 381–82.

44. Skinner, journal, July 21–24, 1759, 381–84; Hayden, journal, July 22–26, 1759; Rufus Putnam, journal, July 22–26, 1759, 88–91; Amherst, journal, July 22, 1759, 142–43.

45. Skinner, journal, July 26–27, 1759, 384–86; Robert Webster, diary, July 26, 1759, Fort Ticonderoga Museum; Hayden, journal, July 27, 1759; Rufus Putnam, journal, July 27, 1759, 91 ("1:00 a.m."); Amherst, journal, July 23–29, 1759, 143–48; Parkman, "Montcalm and Wolfe," 1360–63 ("fall of Ticonderoga"); Anderson, *Crucible of War*, 340–43; Humphreys, *An Essay*, 53. Author's Note: Sergeant Robert Webster was a member of the Seventh Company under the command of Capt. David Holmes of Woodstock, Connecticut. Bates, *Rolls of Connecticut Men*, 2:167–68.

46. Webster, diary, August 15, 1759, Fort Ticonderoga Museum ("exhausted"); Amherst, journal, August 4, 1759, 150–52 ("partially blown up") and August 22, 1759, 159–60 ("Putnam's post"); John Hawks, journal, August 8, 1759, Hugh Hastings, ed., *Orderly Book and Journal of Major John Hawks: On the Ticonderoga–Crown Point Campaign, Under General Jeffery Amherst, 1759–1760* (New York: Society of Colonial Wars, 1911), 59–60.

47. Anderson, *Crucible of War*, 333–38 ("capture of Fort Niagara"), and 364–65 ("surrender of Quebec"); Parkman, "Montcalm and Wolfe," 1363–68 ("Fort Niagara"); Amherst to Pitt, August 5, 1759, CWP 2:146–48 ("Prideaux"); Amherst, journal, July 28, 1759, 148; Charles Lee to William Bunbury, August 9, 1759, Lee Papers 1:20–22.

48. Amherst, journal, August 8, 1759, 153, September 9, 1759, 166–67, and October 26, 1759, 184–85; Amherst to Pitt, October 22, 1759, CWP 2:187–202 ("road to No 4"); Webster, diary, September 9, 1759, Fort Ticonderoga Museum; Anderson, *Crucible of War*, 343.

49. Amherst to Pitt, December 16, 1759, CWP 2:219–26 ("sick to Albany" and "mutiny"); Webster, diary, October 2 through 7, 1759.

50. Rufus Putnam, journal, November 18 through 25, 1759, 101–103 ("March to Fort at No. 4"); Webster, diary, October 26 through November 16, 1759.

51. Amherst, journal, November 24–25, 1759, 193–94 ("Fitch's Regiment"); Thomas Fitch, FP 2:38–39 ("Fort at No. 4"); Barbour Collection, "Pomfret," CSLA ("Daniel"); Livingston, *Israel Putnam*, 106 ("Daniel").

52. Jeffery Amherst to Thomas Fitch, February 14, 1760, and Jeffery Amherst to Thomas Fitch, February 21, 1760, FP 2:50–54; Thomas Fitch to William Pitt, April 11, 1760, FP 2:60–61 ("reimbursement").

53. Hoadly, PRCC 11:349–57; Bates, *Rolls of Connecticut Men*, 2:215 ("2nd Company"); Thomas Fitch to Jeffrey Amherst, March 28, 1760, FP 2:57–60.

54. Jeffery Amherst to Thomas Fitch, April 20, 1760, and Thomas Fitch to Jeffery Amherst, April 25, 1760, FP 2:62.

55. Thomas Fitch to Jeffrey Amherst, April 25, 1760, FP 2:63.

56. Jeffery Amherst to Thomas Fitch, April 27, May 11, and June 1, 1760, and Thomas Fitch to Jeffery Amherst, May 23, 1760, FP 2:64–68.

57. Bates, *Rolls of Connecticut Men*, 2:215 ("few new recruits"); Amherst, journal, June 22, 1760, 212; Amherst to Pitt, June 21, 1760, CWP 2:305–309.

58. Parkman, "Montcalm and Wolfe," 1444 ("three-pronged plan"); Anderson, *Crucible of War*, 364–65 ("surrender of Quebec"), and 400–403 ("three-pronged plan"); Humphreys, *An Essay*, 53–54.

59. Amherst, journal, 221.

60. Amherst, journal, August 10 through 17, 1760, 227–32; Amherst to Pitt, August 26, 1760, CWP 2:324–29; Parkman, "Montcalm and Wolfe," 1449 ("Ottawa"); Humphreys, *An Essay*, 53–54 ("two vessels"). Author's Note: Amherst makes no mention of Putnam's stratagem with the first boat in either his journal or his letter to Pitt, however, whether or not Putnam had a hand in the success, it is clear from his report that one enemy vessel did run aground, which is consistent with Humphreys' account.

61. Amherst, journal, August 18–26, 1760, 232–40; Amherst to Pitt, August 26, 1760, CWP 2:324–29.

62. Parkman, "Montcalm and Wolfe," 1449–50 ("Fort Lévis"); Anderson, *Crucible of War*, 401–402; Humphreys, *An Essay*, 54–55. Author's Note: According to Humphreys, Putnam suggested that before an assault on the fort, the whaleboats be fitted out with a long plank to drop on the abatis and allow the attackers to cross over it. Once again, it is possible that Putnam had made such a suggestion at an officer's meeting, but that it was never acted upon. For another, Amherst could well have harbored some prejudice regarding Provincial officers, particularly a lieutenant colonel like Putnam. Amherst makes no mention of Putnam. He does write that while the Grenadiers were poised to stage the landing at Fort Lévis, on August 20, he had also called up both David Wooster's and Eleazar Fitch's regiments from Oswegatchi, so Putnam would have been present six days prior to the planned assault. In any event, the fort surrendered prior to the planned amphibious infantry assault. Amherst later renamed it Fort William Augustus. Amherst, journal, August 20, 1760, 235–36 ("Wooster and Fitch").

63. Amherst, journal, August 31 to September 4, 1760, 241–44; Amherst to Pitt, September 8, 1760, CWP 2:329–33.

64. Amherst to Pitt, September 8, 1760, CWP 2:329–33; Samuel Jenks, September 8, 1760, *The Diary of Captain Samuel Jenks, During the French and Indian War, 1760* (Cambridge, MA: Harvard University Press, 1890), 28 ("rain"); Parkman, "Montcalm and Wolfe," 1450–52; Anderson, *Crucible of War*, 405–409.

65. Amherst, journal, September 11, 1760, 248–49; Humphreys, *An Essay*, 55.

66. Hoadly, PRCC 11:478–87; Bates, *Rolls of Connecticut Men*, 2:239–41 ("2nd Company"); Amherst, journal, June 8, 1761, 266.

67. Amherst to Fitch, October 11, 1761; Fitch to Amherst, October 19, 1761, and October 27, 1761, FP 2:146–48.

68. Barbour Collection, "Pomfret," CSLA ("David" and "Peggy"); Livingston, *Israel Putnam*, 116; Baker, *Connecticut Families*, 109 ("David"); Muster Roll, November 23, 1761, FP 2:161–62. Author's Note: While the language in the church record calls Peggy a "servant," it is clear from other evidence that she was, in fact, a slave and the word was simply a euphemism.

CHAPTER 5

1. Amherst, journal, February 19, 1761, 279; Anderson, *Crucible of War*, 497–99.
2. Hoadly, PRCC 11:612–21; Bates, *Rolls of Connecticut Men*, 2:298–301; Clark, *Phineas Lyman*, 57.
3. Clark, *Phineas Lyman*, 57–58; William Starr Myers, ed., "Log of an American Marine in 1762 on a British Fighting Ship," *Journal of American History* 3 (1909): 114.
4. Anderson, *Crucible of War*, 499; "An Authentic Journal of the Siege of Havana by an Officer," June 2, 1762, Edward Everett Hale, Sr., ed., *The Capture of Havana in 1762 by the Forces of George III: Being Two Authentic Reports of the Siege and Capture of Havana by the Combined Forces of Great Britain and the American Colonies* (Cambridge, MA: Cooperative Printing Society, 1898), 11 ("Spanish unaware").
5. "Journal of the Siege," June 7 and 15, 1762, 12–13 and 17–18; Anderson, *Crucible of War*, 499–501.
6. "Journal of the Siege," June 11, 1762, 16–19 and 18; Patrick McKellar, "A Correct Journal of the Landing of His Majesty's Forces on the Island of Cuba; and of the Siege and Surrender of the Havannah, June 8 through 11, 1762," Hale, ed., *The Capture of Havana in 1762 by the Forces of George III*, 4–7.
7. "Journal of the Siege," June 10 and 14, 1762, 15–17.
8. "Journal of the Siege," June 25 to 27, June 29, July 1, and July 4, 1762, 19–23 and 24–25 ("more resolute"); McKellar, "A Correct Journal," July 1, 1762, 11.
9. "Journal of the Siege," June 16–19 ("two or three men"), July 4 ("succumbed to heat"), July 8 and 9 ("infinite numbers"), July 13, 1762 ("reduced guard"), and July 23 through 27, 1762 ("5,000"), 18, 24–28, and 31–32; McKellar, "A Correct Journal," June 3, 1762, 9 ("500 slaves").
10. "Journal of the Siege," July 8 and 9, and 16 through 18, and July 22, 1762, 26–31; McKellar, "A Correct Journal," July 22, 1762, 19–20.
11. Myers, "Log of an American Marine," June 11 and 16, 1762, 114; Amherst, journal, June 4 through 11, 1761, 282–84; Clark, *Phineas Lyman*, 57–58.
12. Myers, "Log of an American Marine," July 19, 1762, 114. Absent a copy of the ship's manifest, we do not know for sure if this was the vessel that carried Putnam and part of the Connecticut Regiment. While Humphreys does not name the transport, Swann's eyewitness account dovetails closely with Putnam's experience as related by Humphreys. Also, Swann was part of that Connecticut Regiment, so it stands to reason that the Connecticut troops sailed with the first convoy. Later, Swann's own transport (*Swallow*) and several others, as well as the warship *Chesterfield*, would strike a reef in high seas in the Old Bahama Channel at Cayo Confites on July 23 and sink, necessitating their own rescue. Swann specifically mentions General Lyman and Majors Durkee and Hierlihy as being shipwrecked with him on Sugar Key, but he makes no mention

of Lieutenant Colonel Putnam, who, as second-in-command of the regiment, would naturally have been mentioned if he was there with them. This should not be surprising, as it would also be fair to assume that, as a prudent measure, Lyman and Putnam would sail on different vessels. No mention of the *Juno*'s sinking is made by the anonymous diarist, who corroborates Swann in other respects. In a letter to Amherst, Lyman himself mentions that he was shipwrecked, but from Swann, we know that it was on Sugar Key near Cayo Confites, and not farther east. Clark, *Phineas Lyman*, 58. Accordingly, since the first shipwreck was clearly a separate incident, I have assumed that Putnam's transport was the *Juno*.

13. Humphreys, *An Essay*, 56–57; Livingston, *Israel Putnam*, 118–20.

14. Myers, "Log of an American Marine," July 23 and August 1, 1762, 114–15. Lieutenant Swann writes that on August 1 he saw the *Falls* and *Enterprize* with the survivors from *Juno* aboard sail past on their way to Havana, five day's sail west from Cayo Confites. Thus, Putnam and his men would have arrived at Havana sometime around August 6, in time to take part in the siege of Havana and the Punta.

15. McKellar, "A Correct Journal," July 30, 1762, 23–24; "Journal of the Siege," July 30–31, 1762, 33–35.

16. "Journal of the Siege," July 28–29, 1762, 32–33; Myers, "Log of an American Marine," 114; McKellar, "A Correct Journal," July 28, 1762, 22; Levi Redfield, *A Succinct Account of the Memorable Events and Remarkable Occurrences in the Life of Levi Redfield, Late of Connecticut, now Residing in Brattleboro, Ver.* (Brattleboro, VT: B. Smead, 1798), 6–8.

17. Amherst, journal, July 5, 1762, 286–87; "Journal of the Siege," August 2, 1762, 36–37; Anderson, *Crucible of War*, 500–501.

18. Myers, "Log of an American Marine," August 4 and 9, 1762, 115; Redfield, *A Succinct Account*, 8. Author's Note: Redfield's memoir, which was written thirty-six years after the fact, says August 10.

19. "Journal of the Siege," August 1 through 13, 1762, 37–40; McKellar, "A Correct Journal," August 1 and 5, 1762, 24 and 26.

20. Myers, "Log of an American Marine," August 10, 1762, 115; McKellar, "A Correct Journal," August 9–10, 1762, 28–29.

21. "Journal of the Siege," August 10 through 13, 1762, 35–38; McKellar, "A Correct Journal," August 10 through 13, 1762, 28–30; Anderson, *Crucible of War*, 501.

22. Israel Putnam, "Orderly Book of the Havana Expedition," August 25–26, 1762, Albert C. Bates, ed., *The Two Putnams: Israel and Rufus in the Havana Campaign 1762 and in the Mississippi Expedition 1772–73 with Some Account of The Company of Military Adventurers* (Hartford, CT: Connecticut Historical Society, 1931), 57–59.

23. Bates, "Historical Introduction," *The Two Putnams*, 5–9; Clark, *Phineas Lyman*, 59; Graham, journal, September 28–October 19, 1762, 12 and 17–18; according to the *Pictorial History of England*, field officers like Putnam received 564£ 14s 6d. McKellar, "A Correct Journal," Appendix.

24. Nearly 150 years later in Cuba, American troops would experience much the same effects from tropical disease, particularly yellow fever, as effective troop strength dropped. The situation became so bad that senior officers prevailed upon Lt. Col. Theodore Roo-

sevelt to write what would later become known as the "Round Robin" letter requesting immediate relief. This caused a quite a stir in Washington but proved effective in obtaining immediate orders to withdraw the initial contingent of units that had been deployed to Cuba. David F. Trask, *The War with Spain in 1898* (Lincoln: University of Nebraska Press, 1996), 331–32.

25. John Graham, journal, September 25, 1762, *Extracts from the Journal of the Reverend John Graham, Chaplain of the First Connecticut Regiment, Colonel Lyman, From September 25th to October 19th 1762, at the Siege of Havana* (New York: Society of Colonial Wars in the State of New York, 1896), 8–9; Israel Putnam, "Orderly Book," August 29 and September 3, 15–16, and 29, 1762 ("replacements"); September 26 and September 5 and 8, 1762 ("notice of auction"); and September 13, 1762, 78–80 ("guard mount").

26. Graham, journal, September 25 and 30, 1762, 8–9 and 12–13. Author's Note: While Graham does not mention Putnam by name, he refers to "the 2d in Command in the Regiment."

27. Graham, journal, October 7 and 11, 1762, 15–16; Clark, *Phineas Lyman*, 58 ("spoiled provisions"); Israel Putnam, "Orderly Book," August 31, September 2, 23, and 28, 1762, 64–66, 68–69 ("patrols"), 90–91, and 96–97.

28. Livingston, *Israel Putnam*, 126–27. Author's Note: The U.S. Census for 1790 lists Israel Putnam as Head of Household and includes one slave, possibly Dick. 1790 U.S. Census, State of Connecticut, Windham County, Town of "Brooklyne." According to the same census, there were 2,764 slaves living in Connecticut, which represented 1.2 percent of the population.

29. Jonathan Trumbull, Sr. to William Samuel Johnson, December 12, 1769, "Trumbull Papers, Early Miscellaneous Papers," *Collections of the Massachusetts Historical Society*, Fifth Series, vol. 9 (Cambridge, MA: University Press, 1885), 388–91 (hereafter MHS5).

30. Graham, journal, October 3 and 10, 1762, 14–15.

31. Myers, "Log of an American Marine," October 11, 19, and 22, 1762, 116–17; Graham, *Extracts*, October 10 and 21, 1762; Israel Putnam, "Orderly Book," October 14, 1762, 105–110; Trumbull, Sr. to Johnson, December 12, 1769, "Trumbull Papers," MHS5 9:388–91. Author's Note: (1) Originally, 109 men enlisted in his company, but 11 deserted and 2 were arrested by the sheriff before sailing for Cuba. Bates, *Rolls of Connecticut Men*, 2:299–301; (2) According to Amherst, one-quarter of the deaths occurred during the voyage home. Amherst, journal, November 28, 1762; and (3) In May 1766, the General Assembly voted to pay Dana's estate the sum of £15 proclamation money or bills "towards the defraying of the expense of the deceased incurred in his sickness." Charles J. Hoadly, ed., *The Public Records of the Colony of Connecticut, From May, 1762, to October, 1767, Inclusive*, vol. 12 (Hartford, CT: Case, Lockwood, 1881), 487 ("Ensign Dana").

32. Myers, "Log of an American Marine," November 22, 1762, 117; Amherst, journal, November 11, 1762, 298.

33. Anderson, *Crucible of War*, 505–506; Clark, *Phineas Lyman*, 59–60.

34. Trumbull, Sr. to Johnson, December 12, 1769, "Trumbull Papers," MHS5 9:388–91.

C<small>HAPTER</small> 6

1. Anderson, *Crucible of War*, 503–506; Bernard Bailyn, *Voyagers to the West: A Passage in the Peopling of America on the Eve of the Revolution* (New York: Vintage, 1988), 485 ("return of Cuba"); Paul E. Hoffman, *Florida's Frontiers* (Bloomington: Indiana University Press, 2002), 208–209.

2. Clark, *Phineas Lyman*, 60.

3. Bates, "Historical Introduction," 9–11; Franklin Bowditch Dexter, ed., *Extracts from the Itineraries and Other Miscellanies of Ezra Stiles, D.D., LL.D., 1755–1794, with a Selection from His Correspondence* (New Haven, CT: Yale University Press, 1916), 218; Anderson, *Crucible of War*, 595–96; Bernard Bailyn, *The Peopling of North America: An Introduction* (New York: Vintage, 1988), 66–75 ("speculation").

4. Bates, "Historical Introduction," 10–11; Clark, *Phineas Lyman*, 61.

5. Amherst, journal, July 23, 1763, 312–13 ("Pitt Packet"); Bates, "Historical Introduction," 11; Clark, *Phineas Lyman*, 61–62.

6. Colin G. Calloway, *The Scratch of a Pen: 1763 and the Transformation of North America* (New York: Oxford University Press, 2006), 92–94; Anderson, *Crucible of War*, 560–71.

7. Bates, "Historical Introduction," 12–14; Calloway, *Scratch of a Pen*, 94.

8. Calloway, *Scratch of a Pen*, 92–94.

9. Anderson, *Crucible of War*, 469–71 ("Amherst's new policies").

10. Anderson, *Crucible of War*, 535–38 ("rise of Pontiac"); Alvin M. Josephy Jr., *The Patriot Chiefs: A Chronicle of American Indian Resistance* (New York: Viking, 1969), 98–100, and 108–112; Francis Parkman, *The Conspiracy of Pontiac* (New York: Library of America, 1991), 483–87.

11. Calloway, *Scratch of a Pen*, 70–72 ("seven posts"); Anderson, *Crucible of War*, 538–46 ("fall of posts"); Josephy, *Patriot Chiefs*, 117–19 ("loss of posts").

12. Josephy, *Patriot Chiefs*, 119 ("ambitious and impulsive").

13. Amherst, journal, September 2, 1763, 319–20; Parkman, *Conspiracy of Pontiac*, 570–76; Anderson, *Crucible of War*, 547–48; Josephy, *Patriot Chiefs*, 120–21 ("Bloody Run"); Humphreys, *An Essay*, 57–58 ("death of Dalyell").

14. Anderson, *Crucible of War*, 548.

15. Amherst, journal, November 17, 22, 24, and 30, 1763, 324–25; Anderson, *Crucible of War*, 617–19 ("cautious"). The official transfer of command would take place on December 9, 1764, after the expedition had returned. John Montresor, journal, December 9, 1764, 321 ("orders this day").

16. Lyman to Durkee, November 3, 1763, quoted in Bates, "Historical Introduction," 14–15.

17. Joseph Trumbull to Jonathan Trumbull, January ___, 1764, quoted in Clark, *Phineas Lyman*, 65–66. Author's Note: The issue remained unsolved as late as 1773, as a notice appeared in the *Norwich Packet* dated December 13 calling for a meeting at the home of John Durkee, "to enquire why the last dividend of their prize money has not been paid." Frances Manwaring Caulkins, *History of Norwich, Connecticut* (Hartford, CT: Case, Lockwood & Brainard, 1873), 358.

18. Hoadly, PRCC 12:232–34 ("major") and 12:241–49 ("lt. col."); Livingston, *Israel Putnam*, 129–31 ("commands battalion") and 158 ("Selectman").

19. Humphreys, *An Essay*, 48 ("capture of Fort Frontenac") and 57; Livingston, *Israel Putnam*, 131–32 ("commands regiment"); Parkman, *Conspiracy of Pontiac*, 735–36; Josephy, *Patriot Chiefs*, 126 ("1,200 men").

20. Charles Lee to William Bunbury, August 9, 1759, Lee Papers, 1:20–22 ("most magnificent"); Livingston, *Israel Putnam*, 132–33; John Montresor, journal, July 16, 1764, 272 ("Ojibway").

21. John Montresor, journal, July 16, 1764, 272 ("500 men"); Amherst, journal, September 30, 1763, 322 ("Devil's Hole"); Livingston, *Israel Putnam*, 132.

22. John Montresor, journal, July 16–18, 1764, 272–73; Fort Schlosser was built by the British about 1760 near the site of an abandoned French post called La Petite Niagara or more colloquially, Fort du Portage, to guard the upper end of the portage around Niagara Falls. An old stone chimney is all that remains (a part of the French fort later incorporated within Fort Schlosser) on the site, which is now located within the limits of the city of Niagara Falls, New York. New York State Military Museum and Veterans Research Center, "Fort Schlosser," https://dmna.ny.gov/forts/fortsQ_S/schlosserFort.htm. Accessed 2/2/2019.

23. John Montresor, journal, July 18 through August 9, 1764, 273–79; Livingston, *Israel Putnam*, 133.

24. Livingston, *Israel Putnam*, 134.

25. Parkman, *Conspiracy of Pontiac*, 746 ("You have concluded"); John Montresor, journal, September 25, 1764, 298–99 ("disapprobation of the peace concluded").

26. Livingston, *Israel Putnam*, 135.

27. John Montresor, journal, August 31 and September 7, 1764, 286–87 ("narrow ax men"). *Île aux* Cochons was so called by the early French settlers who let their pigs and other livestock roam the island. It was later named "Belle Isle" and is now a municipal park managed by the state of Michigan located within the city of Detroit.

28. Humphreys, *An Essay*, 58 ("accept reality"); John Montresor, journal, September 14 through October 17, 1764, 291–311 ("Sandusky"); Livingston, *Israel Putnam*, 138–44.

29. Putnam to Durkee, October 7, 1754, *The Connecticut Courant*, December 17, 1764 ("illy-used").

30. Israel Putnam to John Durkee, October 7, 1754, *The Connecticut Courant*, December 17, 1764; Bates, "Historical Introduction," 14–16 ("Bull's Tavern").

31. John Montresor, journal, October 18 through November 3, 1764, 311–18; Livingston, *Israel Putnam*, 145; Parkman, *Conspiracy of Pontiac*, 759–60 ("perished miserably in the woods").

32. John Montresor, journal, November 3 and 4, 1764, 318; Livingston, *Israel Putnam*, 1901), 145.

33. John Montresor, journal, November 7 through 11, 1764, 319–21 ("perfect Tempest with a snow drift"); Livingston, *Israel Putnam*, 145–46. Livingston states that the flotilla left Fort Niagara on November 8, but Montresor's journal clearly states that it was the following day.

34. John Montresor, journal, November 12 through 19, 1764, 321 ("arrived Albany"); Livingston, *Israel Putnam*, 146.

35. Anderson, *Crucible of War*, 288.

CHAPTER 7

1. Barbour Collection, "Pomfret," CSLA ("Peter Schuyler," "Elizabeth," and "Hannah"); Livingston, *Israel Putnam*, 147–48; Hubbard, *Major General Israel Putnam*, 49. In addition to Israel Jr., Putnam's eldest daughter, Hannah, had married John Winchester Dana and was no longer living at home.

2. Livingston, *Israel Putnam*, 158 ("Selectman"). The office of selectman is one that originated in early colonial New England, as voters at the annual town meeting chose one or more responsible (i.e., "select") men to handle the day-to-day business of the community for the following year. The practice persists to this day throughout New England. Demos, *A Little Commonwealth*, 7–8; Louis Grosvenor, *The Life and Character of Maj. General Putnam: An Address Delivered at a Meeting of the Descendants of Maj. General Israel Putnam* (Boston, MA: Farwell & Company, 1855), 16 ("profession of faith").

3. Anderson, *Crucible of War*, 560–71 and 585–86. According to Anderson, the colonies met 80 to 90 percent of their levies, but the British subsidies amounted to only 40 percent of the actual costs; Thomas Fitch, "A Short Narrative of the General Conduct of Connecticut Relating to the War and Since the Year 1755," FP 1:349 (discussing the financial burden of the colony); Nathan Whiting to Ezra Stiles, March 26, 1761, Dexter, ed., *Extracts*, 104.

4. Draper, *Struggle for Power*, 218 and 270–71; Anderson, *Crucible of War*, 572–80 ("Sugar Act") and 641–51; Bruce Frohnen, ed., "The Stamp Act, March 22, 1764," *The American Republic: Primary Sources* (Indianapolis, IN: Liberty Fund, 2002), 110–14.

5. Andrew David Edwards, "Grenville's Silver Hammer: The Problem of Money in the Stamp Act Crisis," *Journal of American History* (September 2017): 346–49; George Washington to Francis Dandridge, September 20, 1765, *Founders Online*, National Archives, accessed September 29, 2019, https://founders.archives.gov/documents/Washington/02-07-02-0250.

6. Thomas Fitch, "Reasons Why the British Colonies in America Should not be Charged with Internal Taxes by Authority of Parliament," Hoadly, PRCC 12:662.

7. Fitch, "Reasons Why," Hoadly, PRCC 12:659; John Dickinson, "Letter VII," *Letters from a Farmer in Pennsylvania to the Inhabitants of the British Colonies*, Forrest McDonald, ed., *Empire and Nation: John Dickinson, Letters from a Farmer in Pennsylvania; Richard Henry Lee, Letters from the Federal Farmer*, second edition (Indianapolis, IN: Liberty Fund, 1999), 38–45.

8. Jared Ingersoll to Thomas Fitch, February 11, 1765, FP 2:317–26.

9. Jill Lepore, "Back Issues," *New Yorker* 84, no. 46 (January 26, 2009): 68–73 ("Franklin"); Jeffrey L. Pasley, *The Tyranny of Printers: Newspaper Politics in the Early American Republic* (Charlottesville: University of Virginia Press, 2001), 36.

10. John Ferling, *A Leap in the Dark: The Struggle to Create the American Republic* (New York: Oxford University Press, 2003), 54 ("child Independence").

11. Claire Priest and Justin du Rivage, "The Stamp Act and the Political Origins of American Legal and Economic Institutions" (2015). *Faculty Scholarship Series* 4934. https://digitalcommons.law.yale.edu/fss_papers/4934.

12. Barnet Schecter, *The Battle for New York: The City at the Heart of the American Revolution* (New York: Walker & Co., 2002), 22–23 ("Isaac Barré"); Livingston, *Israel*

Putnam, 154 ("committee of eight"). It is one of the rich ironies of history that the term "Sons of Liberty" was coined by a British parliamentarian and introduced in America by Jared Ingersoll, then acting as a colonial agent in London and later appointed as a stamp agent in Connecticut. The latter sent a letter to Gov. Thomas Fitch, in which he quotes Barré, which phrase was, in turn, adopted by the forces in opposition to the Stamp Act. Ingersoll to Fitch, February 11, 1765, FP 2:317–26.

13. David Colden to Jared Ingersoll, October 28, 1765, FP 2:367–68. The *Gaspee* was later captured and burned in Narragansett Bay on June 10, 1772, by a group of Rhode Island citizens.

14. Humphreys, *An Essay*, 61–62 ("leveled with the dust"); Livingston, *Israel Putnam*, 152–53 ("late 1765").

15. "General Israel Putnam," *Hartford Daily Courant*, November 1, 1855, p. 2; Bayles, *History of Windham County*, 62–63; Livingston, *Israel Putnam*, 151–53.

16. John Montresor, journal, March 24, 1764, 355 ("10,000 men"); Humphreys, *An Essay*, 62 ("no stamped paper in Connecticut"); Richard M. Ketchum, *Divided Loyalties: How the American Revolution Came to New York* (New York: Henry Holt, 2002), 166.

17. Hoadly, PRCC 12:451–52 ("May") and 12:493–94 ("October"); Livingston, *Israel Putnam*, 154 ("General Assembly"); Humphreys, *An Essay*, 62 ("injuries").

18. John Montresor, journal, February 24, 1764, 350 ("utmost lives and fortunes"); Schecter, *The Battle for New York*, 25 ("repeal"); Rick Atkinson, *The British Are Coming: The War for America, Lexington to Princeton, 1775–1777* (New York: Henry Holt, 2019), 8 ("£45").

19. Hoadly, PRCC 12:541 ("January") and 12:545–46 ("May"); Barber Collection, "Pomfret," CSLA ("remarriage"); Livingston, *Israel Putnam*, 155; Baker, *Connecticut Families of the Revolution*, 109–110; Mercy Otis Warren to Abigail Adams, April 17, 1776, Founders Online, National Archives, http://founders.archives.gov/documents/Adams/04-01-02-0250.

20. Livingston, *Israel Putnam*, 155–58; Hoadly, PRCC 12:605–607 ("October").

21. Livingston, *Israel Putnam*, 158–61.

22. Charles J. Hoadly, *The Public Records of the Colony of Connecticut, From May, 1768, to May, 1772, Inclusive*, vol. 13 (Hartford, CT: Case, Lockwood, 1885), 631 ("Lovett's Bridge"). Two years earlier, in 1770, Putnam, along with Seth Paine and Samuel Williams, were appointed a committee to oversee "the rebuilding of Danielson's Bridge over the Quinebaug River." Livingston, *Israel Putnam*, 158–59.

23. Caulkins, *History of Norwich*, 369–70.

CHAPTER 8

1. Hoffman, *Florida's Frontiers*, 211 ("headrights and grants"); Calloway, *Scratch of a Pen*, 94 ("grants"); Clarence E. Carter, "Some Aspects of British Administration in West Florida," *The Mississippi Valley Historical Review* 1 (June 1914 to March 1915): 369 ("grants").

2. Carter, "Some Aspects of British Administration," 365 ("original line").

3. Carter, "Some Aspects of British Administration," 365–67 ("reset northern boundary"); Dunbar Rowland, ed., *Encyclopedia of Mississippi History: Comprising Sketches of*

Counties, Towns, Events, Institutions and Persons, vol. 2 (Madison, WI: Selwyn A. Brant, 1907), 997–98 (s.v. "Yazoo-Chattahoochee Line").

4. Bailyn, *Voyagers to the West*, 29–32 ("Hillsborough") and 484–85; Carter, "Some Aspects of British Administration," 367–68 ("20,000 acres").

5. Horace Walpole to Earl of Dartmouth, August 24, 1772, *The Connecticut Courant*, November 3–9, 1772, p. 2. Historian Malcolm Rohrbough's study of trans-Appalachian settlement demonstrates the initial need for security before the elements of a stable government, including courts and schools, can take root. Malcolm J. Rohrbough, *Trans-Appalachian Frontier: Peoples, Societies, and Institutions, 1775–1850* (Bloomington: Indiana University Press, 2008), 22–49.

6. John Francis Hamtramck Claiborne, *Mississippi as a Province, Territory and State with Biographical Notices of Eminent Citizens*, vol. 1 (Jackson, MS: Power & Barksdale, 1880), 108 ("Thaddeus"); Stiles, *The Literary Diary*, October 24, 1772, and November 8, 1774, 296 ("pension") and 475–76 ("disappointed and in debt"); Clark, *Phineas Lyman*, 78 ("much distressed"); Stiles, *Literary Diary*, 315 (quoting from memoir of Mr. Marchant, January 29, 1773); *The Connecticut Courant*, December 1, 1772, p. 4 ("in September").

7. *The Connecticut Courant*, October 20–27, 1772, p. 4 ("call of meeting").

8. *The Connecticut Courant*, December 1–8, 1772, p. 4; Bates, "Historical Introduction," 19–22; Livingston, *Israel Putnam*, 162–63.

9. Rufus Putnam, journal (longer), December 11–17, 1772, *The Two Putnams: Israel and Rufus in the Havana Expedition 1762 and in the Mississippi River Exploration 1772–73 with Some Account of The Company of Military Adventurers* (Hartford, CT: Connecticut Historical Society, 1931), 146.

10. Rufus Putnam, journal (longer), December 11–17, 1772, 143. Rufus Putnam mentions meeting at Israel's home in Brooklyn ("Broolin") before heading to West Florida. Brooklyn did not separate from the towns of Pomfret and Canterbury until 1786, when it was incorporated. Since 1754 it was considered a separate parish lying within the boundaries of both Pomfret and Canterbury called Brooklyn Society. John Warner Barber, *Connecticut Historical Collections: Containing General Collection of Interesting Facts, Traditions, Biographical Sketches, Anecdotes, etc. Relating to the History and Antiquities of Every Town in Connecticut with Geographical Descriptions* (Storrs, CT: Bibliopola Press, 1999), 413–16. Three years later, Coit, a third-generation shipbuilder and lawyer, who had lost an eye in an accident, raised an independent company of New London mariners that served at the siege of Boston. He later become a successful privateer. The home is located at 92 Washington Street (corner of Washington and Coit Streets) in present downtown New London. The home formerly faced the water at Bream Cove, which began to silt up and was eventually filled in during the nineteenth century. Richard Curland, "Historically Speaking: New London Privateer Captain Captured British Ships," *Norwich (CT) Bulletin*, June 3, 2018, https://norwichbulletin.com/news/20180603. Accessed March 28, 2020; Samuel Swett, *History of Bunker Hill Battle, with a Plan* (Boston, MA: Munroe and Francis, 1827), 7 ("independent company"); Joseph Reed to Samuel B. Webb, January 16, 1776, Worthington Chauncey Ford, ed., *Correspondence and Journals of Samuel Blachley Webb*, vol. 1, 1772–1777 (New York: Wickersham Press, 1893), 126–28 ("privateer").

11. Israel Putnam, journal, December 20, 1772, *The Two Putnams*, 113; Rufus Putnam, journal (longer), December 18–20, 1772, 143–44; Livingston, *Israel Putnam*, 163.

12. Israel Putnam, journal, December 21, 1772, to January 10, 1773, 113–15; Rufus Putnam, journal (longer), December 21, 1772 to January 10, 1773, 144–46; Livingston, *Israel Putnam*, 163–65.

13. Rufus Putnam, journal (longer), January 25, 1773, 146 ("sea sickness"); Israel Putnam, journal, January 11–February 3, 1773, 115–20; Bates, "Historical Introduction," 28–29.

14. Israel Putnam, journal, February 8–9, 1773, 121–22; Rufus Putnam, journal (longer), March 8–9, 1773, 151–52.

15. Israel Putnam, journal, February 9 to March 1, 1773, 122–28; Rufus Putnam, journal (longer), February 9–March 1, 1773, 152–55; Rufus Putnam, *Memoirs*, 37–38.

16. Israel Putnam, journal, March 1 through 3, 1773, 129–30; Rufus Putnam, journal (longer), March 1 through 3, 1773, 155–56.

17. Clinton L. Howard, "Colonial Pensacola: The British Period, Part III: The Administration of Governor Chester, 1770–1781," *The Florida Historical Quarterly* 19, no. 4 (April 1941): 369–70, 378, and 385 ("troops"); Israel Putnam, journal, March 3, 1773 ("everything in my power").

18. Israel Putnam, journal, March 3, 5, 9, and 12, 1773, 129–32; Rufus Putnam, journal (longer), March 3, 5, and 12, 1773, 155–58; Rufus Putnam, *Memoirs*, 38–39; Bates, "Historical Introduction," 29 ("take up lands").

19. Israel Putnam, journal, March 1–18, 1773, 128–33; Rufus Putnam, journal (longer), March 1–18, 1773, 155–59; Rufus Putnam, *Memoirs*, 38–39 ("Pensacola"); Livingston, *Israel Putnam*, 167–68 ("Haldimand and Small").

20. Rufus Putnam, *Memoirs*, 39; Israel Putnam, journal, March 11 and 15, 1773, 131–32 ("Monsieur Caters"); Rufus Putnam, journal (longer), March 15, 1773.

21. Israel Putnam, journal, March 22–28, 135–38; Rufus Putnam, journal (longer), March 21–30, 1773, 160–66; Rufus Putnam, *Memoirs*, 40–41; Livingston, *Israel Putnam*, 168.

22. Rufus Putnam, journal (longer), March 31 to April 1, 1773, 167; Rufus Putnam, *Memoirs*, 40–41; Livingston, *Israel Putnam*, 168.

23. Rufus Putnam, journal (longer), April 2–8, 1773, 167–70.

24. Rufus Putnam, journal (longer), April 6, 1773, 168.

25. Rufus Putnam, journal (longer), April 8–25, 1773, 170–81.

26. Rufus Putnam, journal (longer), April 26–28, 1773, 181–84.

27. Rufus Putnam, journal (longer), April; 28 to May 2, 1773, 183–86.

28. Rufus Putnam, journal (longer), May 3–5, 1773, 187–90; Rufus Putnam, *Memoirs*, 45.

29. Rufus Putnam, journal (longer), May 5, 1773, 189–92.

30. Rufus Putnam, journal (longer), May 6–8, 1773, 192–95; Rufus Putnam, *Memoirs*, 45–46.

31. Rufus Putnam, journal (longer), May 9–12, 1773, 195–99; Rufus Putnam, *Memoirs*, 45–46; Howard, "Colonial Pensacola," Part III, 375–76 ("encroachment") and 385–86 ("huts").

32. Rufus Putnam, journal (longer), May 13–14, 1773, 198–203; Rufus Putnam, *Memoirs*, 46–47. Author's Note: Eighty-nine years later, at the Battle of Port Gibson, south of Vicksburg, Grant's army would encounter the same canebrakes and broken ground as Putnam's party, which the Confederates used to their advantage. Michael B. Ballard, *Vicksburg: The Campaign that Opened the Mississippi* (Chapel Hill: University of North Carolina Press, 2004), 223–24.

33. Rufus Putnam, journal (longer), May 16, 1773, 202–203; Rufus Putnam, *Memoirs*, 48.

34. Rufus Putnam, journal (longer), May 17–19, 1773, 203–206; Rufus Putnam, *Memoirs*, 48–50.

35. Rufus Putnam, journal (longer), May 21 to June 30, 1773, 208 and 214–25; Rufus Putnam, *Memoirs*, 48–50.

36. Rufus Putnam, journal (longer), July 1–10, 1773, 219–28; Rufus Putnam, *Memoirs*, 50–51; Bailyn, *Voyagers to the West*, 486 ("nineteen townships").

37. Rufus Putnam, journal (longer), July 11 to August 12, 1773, 228–33; Rufus Putnam, *Memoirs*, 50–53.

38. Bailyn, *Voyagers to the West*, 55–56 ("sold in small lots"); Rufus Putnam, *Memoirs*, 53. Author's Note: Rufus Putnam refers to the Order of the King in Council as being received by the governor in October 1773, but see Bailyn, who refers to an order by the Privy Council dated April 7, 1773, prohibiting settlement. This is likely the same order, as there was a long lag time in orders reaching West Florida. Rufus Putnam is consistent with Bailyn when he says that on arrival in West Florida the New Englanders were permitted to settle on vacant lands. This was, no doubt, because of the revised policy of February 1774. Robert V. Haynes, "Mississippi Under British Rule: British West Florida," Mississippi History Now (September 2000), https://,historynow.mdah.state.us/articles/66/british-west-florida. Accessed March 29, 2020.

39. Stiles, *The Literary Diary*, August 24, 1773, 409 ("wilderness is all alive"); Howard, Colonial Pensacola, Part III, 385–87 ("1776").

40. *The Connecticut Courant*, August 10–16, 1773, p. 3; Firmin A. Rozier, *Rozier's History of the Early Settlement of the Mississippi Valley* (St. Louis, MO: G. A. Pierrot & Son, 1890), 59–63; William C. Davis, *A Way Through the Wilderness: The Natchez Trace and the Civilization of the Southern Frontier* (New York: HarperCollins, 1995), 272–75; Jonathan Daniels, *The Devil's Backbone: The Story of the Natchez Trace* (New York: McGraw-Hill, 1962), 31.

41. *Connecticut Courant*, December 14–20, 1773 ("Middletown") and April 26–May 2, 1774; Clark, *Phineas Lyman*, 82–83.

42. Anthony Haswell, ed., *Memoirs and Adventures of Captain Matthew Phelps* (Bennington, VT: Anthony Haswell, 1802), 16, 56 ("Eleanor sails from Middletown"), and 72–73 ("death of Eleanor Lyman"); *Connecticut Courant*, April 26–May 2, 1774, p. 3 ("Pensacola"); Clark, *Phineas Lyman*, 84; Bates, "Historical Introduction," 45; Bailyn, *Voyagers to the West*, 486–88 ("migration"). Author's Note: Citing the journal of Matthew Phelps, a fellow traveler, Delphina Clark states that Eleanor Lyman and her brother Timothy Dwight left Middletown with a group of settlers from Massachusetts on May

1, 1776. This is supported by Claiborne in his book *Mississippi*. Both Bailyn and Bates are in error when they state that she left in the summer of 1775.

43. Stiles, *Literary Diary*, November 8, 1774, 475–76 ("inglorious"); Daniels, *The Devil's Backbone*, 29–30 ("Georgiana"); Claiborne, *Mississippi*, 107 ("patent finally issued"), 107.

44. *Encyclopedia of Mississippi History*, vol, 2, s.v. "Revolt of 1781," 540–44; Daniels, *The Devil's Backbone*, 30–31, 35–38, and 43; Davis, *A Way Through the Wilderness*, 9–10.

45. Humphreys, *An Essay*, 63 ("men with provisions"). It would be logical, but not confirmed, that Israel and Rufus could well have staked out claims on part of the lands that they had surveyed, with the idea of returning at some point or, as more likely, selling them.

Chapter 9

1. Robert Middlekauff, *The Glorious Cause: The American Revolution, 1763–1789* (New York: Oxford University Press, 1982), 221–27.

2. Benson Bobrick, *Angel in the Whirlwind: The Triumph of the American Revolution* (New York: Simon & Schuster, 1997), 89–93; Livingston, *Israel Putnam*, 174–75; James L. Nelson, *With Fire and Sword: The Battle of Bunker Hill and the Beginning of the American Revolution* (New York: St. Martin, 2011), 99–100 ("130 sheep"); Bayles, *History of Windham County*, 63–64 ("258 sheep"); Galvin, *The Minute Men*, 77 ("Salem").

3. Israel Putnam, et al. to Samuel Adams, August 11, 1774, quoted in full in Livingston, *Israel Putnam*, 175–76. Author's Note: Daniel Tyler Jr. was the father of Daniel Tyler III, who married Israel Putnam's daughter Mehitable. Baker, *Connecticut Families of the Revolution*, 109.

4. Joseph Warren to Samuel Adams, August 15, 1774, quoted in Richard Frothingham, *Life and Times of Joseph Warren* (Boston, MA: Little, Brown, 1865), 339–40; Livingston, *Israel Putnam*, 177.

5. Thomas Young to [not named], August 19, 1774, quoted in Frothingham, *Life and Times of Joseph Warren*, 340; Humphreys, *An Essay*, 64–66 ("questioned by officers"); Atkinson, *The British Are Coming*, 496 ("James Grant").

6. John Montresor, journal, December 9, 1764, 135–36 ("one dollar a day").

7. Thomas Young to [not named], August 19, 1774, quoted in Frothingham, *Life and Times of Joseph Warren*, 340.

8. David Hackett Fischer, *Paul Revere's Ride* (New York: Oxford University Press, 1994), 44–46; Galvin, *The Minute Men*, 46–47; Nathaniel Philbrick, *Bunker Hill: A City, a Siege, a Revolution* (New York: Penguin, 2014), 64–65.

9. Fischer, *Paul Revere's Ride*, 46–50; Galvin, *The Minute Men*, 47–49 and 68–76 ("other British raids"); Draper, *A Struggle for Power*, 465 ("depth of resolve").

10. Israel Putnam to Aaron Cleveland, September 3, 1774, "Correspondence of Silas Deane, Delegate to the Congress at Philadelphia, 1774–76," *Collections of the Connecticut Historical Society*, vol. 2 (Hartford, CT: Case, Lockwood, 1870), 156–57; Caulkins, *History of Norwich, 376–77* ("Powder Alarm"); John Adams, diary, September 6, 1774, FONA Adams:01-02-02-0004-0006, last modified June 13, 2018; Silas Deane to Elizabeth Deane, September 8, 1774, "The Deane Papers," vol. 1, *Collections of the New York Historical Society for the Year 1886* (New York: New York Historical Society, 1887), 5–22

(hereafter "Deane Papers") ("blundering story"); Philbrick, *Bunker Hill*, 74; Livingston, *Israel Putnam.*

11. Israel Putnam, "Open Letter," October 3, 1774, Peter Force, *American Archives: Fourth Series, Containing a Documentary History of the English Colonies in North America, from the King's Message to Parliament, of March 7, 1774, to the Declaration of Independence by the United States*, vol. 1 (Washington, DC: Clarke and Force, 1837), 942 (hereafter AA4); William Cooper to Israel Putnam, September 7, 1774, AA4 1:783–84.

12. Israel Putnam to Captain Trumbull, September 11, 1774, AA4 1:783.

13. John Barker, diary, April 18 and 19, 1775, Elizabeth Ellery Dana, ed., *The British in Boston: Being the Diary of Lieutenant John Barker of the King's Own Regiment from November 15, 1774 to May 31, 1776* (Cambridge, MA: Harvard University Press, 1924), 31–32, Galvin, *The Minute Men*, 128 ("eight dead and nine wounded"); Fischer, *Paul Revere's Ride*, 197–98.

14. Galvin, *The Minute Men*, 147–55; Fischer, *Paul Revere's Ride*, 208–15.

15. Amos Farnsworth, diary, April 19, 1775, Samuel A. Green, ed., *Three Military Diaries Kept by Groton Soldiers in Different Wars* (Cambridge, MA: Harvard University Press, 1901), 83 ("many dead").

16. Humphreys, *An Essay*, 67; Daniel Putnam, "Colonel Daniel Putnam's Letter Relative to the Battle of Bunker Hill and General Israel Putnam," August 1825, *Collections of the Connecticut Historical Society*, vol. 1 (Hartford, CT: The Society, 1860), 231.

17. Bayles, *History of Windham County*, 67–68.

18. Fischer, *Paul Revere's Ride*, 324 ("11:00 a.m."); Humphreys, *An Essay*, 67; Nelson, *With Fire and Sword*, 203 ("a rabble in arms"); Israel Putnam to Ebenezer Williams, April 21, 1775, reprinted in the *Hartford Courant*, February 24, 1914, p. 12; Swett, *History of Bunker Hill Battery*, 7 ("Council of War"); Paul Lockhart, *The Whites of Their Eyes: Bunker Hill, the First American Army, and the Emergence of George Washington* (New York: Harper-Collins, 2011), 148–50.

19. Experience Storrs, diary, April 20 and 21, 1775, Wladimir Hagelin and Ralph A. Brown, eds., "Connecticut Farmers at Bunker Hill: The Diary of Colonel Experience Storrs," *The New England Quarterly* 28, vol. 1 (March 1955): 84.

20. Storrs, diary, April 22 to 25, 1775, 84–85.

21. Worthington Chauncey Ford, ed., *Correspondence and Journals of Samuel Blachley Webb*, vols. 1–3, 1772–1806 (New York: Wickersham Press, 1893–1894) (hereafter *Correspondence and Journals*).

22. Charles J. Hoadly, ed., *The Public Records of the Colony of Connecticut, From October, 1772, to April, 1775, Inclusive*, vol. 14 (Hartford, CT: Case, Lockwood, 1887), 413 and 422–25.

23. Henry P. Johnston, ed., *Record of Connecticut Men in the Military and Naval Service During the War of the Revolution, 1775–1783*, Part 1 (Hartford, CT: Case, Lockwood & Brainard, 1889), 53–54; French, journal, April 1, 1776, CHS 1:197.

24. Daniel Putnam, Letter, August 1825, 323, 236, and 238–39; Elizabeth Inman to Her Friends in Boston, April 22, 1775, Nina Moore Tiffany and Susan I. Leslie, ed., *Letters of James Murray, Loyalist* (Boston, MA: Printed not published, 1901), 183–85; Lockhart, *The Whites of Their Eyes*, 99–100; Livingston, *Israel Putnam*, 197 ("Borland House").

25. Jedediah Huntington to Jonathan Trumbull, Jr., MSH5 9:495–96); Catherine Drinker Bowen, *John Adams and the American Revolution* (Boston, MA: Little, Brown, 1950), 529 ("cooked meat").

26. De Forest, *Seth Pomeroy: Sometime General in the Colonial Service*, 164.

27. Farnsworth, diary, May 13, 1775, 85 ("shoe [show] themselves to the Regulars"); Philbrick, *Bunker Hill*, 170, 182, and 195; Richard M. Ketchum, *The Decisive Day: The Battle for Bunker Hill* (New York: Henry Holt, 1999), 78 ("Bunker Hill"); Livingston, *Israel Putnam*, 199–200 ("dig a ditch") and 201 ("marched up Bunker Hill"); Jedediah Huntington to Jonathan Trumbull, Sr., August 14, 1775, MHS5 9:497–98 ("floating batteries").

28. Barker, diary, May 20 and 21, 1775, 48–49.

29. Farnsworth, diary, May 27, 1775, 86–87; Barker, diary, May 28, 1775, 50–51.

30. Humphreys, *An Essay*, 70–71; Livingston, *Israel Putnam*, 202–204; Farnsworth, diary, May 27, 1775, 86–87 ("balls sung"); Barker, diary, May 28, 1775, 50–51. (Barker, who was not present, writes that the British set fire to the vessel and abandoned her, while Farnsworth, who was present, writes that "we Sot fiar to hur." However, in his diary entry for May 30, Barker does confirm that the vessel was "burnt by the Yankies."); Philbrick, *Bunker Hill*, 183–87; Ketchum, *The Decisive Day*, 67–68 ("Grape Island") and 68–72 ("Noddle's Island"); Lockhart, *The Whites of Their Eyes*, 162–68; Nelson, *With Fire and Sword*, 188–94; Atkinson, *The British Are Coming*, 86–90.

31. Humphreys, *An Essay*, 70–71; Livingston, *Israel Putnam*, 204; Philbrick, *Bunker Hill*, 186 ("nothing between"); Mercy Otis Warren, *History of the Rise, Progress and Termination of the American Revolution*, vol. 1 (Indianapolis, IN: Liberty Fund, 1994), 107.

32. Swett, *History of Bunker Hill*, 7; Livingston, *Israel Putnam*, 207–208.

33. Swett, *History of Bunker Hill*, 15.

34. Resolutions, Massachusetts Committee of Safety, June 15, 1775, quoted in full in Swett, *History of Bunker Hill*, 17–18; Christopher Ward, *The War of the Revolution*, vol. 1 (New York: Macmillan, 1952), 74 ("cover those").

35. William Prescott to John Adams, August 25, 1775, FONA Adams:06-03-02-0070; Storrs, diary, June 16, 1775, 92 ("31 men")

36. Swett, *History of Bunker Hill*, 19–20; Daniel Putnam to President and Directors of the Bunker Hill Monument Association, August 1825, CHS 1:239; Tiffany, *Letters of James Murray*, 213 ("family tradition").

37. William Prescott to John Adams, August 25, 1775, FONA Adams:06-03-02-0070; Richard Wheeler, *Voices of 1776: The Story of the American Revolution in the Words of Those Who Were There* (New York: Meridian, 1991), 39–40; Atkinson, *The British Are Coming*, 94.

38. Daniel Putnam to President and Directors, CHS 1:245.

39. Daniel Putnam to President and Directors, CHS 1:245; Lockhart, *The Whites of Their Eyes*, 229–33 ("Ward").

40. Storrs, diary, June 17, 1775, 92.

41. William Abbatt, ed., *Memoirs of Major-General William Heath by Himself* (New York: William Abbatt, 1901), 13; quoting Thomas Kittredge, Swett, *Bunker Hill*, Note A, p. 9 ("11:00 a.m.").

42. Thomas Grosvenor to Daniel Putnam, April 30, 1818, quoted in Daniel Putnam, *A Letter to Major-General Dearborn Repelling His Unprovoked Attack on the Character of the Late Major-General Israel Putnam, and Containing Some Anecdotes Relating to the Battle of Bunker Hill Not Generally Known* (Boston, MA: Munroe & Francis, 1818), 6–7; Daniel Putnam to President and Directors, CHS 1:246.

43. Nelson, *With Fire & Sword*, 254–55 ("Knowlton"); Lockhart, *The Whites of Their Eyes*, 248–51; Philbrick, *Bunker Hill*, 211–13. Author's Note: Just before Putnam issued his orders to Captains Knowlton and Trevett, Prescott had ordered Trevett, with the support of Knowlton, to go forward and oppose the British landing. This would have been an extremely foolhardy contest, as the British would soon amass a 10 to 1 advantage against that small force. According to Prescott, Trevett and Knowlton "followed a different course . . . which I suppose to Bunker's Hill." This would confirm that Putnam issued orders to the two officers, and moreover, that Prescott did not command the entire battlefield. William Prescott to John Adams, August 25, 1775, FONA Adams:06-03-02-0070.

44. William Prescott to John Adams, August 25, 1775, FONA Adams:06-03-02-0070 ("2:00 p.m."); Farnsworth, diary, July 17, 1775, 89 ("1:00 p.m."); John Chester to [Joseph Fish], July 22, 1775, Webb, *Correspondence and Journals*, 1:89 ("Israel Putnam, Jr."); Storrs, diary, June 17, 1775, 92.

45. John Chester to [Joseph Fish], July 22, 1775, Webb, *Correspondence and Journals*, 1:87–90 ("Israel Putnam, Jr."); William Coit, June 17, 1775, "Orderly Book for Cap't William Coits Company Campt at Cambridge, April 23d AD 1775," Connecticut Historical Society. "Orderly Book and Journals Kept by Connecticut Men While Taking part in the American Revolution, 1775–1778," *Collections of the Connecticut Historical Society*, vol. 7 (Hartford, CT: Connecticut Historical Society, 1899), 22.

46. Dearborn, *Account of the Battle of Bunker's Hill*, 3; quoting Richard Gilchrist, Swett, *Bunker Hill*, "Notes to the Sketch of Bunker Hill Battle," Note A, p. 10 ("push on"); Swett, *History of Bunker Hill*, 28; Lockhart, *The Whites of Their Eyes*, 256–59 ("Stark"); Philbrick, *Bunker Hill*, 212–15.

47. De Forest, *The Journals and Papers of Seth Pomeroy*, 164–65.

48. De Forest, *The Journals and Papers of Seth Pomeroy*, 164–65.

49. Daniel Putnam to John Adams, May 21, 1818, FONA Adams:99-02-02-6897, accessed September 29, 2019.

50. Barker, diary, June 17, 1775, 60–61; William Prescott to John Adams, August 25, 1775, FONA Adams:06-03-02-0070; John Chester to [Joseph Fish], July 22, 1775, Webb, *Correspondence and Journals*, 1:87–90; John Waller to Jacob Waller, June 22, 1775, quoted in full in Samuel Adams Drake, *Bunker Hill: The Story Told in Letters from the Battle Field by British Officers Engaged* (Boston, MA: Nichols & Hall, 1875), 29 ("astonishing").

51. Nelson, *With Fire & Sword*, 243–45 and 274–75 ("offers encouragement"); Atkinson, *The British Are Coming*, 99–100 ("back and forth").

52. Quoting Abner Allen, Philip Bagley, Reuben Kemp, and Simeon Noyes in Samuel Swett, ed., *Notes to His Sketch of the Bunker Hill Battle*, Note A (Boston, MA: Munroe and Francis, 1825), 1–20.

53. Quoting Isaac Bassett and John Holden, Swett, *Bunker Hill*, Note A, pp. 5 and 12.

54. Samuel B. Webb and John Chester to Joseph Webb, June 19, 1775, Webb, *Correspondence and Journals*, 1:63–69.

55. Samuel B. Webb and John Chester to Joseph Webb, June 19, 1775, Webb, *Correspondence and Journals*, 1:63–69.

56. William Prescott to John Adams, August 25, 1775, FONA Adams:06-03-02-0070; Atkinson, *The British Are Coming*, 107–109.

57. John Waller to Jacob Waller, June 22, 1775, Drake, *Bunker Hill*, 28; Tarbox, *Life of Israel Putnam*, 162 ("Waller"); Farnsworth, diary, June 17, 1775, 89–90 ("Althoe thay fell").

58. Thomas Grosvenor to Daniel Putnam, April 30, 1818, quoted in Putnam, *A Letter to Major-General Dearborn*, 6–7; Nelson, *With Fire and Sword*, 276–80 and 303–304; Lockhart, *The Whites of Their Eyes*, 302 ("orderly retreat"); Atkinson, *The British Are Coming*, 109 ("orderly retreat").

59. Quoting Anderson Miner, Colonel Wade, and Frances Green, Swett, *Bunker Hill*, Note A, pp. 6, 14, and 19.

60. Samuel B. Webb and John Chester to Joseph Webb, June 19, 1775, Webb, *Correspondence and Journals*, 1:63–69; Quoting James Clark, Swett, *Bunker Hill*, Note A, p. 7. ("actively managing"); Swett, *Bunker Hill*, 44 ("Clark"); Daniel Putnam, *A Letter to Major-General Dearborn*, 7 ("cover retreat").

61. Samuel B. Webb and John Chester to Joseph Webb, June 19, 1775, Webb, *Correspondence and Journals*, 1:63–69; John Waller to Jacob Waller, June 22, 1775, Drake, *Bunker Hill*, 28 ("suffered exceedingly"); John Chester to [Joseph Fish], July 22, 1775, Webb, *Correspondence and Journals*, 1:87–90 ("six minutes"); Thomas Grosvenor to Daniel Putnam, April 30, 1818, quoted in Daniel Putnam, *A Letter to Major-General Dearborn*, 6–7; Atkinson, *The British Are Coming*, 108–109.

62. Samuel Holden Parsons to Mehitable Parsons, June 21, 1775, quoted in full in Charles S. Hall, *Life and Letters of Samuel Holden Parsons, Major General in the Continental Army and Chief Judge of the Northwestern Territory, 1737–1789* (Binghamton, NY: Otseningo Publishing Co., 1905), 31–32 ("Captain Chester").

63. Samuel Parsons to Mehitable Parsons, Hall, *Life and Letters*, 31–32.

64. Samuel B. Webb to Silas Deane, July 11, 1775, Webb, *Correspondence and Journals*, 1:73–79; Galvin, *The Minute Men*, 230 ("Montresor").

65. John Trumbull to Daniel Putnam, March 30, 1818, quoted in Putnam, *A Letter to Major-General Dearborn*, 8–9. Author's Note: In an account purportedly written by a Lt. John Clarke, he wrote that a wounded Doctor Warren appealed to a soldier not to run him through with his bayonet, as he would soon die of his wounds. The soldier ignored him, drove the bayonet home, and stripped Warren of his elegant clothing. Clarke's account is suspect, yet it has an element of truth, in that it does place the mortally wounded man outside the redoubt, bayonetted as he lay dying. John Clarke, "An Authentic and Impartial Narrative of the Battle Fought on the 17th of June, 1775," Drake, *Bunker Hill*, 1n14 and 50.

66. John Trumbull to Daniel Putnam, March 30, 1818, quoted in Putnam, *A Letter to Major-General Dearborn*, 8–9; Daniel Putnam to John Adams, May 21, 1818, FONA Adams:99-02-02-6897, accessed September 29, 2019; Grosvenor, "An Address," 15

("spare that man"). Author's Note: In London during the summer of 1786, in a conversation with the artist John Trumbull, Small recollected that he had heard Putnam's voice as he [Small] stood alone near the redoubt after the failure of the second attempt to storm it. There is no evidence that Putnam was in the redoubt at that time, let alone close enough to see his friend there. What is clear is that Small did see the mortally wounded Warren outside of the redoubt during the retreat and spoke to the dying man. At the same time, it is more likely that Putnam, who was already nearby because he was urging men forward to cover the retreat, spoke the words to spare Small's life. To the end of his life, Small remained convinced that Putnam had spared his life.

67. Joshua Huntington to Jabez Huntington, June 22, 1775, *Huntington Papers: Correspondence of the Brothers Joshua and Jedediah Huntington During the Period of the American Revolution*, part 1 (Hartford: Connecticut Historical Society, 1923), 19 (hereafter *Huntington Papers*); Lockhart, *The Whites of Their Eyes*, 316 ("hasty burial"). The body of Dr. Warren would be disinterred in late March 1776, shortly after the British had left town, and it was reburied following a procession of notables and proper ceremony at King's Chapel on Monday, April 8. The corpse was badly decomposed, having been hastily buried, and Warren was identified by some bridgework he had received shortly before he had died. *Connecticut Courant and Weekly Hartford Intelligencer*, April 29, 1776, p. 2.

68. Draper, *A Struggle for Power*, 503 ("casualties"); Lockhart, *The Whites of Their Eyes*, 306–307, 314, and 316 ("hasty burial"); Philbrick, *Bunker Hill*, 250 (115 killed, 305 wounded); Atkinson, *The British Are Coming*, 109 ("such carnage").

69. Seanegan P. Sculley, *Contest for Liberty: Military Leadership in the Continental Army, 1775–1783* (Yardley, PA: Westholme Publishing, 2019), 102; Atkinson, *The British Are Coming*, 228–37; Middlekauff: *The Glorious Cause*, 60 ("a quarter"). Atkinson's figure would square with Fred Anderson's estimate that by the end of the French and Indian War, a decade earlier, between 40 to 60 percent of the men of military age from Massachusetts and Connecticut had served. Anderson, *Crucible of War*, 288.

70. Quoting Rev. Daniel Chaplin and Rev. John Bullard, Swett, *Bunker Hill*, Note A, pp. 9–10; Sculley, *Contest for Liberty*, xxvii.

71. Middlekauff: *The Glorious Cause*, 106–107 ("failure to resupply").

72. Quoting *Ecclesiastes* 9:11. Abigail Adams to John Adams, June 18, 1775, FONA Adams:04-01-02-0150 (version of January 18, 2019).

73. Jedediah Huntington to Jonathan Trumbull, Sr., August 10, 1775, Jedediah Huntington to Jonathan Trumbull, Sr., August 14, 1775, and Jedediah Huntington to Jonathan Trumbull, Sr., August 17, 1775, MHS5 9:496–99.

74. Atkinson, *The British Are Coming*, 116–18.

75. Eliphalet Dyer to Joseph Trumbull, June 20, 1775, Paul H. Smith, ed., *Letters of Delegates to Congress, 1774–1789*, vol. 1 (August 1774–August 1775) (Washington, DC: Library of Congress, 1976–2000), 521–22 (hereafter *Letters of Delegates*).

76. Taaffe, *Washington's Revolutionary War Generals*, 14–16; Robert K. Wright Jr., *The Continental Army* (Washington, DC: Center of Military History, United States Army, 1983), 27.

77. Jonathan Trumbull, Sr. to George Washington, July 13, 1775, "Trumbull and Washington Letters," MHS5 10:1.

78. George Washington to John Hancock (president of the Continental Congress), July 10, 1775, Jared Sparks, ed., *The Writings of George Washington; Being His Correspondence, Addresses, Messages, and Other Papers, Official and Private, Selected and Published from the Original Manuscripts; with a Life of the Author, Notes, and Illustrations*, vol. 3 (Boston, MA: Russell, Odiorne, 1834), 17–26; Samuel B. Webb to Silas Deane, July 11, 1775, Webb, *Correspondence and Journals*, vol. 1, 79–82. Author's Note: There seems to be some confusion among historians about when Washington arrived in Cambridge to take command of the army. On Sunday, July 2, he and his entourage arrived in Watertown, Massachusetts, three miles east of Cambridge, where he most likely spent the night. The following day, Monday, July 3, he was escorted to Cambridge. I have relied upon Washington's own words. Ketchum, *Divided Loyalties*, 351 ("Watertown on July 2").

79. Taaffe, *Washington's Revolutionary War Generals*, 14–17 ("selection"); Livingston, *Israel Putnam*, 205 ("success at Noddle's Island"); Silas Deane to Elizabeth Deane, July 15, 1775, and Silas Deane to Elizabeth Deane, July 20, 1775, "Deane Papers" 1:71–74). Author's Note: Some delegates anticipated that Spencer would have a problem with Putnam's appointment. Eliphalet Dyer to Joseph Trumbull, June 20, 1775, Smith, *Letters of Delegates*, 1:521–22.

80. Taaffe, *Washington's Revolutionary War Generals*, 7 and 259 ("seniority and merit").

81. General Orders, August 9, 1775, FONA Washington:03-01-02-0179; Cox, *A Proper Sense of Honor*, 21–26 ("gentlemen"); Sculley, *Contest for Liberty*, 94; John A. Ruddiman, *Becoming Men of Some Consequence: Youth and Military Service in the Revolutionary War* (Charlottesville: University of Virginia Press, 2014), 30–31 and 47 ("fewer means").

82. Letter signed by "A Friend of Truth," *The Connecticut Courant and Intelligencer*, July 31, 1775, p. 3.

83. William Heath to John Adams, October 23, 1775, FONA Adams:06-03-02-0118.

84. Silas Deane to Elizabeth Deane, July 20, 1775, "Deane Papers" 1:73–74.

85. John Chester to Samuel B. Webb, August 11, 1775, Webb, *Correspondence and Journals*, 1:90–91 ("big bellied"); Charles Lee to Israel Putnam, October 19, 1775, reprinted in Tarbox, *Life of Israel Putnam*, 121.

86. Silas Deane to Samuel B. Webb, June 22, 1775, and Samuel B. Webb to Silas Deane, July 11, 1775, Webb, *Correspondence and Journals*, 1:71–72 and 73–82; General Orders, July 22, 1775, FONA Washington:03-01-02-0091.

87. Humphreys, *An Essay*, 68 ("Gage's offer"); Daniel Putnam to John Adams, May 21, 1818, FONA Adams:00-02-02-6897, accessed September 29, 2019.

88. *The Connecticut Courant and Weekly Hartford Intelligencer*, July 24, 1775, p. 2; "The Flag of the United States," *Hartford Daily Courant*, June 13, 1877, p. 2; Philbrick, *Bunker Hill*, 265 ("mast from *Diana*"). Author's Note: Putnam was always looking for an opportunity to prick the British occupiers to gain the psychological edge. One night in late October 1775, he ordered some floating batteries to fire into Boston. In doing so, he disrupted a ball as well as a play being staged by the army. The resulting alert meant no sleep for the balance of the night. Unfortunately, it is likely that more casualties were suffered by the Americans, when one of the guns split, killing two and wounding six members of the battery. James Warren to John Adams, October 20, 1775, FONA Adams:06-03-02-0113, last modified June 13, 2018.

89. General Orders, July 22, 1775, FONA Washington:03-01-02-0091. Joshua Huntington to Jabez Huntington, September 25, 1775, *Huntington Papers*, 1:22–23.

90. Ebenezer David to Nicholas Brown, January 29, 1776, Jeannette D. Black and William Greene Roelker, eds., *A Rhode Island Chaplain in the Revolution: Letters of Ebenezer David to Nicholas Brown 1775–1778* (Providence: Rhode Island Society of the Cincinnati, 1949), 9–13.

91. Joshua Huntington to Jabez Huntington, November 22, 1775, *Huntington Papers*, 1:24.

92. George Washington to Jonathan Trumbull, Sr., December 2, 1775, FONA Washington:03-02-02-0428; Experience Storrs to George Washington, October 23, 1775, FONA Washington:03-02-02-0199; Charles Webb to George Washington, October 23, 1775, FONA Washington:03-02-02-0203; Samuel Holden Parsons to George Washington, October 23, 1775, FONA Washington:03-02-02-0198; George Washington to John Hancock, December 4, 1775, FONA Washington:03-02-02-0437.

93. Bill of Sale, November 22, 1775, Worthington Chauncey Ford, ed., *Family Letters of Samuel Blachley Webb 1764–1807* (Cambridge, MA: University Press, 1912.

94. Nathanael Greene to Henry Ward, December 18, 1775, AA4 4:311–12 ("scurvy"); George Washington to Joseph Reed, November 30, 1775, FONA Washington:03-02-02-0419; George Washington to Philip Schuyler, November 30, 1775, FONA Washington:03-02-02-0408; George Washington to John Hancock, December 4, 1775, FONA Washington:03-02-02-0437.

95. Simeon Lyman, "Journal of Simeon Lyman of Sharon, Aug. 10 to Dec. 28, 1775," *Collections of the Connecticut Historical Society*, vol 7 (Hartford: Connecticut Historical Society, 1899), 129–30 ("Congress"); Israel Angell to Brother, December 1, 1775, Edward Field, ed., *Diary of Colonel Israel Angell, Commanding the Second Rhode Island Continental Regiment During the American Revolution, 1778–1781* (Providence, RI: Preston and Rounds, 1899), x–xi; Samuel B. Webb, journal, March 3, 1776, 133; Atkinson, *The British Are Coming*, 226–27.

96. Joseph Reed to Samuel B. Webb, January 16, 1776, Webb, *Correspondence and Journals*, 126–28; "Extract of Letter from Beverly (MA)," December 18, 1775, AA4 4:313–14 ("Manly's exploits"); George Washington to John Hancock, December 18, 1775, AA4 4:314–15 ("Manly"); Atkinson, *The British Are Coming*, 228.

97. Barker, diary, December 18 and 19, 1775, 68–69; "Extract of a Letter from Cambridge," December 18, 1775, AA4 4:313; George Washington to John Hancock, December 18, 1775, AA4 4:314–15; William Abbat, ed., *Memoirs of Major-General William Heath by Himself* (New York: William Abbatt, 1901), 25–27.

98. Extract of a Letter to a "Gentleman in Philadelphia," January 9, 1776; George Washington to John Hancock, *Report to Congress*, January 11, 1776; General Orders, January 9, 1776; and two unidentified Boston newspaper accounts dated January 11, 1776, AA4 4:612–13 and 4:629–32; George Washington to Joseph Reed, January 14, 1776, *George Washington: Writings*, 200–205; Ebenezer David to Nicholas Brown, January 8, 1776, *A Rhode Island Chaplain*, 7–9 ("merry as you please"); Livingston, *Israel Putnam*, 265–66.

99. Samuel Shaw to Francis Shaw, February 14, 1776 (extract), Josiah Quincy, *The Journals of Major Samuel Shaw, the First American Consul at Canton. With a Life of the Author, by Josiah Quincy* (Boston, MA: Crosby & Nichols, 1847), 7–8 ("Jesus bless you!"); Atkinson, *The British Are Coming,* 220–22.

100. Ebenezer David to Nicholas Brown, January 29, 1776, *A Rhode Island Chaplain,* 9–13 ("parked at Framingham"); Atkinson, *The British Are Coming,* 228–37; Middlekauff: *The Glorious Cause,* 276–77; Philip Schuyler to George Washington, January 5–7, 1776, FONA Washington:03-03-02-0021.

101. George Washington to John Hancock, January 11, 1776, AA4 4:629–30; Humphreys, *An Essay,* 77; Fischer, *Paul Revere's Ride,* 262–63 ("food shortages").

102. Atkinson, *The British Are Coming,* 238 and 257–59.

103. Samuel B. Webb, journal, March 1 and March 4–5, 1776, 128–34 ("vast number"); Ebenezer Huntington to Jabez Huntington, March 4 and March 7, 1776, *Letters Written by Ebenezer Huntington During the Revolution* (New York: C. F. Hartman, 1915), 30–31; John Sullivan to John Adams, March 15-19, 1776, FONA Adams:06-04-02-0021 ("utmost consternation").

104. Samuel B. Webb, journal, March 3 and 4, 1776, 133–34; Atkinson, *The British Are Coming,* 257–59.

105. "Plan for Attacking Boston," February 18–25, 1776, FONA Washington:03-03-02-0237, last modified June 13, 2018; Samuel B. Webb, journal, March 5 and 6, 1776, 134–36; Barker, diary, March 5, 1776, 70; John Sullivan to John Adams, March 15–19, 1776, FONA Adams:06-04-02-0021; Ebenezer Huntington to Jabez Huntington, March 7, 1776, *Letters by Ebenezer Huntington,* 31; Ebenezer David to Nicholas Brown, March 10, 1776, *A Rhode Island Chaplain,* 16–17; Middlekauff: *The Glorious Cause,* 310.

106. Barker, diary, March 17, 1776, 71–72; Ebenezer Huntington to Jabez Huntington, March 21, 1776, *Letters Written by Ebenezer Huntington,* 32–33; Samuel Richards, *Diary of Samuel Richards, Captain of Connecticut Line, War of Revolution, 1775–1781* (Philadelphia, PA: Leeds & Biddle, 1909), 28; Humphreys, *An Essay,* 77; Atkinson, *The British Are Coming,* 262–68; Middlekauff: *The Glorious Cause,* 310–11.

107. John Montresor, journal, 120–21 ("blew to pieces"); Barker, diary, March 17, 1776, 71–72; *The Connecticut Courant and Hartford Weekly Intelligencer,* April 15, 1776 ("Putnam enters Boston").

CHAPTER 10

1. George Washington, Orders and Instructions for Major General Charles Lee, January 8, 1776, Lee Papers 2:236–37; George Washington, Orders and Instructions for Major General Israel Putnam, March 29, 1776, FONA Washington:03-03-02-0421; Humphreys, *An Essay,* 77–79.

2. "Instructions and Orders for Brigadier-General Heath," March 19, 1776, AA4 5:422; *A Rhode Island Chaplain,* 19–20. The introductory essay to the section "New York and Brooklyn, Letter VII, May 1776" indicates that the men marched from Norwich to New London, where they boarded open boats for the three-day journey to New York. This would seem to conflict somewhat with Washington's original orders.

3. William Douglas to Hannah Douglas, July 20, 1776, "Revolutionary War Letters of Colonel William Douglas," *The New York Historical Society Bulletin* 13, no. 1 (April 1929): 37–38 (hereafter "Revolutionary War Letters," NYHS13); Barnet Schecter, *The Battle for New York: The City at the Heart of the Revolution* (New York: Walker, 2002), 98 ("William Douglas"); Joseph Plumb Martin, *Narrative of a Revolutionary Soldier: Some of the Adventures, Dangers, and Sufferings of Joseph Plumb Martin* (New York: Signet, 2010), 16–18. Author's Note: Typically, a colonel is the ranking officer in a regiment, however, the seven subordinate units of Connecticut State Troops (sometimes referred to as "Levies") in Brig. Gen. James Wadsworth's brigade were designated as the first through sixth (together with an un-numbered one) battalions. Johnston, *Record of Connecticut Men*, 392.

4. French, journal, no. 2, April 1, 1776, 197 ("Wethersfield"); General Orders, April 7, 1776, AA4 5:796; Israel Putnam to John Hancock, April 4, 1776, AA4 5:787; John Hancock to Israel Putnam, April 10, 1776, AA4 5:843; Livingston, *Israel Putnam*, 287 ("Kennedy House").

5. General Orders, April 7, 1776, AA4 5:796.

6. George Washington to Artemas Ward, May 28, 1776, FONA Washington:03-04-02-0326 ("lead"); Samuel Blachley Webb, Plan of Operations, April 6/7, 1776, Webb, *Correspondence and Journals*, 1:140–41.

7. Martin, *Narrative of a Revolutionary Soldier*, 19–21.

8. George Washington to Israel Putnam, May 21, 1776, FONA Washington:03-04-02-0294; Reverend Shewkirk, diary, June 13, 1776, A. A. Reinke, "Occupation of New York City by the British, 1776," extract cited in Henry P. Johnston, *The Campaign of 1776 Around New York and Brooklyn, Including a New and Circumstantial Account of the Battle of Long Island and the Loss of New York*, part 2 (Brooklyn, NY: Long Island Historical Society, 1878), 108; Anonymous letter writer quoted in Washington Irving, *Life of George Washington* (New York: G. P. Putnam, 1856), 192 ("so little mischief"); Atkinson, *The British Are Coming*, 312 ("anti-Tory mobs").

9. William Tudor to John Adams, September 23, 1776, FONA Adams:06-05-02-0019.

10. Jedediah Huntington to Joshua Huntington, April 26, 1776, *Huntington Papers*, 2:281–82.

11. Israel Putnam to George Washington, April 7, 1776, AA4 5:811; General Orders, June 28, 1776, AA4 6:1147–49 ("sandbags and hogsheads"); Livingston, *Israel Putnam*, 276 ("Governor's Island").

12. Samuel Shaw to Francis Shaw, May 3, 1776 (extract), The *Journals of Major Samuel Shaw*, 11–12.

13. Joseph Reed to Samuel B. Webb, January 16, 1776, Webb, *Correspondence and Journals*, 1:126–27; "The Book of Scottish Song/Maggie Lauder," https://en.wikisource .org/w/index.php?title=The_Book_of_Scottish_Song/Maggie_Lauder&oldid=6785750. Last edited April 30, 2017.

14. Caleb Gibbs to Penelope Gibbs, June 18, 1776, extract quoted in Livingston, *Israel Putnam*, 279–80.

15. General Orders, June 21 and 22, 1776, AA4 6:1146; Webb, journal, June 21, 1776, Webb, *Correspondence and Journals*, 1:148–49; Livingston, *Israel Putnam*, 280 ("Burr

appointed"); Baker, *Connecticut Families of the Revolution*, 119–20; Thomas Fleming, *The Duel: Alexander Hamilton, Aaron Burr, and the Future of America* (New York: Basic, 1999), 80, 85, and 405; Clark, *Phineas Lyman*, 3–4. Author's Note: Burr also had several other family connections that held him in good stead. For one, his mother's sister Mary had married Timothy Dwight III, who had joined Phineas Lyman on his ill-fated Natchez expedition, and who would also die in Mississippi shortly after settling there. His first cousin, Eleanor, had married Phineas Lyman. During the Revolution, her brother, Timothy Dwight IV, would serve as a chaplain in a Connecticut regiment led by Brig. Gen. Samuel H. Parsons. Dwight would later serve as president of Yale.

16. General Orders, March 11, 1776, AA4 5:207.

17. Proceedings of a General Court Martial of the Line, June 26, 1776, AA4 6:1084–86; George Washington, Warrant and Order to Provost Marshall, June 28, 1776, AA4 6:1119–20; Webb, *Correspondence and Journals*, June 21, 24, and 28, 1776, 1:148–50; Atkinson, *The British Are Coming*, 313–16.

18. General Orders, AA4 6:1148; William Tudor to John Adams, July 7, 1776, FONA Adams:06-04-02-0152; Ebenezer Huntington to Jabez Huntington, June 23, 1776, *Letters Written by Ebenezer Huntington*, 35.

19. Robert Rogers to George Washington, December 14, 1775, FONA Washington:03-02-02-0505.

20. Eleazar Wheelock to George Washington, December 2, 1775, FONA Washington:03-0202-0429; George Washington to John Sullivan, December 17, 1775, FONA Washington:03-02-02-0522; George Washington to Philip Schuyler, December 18, 1775, FONA Washington:03-02-02-0531; Philip Schuyler to George Washington, January 5-7, 1776, FONA Washington:03-02-02-0021.

21. George Washington to John Hancock, June 27, 1776, FONA Washington:03-05-02-0079; Thomas B. Allen, *Tories: Fighting for the King in America's First Civil War* (New York: Harper, 2010), 177–78 ("Queen's American Rangers"). Author's Note: Apparently Rogers did not enjoy the respect of many British officers, as was apparent from an interaction observed by American officers under a flag of truce near Peekskill that November when he interrupted the meeting and was summarily dismissed with harsh and insulting words by the senior British officer present. Ebenezer Huntington to Jabez Huntington, November 1, 1776, *Letters Written by Ebenezer Huntington*, 50–51.

22. "Minutes of a Conference of General Officers," July 8, 1776, AA5 1:224. Author's Note: At the request of Congress, Washington ordered Putnam to prepare the way for the construction of fire rafts by purchasing lumber and hiring carpenters to build them. These, too, proved largely ineffective. George Washington to Israel Putnam, June 3, 1776, FONA Washington:03-04-02-0343.

23. Israel Putnam to Horatio Gates, July 26, 1776, (extract) quoted in Livingston, *Israel Putnam*, 282; Horatio Gates to Israel Putnam, August 11, 1776, AA5 1:900.

24. Jedediah Huntington to Jabez Huntington, August 5, 1776, *Huntington Papers*, 2:317; Atkinson, *The British Are Coming*, 359–60 ("fire ships"); Schechter, *The Battle for New York*, 114–15 ("August 16").

25. Atkinson, *The British Are Coming*, 432–35; Schecter, *The Battle for New York*, 244–45 ("ineffective"); Samuel Shaw to Francis Shaw, October 9, 1776, *Journals of Major Samuel Shaw*, 23 ("failure of the *cheval de frise*").

26. Terry Golway, *Washington's General: Nathanael Greene and the Triumph of the American Revolution* (New York: Henry Holt, 2005), 99–100; George Washington to Nathanael Greene, November 8, 1776, FONA Washington:03-07-02-0078; Nathanael Greene to George Washington, November 9, 1776, FONA Washington:03-07-02-0085.

27. Webb, journal, July 9 and 10, 1776, *Correspondence and Journals*, 153; Atkinson, *The British Are Coming*, 349.

28. Atkinson, *The British Are Coming*, 349–50. Author's Note: Along the way, the drivers pulled their wagons up in front of a tavern owned by Clapp Raymond in Wilton Parish (then part of Norwalk, Connecticut) on the Danbury Road, and they went in to spend the night. Meanwhile, outside, some local Tories, aware of the destination of the load, began to take as many pieces of lead as they could from the wagons and threw some of them into a nearby swamp, while others secreted some on nearby properties. The unsuspecting drivers resumed their journey the next morning with a somewhat lightened load. The cargo reached its destination, and the balls were later returned to the king's men through the barrels of the Patriots' muskets. Years later, a treasure seeker using a metal detector located several pieces of the statue, which he sold to a museum. The subsequent lawsuit was decided in favor of the landowner by the Connecticut Supreme Court in *Favorite v. Miller*, 176 Conn. 310 (1978). Robert H. Russell, *Wilton, Connecticut: Three Centuries of People, Place, and Progress* (Wilton, CT: Wilton Historical Society, 2004), 116–20.

29. Margaret Moncrieffe Coughlan, *Memoirs of Mrs. Coughlan (Daughter of the late Major Moncrieffe) Written by Herself, and Dedicated to the British Nation; Being Interspersed with Anecdotes of the Late American and Present French War, with Remarks Moral and Political in Two Volumes*, vol. 1 (London: C. and G. Kearsley, 1794), 20–29.

30. Livingston, *Israel Putnam*, 285.

31. Israel Putnam to Margaret Moncrieffe, July 26, 1776, AA5 1:471.

32. Coughlan, *Memoirs*, 30–32.

33. Coughlan, *Memoirs*, 33–35.

34. Coughlan, *Memoirs*, 36–37.

35. Coughlan, *Memoirs*, 38 and 44–47; Russell Shorto, *Revolution Song: The Story of America's Founding in Six Remarkable Lives* (New York: Norton, 2018), 262–63.

36. Coughlan, *Memoirs*, 48–58.

37. Schecter, *The Battle for New York*, 100–101 and 110–11; John J. Gallagher, *The Battle of Brooklyn, 1776* (Rockville Center, NY: Sarpedon, 1999), 61–63; Atkinson, *The British Are Coming*, 317–21.

38. General Orders, April 30, 1776, Johnston, *The Campaign of 1776*, Documents, 5–6; Ebenezer David to Nicholas Brown, May 4, 1776, *A Rhode Island Chaplain in the Revolution*, 20–22; Atkinson, *The British Are Coming*, 364 ("Greene's Plan").

39. General Orders, August 20, 1776, AA5 1:1139–40; Joseph Reed to Esther de Berdt Reed, August 23–24, 1776, William B. Reed, ed., *Life and Correspondence of Joseph Reed: Military Secretary of Washington, at Cambridge; Adjutant General of the Continental Army; Member of Congress of the United States; and President of the Executive Council of the State of Pennsylvania, By His Grandson, William B. Reed*, vol. 1 (Philadelphia, PA: Lindsay and Blakiston, 1847), 219–20.

40. George Washington to William Heath, August 22, 1776, George Washington to William Heath, August 23, 1776, and George Washington to John Hancock, President of Congress, August 23, 1776, John C. Fitzpatrick, ed., *The Writings of George Washington from the Original Manuscript Sources, 1775–1799*, vol. 5, May, 1776–August, 1776 (Washington, DC: Government Printing Office, 1932), 473–77; Ebenezer Huntington to Jabez Huntington, August 23, 1776, *Letters written by Ebenezer Huntington*, 41.

41. Joseph Reed to William Livingston, August 30, 1776, AA5 1:1231–32 ("soothe and soften").

42. Gallagher, *The Battle of Brooklyn*, 97; Joseph Trumbull to Jonathan Trumbull, Jr., August 27, 1776, Johnston, *Campaign of 1776*, part 2, 40.

43. Orders: To Major General Putnam, August 25, 1776, AA5 1:1149–50.

44. Samuel Miles, journal, Johnston, *The Campaign of 1776*, part 2, 60–63 ("warning to Sullivan"); Atkinson, *The British Are Coming*, 363–65; Gallagher, *The Battle of Brooklyn*, 99–100; John Buchanan, *The Road to Valley Forge: How Washington Built the Army That Won the Revolution* (New York: Wiley, 2004), 47–48.

45. David Hackett Fischer, *Washington's Crossing* (New York: Oxford University Press, 2004), 158 ("strong supporter"); George Washington to Jonathan Trumbull, July 7, 1776, AA5 1:106–107; George Washington to Thomas Seymour, July 8, 1776, AA5 1:124–25; Thomas Seymour to Jonathan Trumbull, July 11, 1776, AA5 1:204–206; George Washington to Jonathan Trumbull, July 9, 1776, AA5 1:142.

46. Minutes of a Conference of General Officers, July 8, 1776, AA5 1:224; Jonathan Trumbull to George Washington, July 17, 1776, AA5 1:400–401; Samuel B. Webb to Jonathan Trumbull, July 18, 1776, Webb, *Correspondence and Journals*, 1:159–60; George Washington to Jonathan Trumbull, July 18, 1778, AA5 1:414; James Wadsworth to Jonathan Trumbull, July 18, 1776, AA5 1:417; Thomas Seymour et al. to George Washington, July 16, 1776, FONA Washington:03-05-02-0244; George Washington to John Hancock, FONA Washington:03-05-02-0261; William Douglas to Hannah Douglas, July 27, 1776, "Revolutionary War Letters," NYHS13, 1:38–39 ("displeased"); Fischer, *Washington's Crossing*, 85–86 and 93–94; Gallagher, *The Battle of Brooklyn*, 100.

47. Schecter, *The Battle for New York*, 135–37; Atkinson, *The British Are Coming*, 366–67.

48. Samuel Holden Parsons to John Adams, August 29, 1776, FONA Adams:06-05-02-0002; Jedediah Huntington to Jabez Huntington, August 26, 1776, *Huntington Papers*, 2:322 ("fever").

49. Lord Stirling to George Washington, August 29, 1776, AA5 1:1245–46; Gallagher, *The Battle of Brooklyn*, 110; Buchanan, *The Road to Valley Forge*, 50–51. Author's Note: Some authors (e.g., Gallagher) have said that Putnam rode to Stirling's headquarters on August 27 to issue his orders. However, Stirling told Washington that, "I was *called up* and informed by General Putnam." (Emphasis added) I have interpreted that to mean that he was summoned to Putnam's headquarters.

50. Stirling to Washington, August 29, 1776, AA5 1:1245–46; Samuel J. Atlee, Journal of the Transactions of August 27, 1776, Upon Long-Island, August 27, 1776, AA5 1:1251–55; William Howe to George Germain, September 3, 1776, AA5 1:1256–58.

51. Gallagher, *The Battle of Brooklyn*, 110.

52. Gallagher, *The Battle of Brooklyn*, 110–11; Martin, *Narrative of a Revolutionary Soldier*, 21–23.

53. William Howe to George Germain, September 3, 1776, AA5 1:1256–58; "Extract of a Letter from Long Island," August 28, 1776, AA5 1:1195–96; Samuel Miles, journal, Johnston, *The Campaign of 1776*, part 2, 60–63. Author's Note: General Parsons was quick to unfairly accuse the Pennsylvania and New York soldiers who were standing guard at the Narrows near the Red Lion of cowardice and Col. Samuel Miles of negligence in allowing Clinton to have gotten so far behind the American line. Samuel Holden Parsons to John Adams, September 17, 1776, and October 8, 1776, FONA Adams:06-05-02-0015 and 06-05-02-0025. His account does not square with those of Colonel Atlee and Lord Stirling.

54. "Extract of a Letter from an Officer in General Frasier's Battalion," September 3, 1776, AA5 1:1250–51. That same officer wrote that the Hessians had been told in advance that the Americans would not give any quarter to them, thus inciting them to act dishonorably.

55. Joseph Reed to William Livingston, August 30, 1776, AA5 1:1231–32; Gallagher, *The Battle of Brooklyn*, 127–30 and 133, Atkinson. *The British Are Coming*, 370–71.

56. Martin, *Narrative of a Revolutionary Soldier*, 24–25 ("drowned"); "Extract of a Letter from an Officer in the Maryland Battalion," Wednesday Morning, Daybreak, August 28, 1776, AA5 1:1195; Samuel Holden Parsons to John Adams, August 29, 1776, FONA Adams:06-05-02-0002; Ebenezer Huntington to Jabez Huntington, August 31, 1776, *Letters*, 42.

57. William Douglas to Hannah Douglas, August 31, 1776, "Revolutionary War Letters," NYHS13, 3:118–19.

58. William Howe to George Germain, September 3, 1776, AA5 1:1256–58 ("six hundred yards"); Gold Selleck Silliman to _____, August 29, 1776, quoted in Livingston, *Israel Putnam*, 305–306; Joseph Reed to William Livingston, August 30, 1776, AA5 1:1231–32.

59. Samuel Greene, quoted in *The Hartford Courant*, June 25, 1888 ("God take it all!").

60. AA5 1:1246.

61. William Douglas to Hannah Douglas, August 31, 1776, "Revolutionary War Letters," NYHS13, 3:118–19; Benjamin Tallmadge, *Memoir of Colonel Benjamin Tallmadge* (New York: Gilliss Press, 1904), 12–14; "Extract of a Letter from New York," Friday Morning, August 30, 1776, AA5 1:1233; "Extract of a Letter from New York," August 31, 1776, AA5 1:1249; Atkinson, *The British Are Coming*, 376–77.

62. Atkinson, *The British Are Coming*, 372 ("prisoners").

63. Wheeler, *Voices of 1776*, 138.

64. Nathanael Greene to George Washington, September 5, 1776, FONA Washington:06-06-02-0180; George Washington Greene, *The Life of Nathanael Greene, Major-General in the Army of the Revolution*, vol. 2 (New York: Hurd and Houghton, 1871), 214–16; "Petition of Major-General Greene and others for a reconsideration of the Proceedings of a Council of General Officers," September 11, 1776, AA5 2:326–27; "Proceedings of a Council of General Officers," September 12, 1776, AA5 2:329–30.

65. Livingston, *Israel Putnam*, 307; Schechter, *The Battle for New York*, 170–71; Henry Phelps Johnston, *The Battle of Harlem Heights, September 16, 1776: With a Review of the Events of the Campaign* (New York: Columbia University Press, 1897), 28–29.

66. Greene, *The Battle of Brooklyn*, 157; Schecter, *The Battle for New York*, 171–74 ("God curse 'em"); Atkinson, *The British Are Coming*, 380–82; Humphreys, *An Essay*, Livingston, *Israel Putnam*, 82–87 and 283–84.

67. Johnston, *The Campaign of 1776*, 232; Livingston, *Israel Putnam*, 307.

68. Caesar Rodney to Thomas McKean and George Read, September 18, 1776, *Letters of the Delegates*, 5:197–98 ("as if the devil"); Martin, *Narrative of a Revolutionary Soldier*, 30–31.

69. William Douglas to Hannah Douglas, September 18, 1776, NYHS13, 3:122.

70. Joshua Huntington to Jabez Huntington, September 20, 1776, *Huntington Papers*, 1:44–45; Tallmadge, *Memoir*, 15.

71. Schecter, *The Battle for New York*, 187–93; Middlekauff, *The Glorious Cause*, 348; George Washington to John Augustine Washington, September 26, 1776, John Rhode-hamel, ed., *George Washington: Writings* (New York: Library of America, 1997), 244–48 ("surprise and Mortification"); Hubbard, *Major General Israel Putnam*, 121–23; James Thomas Flexner, *Washington: The Indispensable Man* (Boston: Little, Brown, 1974), 84 ("are these the men"); George Washington Greene, *Life of Nathanael Greene*, 216.

72. George Washington to President of Congress (John Hancock), Report, September 17, 1776, AA5 2:351; "Testimony of Samuel Holden Parsons," John Morin Scott, Report of the Evidence Taken at the Court of Inquiry, October 26, 1776, AA5 2:1251–54; Schecter, *The Battle for New York*, 185–86; John Buchanan, *The Road to Valley Forge*, 85 ("Parsons"); Nathanael Greene to Nicholas Cooke, September 17, 1776, AA5 2:369–70 ("a miserable, disorderly retreat"); Hezekiah Munsell, Recollections, Henry R. Stiles, *The History of Ancient Windsor, Connecticut, Including East Windsor, South Windsor, and Elling-ton, Prior to 1768, the Date of Their Separation from the Old Town; and Windsor, Bloomfield and Windsor Locks, to the Present Time: Also the Genealogies and Genealogical Notes of Those Families Which Settled Within the Limits of Ancient Windsor, Connecticut, Prior to 1800* (New York: Charles B. Norton, 1859), 715 ("Putnam returning"). Author's Note: Putnam's division consisted of five brigades: Gold Selleck Silliman, James Clinton, John Morin Scott, Samuel Holden Parsons, and John Fellows. Their area of responsibility was Lower Manhattan and the East River from Corlear's Hook on the south to approximately present-day 15th Street. Above that was Joseph Spencer's division with coverage north to Horen's Hook at the Harlem River. Part of Spencer's responsibility was at Kip's Bay where Douglas and his Connecticut Militia (James Wadsworth's brigade) were stationed. I have been unable to determine the movement of Scott and Clinton on September 15, and I have assumed that they had already retreated up the Bloomingdale Road to Harlem, since they do not appear to have been involved in any fighting or the ensuing panic. Livingston, *Israel Putnam*, 307; Johnston, *The Campaign of 1776*, 237 ("Bloomingdale Road").

73. Caesar Rodney to Thomas McKean and George Read, September 18, 1776, *Letters of the Delegates*, 5:197-98; Frank Landon Humphreys, *Life and Times of David Humphreys: Soldier—Statesman—Poet, "Belov'd of Washington"* (New York: G. P. Putnam's Sons, 1917), 66; Humphreys, *An Essay*, 89–90; Schecter, *The Battle for New York*, 188–89; Middlekauff,

The Glorious Cause, 348–49; Hubbard, *Major General Israel Putnam*, 123–25; Livingston, *Israel Putnam*, 307–12.

74. Gold Selleck Silliman to Mary Silliman, September 15-16, 1776, and September 17, 1776, Silliman Family Papers, Manuscripts and Archives, Yale University Library.

75. Humphreys, *An Essay*, 92–93.

76. Samuel Shaw to His Parents, September 18, 1776 (extract), *The Journals of Major Samuel Shaw*, 19–20; Extract of a Letter from Harlem, September 16, 1776, AA5 1:352 ("Henry Knox"); Atkinson, *The British Are Coming*, 393 ("Henry Knox"). Author's Note: William Tudor, the judge advocate, had an experience like that of Henry Knox. Caught in Lower Manhattan three hours after the British had landed at Kip's Bay, he was unable to find a boat and incapable of swimming the Hudson River, so he took to the woods, evading British patrols. Tudor made it safely to the American lines, greatly relieved that he had only lost some of his baggage. William Tudor to John Adams, September 23, 1776, FONA Adams:06-05-02-0019.

77. Fischer, *Washington's Crossing*, 104; Schecter, *The Battle for New York*, 189–90; Buchanan, *The Road to Valley Forge*, 86–87 ("cautious"); Livingston, *Israel Putnam*, 310–11 ("Mary Lindley Murray").

78. George Washington to John Hancock, September 18, 1776, 5AA 2:380–81; Buchanan, *The Road to Valley Forge*, 88–90; Joseph Reed to Esther de Berdt Reed, September [no date], 1776, *Life and Correspondence of Joseph Reed*, 337–38 ("animate troops"); Nathanael Greene to Governor Nicholas Cooke, September 17, 1776, 5AA 2:369–70 ("spirited conduct"); Gold Selleck Silliman to Mary Silliman, September 17, 1776, Silliman Family Papers ("Putnam"); Livingston, *Israel Putnam*, 312–17; Martin, *Narrative of a Revolutionary Soldier*, 37 ("nineteen bullet holes"). Author's Note: Accounts vary as to who delivered the order to Knowlton. I am assuming that Washington issued it and Putnam delivered it. Oliver Burnham, one of Knowlton's Rangers, recollected that: "Soon after we met our army, General Putnam came up to Colonel Knowlton, and directed him to take the left flank, and the troops marched to meet the enemy." Henry P. Johnston, *The Battle of Harlem Heights*, 178.

79. General Orders, September 17, 1776, AA5 2:382 ("an honor to any country"); Gold Selleck Silliman to Mary Silliman, November 16, 1776, Silliman Family Papers; Livingston, *Israel Putnam*, 312–17; Humphreys, *An Essay*, 94–96; Schecter, *The Battle for New York*, 196–203; Atkinson, *The British Are Coming*, 394–97.

80. General Orders, AA5 2:381–82.

81. John Chester to Joseph Webb, October 3, 1776, (extract) quoted in Johnston, *The Campaign of 1776*, 2:98–99.

82. Martin, *Narrative of a Revolutionary Soldier*, 43–44.

83. William Douglas to Hannah Douglas, October 25, 1776, "Revolutionary War Letters," NYHS13, 4:160–61; Atkinson, *The British Are Coming*, 438–42; Humphreys, *An Essay*, 97. Throg's Neck was named for a John Throgmorton, an early settler in that area of New Amsterdam. Walter D. Edmonds, *The Musket and the Cross: The Struggle of France and England for North America* (Boston, MA: Little, Brown, 1968), 275.

84. Tallmadge, *Memoir*, 16–18; Martin, *Narrative of a Revolutionary Soldier*, 46–48.

85. Atkinson, *The British Are Coming*, 442–47; Tallmadge, *Memoir*, 18–19; "Extract of a Letter to a Gentleman in Annapolis," October 29, 1776, AA5 2:1284; Rufus Putnam, *Memoirs*, 64–65; Martin, *Narrative of a Revolutionary Soldier*, 116–17 ("hastily buried"). Martin and his comrades returned to the scene of the battle one year later and noted that: "Some of the bodies had been so slightly buried that the dogs or hogs, or both, had dug them out of the ground. The skulls and other bones, and hair were scattered about the place."

86. "Minutes of the Council of War," November 6, 1776, 5AA 3:543–44; Tallmadge, *Memoir*, 19.

87. George Washington to Israel Putnam, November 9, 1776 ("not a moments time"), FONA Washington:03-07-01-0091; Humphreys, *An Essay*, 97 ("western side of the Hudson"); Thomas Mifflin to President of Congress [John Hancock], November 10, 1776, AA5 3:634; Samuel Shaw to [parents], October 31, 1776, *The Journals of Major Samuel Shaw*, 25; Atkinson, *The British Are Coming*, 453.

88. Schecter, *The Battle for New York*, 246–47.

89. Nathanael Greene to Henry Knox, November 17, 1776, Johnston, *The Campaign of 1776*, part 2, 100–101; Tallmadge, *Memoir*, 19–20; Henry B. Carrington, *Battles of the American Revolution, 1775–1781* (New York: A. S. Barnes, 1876), 249; Fischer, *Washington's Crossing*, 111–14; Schecter, *The Battle for New York*, 247–55; Buchanan, *The Road to Valley Forge*, 114–18.

90. John S. Pancake, *1777: The Year of the Hangman* (Tuscaloosa: University of Alabama Press, 1992), 45; Nathanael Greene to Henry Knox, November 17, 1776, Johnston, *The Campaign of 1776*, part 2, 100–101.

91. William Douglas to Hannah Douglas, September 26, 1776, "Revolutionary War Letters," NYHS13, 4:157–58; Samuel Holden Parsons to John Adams, September 17, 1776 and October 8, 1776, FONA Adams:06-05-02-0015 and Adams:06-05-02-0025; Daniel Brodhead to [Unnamed], September 5, 1776, Johnston, *The Campaign of 1776*, part 2, 63–66.

92. John Sullivan to [un-named], October 25, 1777, *Memoirs of the Long Island Historical Society*, vol. 2, 369–72; Samuel Miles, journal, Johnston, *The Campaign of 1776*, part 2, 60–63; Gallagher, *The Battle of Brooklyn*, 114.

93. William Douglas to Hannah Douglas, December 5, 1776, Douglas Letters, Litchfield Historical Society.

CHAPTER 11

1. Benjamin Rumsey to Maryland Council of Safety, November 13, 1776, *Letters of Delegates*, 5:478–79 ("crossed over"); Samuel B. Webb to Joseph Trumbull, November 24, 1776, Webb, *Correspondence and Journals*, 1:174–75.

2. William Hooper to Joseph Hewes, January 1, 1777, *Letters of Delegates*, 6:7–8 ("Lee's capture"); Israel Putnam to George Washington, December 12, 1776, FONA Washington:03-07-02-0250, accessed September 29, 2019 ("all the Craft"); Fischer, *Washington's Crossing*, 148–49; Atkinson, *The British Are Coming*, 491–92.

3. Atkinson, *The British Are Coming*, 499–500.

4. George Washington to President of Congress (John Hancock), December 9, 1776, AA5 3:1137–38 ("Putnam to Philadelphia"); Israel Putnam, General Orders, December 12, 1776, AA5 3:1180–81; Israel Putnam to George Washington, December 12, 1776, FONA Washington:03-07-02-0250, accessed September 29, 2019; George Washington to Israel Putnam, December 25, 1776, FONA Washington:03-07-02-0346, accessed September 29, 2019. Author's Note: In a letter to John Hancock, Washington refers to a "clever" French engineer in Philadelphia. It is believed that the "French" engineer was actually Andre Thaddeus Kosciuszko (1746–1817), a Polish national and military officer. George Washington to John Hancock, December 20, 1776, FONA Washington:03-07-02-0305.

5. Israel Putnam, General Orders, December 13, 1776, AA5 3:1200; John Bayard to Council of Safety, December 13, 1776, Samuel Hazard, ed., *Pennsylvania Archives: Selected and Arranged from Original Documents in the Office of the Secretary of the Commonwealth, Conformably to Acts of the General Assembly, February 15, 1851, and March 1, 1853*, First Series, Vol. 5 (Philadelphia, PA: Joseph Severns & Co., 1853), 107–108 (hereafter PA1) ("rumor").

6. George Washington to Israel Putnam, December 21, 1776, FONA Washington:03-07-02-0317, accessed September 29, 2019.

7. General Orders, December 13, 1776, AA5 3:1200 ("conscientious scruples"); Livingston, *Israel Putnam*, 330–31 ("drones"); Joseph Pennell to Council of Safety, December 30, 1776, PA1 5:143 ("bar iron").

8. George Washington to President of Congress (John Hancock), December 9, 1776, AA5 3:1137–38 ("Delaware to the Schuylkill"); General Orders, December 14, 1776, AA5 3:1214 ("currency").

9. Elbridge Gerry to James Warren, December 23, 1776; William Hooper to Joseph Hewes, January 1, 1777; and John Hancock to Robert Treat Paine, January 13, 1777, *Letters of Delegates*, 5:640–42, 6:7–8, and 6:90–93.

10. Oliver Wolcott to [unnamed], December 13, 1776, quoted in Livingston, *Israel Putnam*, 331–32 ("last extremity" and "exhaustion"); George Washington to Israel Putnam, December 25, 1776, AA5 3:1420 ("much improved").

11. In 1969, Laurence J. Peter sagely but humorously observed: "In a hierarchy, every employee tends to rise to his level of incompetence." *The Peter Principle*. While I would never refer to Putnam as "incompetent," given his experience and his personality, he was less suited for some assignments than others, as he often tended to lose sight of the big picture and, more important, his place in it. When he proposed an attack on New York City, his friend Horatio Gates had to remind him that without a fleet to match the British, he could not hold the city were he to capture it. Putnam got the point and abandoned that plan.

12. Joseph Reed to George Washington, December 22, 1776, FONA Washington:03-07-02-0324.

13. Robert Morris to Silas Deane, January 8, 1777, *Letters of Delegates*, 6:58–68; Fischer, *Washington's Crossing*, 210 and 214; Atkinson, *The British Are Coming*, 520.

14. Livingston, *Israel Putnam*, 333–34.

15. Samuel Griffin to Israel Putnam, December 21, 1776, PA1 5:127; Joseph Reed to George Washington, December 22, 1776, FONA Washington:03-07-02-0324; Fischer, *Washington's Crossing*, 198–200; Atkinson, *The British Are Coming*, 513.

16. Robert Morris to Silas Deane, January 8, 1777, *Letters of Delegates*, 6:58–68; Middlekauff, *The Glorious Cause*, 359–60; Atkinson, *The British Are Coming*, 519–26; Fischer, *Washington's Crossing*, 234–54.

17. James Ewing to Thomas Wharton, Jr. (President of the Council of Safety), Order, December 30, 1776 ("sending prisoners"), and Address of Council of Safety, December 31, 1776, PA1 5:146 ("suitable quarters"); Fischer, *Washington's Crossing*, 254–55 ("896 officers and men"); Livingston, *Israel Putnam*, 335–36 ("old gray-beard").

18. Executive Committee to John Hancock, January 6, 1777, *Letters of Delegates*, 6:37–39.

19. Middlekauff, *The Glorious Cause*, 360–62; Atkinson, *The British Are Coming*, 543–49; Fischer, *Washington's Crossing*, 324–40.

20. Joseph Reed to Israel Putnam, January 2, 1777, quoted in full in Livingston, *Israel Putnam*, 337; Executive Committee to John Hancock, January 6 and 8, 1777, *Letters of Delegates*, 6:37–39 and 6:50–51.

21. Israel Putnam to Council of Safety, January 5, 1777, Israel Putnam to Council of Safety, January 6, 1777, Israel Putnam to Council of Safety, January 7, 1777, and Israel Putnam to Council of Safety, January 9, 1777, PA1 5:163, 5:168–69, 5:171, and 5:177; George Washington to Israel Putnam, January 7, 1777, FONA Washington:03-07-02-0416.

22. George Washington to Joseph Reed, January 15, 1777, FONA Washington:03-08-02-0082; Israel Putnam to the Council of Safety, January 6, 1777, PA1 5:168-69.

23. George Washington to Joseph Reed, January 15, 1777, FONA Washington:03-08-02-0082; Livingston, *Israel Putnam*, 337–40. Author's Note: There would appear to be a misapprehension on the part of both the Board of War and the Executive Committee of Congress as to how many troops Putnam had at Princeton at this time. Both grossly estimated that he had "not less than 6,000 men." Executive Committee to John Hancock, January 22, 1777, and Board of War to the Executive Committee, January 25, 1777, *Letters of Delegates*, 6:130–31 and 6:144; Israel Putnam to Council of Safety, January 31, 1777, PA1 5:208–209.

24. Humphreys, *An Essay*, 102–103; Livingston, *Israel Putnam*, 340–41.

25. Israel Putnam to Council of Safety, February 8, 1777, and Daniel Putnam, aide to General Putnam to Commanding Officer of the Prison, February 8, 1777, PA1 5:215–16.

26. George Washington to William Livingston, January 24, 1777, Carl E. Prince, ed., *The Papers of William Livingston*, vol. 1 (June 1774–June 1777) (Trenton: New Jersey Historical Commission, 1979), 202 (hereafter *Livingston Papers*); Israel Putnam to William Livingston, February 10, 1777, *Livingston Papers* 1:220–21 ("no man's interest").

27. Israel Putnam to William Livingston, February 10, 1777, *Livingston Papers* 1:220–21.

28. William Livingston to Israel Putnam, February 13, 1777, *Livingston Papers* 1:221–23 ("men not money"); Israel Putnam to William Livingston, February 18, 1777, *Livingston Papers* 1:241–42 ("no sum").

29. Israel Putnam to William Livingston, February 18, 1777, *Livingston Papers* 1:241–42; William Livingston to Israel Putnam, February 13, 1777, *Livingston Papers* 1:221–23.

30. George Washington to Israel Putnam, February 22, 1777, FONA Washington:03-08-02-0448.

31. Israel Putnam to George Washington, February 26, 1777, FONA Washington:03-08-02-0479; George Washington to Israel Putnam, February 28, 1777, FONA Washington:03-08-02-0492.

32. George Washington to John Sullivan, February 3, 1777, FONA Washington:03-08-02-0252, accessed September 29, 2019; Israel Putnam to George Washington, February 8, 1777, FONA Washington:03-08-02-0292, accessed September 29, 2019; Mark Edward Lender, *Cabal: The Plot Against General Washington* (Yardley, PA: Westholme Publishing, 2019), 6 ("Forage War").

33. Israel Putnam to Major Boggs, Order, February 19, 1777, PA1 5:232; Israel Putnam to William Livingston, February 18, 1777, *Livingston Papers* 1:241–42; William Livingston to the Assembly, February 22, 1777, *Livingston Papers* 1:249; Livingston, *Israel Putnam*, 341–43 ("Stockton").

34. Israel Putnam to John Hancock (President of Congress), April 8, 1777, PA1 5:300; Mann Page to John Page, April 9, 1777, *Letters of Delegates*, 6:559–60.

35. Seth Pomeroy to a Son, February 11, 1777, *The Journals and Papers of Seth Pomeroy*, 163 and 171. An anvil-shaped monument dedicated to Pomeroy was erected in the Old Cemetery off Locust Street in Cortlandt, New York, where he lies in an unmarked grave.

36. George Washington to Benedict Arnold, May 8, 1777, FONA Washington:03-09-02-0357; George Washington to Israel Putnam, May 12, 1777, FONA Washington:03-09-02-0398; George Washington to John Sullivan, May 15, 1777, FONA Washington:03-09-02-0432; George Washington to Alexander McDougall, May 16, 1777, FONA Washington:03-09-02-0437; Nathaniel Philbrick, *Valiant Ambition: George Washington, Benedict Arnold, and the Fate of the American Revolution* (New York: Viking, 2016), 100–101 ("perceived slights"); Bobrick, *Angel in the Whirlwind*, 238–39 ("Arnold").

37. Jedediah Huntington to Andrew Huntington, July 20/23, 1777, *Huntington Papers*, 2:351–55; Abraham King, Administrator of John Mandeville, Report, Court of Claims No. 130, *Reports from the Court of Claims Submitted to the House of Representatives During the First Session of the Thirty-Fifth Congress, 1857–58*, vol. 2 (Washington, DC: James B. Steedman, 1858), 77–91.

38. Pancake, *1777: The Year of the Hangman*, 92.

39. Alexander Hamilton to Israel Putnam, June 2, 1777, FONA Hamilton:01-01-02-0176; Alexander Hamilton to Israel Putnam, June 9, 1777, FONA Hamilton:01-01-02-0184.

40. Israel Angell to Nicholas Cooke, August 27, 1777, *Diary of Israel Angell*, xii–xiii.

41. Jedediah Huntington to Andrew Huntington, August 12, 1777, *Huntington Papers*, 2:363.

42. Worthington Chauncey Ford, ed., *General Orders Issued by Major-General Israel Putnam When in Command of the Highlands, in the Summer and Fall of 1777* (Brooklyn, NY: Historical Printing Club, 1893), June 8, 1777, 8–10; Cox, *A Proper Sense of Honor*, 86 ("disparity in punishment").

43. Harry M. Ward, *Between the Lines: Banditti of the American Revolution* (Westport, CT: Praeger, 2002), 17–21.

44. Ford, *General Orders Issued by Major-General Israel Putnam*, July 18 and July 24, 1777, 31 and 37–38; Jedediah Huntington to Andrew Huntington, July 20–23, 1777, *Huntington Papers*, 2:351–53.

45. Israel Putnam to George Washington, July 19, 1777, FONA Washington:03-10-02-0333, last modified June 13, 2018; Israel Putnam to George Washington, July 26, 1777, FONA Washington:03-10-02-0421, last modified June 13, 2018; Israel Putnam to George Washington, August 15, 1777, FONA Washington:03-10-02-0615, last modified June 13, 2018.

46. Humphreys, *An Essay*, 113; Livingston, *Israel Putnam*, 349–51; Hubbard, *Major General Israel Putnam*, 141–42; General Orders, August 7, 1777, 48–49 (see footnote). Author's Note: The date and text of Putnam's response vary with the source. Accordingly, rather than guess, I have left it blank. It is, however, certain that the exchange occurred prior to the actual execution date. Unlike most sources, the footnote states that the reply was made to Gen. Henry Clinton. I have followed David Humphreys' account.

47. Jedediah Huntington to Joshua Huntington, August 9, 1777, *Huntington Papers*, 2:361–62; Ford, *General Orders*, August 7, 1777, 48–49.

48. Israel Putnam, "Sentencing Statement," July 27, 1777, *Calendar of Historical Manuscripts Relating to the War of the Revolution, in the Office of the Secretary of State, Albany, N.Y.*, vol. 2 (Albany, NY: Weed, Parsons and Company, 1868), 258–60.

49. *Record of Service of Connecticut Men*, "Third Regiment, 1775," 53.

50. George Washington to Jonathan Trumbull, Sr., December 15, 1775, FONA Washington:03-02-02-0510; George Washington and Israel Putnam to First Church of Woodstock, March 24, 1776, FONA Washington:03-03-02-0395.

51. Nathanael Greene to John Adams, May 2, 1777, FONA Adams:06-05-02-0103.

52. Ford, *General Orders*, July 11, 1777, 25 ("religious services"); Jedediah Huntington to Jabez Huntington, July 28, 1777, *Huntington Papers*, 2:355–57; Jedediah Huntington to Jabez Huntington, July 29, 1777, *Huntington Papers*, 2:357–58; Roy J. Honeywell, *Chaplains of the United States Army* (Washington, DC: Government Printing Office, 1958), 73.

53. Pancake, *1777: The Year of the Hangman*, 229 ("deferential request").

54. General Orders, August 26, 1777, Webb, *Correspondence and Journals*, 1:279.

55. John Hancock to Israel Putnam, September 9, 1777; John Hancock to George Washington, September 9, 1777; and John Hancock to Israel Putnam, September 12, 1777, *Letters of the Delegates*, 7:639–40 and 7:653.

56. Israel Putnam to "Gentlemen" [Council of Safety], [1777], CSLA #973.3.

57. George Washington to Israel Putnam, September 14, 1777, FONA Washington:03-11-02-0225. Author's Note: On August 1, Washington begged Governor Clinton to assume the defense of Fort Montgomery, if possible, and to "immediately call in every man in the militia you possibly can." George Washington to George Clinton, August 1, 1777, Hugh Hastings, ed., *Public Papers of George Clinton, First Governor of New York, 1777—1795—1801—1804*, vol. 2 (New York: Wynkoop Hallenbeck Crawford Co., 1900), 185.

58. Israel Putnam to Jonathan Trumbull, Sr., September 15, 1777, "Trumbull Papers," MHS7 2:145–48. Author's Note: Late the night before, Putnam had sent a letter

addressed to "Colonels and Other Officers of the Army and Militia of Connecticut," exhorting them in forceful prose to "immediately repair to" Peekskill. He asked them to, "unitedly exert ourselves like freemen, put a speedy end to those unnatural disturbers of our peace, and, with them, a period of this unhappy and bloody war, which now ravages and desolates our country, and threatens its inhabitants and their posterity with the most dismal ruin and abject slavery." He ended the letter with a call to patriotism: "Awake, then to virtue and to great military exertion, and we shall put a speedy and happy issue to this mighty contest." Quoted in full in Livingston, *Israel Putnam*, 352–53.

59. Israel Putnam to Jonathan Trumbull, Sr., September 17, 1777, "Trumbull Papers," MHS7 2:148–50.

60. Worthington Chauncey Ford, ed., *Defenses of Philadelphia in 1777* (Brooklyn, NY: Historical Printing Club, 1897), 51–54.

61. Israel Putnam to George Clinton, September 29, 1777, Jared Sparks, ed., *Correspondence of the American Revolution Being Letters of Eminent Men to George Washington from the Time of His Taking Command of the Army to the End of His Presidency*, vol. 2 (Boston, MA: Little, Brown, 1853), 536–37; General Horatio Gates had also gleaned from his sources that: "General Burgoyne expects a violent effort will be made by General Clinton to force the posts of the Highlands and unbar the door which the army under his (Burgoyne's) command have not yet been able to break open." He passed this information on to Governor Clinton to pass on to Putnam. Horatio Gates to Jonathan Trumbull, Sr., October 5, 1777, "Trumbull Papers," MHS7 2:151–52.

62. Israel Putnam to George Washington, October 2, 1777, FONA, Washington:03-11-02-0398.

63. Pancake, *1777: The Year of the Hangman*, 141–45.

64. William B. Willcox, ed., *The American Rebellion: Sir Henry Clinton's Narrative of His Campaigns, 1775–1782, with an Appendix of Documents* (New Haven, CT: Yale University Press, 1954), 62–64, 72, and 81 ("any diversion" and "influx of British troops"); Israel Putnam to Jonathan Trumbull, Sr., September 17, 1777, "Trumbull Papers," MHS7 2:148–50 ("British reinforcements").

65. Israel Putnam to George Clinton, October 4, 1777, Sparks, *Correspondence of the American Revolution*, 537.

66. Israel Putnam to George Washington, October 8, 1777 (two letters), FONA Washington: 03-11-02-0461 and Washington:03-11-02-0462; Henry Laurens to the Marquis de Lafayette, October 12, 1777, *Letters of Delegates*, 8:115–16; Israel Putnam to George Clinton, October 6, 1777, Sparks, *Correspondence of the American Revolution*, 538; Willcox, *The American Rebellion*, 72–73; Frank L. Humphreys, *Life and Times*, 104–105.

67. George Clinton, Report to Council of Safety, October 7, 1777, *Public Papers*, vol. 2, 380–83; Israel Putnam to George Washington, October 8, 1777 (two letters), FONA Washington:03-11-02-0461 and Washington:03-11-02-0462; Samuel Parsons to Jonathan Trumbull, Sr., October 7, 1777, "Trumbull Papers," MHS7 2:154–55; George Clinton to George Washington, October 9, 1777, FONA Washington:03-11-02-0468; Richards, *Diary of Samuel Richards*, 50 ("Col. Meigs"); Willcox, *The American Rebellion*, 75–76; Frank L. Humphreys, *Life and Times*, 106–107; David Humphreys, *An Essay*, 114–15. Author's Note: In response to some early accounts that the loss of Fort Mont-

gomery was Putnam's fault due to his failure to send reinforcements, an extract from an open letter to Putnam, attributable to his longtime friend Col. John Durkee, was published, in which he offered a spirited defense of the general. In brief, he states from firsthand knowledge that while Governor Clinton's requests for reinforcements arrived late in the afternoon, Putnam acted quickly to pull together a relief force. Furthermore, as the first unit was about to board boats, the fort had surrendered. "Letter from an Officer of Distinction in the Army" (John Durkee), *Hartford Courant*, November 18, 1777, p. 3.

68. Samuel H. Parsons to Jonathan Trumbull, Sr., October 7, 1777, "Trumbull Papers," MHS7 2:154–55; Israel Putnam to George Washington, October 8, 1777, FONA Washington:03-11-02-0462; Israel Putnam to George Washington, October 16, 1777, FONA Washington:03-11-02-0540; Israel Putnam to George Clinton, October 8, 1777, *Public Papers*, 384–86; Horatio Gates to Israel Putnam, November 2, 1777, "Trumbull Papers," MHS7 2:181 ("Mrs. Robinson"); Livingston, *Israel Putnam*, 357–58. Author's Note: After he was appointed to command West Point, Maj. Gen. Benedict Arnold, along with his wife and child, occupied the house. It was from the landing there that he boarded his barge that took him downriver to the *Vulture* after his treachery was discovered. Philbrick, *Valiant Ambition*, 277, 283, and 309–10.

69. George Washington to Israel Putnam, October 8, 1777 (two letters), FONA Washington:03-11-02-0459 and Washington:03-11-02-0460; Israel Putnam to George Washington October 8, 1777, FONA Washington:03-11-02-0461.

70. George Washington to Israel Putnam, October 1, 1777, FONA Washington:03-11-02-0393; Israel Putnam to George Washington, October 8, 1777, FONA Washington:03-11-02-0462; Israel Putnam to George Washington, October 10, 1777, FONA Washington:03-11-02-0486, last modified June 13, 2018; Willcox, *The American Rebellion*, 76–78 ("Fort Constitution and Continental Village").

71. Israel Putnam to George Washington, October 16, 1777, FONA Washington:03-11-02-0540, last modified June 13, 2018; Israel Putnam to Horatio Gates, October 9, 1777, and Israel Putnam to George Clinton, October 9, 1777, Sparks, *Correspondence of the American Revolution*, 538–39 ("arrival of militia"); George Clinton to Council of Safety, October 10, 1777, *Public Papers*, 387–89.

72. George Clinton to Council of Safety, October 10, 1777, *Public Papers*, 402–403; Israel Putnam to George Clinton, October 9, 1777, Sparks, *Correspondence of the American Revolution*, 540 ("Brinkerhoff"); George Clinton to Jacobus Swarthoutd, October 10, 1777, *Public Papers*, 410–11.

73. Israel Putnam to George Washington, October 16, 1777, FONA Washington:03-11-02-0540, last modified June 13, 2018; Israel Putnam to John Hancock, October 16, 1777, Webb, *Correspondence and Journals*, 1:362; O'Callaghan, *Documentary History*, 4:409n1 ("family vault"); Livingston, *Israel Putnam*, 357–59; Cox, *A Proper Sense of Honor*, 169 ("social convention").

74. George Washington to Israel Putnam, October 19, 1777, Rhodehamel, *George Washington: Writings*, 279.

75. Willcox, *The American Rebellion*, 80; George Clinton to Israel Putnam, October 17, 1777, Webb, *Correspondence and Journals*, 363 ("Kingston"); George Clinton to Israel

Putnam, October 18, 1777, Webb, *Correspondence and Journals*, 1:364–65 ("Hurley" and "Kingston").

76. George Clinton to Horatio Gates, October 21, 1777, Webb, *Correspondence and Journals*, 1:366–67; George Clinton to George Washington, October 20, 1777, FONA Washington:03-11-02-0572. Author's Note: In a letter to Washington dated December 20, 1777, George Clinton would repeat the charge that Kingston could have been saved if only Putnam had "prudently disposed" of his forces, which claims included the Militia. However, the Connecticut Militia arrived in batches starting between October 7 and 8, at which time Putnam promptly dispatched four hundred Continentals to Clinton, as well as an additional regiment of Dutchess County Militia on October 9. Deborah Putnam died on October 14, and Putnam returned to Fishkill following the funeral after sending Parsons south to retake Peekskill. Kingston, thirty miles north of Fishkill, and on the west side of the Hudson, was destroyed on October 15. It is unlikely that Putnam would have had means to get sufficient troops there in time, let alone anticipate that the town would be the next objective of Generals Clinton and Vaughn. George Clinton to George Washington, December 20, 1777, FONA Washington:03-12-02-0587.

77. Willcox, *The American Rebellion*, 80–81 ("desperate"); John Vaughn, Report, October 17, 1777, James Wallace to William Hotham, October 17, 1777, and Council of Safety of New York to the New York Delegates in Congress, October 22, 1777, Webb, *Correspondence and Journals*, 1:363–64 and 1:368–69; William Hotham to Richard Howe, October 21, 1777, Webb, *Correspondence and Journals*, 1:367–68; Schecter, *The Battle for New York*, 293–96.

78. Israel Putnam to George Clinton, October 15, 1777; Israel Putnam to George Clinton, October 16, 1777; and George Clinton to Israel Putnam, October 17, 1777, Sparks, *Correspondence of the American Revolution*, 542–44; Israel Putnam to George Clinton, October 18, 1777, *Public Papers*, 460–61 ("cooperation").

79. Israel Putnam to George Clinton, October 20, 1777, Sparks, *Correspondence of the American Revolution*, 544.

80. Israel Putnam to George Washington, October 25, 1777, FONA Washington:03-11-02-0635; Israel Putnam to George Washington, October 27, 1777, FONA Washington:03-12-02-0029; Israel Putnam to George Washington, October 16, 1777, FONA Washington:03-11-02-0540 ("Kingsbridge"); General Orders, October 26, 1777, Worthington Chauncey Ford, *General Orders Issued by Major-General William Heath When in Command of the Eastern Department, 23 May, 1777–3 October, 1777, with Some Fragmentary Orders by Major-General Putnam and Lt. Col. Wm. S. Smith* (Brooklyn, NY: Historical Printing Club, 1890), 95–96.

81. General Orders, October 27, 1777, Ford, *General Orders Issued by Major-General William Heath*, 97–98; Israel Putnam to George Clinton, October 27, 1777, and George Clinton to Israel Putnam, October 27, 1777, Sparks, *Correspondence of the American Revolution*, 544–45 ("advice and counsel") and 545.

82. George Washington to William Livingston, October 8, 1777, FONA Washington:03-11-02-0457; Council of Safety of New York to the New York Delegates in Congress, October 22, 1777, Webb, *Correspondence and Journals*, 1:368–69.

83. Samuel Shaw to Francis and Mary Shaw, October 13, 1777, *The Journals of Major Samuel Shaw*, 40–43.

84. George Washington to Israel Putnam, November 4, 1777, FONA Washington:03-12-02-0113; Horatio Gates to Israel Putnam, November 2, 1777, "Trumbull Papers," MHS7 2:181.

85. Israel Putnam to Horatio Gates, October 31, 1777, and Proceedings of a Council of War, October 31, 1777, "Trumbull Papers," MHS7 2:179–81; George Washington to Israel Putnam, November 4, 1777, FONA Washington:03-12-02-0113.

86. George Washington to Israel Putnam, October 26, 1777, FONA Washington:03-12-02-0013; Israel Putnam to George Washington, October 26, 1777, FONA Washington:03-12-02-0029.

87. George Washington to Israel Putnam, October 26, 1777, FONA Washington:03-12-02-0013 ("have not received"); George Washington to Alexander Hamilton, October 30, 1777, FONA Hamilton:01-01-02-0331.

88. George Washington to Israel Putnam, October 30, 1777, FONA Washington:03-12-02-0055; George Washington to Israel Putnam, October 31, 1777, FONA Washington:03-12-02-0063.

89. Alexander Hamilton to George Washington, November 2, 1777, FONA Hamilton:01-01-02-0332.

90. Israel Putnam to George Washington, November 3, 1777, FONA Washington:03-12-02-0096; George Washington to Israel Putnam, November 4, 1777, FONA Washington:03-12-02-0113; Samuel H. Parsons to Jonathan Trumbull, Sr., November 2, 1777, "Trumbull Papers," MHS7 2:182–84 ("Westchester").

91. Israel Putnam to George Washington, November 7, 1777, FONA Washington:03-12-02-0147.

92. George Washington to Israel Putnam, November 9, 1777, FONA Washington:03-12-02-0175.

93. Alexander Hamilton to George Washington, November 6, 1777, FONA Hamilton:01-01-02-0337.

94. Henry Laurens to George Washington, November 5, 1777, FONA Washington:03-12-02-0122; Resolution, November 5, 1777, *Journals of Congress Containing the Proceedings from January 1, 1777, to January 1, 1778, Published by Order of Congress*, vol. 3 (Philadelphia, PA: John Dunlap, 1778), 474–77, onlinebooks.library.upenn.edu. Accessed July 25, 2020.

95. James Lovell to Horatio Gates, November 5, 1777, *Letters of the Delegates*, 8:237–38.

96. George Clinton to George Washington, October 20, 1777, FONA Washington:03-11-02-0572.

97. Alexander Hamilton to George Washington, November 10, 1777, FONA Hamilton:01-01-02-0339.

98. Alexander Hamilton to Israel Putnam, November 9, 1777, FONA Hamilton:01-01-02-0338.

99. Israel Putnam to George Washington, November 7, 1777, FONA Washington:03-12-02-0147.

100. Alexander Hamilton to Israel Putnam, November 9, 1777, FONA Hamilton:01-01-02-0338, last modified March 30, 2017.

101. Alexander Hamilton to George Washington, November 10, 1777, FONA Hamilton:01-01-02-0339; Peter R. Henriques, *Realistic Visionary: A Portrait of George Washington* (Charlottesville: University of Virginia Press, 2006), 129.

102. Israel Putnam to George Washington, November 14, 1777, FONA Washington:03-12-02-0243.

103. Israel Putnam to George Washington, November 14, 1777, FONA Washington:03-12-02-0243; Alexander Hamilton to George Washington, November 15, 1777, FONA Hamilton:01-01-02-0343; Samuel H. Parsons to Jonathan Trumbull, Sr., November 2, 1777, "Trumbull Papers," MHS7 2:182–84.

104. Alexander Hamilton to George Washington, November 12, 1777, FONA Hamilton:01-01-02-0341.

105. William Alexander ("Lord Stirling") to George Washington, November 3, 1777, FONA Washington:03-12-02-0098; Lender, *Cabal*, 84–91.

106. George Washington to Thomas Conway, November 5, 1777, FONA Washington:03-12-02-0118; Thomas Conway to George Washington, November 5, 1777, FONA Washington:03-12-02-0119; Taaffe, *Washington's Revolutionary War Generals*, 142; Lender, *Cabal*, 73.

107. "Report of the Board of War," November 21, 1777, Ford, *Defenses of Philadelphia in 1777*, 175–76; Lender, *Cabal*, 124.

108. Taaffe, *Washington's Revolutionary War Generals*, 147.

109. George Washington to Israel Putnam, November 19, 1777, FONA Washington:03-12-02-0317; Lender, *Cabal*, 221.

CHAPTER 12

1. George Washington to Israel Putnam, November 4, 1777, FONA Washington:03-12-02-0113.

2. Philemon Dickinson to George Washington, November 1, 1777, FONA Washington:03-12-02-0071.

3. George Washington to Philemon Dickenson, November 4, 1777, FONA Washington:03-12-02-0104; George Washington to Israel Putnam, November 4, 1777, FONA Washington:03-12-02-0113; Israel Putnam to George Clinton, November 10, 1777, Sparks, *Correspondence of the American Revolution*, 550.

4. Philemon Dickenson to George Washington, November 28, 1777, FONA Washington:03-12-02-0423; George Washington to Philemon Dickenson, December 2, 1777, FONA Washingto:03-12-02-0470.

5. Samuel Holden Parsons to George Washington, December 29, 1777, FONA Washington:03-13-02-0046; Samuel Blatchley Webb to George Washington, December 29, 1777, FONA Washington:03-13-02-0051.

6. Israel Putnam to George Washington, December 16, 1777, FONA Washington:03-12-02-0564; Israel Putnam to Samuel Holden Parsons, December 20, 1777, cited in full in Hall, *Life and Letters of Samuel Holden Parsons*, 126–27.

7. George Washington to Israel Putnam, December 27, 1777, FONA Washington:03-13-02-0019; Hall, *Life and Letters of Samuel Holden Parsons*, 133–34 ("diversion at Kingsbridge"); Israel Putnam to George Washington, January 13, 1778, FONA Washington:03-13-02-0190 ("Hessian raid").

8. George Washington to Israel Putnam, November 28, 1777, FONA Washington:03-12-02-0430; General Orders, June 10, 1777, FONA Washington:03-09-02-0655.

9. Humphreys, *An Essay*, 118 ("unconquerable aversion"); Israel Putnam to George Washington, December 16, 1777, FONA Washington:03-12-02-0564, last modified June 13, 2018; George Washington to Israel Putnam, December 27, 1777, FONA Washington:03-13-02-0019.

10. Samuel Holden Parsons to George Washington, February 18, 1778, FONA Washington:03-13-02-0497; George Washington to Samuel Holden Parsons, March 5, 1778, FONA Washington:03-14-02-0054.

11. General Orders, June 10, 1777, FONA Washington:03-09-02-0655 (Emphasis added); George Washington to Israel Putnam, November 28, 1777, FONA Washington:03-12-02-0430.

12. General Orders, August 28 and 31, 1777, Webb, *Correspondence and Journals*, 280–81.

13. General Orders, June 28, September 24, and October 25, 1777, Ford, *Orderly Book*, 15, 78–79, and 85.

14. Israel Putnam to George Washington, December 16, 1777, FONA Washington:03-12-02-0564, last modified June 13, 2018; George Washington to Israel Putnam, December 27, 1777, FONA Washington:03-13-02-0019.

15. George Washington to Israel Putnam, December 2, 1777, FONA Washington:03-12-02-0473.

16. George Washington to Lieutenant Colonel La Radière, October 8, 1777, FONA Washington:03-11-02-0456; George Washington to Israel Putnam, December 2, 1777, FONA Washington:03-12-02-0473; Israel Putnam to George Washington, November 7, 1777, FONA Washington:03-12-02-0147, George Clinton to George Washington, December 20, 1777, FONA Washington:03-12-02-0587.

17. Edward C. Boynton, *History of West Point and Its Military Importance During the American Revolution and the Origin and Progress of the United States Military Academy* (New York: Van Nostrand, 1864), 52–55; Israel Putnam to George Washington, January 13, 1778, FONA Washington:03-13-02-0190. Author's Note: (1) Washington was acting pursuant to a Resolution of Congress dated November 5, 1777, which, among other things, stressed the importance of the Hudson River and the Highlands and authorized General Gates to take charge and build the necessary forts and obstructions. However, since both Clinton and Gates had declined the mission, Washington's natural fallback was Putnam. Resolution, November 5, 1777, *Journals of Congress*, 3:474–77. (2) La Radière's version of events differs somewhat from Putnam's, in that he claims to have requested the select committee, and that of the original group of officers inspecting the site, two of the nine favored Fort Clinton. In the end, although Israel Putnam would lay out the works and begin the project, by coincidence, it was his cousin Col. Rufus Putnam, with the assistance of another foreign engineering officer, Col. Thaddeus

Kościuszko, who would complete it. The fort would later be named for Rufus Putnam by General McDougall. La Radière to George Washington, January 13, 1778, FONA Washington:03-13-02-0187; George Washington to Horatio Gates, September 11, 1778, FONA Washington:03-16-02-0618 ("has chief direction"); Michelle Eberhart, "Fort Putnam—West Point's Hidden Revolutionary Treasure," *Pointer View*, http://www .pointerview.com/2016/06/16/fort-putnam-west-points-hidden-revolutionary-treasure/. Accessed July 1, 2018; Livingston, *Israel Putnam*, 373–74 ("West Point").

18. Richards, diary, February 1778, 53–54; Boynton, *History of West Point*, 55–56; Israel Putnam to George Washington, January 13, 1778, FONA Washington:03-13-02-0190; George Clinton to George Washington, January 16, 1778, FONA Washington:02-13-02-0214.

19. Israel Putnam to George Washington, February 13, 1778, FONA Washington:03-13-02-0443.

20. Israel Putnam to George Washington, February 13, 1778, FONA Washington:03-13-02-0443.

21. Israel Putnam to George Washington, February 13, 1778, FONA Washington:03-13-02-0443.

22. Israel Putnam to George Washington, February 13, 1778, FONA Washington:03-13-02-0443; Livingston, *Israel Putnam*, 376–78 ("recruiting"); George Washington to Alexander McDougall, March 16, 1778, FONA Washington:03-14-02-0167; Samuel Holden Parsons to George Clinton, February 15, 1778, quoted in full in Hall, *Life and Letters of Samuel Holden Parsons*, 143.

23. Samuel Holden Parsons to George Washington, February 18, 1778, FONA Washington:0313-02-0497; George Washington to Robert R. Livingston, March 12, 1778, FONA Washington:03-14-02-0128.

24. Resolution, November 28, 1777, *Journals of Congress Containing the Proceedings from January 1, 1777, to January 1, 1778, Published by Order of Congress*, vol. 3 (Philadelphia, PA: John Dunlap, 1778), 544, onlinebooks.library.upenn.edu. Accessed July 28, 2020; Henry Laurens to George Washington, November 30, 1777, FONA Washington:03-12-02-0437; George Washington to Alexander McDougall, March 16, 1778, FONA Washington:03-14-02-0167; Jedediah Huntington to Jabez Huntington, March 15, 1778 (postscript dated March 17, 1778), *Huntington Papers*, 2:405-406; George Washington to Israel Putnam, March 16, 1778, FONA Washington:03-14-02-0169; Israel Putnam to George Washington, March 29, 1778, FONA Washington:03-14-02-0329.

25. Ann Hawks Hay to George Washington, February 28, 1778, FONA Washington 03-13-02-0594; George Washington to Israel Putnam, March 16, 1778, FONA Washington:03-14-02-0169; George Washington to Samuel Holden Parsons, March 5, 1778, FONA Washington:03-14-02-0054.

26. George Washington to George Clinton, December 3, 1777, FONA Washington:03-12-02-0482; George Clinton to George Washington, December 20, 1777, FONA Washington:03-12-02-0587; Robert R. Livingston to George Washington, January 14, 1778, FONA Washington:03-13-02-0195.

27. George Washington to Robert R. Livingston, March 12, 1778, FONA Washington:03-14-02-0128.

28. George Clinton to George Washington, December 20, 1777, FONA Washington:03-12-02-0587; George Clinton to George Washington, March 5, 1778, FONA Washington:03-14-02-0046.

29. George Clinton to George Washington, December 20, 1777, FONA Washington:03-12-02-0587. Author's Note: Governor Tryon suggested a similar arrangement with Governor Trumbull when he sent a packet of New York newspapers to him. There is no evidence that Trumbull accepted the offer. William Tryon to Jonathan Trumbull, Sr., March 7, 1779, "Trumbull Papers," MHS7 2:369.

30. Humphreys, *An Essay*, 117–18.

31. Daniel Putnam to John Adams, May 21, 1818, FONA Adams:99-02-02-6897.

32. George Washington to Charles Hector, Comte D'Estang, September 20, 1778, Fitzpatrick, *Writings of George Washington*, vol. 12, 472–73 ("shipping"); Israel Putnam to George Washington, March 30, 1779, FONA Washington:03-19-02-0641 ("New York newspaper"); Humphreys, *An Essay*, 118–19 ("Rivington"); Livingston, *Israel Putnam*, 368.

33. Israel Putnam to Governor Jonathan Trumbull, Sr., April 10, 1778, CSLA #973.3 T48; George Washington to Israel Putnam, April 29, 1778, FONA Washington:03-14-02-0607; George Washington to Israel Putnam, May 5, 1778, FONA Washington:03-15-02-0046; General Order, April 21, 1778. Reprinted in *Hartford Courant*, April 23, 1978.

34. George Washington to Gouverneur Morris, May 29, 1778, FONA Washington:03-15-02-0269, last modified June 13, 2018; Resolution, November 5, 1777, *Journals of Congress*, 3:474–77.

35. Israel Putnam to President of Congress (Henry Laurens), June 30, 1778, Webb, *Correspondence and Journals*, 2:113–14.

36. Israel Putnam to President of Congress (Henry Laurens), June 30, 1778, Webb, *Correspondence and Journals*, 2:113–14; Henry Laurens to Israel Putnam, July 8, 1778, *Letters of the Delegates*, 10:239–40.

37. Order, July 8, 1778, Order, August 4, 1778, and Resolution, August 17, 1778, *Journals of Congress Containing the Proceedings from January 1, 1778, to January 1, 1779, Published by Order of Congress*, vol. 4 (Philadelphia, PA: David C. Claypoole, 1779), 397–98, 441, and 476–77, onlinebooks.library.upenn.edu. Accessed July 30, 2020.

38. Cox, *A Proper Sense of Honor*, 38; Sculley, *Contest for Liberty*, x–xi; Israel Putnam to The Printers of the Connecticut Courant, August 22, 1778, *Connecticut Courant and Weekly Intelligencer*, September 1, 1778.

39. Henry Laurens to George Clinton, September 27, 1778, *Letters of the Delegates*, 10:702–703 (See Note 1).

40. Taafe, *Washington's Revolutionary War Generals*, 16971 ("Maj. Gen. Lee"); Patrick K. O'Donnell, *Washington's Immortals: The Untold Story of an Elite Regiment Who Changed the Course of the Revolution* (New York: Grove Press, 2017), 199 ("Maj. Gen. Lee"); Humphreys, *An Essay*, 120; Livingston, *Israel Putnam*, 378–79.

41. Robert Troup to John Jay, June 29, 1778, FONA Jay:01-01-02-0310 ("Putnamized").

42. Israel Putnam to George Washington, September 2, 1778, FONA Washington:03-16-02-0525.

43. General Orders, September 15, 1778, FONA Washington:03-17-02-0001; George Washington to Israel Putnam, September 15, 1778, FONA Washington:03-17-02-0013; George Washington to Israel Putnam, September 19, 1778, FONA Washington:03-17-02-0052; George Washington to President of Congress [Henry Laurens], September 23, 1778, Fitzpatrick, *Writings of Washington*, vol. 12, 489–93.

44. James Thatcher, *Military Journal During the Revolutionary War from 1775 to 1783, Describing Interesting Events and Transactions of the Period, with numerous Historical Facts and Anecdotes, from the Original Manuscript, to which is Added an Appendix, Containing Biographical Sketches of Several General Officers* (Boston, MA: Richardson and Lord, 1823), 176–77.

45. Israel Putnam to George Washington, September 24, 1778, FONA Washington:03-17-02-0112, last modified June 13, 2018; George Washington to Israel Putnam, September 25, 1778, FONA Washington:03-15-02-0121, last modified June 13, 2018; Israel Putnam to George Washington, September 27, 1778, FONA Washington:03-17-02-0151 ("fatigue parties"); George Washington to Israel Putnam, September 27, 1778, FONA Washington:03-17-02-0150 ("Woodford"); Israel Putnam to George Washington, September 28, 1778, FONA Washington:03-17-02-0166 ("Baylor's Dragoons"); Buchanan, *The Road to Valley Forge*, 262.

46. Thatcher, *Military Journal*, 184.

47. George Washington to Israel Putnam, November 20, 1778, FONA Washington:03-18-02-0250; George Washington to Israel Putnam, November 27, 1778, FONA Washington:03-18-02-0338; Frank Langdon Humphreys, *Life and Times of David Humphreys*, 120–21; Livingston, *Israel Putnam*, 382–83 ("Redding").

48. Jedediah Huntington to Andrew Huntington, December 2/7, 1778, and Jedediah Huntington to Jabez Huntington, December 23, 1778, *Huntington Papers*, 2:421–22 and 2:424; George Washington to Israel Putnam, November 25, 1779, FONA Washington:03-18-02-0314; Frank L. Humphreys, *Life and Times of David Humphreys*, 120–21. Author's Note: For a description of how a typical hut was constructed, see Martin, *A Narrative of a Revolutionary Soldier*, 144–46.

49. George Washington to Israel Putnam, November 27, 1778, FONA Washington:0318-02-0338; Israel Putnam to George Washington, December 17, 1778, FONA Washington:03-18-02-0502; George Washington to Israel Putnam, December 26, 1778, FONA Washington:03-18-02-0575.

50. George Washington to Israel Putnam, November 27, 1778, FONA Washington:0318-02-0338; Israel Putnam to George Washington, December 17, 1778, FONA Washington:03-18-02-0502; Samuel Holden Parsons to George Washington, December 23, 1778, FONA Washington:03-18-02-0554 ("delicate situation").

51. George Washington to Israel Putnam, November 27, 1778, FONA Washington:0318-02-0338.

52. George Washington to Israel Putnam, November 27, 1778, FONA Washington:0318-02-0338; George Washington to Israel Putnam, December 20, 1778, FONA Washington:03-18-02-0537.

53. Frank L. Humphreys, *Life and Times of David Humphreys*, 121 ("inflation"); O'Donnell, *Washington's Immortals*, 203.

54. Samuel Holden Parsons to George Washington, December 23, 1778, FONA Washington:03-18-02-0554; Israel Putnam to George Washington, December 23, 1778, FONA Washington:03-18-02-0555.

55. George Washington to Israel Putnam, January 8, 1779, FONA Washington:03-18-02-0663; Israel Putnam to George Washington, January 24, 1779, FONA Washington:03-19-02-0059 ("route to Redding"). Author's Note: (1) Jedediah Huntington had had a similar exchange in November with Washington in which he suggested some partiality in the distribution of clothing. Washington's pointed response caused Huntington to assure Washington that no such implication was intended. George Washington to Jedediah Huntington, November 19, 1778, FONA Washington:03-18-02-0216; Jedediah Huntington to George Washington, November 20, 1778, FONA Washington:03-18-02-0240; (2) On November 29, 1778, Washington had directed Major Bigelow to transfer all clothing form Hartford to Fishkill "as expeditiously as possible." George Washington to John Bigelow, November 29, 1778, FONA Washington:03-18-02-0352.

56. Sculley, *Contest for Liberty*, 10–11, 74–76, and 94; Ruddiman, *Becoming Men of Some Consequence*, 12; Middlekauff, *The Glorious Cause*, 504–508.

57. George Washington to Israel Putnam, January 18, 1779, FONA Washington:03-19-02-0021; Cox, *A Proper Sense of Honor*, 74–75 and 247; Ruddiman, *Becoming Men of Some Consequence*, 86–87; O'Donnell, *Washington's Immortals*, 204.

58. Nathaniel Webb, "Petition, to his Excellency Gov. Trumbull," Orderly Book, December 27, 1778, *The New England Genealogical & Historical Register and Antiquarian Journal* 27, no. 1 (January 1873): 58–60.

59. Israel Putnam to George Washington, January 5, 1779, FONA Washington:03-18-02-0647, last modified June 13, 2018; Humphreys, *An Essay*, 121–22; John Fell, diary, January 9, 1779, *Letters of the Delegates* 11:439; Taaffe, *Washington's Revolutionary War Generals*, 186; Livingston, *Israel Putnam*, 384–85 ("mutiny").

60. Samuel Holden Parsons to George Washington, February 3, 1779, quoted in full in Hall, *Life and Letters of Samuel Holden Parsons*, 209–11; Martin, *A Narrative of a Revolutionary Soldier*, 130–32.

61. Webb, "Petition, to his Excellency Gov. Trumbull;" Israel Putnam to Jonathan Trumbull, Sr., January 1779, "Trumbull Papers," MHS7 2:339–40.

62. Israel Putnam to Jonathan Trumbull, Sr., January 1779, "Trumbull Papers," MHS7 2:339–40; Sculley, *Contest for Liberty*, 43 ("inflation"); Ruddiman, *Becoming Men of Some Consequence*, 51 ("inflation"); Ralph Ketcham, *James Madison, A Biography* (Charlottesville: University Press of Virginia, 1994), 85 (effects of inflation).

63. George Washington to Israel Putnam, January 18, 1779, FONA Washington:03-19-02-0021, last modified June 13, 2018; Israel Putnam to George Washington, January 24, 1779, FONA Washington:03-19-02-0059, last modified June 13, 2018; Samuel H. Parsons, Brigade Order, February 9, 1779, quoted in full in Hall, *Life and Letters of Samuel Holden Parsons*, 215.

64. General Orders, February 4 and 6, 1779, cited in full in Hall, *Life and Letters of Samuel Holden Parsons*, 213–15; Barber, *Connecticut Historical Collections*, 396; Livingston, *Israel Putnam*, 385–88 ("spies").

65. George Washington to Israel Putnam, January 8, 1779, FONA Washington:03-18-02-0663.

66. Israel Putnam to George Washington, March 22, 1779, FONA Washington:03-19-02-0556; George Washington to Israel Putnam, March 27, 1779, FONA Washington:02-19-02-0612. Author's Note: "He who seeks to defend everything; defends nothing." Frederick the Great of Prussia.

67. Willcox, *The American Rebellion*, 131; Israel Putnam to George Washington, March 28, 1779, FONA Washington:03-19-02-0624; Samuel Holden Parsons to George Washington, March 29, 1779, FONA Washington:03-19-02-0632; Israel Putnam to George Washington, March 30, 1779, FONA Washington:03-19-02-0641; Samuel H. Parsons to Jonathan Trumbull, Sr., March 24, 1779, "Trumbull Papers," MHS7 2:373–74; James Wadsworth to Jonathan Trumbull, Sr., April 1, 1779, "Trumbull Papers," MHS7 2:377–79 ("300 to New Haven").

68. Israel Putnam to George Washington, March 2, 1779, FONA Washington:03-19-02-0350, last modified June 13, 2018; Humphreys, *An Essay*, 122; Frank L. Humphreys, *Life and Times of David Humphreys*, 123–24; Livingston, *Israel Putnam*, 388–94 ("escape"). Author's Note: For a description of "Putnam's Hill" then and in 1836, following considerable alterations to the landscape, see Barber, *Connecticut Historical Collections*, 380–82. Today, approximately two dozen original steps remain intact.

69. George Washington to Israel Putnam, February 10, 1779, FONA Washington:03-19-02-0166; Israel Putnam to George Washington, April 1, 1779, FONA Washington:03-19-02-0664; George Washington to Israel Putnam, April 28, 1779, FONA Hamilton:01-02-02-0096 ("Parsons' Brigade"); Livingston, *Israel Putnam*, 394–95.

70. George Washington to Israel Putnam, April 29, 1778, FONA Washington:03-14-02-0607; Israel Putnam to George Washington, May 7, 1779, FONA Washington:03-20-02-0330, last modified June 13, 2018.

71. Hall, *Life and Letters of Samuel Holden Parsons*, 226–27.

72. Livingston, *Israel Putnam*, 378.

73. George Washington to Israel Putnam, May 24, 1779, FONA Washington:03-20-02-0547; George Washington to Israel Putnam, June 2, 1779, FONA Washington:03-21-02-0023; General Order, May 27, 1779, quoted in full in Record of Service of Connecticut Men, 132; Frank Landon Humphreys, *Life and Times of David Humphreys*, 125.

74. General Orders, June 14, 1779, FONA Washington:03-21-02-0141; George Washington to Israel Putnam, June 14, 1779, FONA Washington:03-21-02-0148, last modified June 13, 2018; George Washington to Israel Putnam, June 16, 1779, FONA Washington:03-21-02-0153, last modified June 13, 2018; George Washington to Israel Putnam, June 21, 1779, FONA Hamilton:01-02-02-0239.

75. Willcox, *The American Rebellion*, 122–23; Tallmadge, *Memoir*, 44–45 ("Stony Point"); Alexander Hamilton to Israel Putnam, June 23, 1779, FONA Hamilton:01-02-02-0243; George Washington to Israel Putnam, July 20, 1779, FONA Wash-

ington:03-21-02-0481; Israel Putnam to George Washington, July 21, 1779, FONA Washington:03-21-02-0496.

76. Committee of Fairfield, Connecticut, to Jonathan Trumbull, Sr., July 2, 1779, "Trumbull Papers," MHS7 2:396–98; Andrew Ward to Jonathan Trumbull, Sr., July 7, 1779, "Trumbull Papers," MHS7 2:400–401; Peter Colt to Jonathan Trumbull, Sr., July 8, 1779, "Trumbull Papers," MHS7 2:401–404; Samuel Whiting to Jonathan Trumbull, Sr., July 9, 1779, "Trumbull Papers," MHS7 2:404–405; George Washington to Jonathan Trumbull, Sr., July 7, 1779, FONA Washington:03-21-02-0309; William Tryon to Henry Clinton, July 20, 1779, quoted in full in Willcox, *The American Rebellion*, 411–15; George Washington to Samuel Holden Parsons, July 10, 1779, FONA Washington:03-21-02-0347 ("highest honor"); George Washington to William Heath, July 10, 1779, FONA Washington:03-21-02-0340.

77. Frank Landon Humphreys, *Life and Times of David Humphreys*, 126; Livingston, *Israel Putnam*, 397–99; Humphreys, *An Essay*, 123.

78. Israel Putnam to George Washington, January 4, 1780, FONA Washington:03-24-02-0024, last modified June 13, 2018; James Lovell to Horatio Gates, March 4, 1780, *Letters to the Delegates*, 14:460–61; Humphreys, *An Essay*, 123; Frank Landon Humphreys, *Life and Times of David Humphreys*, 141–42; Hubbard, *Major General Israel Putnam*, 171–72.

79. Israel Putnam to George Washington, May 29, 1780, FONA Washington:99-01-02-01922, last modified June 13, 2018.

80. Israel Putnam to Nathanael Greene, May 29, 1780, quoted in full in Frank Landon Humphreys, *The Life and Times of David Humphreys*, 152–53.

81. Israel Putnam to George Washington, May 29, 1780, FONA Washington:99-01-02-01922, last modified June 13, 2018; George Washington to Israel Putnam, July 5, 1780, quoted in Livingston, *Israel Putnam*, 403.

82. Nathanael Greene to Catherine ("Caty") Greene, September 29, 1780, extract quoted in Greene, *The Life of Nathanael Greene*, vol. 2, 233.

83. Estate of Israel Putnam, Court of Probate, District of Pomfret, June 15, 1790, CSLA. Author's Note: It is possible that he freed "Dick" at some time, perhaps around the time of the Revolution. Curiously, while the U.S. Census for 1790, the year he died, lists his household as having one slave, no slaves are listed in Putnam's estate inventory dated June 12, 1790.

84. Israel Putnam to George Washington, June 2, 1783, FONA Washington:99-01-02-11304, last modified June 13, 2018.

85. George Washington to Israel Putnam, June 2, 1783, FONA Washington:99-01-02-11360, last modified June 13, 2018.

86. Bayles, *History of Windham County*, 569 ("town meeting").

87. Livingston, *Israel Putnam*, 407–409.

88. Douglas Hurt, *The Ohio Frontier: Crucible of the Old Northwest, 1720–1830* (Bloomington: Indiana University Press, 1996), 179–81 ("Ohio Company"); Samuel Prescott Hildreth, *Biographical and Historical Memoirs of the Early Pioneer Settlers of Ohio, with Narratives of Incidents and Occurrences in 1775* (Cincinnati, OH: H. W. Derby, 1852), 372–73. Author's Note: As a young man, Kitt was raised in the Putnam household in

Brooklyn, and he was sometimes referred to as "Kit Putnam." However, once in Ohio, Kitt adopted the name Christopher Malbone, which confirms the fact that he was born on the Malbone Plantation in Pomfret. At some point while living in Ohio, he was treated as a free man, and in November 1802, he cast a vote for delegates to the Territorial Convention, the first free Black man to do so in the Northwest Territory. He is said to have died shortly thereafter. Samuel Prescott Hildreth, *Pioneer History: Being an Account of the First Examinations of the Ohio Valley and the Early Settlements of the Northwest Territory* (Cincinnati, OH: H. W. Derby, 1848), 388–89; David McCullough, *The Pioneers: The Heroic Story of the Settlers Who Brought the American Ideal West* (New York: Simon & Schuster, 2019), 144; Bill Reynolds, *Marietta Times*, https://www.mariettatimes.com/news/2018/02/black-history-month-first-to-vote/. Accessed January 31, 2021.

89. George Washington to Gouverneur Morris, October 13, 1789, Rhodehamel, *George Washington: Writings*, 745–78 (Rhode Island); George Washington to Catharine Macaulay Graham, January 9, 1790, Rhodehamel, *George Washington: Writings*, 751–54 (New England).

90. Joseph J. Ellis, *His Excellency George Washington* (New York: Vintage, 2004),195; Marlowe, *Coaching Roads of Old New England*, 68.

91. *Connecticut Courant and Weekly Intelligencer*, June 7, 1790; Livingston, *Israel Putnam*, 411.

92. Albigence Waldo, Eulogy, *Gazette of the United States*, June 23, 1790, p. 1, LOCD. Albigence Waldo, M.D. (1750–1794) was born in Pomfret, Connecticut. He was a physician who served with Washington's army at Valley Forge during the winter of 1777–1778. Waldo kept a diary of his experiences there.

93. Estate of Israel Putnam, Court of Probate, District of Pomfret, June 15, 1790, CSLA; 1790 U.S. Census, Brooklyn, Windham County, Connecticut. Author's Note: Connecticut adopted a law in 1784 calling for the gradual abolition of slaves born after March 1, 1784, followed by other legislative measures, including an act passed in 1788 to prevent the slave trade. Menschel, "Abolition Without Deliverance, 183–222.

94. To many people, John ("Johnny Appleseed") Chapman would immediately come to mind as the originator of the apple industry in Ohio and other midwestern states. However, Chapman came to Ohio around 1800, and, moreover, he grew trees from seeds gathered from cider mills in western Pennsylvania. He was indeed a prolific nurseryman, however, his trees grown from seed did not always propagate true to the variety. Moreover, trees grown from seed were more likely to produce cider apples. The same could be said for the fifty varieties of apple seeds brought to Ohio by Rufus Putnam when he returned with his family in June 1790. However, the grafted seedlings, carefully wrapped in beeswax by Israel Putnam Jr. and sent to Marietta in 1795, did produce apples true to variety. Accordingly, he and his son Aaron, who planted the seedlings on the family farm at Belpre, could well be looked upon as the fathers of the apple industry there. McCullough, *The Pioneers*, 82 ("fifty varieties"); Hurt, *The Ohio Frontier*, 243–47 ("apples"); Hildreth, *Biographical and Historical Memoirs*, 378 ("beeswax").

CHAPTER 13

1. John Adams to Daniel Putnam, June 5, 1818, FONA Adams:99-02-02-6904.

2. Dearborn, *Account of the Battle of Bunker's Hill*, 4 and 7–8; A. J. Langguth, *Union 1812: The Americans Who Fought the Second War of Independence* (New York: Simon & Schuster, 2006), 233–35; Sarah J. Purcell, *Sealed with Blood: War Sacrifice, and Memory in Revolutionary America* (Philadelphia: University of Pennsylvania Press, 2010), 161–62 and 164–68; Donald R. Hickey, *The War of 1812: A Forgotten Conflict* (Urbana: University of Illinois Press, 1989), 128 and 305.

3. Robert E. Cray Jr., "Bunker Hill Refought: Memory Wars and Partisan Conflicts, 1775–1825," *Historical Journal of Massachusetts* 29, no. 1 (Winter 2001): 25, 33; Cox, *A Proper Sense of Honor*, 243.

4. Cray, "Bunker Hill Refought," 49–52; Robert V. Remini, *Daniel Webster: The Man and His Times* (New York: Norton, 1997), 250–51; Fellows, *The Veil Removed*.

5. Forrest McDonald, ed., *Empire and Nation: Letters from a Farmer in Pennsylvania, John Dickinson; Letters from the Federal Farmer, Richard Henry Lee*, second edition (Indianapolis, IN: Liberty Fund, 1999), 77–79.

6. Middlekauff, *The Glorious Cause*, 282.

7. Silas Deane to Elizabeth Deane, July 20, 1775, "Deane Papers" 1:73–76.

8. John Adams to Abigail Adams, February 21, 1777, FONA Adams:04-02-02-0121; Taaffe, *Washington's Revolutionary War Generals*, 266.

9. Purcell, *Sealed with Blood*, 169–70.

Abbreviations

AA:	American Archives (Fourth and Fifth Series)
CHS:	Connecticut Historical Society
CSLA:	Connecticut State Library and Archives
CWP:	Correspondence of William Pitt
DCHNY:	Documents Related to the Colonial History of the State of New York
FONA:	Founders Online, National Archives
FP:	Fitch Papers
FTM:	Fort Ticonderoga Museum
LOCD:	Library of Congress Digital Newspapers
MHS:	Massachusetts Historical Society
PA:	Pennsylvania Archives (First Series)
PRCC:	Public Records of the Colony of Connecticut
WHS:	Windsor Historical Society

Bibliography

Manuscript and Archival Sources
Connecticut State Library and Archives, Hartford, CT
    Barbour Collection
    Estate of Israel Putnam
Fort Ticonderoga Museum, Ticonderoga, NY
    Charles Lee Correspondence
    Diary of Robert Webster
    Manuscript Collection
Library of Congress, Washington, DC
    Photographs
Litchfield Historical Society, Litchfield, CT
    William Douglas Letters
National Archives and Records Administration, Washington, DC
Founders Online, Adams, Hamilton, and Washington Papers
Stirling Memorial Library, Yale University, Manuscripts and Archives, New Haven, CT
    Silliman Family Papers

Primary Sources
Abbatt, William, ed. *Memoirs of Major-General William Heath by Himself.* New York: William Abbatt, 1901.

André, John. *Major André's Journal: Operations of the British Army under Lieutenant Generals Sir William Howe and Sir Henry Clinton, June 1777 to November 1778.* Tarrytown, NY: William Abbatt, 1930.

Bates, Albert C., ed. *Rolls of Connecticut Men in the French and Indian War, 1755–1762,* vol. 1, 1755–1757. Hartford, CT: Case, Lockwood, 1903.

———. *Rolls of Connecticut Men in the French and Indian War, 1755–1762,* vol. 2, 1758–1762. Hartford, CT: Case, Lockwood, 1905.

———. *The Two Putnams: Israel and Rufus in the Havana Campaign 1762 and in the Mississippi Expedition 1772–73 with Some Account of The Company of Military Adventurers.* Hartford: Connecticut Historical Society, 1931.

———. *The Fitch Papers: Correspondence and Documents During Thomas Fitch's Governorship of the Colony of Connecticut, 1754–1766,* vol. 1, May 1754–December 1758. Hartford: Hartford Printing Co., 1918.

_____. *The Fitch Papers: Correspondence and Documents During Thomas Fitch's Governorship of the Colony of Connecticut, 1754–1766*, vol. 2, January 1759–May 1766. Hartford: Connecticut Historical Society, 1920.

Black, Jeannette D., and William Greene Roelker, eds. *A Rhode Island Chaplain in the Revolution: Letters of Ebenezer David to Nicholas Brown, 1775–1778*. Providence: Rhode Island Society of the Cincinnati, 1949.

Brown, Lloyd A., and Howard H. Peckham, eds. *Revolutionary War Journals of Henry Dearborn 1775–1783*. Chicago, IL: Caxton Club, 1939.

Buell, Rowena, ed. *The Memoirs of Rufus Putnam and Certain Official Papers and Correspondence*. Boston: Houghton, Mifflin, 1903.

Calendar of Historical Manuscripts Relating to the War of the Revolution, in the Office of the Secretary of State, Albany, N.Y., vol. 2. Albany, NY: Weed, Parsons and Company, 1868.

Connecticut Historical Society. "Orderly Book and Journals Kept by Connecticut Men While Taking part in the American Revolution, 1775–1778," *Collections of the Connecticut Historical Society*, vol. 7. Hartford, CT: Connecticut Historical Society, 1899.

Dana, Elizabeth Ellery. *The British in Boston: Being the Diary of Lieutenant John Barker of the King's Own Regiment from November 15, 1774 to May 31, 1776*. Cambridge, MA: Harvard University Press.

Dawes, E. C. *Journal of Gen. Rufus Putnam Kept in Northern New York During Four Campaigns of the Old French and Indian War, 1757–1760*. Albany, NY: Joel Munsell's Sons, 1886.

Deane, Silas. "The Deane Papers, vol 1 (1774–1777)," *Collections of the New York Historical Society for the Year 1886*. New York: New York Historical Society, 1887.

_____. "Correspondence of Silas Deane, Delegate to the Congress at Philadelphia, 1774–76," *Collections of the Connecticut Historical Society*, vol. 2. Hartford, CT: Case, Lockwood, 1870.

Dearborn, Henry. *Account of the Battle of Bunker's Hill*. Boston: Munroe & Francis, 1818.

De Forest, Louis Effingham, ed. *The Journals and Papers of Seth Pomeroy: Sometime General in the Colonial Service*. New Haven, CT: Tuttle, Morehouse, 1926.

Dexter, Franklin Bowditch, ed. *The Literary Diary of Ezra Stiles, D.D., LL.D. President of Yale College, vol. 1, January 1, 1769–March 13, 1776*. New York: Scribner's, 1901.

_____, *Extracts from the Itineraries and Other Miscellanies of Ezra Stiles, D.D., LL.D., 1755–1794, with a Selection from His Correspondence*. New Haven: Yale University Press, 1916.

Douglas, William. "Revolutionary War Letters of Colonel William Douglas," *The New York Historical Society Quarterly Bulletin* 13, nos. 1, 2, 3, and 4 (April 1929, July 1929, October 1929, and January 1930): 37–40, 79–82, 118–22, and 157–62.

Drake, Samuel Adams. *Bunker Hill: The Story Told in Letters from the Battle Field by British Officers Engaged*. Boston, MA: Nichols & Hall, 1875.

Farnsworth, Amos. "Amos Farnsworth's Diary," Samuel A. Green, ed. *Three Military Diaries Kept by Groton Soldiers in Different Wars*. Cambridge, MA: Harvard University Press, 1901.

Field, Edward, ed. *Diary of Colonel Israel Angell, Commanding the Second Rhode Island Continental Regiment During the American Revolution, 1778–1781*. Providence, RI: Preston and Rounds, 1899.

Fitch, Jabez Jr. *The Diary of Jabez Fitch, Jr., in the French and Indian War, 1757*. Fort Edward, NY: New York State French & Indian War 250th Anniversary Commemoration Commission, 2007.

Fitzpatrick, John C., ed. *The Writings of George Washington from the Original Manuscript Sources, 1745–1799*, vols. 1–39. Washington, DC: Government Printing Office, 1931–1944.

Force, Peter, ed. *American Archives: Fourth Series*, vols. 1–6. Washington, DC: M. St. Clair Clarke and Peter Force, 1837–1843.

Force, Peter, ed. *American Archives: Fifth Series*, vols. 1–3. Washington, DC: M. St. Clair Clarke and Peter Force, 1848–1853.

Ford, Worthington Chauncey, ed. *General Orders Issued by Major-General Israel Putnam When in Command of the Highlands, in the Summer and Fall of 1777*. Brooklyn, NY: Historical Printing Club, 1893.

———. *General Orders Issued by Major-General William Heath When in Command of the Eastern Department, 23 May, 1777–3 October, 1777, with Some Fragmentary Orders of Major-General Putnam and Lt. Col. Wm. S. Smith*. Brooklyn, NY: Historical Printing Club, 1890.

———. *Defenses of Philadelphia in 1777*. Brooklyn, NY: Historical Printing Club, 1897.

———. *Correspondence and Journals of Samuel Blachley Webb*, 3 vols. New York: Wickersham Press, 1893–1894.

———. *Family Letters of Samuel Blachley Webb 1764–1807*. Cambridge, MA: University Press, 1912.

French, Christopher. "Major French's Journal, no. 2," *Collections of the Connecticut Historical Society*, vol. 1. Hartford, CT: Connecticut Historical Society, 1860.

Graham, John. *Extracts from the Journal of the Reverend John Graham, Chaplain of the First Connecticut Regiment, Colonel Lyman, from September 25th to October 19th, 1762, at the Siege of Havana*. New York: Society of Colonial Wars in the State of New York, 1896.

Gridley, Luke. *Luke Gridley's Diary of 1757: While in Service in the French and Indian War*. Hartford, CT: Hartford Press, 1907.

Hagelin, Wladimir, and Ralph A. Brown. "Connecticut Farmers at Bunker Hill: The Diary of Experience Storrs," *The New England Quarterly* 28, vol. 1 (March 1955): 72–93.

Hale, Edward Everett, Sr., ed. *The Capture of Havana in 1762 by the Forces of George III: Being Two Authentic Reports of the Siege and Capture of Havana by the Combined Forces of Great Britain and the American Colonies*. Cambridge, MA: Cooperative Printing, 1898.

Hall, Charles S. *Life and Letters of Samuel Holden Parsons, Major General in the Continental Army and Chief Judge of the Northwestern Territory, 1737–1789*. Binghamton, NY: Otseningo Publishing Co., 1905.

Hastings, Hugh, ed. *Public Papers of George Clinton, First Governor of New York, 1777—1795—1801—1804*, vol. 2. New York: Wynkoop Hallenbeck Crawford Co., 1900.

————. *Orderly Book and Journal of Major John Hawks: On the Ticonderoga–Crown Point Campaign, Under General Jeffery Amherst, 1759–1760*. New York: Society of Colonial Wars, 1911.

Haswell, Anthony, ed. *Memoirs and Adventures of Captain Matthew Phelps; Formerly of Harwington in Connecticut, Now a Resident in Newhaven in Vermont: Particularly in Two Voyages, from Connecticut to the River Mississippi, from December 1773 to October 1780*. Bennington, VT: Anthony Haswell, 1802.

Hayden, Augustin. *The French and Indian War Journals of Augustin Hayden, 1758–1759*. Windsor, CT: Windsor Historical Society, 1984.

Hayward, Benjamin. "Diary of Ensign Hayward of Woodstock, Conn., Kept Principally at Fort Edward in 1757." Robert O. Bascom, ed., *The Fort Edward Book: Containing Some Historical Sketches with Illustrations and Family Records*. Fort Edward, NY: James D. Keating, 1903.

Hazard, Samuel, ed. *Pennsylvania Archives: Selected and Arranged from Original Documents in the Office of the Secretary of the Commonwealth, Conformably to Acts of the General Assembly, February 15, 1851, and March 1, 1853*, First Series, vol. 5. Philadelphia, PA: Joseph Severns & Co., 1853.

Henshaw, William. *The Orderly Book of Colonel William Henshaw of the American Army, April 20–Sept. 26, 1775: Including a Memoir by Emory Washburn, and Notes by Charles C. Smith, with Additions by Harriet E. Henshaw*. Boston, MA: A. Williams and Company, 1881.

Hoadly, Charles J., ed. *The Public Records of the Colony of Connecticut, From May, 1751, to February, 1757, Inclusive*, vol. 10. Hartford, CT: Case, Lockwood, 1877.

————. *The Public Records of the Colony of Connecticut, From May, 1757, to March, 1762, Inclusive*, vol. 11. Hartford, CT: Case, Lockwood, 1880.

————. *The Public Records of the Colony of Connecticut, From May, 1762, to October, 1767, Inclusive*, vol. 12. Hartford, CT: Case, Lockwood, 1881.

————. *The Public Records of the Colony of Connecticut, From May, 1768, to May, 1772, Inclusive*, vol. 13. Hartford, CT: Case, Lockwood, 1885.

————. *The Public Records of the Colony of Connecticut, From October, 1772, to April, 1775, Inclusive*, vol. 14. Hartford, CT: Case, Lockwood, 1887.

Holden, David. *Journal Kept by Sergeant David Holden of Groton, Mass. During the Latter Part of the French and Indian War: February 20–November 29, 1760*. Cambridge, MA: Harvard University Press, 1889.

How, David. *Diary of David How: A Private in Colonel Paul Dudley Sargent's Regiment of the Massachusetts Line, in the Army of the American Revolution*. Morrisania, NY: H. D. Houghton, 1865.

Huntington, Ebenezer. *Letters Written by Ebenezer Huntington During the Revolution*. New York: C. F. Heartman, 1915.

Huntington Papers: *Correspondence of the Brothers Joshua and Jedediah Huntington During the Period of the American Revolution*. Parts 1 and 2. Hartford, CT: Connecticut Historical Society, 1923.

Jenks, Samuel. *Diary of Captain Samuel Jenks, During the French and Indian War, 1760.* Cambridge, MA: Harvard University Press, 1890.

Johnston, Henry P., ed. *Record of Connecticut Men in the Military and Naval Service During the War of the Revolution, 1775–1783*, Part 1. Hartford, CT: Case, Lockwood & Brainard, 1889.

Journals of Congress Containing the Proceedings from January 1, 1777, to January 1, 1778, Published by Order of Congress, vol. 3. Philadelphia, PA: John Dunlap, 1778, online books.library.upenn.edu.

Journals of Congress Containing the Proceedings from January 1, 1778, to January 1, 1779, Published by Order of Congress, vol. 4. Philadelphia, PA: David C. Claypoole, 1779, onlinebooks.library.upenn.edu.

Kimball, Gertrude Selwyn, ed. *Correspondence of William Pitt When Secretary of State with Colonial Governors and Military and Naval Commissioners in America*, vols. 1 and 2. New York: Macmillan, 1906.

Lee, Charles. "The Lee Papers, vol. 1, 1754–1776," *Collections of the New York Historical Society for the Year 1871*. New York: Printed for the Society, 1872.

Lyman, Simeon. "Journal of Simeon Lyman of Sharon, Aug. 10 to Dec. 28, 1775." *Collections of the Connecticut Historical Society*, vol 7. Hartford, CT: Connecticut Historical Society, 1899.

Martin, Joseph Plumb. *A Narrative of a Revolutionary Soldier: Some of the Adventures, Dangers, and Sufferings of Joseph Plumb Martin.* New York: Signet, 2010.

O'Callaghan, E. B., ed. *The Documentary History of the State of New York*, vol. 4. Albany, NY: Charles Van Benthuysen, 1851.

Prince, Carl E., ed. *The Papers of William Livingston*, vol. 1 (June 1774–June 1777). Trenton: New Jersey Historical Commission, 1979.

Putnam, Daniel. *A Letter to Major-General Dearborn Repelling His Unprovoked Attack on the Character of the Late Major-General Israel Putnam; and Containing Some Anecdotes Relating to the Battle of Bunker Hill Not Generally Known.* Boston, MA: Munroe & Francis, 1818.

———. "Colonel Daniel Putnam's Letter Relative to the Battle of Bunker Hill and General Israel Putnam," August 1825, *Collections of the Connecticut Historical Society*, vol. 1. Hartford, CT: The Society, 1860.

Quincy, Josiah, ed. *The Journals of Major Samuel Shaw, the First American Consul at Canton. With a Life of the Author, by Josiah Quincy.* Boston, MA: Crosby & Nichols, 1847.

Redfield, Levi. *A Succinct Account of the Memorable Events and Remarkable Occurrences in the Life of Levi Redfield, Late of Connecticut, now Residing in Brattleboro, Ver.* Brattleboro, VT: B. Smead, 1798.

Reed, William B., ed. *Life and Correspondence of Joseph Reed: Military Secretary of Washington, at Cambridge; Adjutant General of the Continental Army; Member of Congress of the United States; and President of the Executive Council of the State of Pennsylvania, By His Grandson, William B. Reed*, vol.1. Philadelphia, PA: Lindsay and Blakiston, 1847.

Richards, Samuel. *Diary of Samuel Richards, Captain of the Connecticut Line, War of the Revolution, 1775–1781.* Philadelphia, PA: Leeds & Biddle, 1909.

Rogers, Robert. *Journals of Major Robert Rogers* (Reprinted from the original edition of 1765). New York: Corinth, 1961.

Scull, G. D., ed. *The Montresor Journals*. New York: New York Historical Society, 1882.

Smith, Paul H. *Letters of Delegates to Congress, 1774–1789*, 6 volumes (January 1–April 30, 1976–2000). Washington, DC: Library of Congress, 1980.

Sparks, Jared, ed. *The Writings of George Washington; Being His Correspondence, Addresses, Messages, and Other Papers, Official and Private, Selected and Published from the Original Manuscripts; with a Life of the Author, Notes, and Illustrations*, vol. 3. Boston, MA: Russell, Odiorne, 1834.

———. *Correspondence of the American Revolution Being Letters of Eminent Men to George Washington from the Time of His Taking Command of the Army to the End of His Presidency*, vol. 2. Boston, MA: Little, Brown, 1853.

Swett, Samuel, ed. *Notes to His Sketch of the Bunker Hill Battle*. Boston, MA: Munroe and Francis, 1825.

Tallmadge, Benjamin. *Memoir of Colonel Benjamin Tallmadge: Edited by Henry Phelps Johnston*. New York, NY: Gilliss Press, 1904.

Thatcher, James. *Military Journal During the American Revolutionary War from 1775 to 1783, Describing Interesting Events and Transactions of the Period, with numerous Historical Facts and Anecdotes, from the Original Manuscript, to which is Added an Appendix, Containing Biographical Sketches of Several General Officers*. Boston, MA: Richardson and Lord, 1823.

Tiffany, Nina Moore, and Susan I. Leslie, ed. *Letters of James Murray, Loyalist*. Boston, MA: Printed not published, 1901.

Trumbull, Jonathan Sr. "The Trumbull Papers, Part 3," *Collections of the Massachusetts Historical Society*, Seventh Series, vol. 2. Cambridge, MA: University Press, 1902.

———. "The Trumbull Papers, Early Miscellaneous Papers," *Collections of the Massachusetts Historical Society*, Fifth Series, vol. 9. Cambridge, MA: University Press, 1885.

Webb, Nathaniel. "Petition, to his Excellency Gov. Trumbull," Orderly Book, December 27, 1778. *The New England Genealogical & Historical Register and Antiquarian Journal* 27, no. 1 (January 1873): 58–60.

Webb, William Seward, ed. *General Orders of 1757 Issued by the Earl of Loudoun and Phineas Lyman in the Campaign Against the French*. New York: Dodd, Mead, 1899.

Webster, John Clarence, ed. *The Journal of Jeffrey Amherst: Recording the Military Career of General Amherst in America from 1758 to 1763*. Toronto: Ryerson Press, 1931.

Wheatland, Henry. *Baptisms at Church in Salem Village, Now North Parish, Danvers*. Salem, MA: Salem Press, 1880.

Willcox, William B., ed. *The American Rebellion: Sir Henry Clinton's Narrative of His Campaigns, 1775–1782, with an Appendix of Original Documents*. New Haven, CT: Yale University Press, 1954.

Wyllys, Hezekiah and John. *The Wyllys Papers: Correspondence and Documents Chiefly of Descendants of Gov. George Wyllys of Connecticut, 1590–1796*. Hartford, CT: Connecticut Historical Society, 1924.

Zaboly, Gary S., ed., "A Royal Artillery Officer with Amherst: The Journal of Captain-Lieutenant Henry Skinner, 1 May–28 July 1759," *The Bulletin of the Fort Ticonderoga Museum* 15, no. 5 (1993): 363–87.

WORKS CONSULTED

Allen, Thomas B. *Tories: Fighting for the King in America's First Civil War*. New York: Harper, 2010.

Ambrose, Stephen E. *Duty, Honor, Country: A History of West Point*. Baltimore, MD: Johns Hopkins University Press, 1999.

Anderson, Fred. *Crucible of War: The Seven Year's War and the Fate of Empire in British North America, 1754–1766*. New York: Knopf, 2000.

Atkinson, Rick. *The British Are Coming: The War for America, Lexington to Princeton, 1775–1777*. New York: Henry Holt, 2019.

Ayres, Harral. *The Great Trail of New England: The Old Connecticut Path*. Boston, MA: Meador Press, 1940.

Bailyn, Bernard. *The Peopling of North America: An Introduction*. New York: Vintage, 1988.
————. *Voyagers to the West: A Passage in the Peopling of America on the Eve of the Revolution*. New York: Vintage, 1988.

Baker, Mark Allen. *Connecticut Families of the Revolution: American Forebears from Burr to Wolcott*. Charleston, SC: History Press, 2014.

Ballard, Michael B. *Vicksburg: The Campaign that Opened the Mississippi*. Chapel Hill: University of North Carolina Press, 2004.

Barber, John Warner. *Connecticut Historical Collections: Containing General Collection of Interesting Facts, Traditions, Biographical Sketches, Anecdotes, etc. Relating to the History and Antiquities of Every Town in Connecticut with Geographical Descriptions*. Storrs, CT: Bibliopola Press, 1999.

Bayles, Richard M., ed. *History of Windham County Connecticut*. New York: W. W. Preston, 1889.

Bobrick, Benson. *Angel in the Whirlwind: The Triumph of the American Revolution*. New York: Simon & Schuster, 1997.

Bowen, Catherine Drinker. *John Adams and the American Revolution*. Boston, MA: Little, Brown, 1950.

Boynton, Edward C. *History of West Point and Its Military Importance During the American Revolution and the Origin and Progress of the United States Military Academy*. New York: Van Nostrand, 1864.

Buchanan, John. *The Road to Valley Forge: How Washington Built the Army That Won the Revolution*. New York: Wiley, 2004.

Calloway, Colin G. *The Scratch of a Pen: 1763 and the Transformation of North America*. New York: Oxford University Press, 2006.

Carrington, Henry B. *Battles of the American Revolution, 1775–1781: Historical and Military Criticism with Topographical Illustrations*. New York: A. S. Barnes, 1876.

Caulkins, Frances Manwaring. *History of Norwich, Connecticut: From Its Possession by the Indians to the Year 1866*. Hartford, CT: Case, Lockwood & Brainard, 1873.

Chambers, John Whiteclay II. *To Raise an Army: The Draft Comes to Modern America*. New York: Free Press, 1987.

Chernow, Ron. *Alexander Hamilton*. New York: Penguin, 2004.

Claiborne, John Francis Hamtramck. *Mississippi, as a Province, Territory and State with Biographical Notices of Eminent Citizens*, vol. 1. Jackson, MS: Power & Barksdale, 1880.

Clark, Delphina L. H. *Phineas Lyman, Connecticut's General*. Springfield, MA: Connecticut Valley Historical Museum, 1964.

Cox, Caroline. *A Proper Sense of Honor: Service and Sacrifice in George Washington's Army*. Chapel Hill: University of North Carolina Press, 2004.

Cutter, William. *The Life of Israel Putnam, Major-General in the Army of the American Revolution*. New York: George F. Cooledge & Brother, 1850.

Daniels, Jonathan. *The Devil's Backbone: The Story of the Natchez Trace*. New York: McGraw-Hill, 1962.

Davis, William C. *A Way Through the Wilderness: The Natchez Trace and the Civilization of the Southern Frontier*. New York: HarperCollins, 1995.

Deetz, James, and Patricia Scott Deetz. *The Times of Their Lives: Life, Love, and Death in Plymouth Colony*. New York: W. H. Freeman, 2000.

Demos, John. *A Little Commonwealth: Family Life in Plymouth Colony*. New York: Oxford University Press, 2000.

Destler, Chester M. *Connecticut: The Provisions State*. Chester, CT: Pequot Press, 1973.

Drake, Samuel Adams. *General Israel Putnam the Commander at Bunker Hill*. Boston, MA: Nichols & Hall, 1875.

Draper, Theodore. *A Struggle for Power: The American Revolution*. New York: Times Books, 1996.

Edmonds, Walter D. *The Musket and the Cross: The Struggle of France and England for North America*. Boston, MA: Little, Brown, 1968.

Ellis, Joseph J. *His Excellency George Washington*. New York: Vintage, 2004.

Fellows, John. *The Veil Removed; or Reflections on David Humphreys' Essay on the Life of Israel Putnam. Also, Notices of Oliver W. B. Peabody's Life of Same, S. Swett's Sketch of Bunker Hill Battle, etc.* New York: J. D. Lockwood, 1843.

Ferling, John. *A Leap in the Dark: The Struggle to Create the American Republic*. New York: Oxford University Press, 2003.

Fischer, David Hackett. *Albion's Seed: Four British Folkways in America*. New York: Oxford University Press, 1989.

————. *Paul Revere's Ride*. New York: Oxford University Press, 1994.

————. *Washington's Crossing*. New York: Oxford University Press, 2004.

————. *Champlain's Dream*. New York: Simon & Schuster, 2008.

Fleming, Thomas. *Washington's Secret War: The Hidden History of Valley Forge*. New York: HarperCollins, 2005.

————. *The Duel: Alexander Hamilton, Aaron Burr, and the Future of America*. New York: Basic, 1999.

Flexner, James Thomas. *Washington: The Indispensable Man*. Boston, MA: Little, Brown, 1974.

Fowler, William Chauncey. *History of Durham, Connecticut*. Hartford, CT: Wiley, Waterman, 1866.

Frohnen, Bruce, ed. *The American Republic: Primary Sources*. Indianapolis, IN: Liberty Fund, 2002.

Frothingham, Richard. *Life and Times of Joseph Warren*. Boston, MA: Little, Brown, 1865.

Gallagher, John J. *The Battle of Brooklyn, 1776*. Rockville Center, NY: Sarpedon, 1999.

Galvin, John R. *The Minute Men: The First Fight: Myths and Realities of the American Revolution*. Washington, DC: Potomac, 2006.

Golway, Terry, *Washington's General: Nathanael Greene and the Triumph of the American Revolution*. New York: Henry Holt, 2005.

Greene, George Washington. *The Life of Nathanael Greene, Major-General in the Army of the Revolution*, vol. 2. New York: Hurd and Houghton, 1871.

Grosvenor, Louis. *The Life and Character of Maj. General Putnam: An Address Delivered at a Meeting of the Descendants of Maj. General Israel Putnam*. Boston, MA: Farwell & Company, 1855.

Henriques, Peter R. *Realistic Visionary: A Portrait of George Washington*. Charlottesville: University of Virginia Press, 2006.

Hibbert, Christopher. *Redcoats and Rebels: The American Revolution Through British Eyes*. New York: Avon, 1991.

Hickey, Donald R. *The War of 1812: A Forgotten Conflict*. Urbana: University of Illinois Press, 1989.

Hildreth, Samuel Prescott. *Pioneer History: Being an Account of the First Examinations of the Ohio Valley, and the Early Settlements of the Northwest Territory*. Cincinnati, OH: H. W. Derby, 1848.

————. *Biographical and Historical Memoirs of the Early Pioneer Settlers of Ohio, with Narratives of Incidents and Occurrences in 1775*. Cincinnati, OH: H. W. Derby, 1852.

Hill, George Canning. *Gen. Israel Putnam ("Old Put"): A Biography*. Boston, MA: E. O. Libby, 1858.

Hoffman, Paul E. *Florida's Frontiers*. Bloomington: Indiana University Press, 2002.

Holbrook, Stewart H. *The Old Post Road: The Story of the Boston Post Road*. New York: McGraw-Hill, 1962.

Hubbard, Robert Ernest. *Major General Israel Putnam: Hero of the American Revolution*. Jefferson, NC: McFarland, 2017.

Humphreys, David. *An Essay on the Life of the Honorable Major General Israel Putnam*. Indianapolis, IN: Liberty Fund, 2000.

Humphreys, Frank Landon. *Life and Times of David Humphreys, Soldier—Statesman—Poet, "Belov'd of Washington."* 2 vols. New York: G. P. Putnam's Sons, 1917.

Hurt, Douglas. *The Ohio Frontier: Crucible of the Old Northwest, 1720–1830*. Bloomington: Indiana University Press, 1996.

Irving, Washington. *Life of George Washington*, vol. 2. New York: G. P. Putnam, 1856.

Jaffe, Eric. *The King's Best Highway: The Lost History of the Boston Post Road, the Route That Made America*. New York: Scribner, 2010.

Johnston, Henry Phelps. *The Battle of Harlem Heights, September 16, 1776: With a Review of the Events of the Campaign*. New York: Columbia University Press, 1897.

———. *The Campaign of 1776 Around New York and Brooklyn, Including a New and Circumstantial Account of the Battle of Long Island and the Loss of New York: With a Review of Events to the Close of the Year*. Two Parts. Brooklyn, NY: Long Island Historical Society, 1878.

Josephy, Alvin M. Jr. *The Patriot Chiefs: A Chronical of Indian Resistance*. New York: Viking, 1969.

Ketcham, Ralph. *James Madison, A Biography*. Charlottesville: University of Virginia Press, 1994.

Ketchum, Richard M. *The Decisive Day: The Battle for Bunker Hill*. New York: Henry Holt, 1999.

———. *Divided Loyalties: How the American Revolution Came to New York*. New York: Henry Holt, 2002.

———. *Saratoga: Turning Point of America's Revolutionary War*. New York: Henry Holt, 1997.

Kwasny, Mark V. *Washington's Partisan War, 1775–1783*. Kent, OH: Kent State University Press, 1996.

Langguth, A. J. *Union 1812: The Americans Who Fought the Second War of Independence*. New York: Simon & Schuster, 2006.

Lee, Charles. "The Lee Papers, vols 1–3." *Collections of the New York Historical Society for the Years 1871–1873*. New York: New York Historical Society, 1872–1874.

Lender, Mark Edward. *Cabal: The Plot Against General Washington*. Yardley, PA: Westholme Publishing, 2019.

Lepore, Jill. *The Name of War: King Philip's War and the Origins of American Identity*. New York: Knopf, 1998.

Livingston, William Farrand. *Israel Putnam: Pioneer, Ranger, and Major General, 1718–1790*. New York: G. P. Putnam's Sons, 1901.

Lockhart, Paul. *The Whites of Their Eyes: Bunker Hill, the First American Army, and the Emergence of George Washington*. New York. HarperCollins, 2011.

Marlowe, George Francis. *Coaching Roads of Old New England: Their Inns and Taverns and Their Stories*. New York: Macmillan, 1945.

McCullough, David. *1776*. New York: Simon & Schuster, 2005.

———. *The Pioneers: The Heroic Story of the Settlers Who Brought the American Ideal West*. New York: Simon & Schuster, 2019.

McDonald, Forrest, ed. *Empire and Nation: Letters from a Farmer in Pennsylvania, John Dickinson; Letters from the Federal Farmer, Richard Henry Lee*, second edition. Indianapolis, IN: Liberty Fund, 1999.

Middlekauff, Robert. *The Glorious Cause: The American Revolution, 1763–1789*. New York: Oxford University Press, 1982.

Morgan, Edmund S. *The Genuine Article: A Historian Looks at Early America*. New York: Norton, 2004.

Morgan, Ted. *Wilderness at Dawn: The Settling of the North American Continent*. New York: Simon & Schuster, 1993.

———. *A Shovel of Stars: The Making of the American West 1800 to the Present*. New York: Simon & Schuster, 1995.

Murray, Stuart. *America's Song: The Story of "Yankee Doodle."* Bennington, VT: Images from the Past, 1999.

Nelson, James L. *With Fire and Sword: The Battle of Bunker Hill and the Beginning of the American Revolution.* New York: St. Martin, 2011.

Norton, Mary Beth. *Liberty's Daughters: The Revolutionary Experience of American Women, 1750–1800.* Boston, MA: Little, Brown, 1980.

O'Donnell, Patrick K. *Washington's Immortals: The Untold Story of an Elite Regiment Who Changed the Course of the Revolution.* New York: Grove Press, 2017.

Pancake, John S. *1777: The Year of the Hangman.* Tuscaloosa: University of Alabama Press, 1992.

Parkman, Francis. *The Oregon Trail and the Conspiracy of Pontiac.* New York: Library of America, 1991.

————. "Montcalm and Wolfe." In *France and England in North America*, vol. 2. New York: Library of America, 1983.

Pasley, Jeffrey L. *The Tyranny of Printers: Newspaper Politics in the Early American Republic.* Charlottesville: University of Virginia Press, 2001.

Philbrick, Nathaniel. *Valiant Ambition: George Washington, Benedict Arnold, and the Fate of the American Revolution.* New York: Viking, 2016.

————. *Bunker Hill: A City, a Siege, a Revolution.* New York: Penguin, 2014.

Pulsifer, David. *An Account of the Battle of Bunker Hill.* Boston, MA: A. Williams, 1875.

Purcell, Sarah J. *Sealed with Blood: War, Sacrifice, and Memory in Revolutionary America.* Philadelphia: University of Pennsylvania Press, 2010.

Randall, Willard Sterne. *Alexander Hamilton: A Life.* New York: Perennial, 2004.

Remini, Robert V. *Daniel Webster: The Man and His Times.* New York: Norton, 1997.

Rhodehamel, John. *George Washington: The Wonder of the Age.* New Haven, CT: Yale University Press, 2017.

————, ed. *George Washington: Writings.* New York: Library of America, 1997.

Rohrbough, Malcolm J. *Trans–Appalachian Frontier: Peoples, Societies, and Institutions, 1775–1850.* Bloomington: Indiana University Press, 2008.

Ross, John F. *War on the Run: The Epic Story of Robert Rogers and the Conquest of America's First Frontier.* New York: Bantam, 2011.

Rowland, Dunbar, ed. *Encyclopedia of Mississippi History: Comprising Sketches of Counties, Towns, Events, Institutions and Persons*, vol. 2. Madison, WI: Selwyn A. Brant, 1907.

Rozier, Firmin A. *Rozier's History of the Early Settlement of the Mississippi Valley.* St. Louis, MO: G. A. Pierrot & Son, 1890.

Ruddiman, John A. *Becoming Men of Some Consequence: Youth and Service in the Revolutionary War.* Charlottesville: University of Virginia Press, 2014.

Russell, Robert H. *Wilton Connecticut: Three Centuries of People, Places, and Progress.* Wilton, CT: Wilton Historical Society, 2004.

Schecter, Barnet. *The Battle for New York: The City at the Heart of the American Revolution.* New York: Walker & Co., 2002.

Sculley, Seanegan P. *A Contest for Liberty: Military Leadership in the Continental Army, 1775–1783.* Yardley, PA: Westholme Publishing, 2019.

Shorto, Russell. *Revolution Song: The Story of America's Founding in Six Remarkable Lives.* New York: Norton, 2018.

Steele, Ian K. *Betrayals: Fort William Henry and the "Massacre."* New York: Oxford University Press, 1993.

Stiles, Henry R. *The History of Ancient Windsor, Connecticut, Including East Windsor, South Windsor, and Ellington, Prior to 1768, the Date of Their Separation from the Old Town; and Windsor, Bloomfield and Windsor Locks, to the Present Time: Also the Genealogies and Genealogical Notes of Those Families Which Settled Within the Limits of Ancient Windsor, Connecticut, Prior to 1800.* New York: Charles B. Norton, 1859.

Swett, Samuel. *History of Bunker Hill Battle, with a Plan,* third ed. Boston, MA: Munroe and Francis, 1827.

Taaffe, Stephen R. *Washington's Revolutionary War Generals.* Norman: University of Oklahoma Press, 2019.

Tarbox, Increase N. *Life of Israel Putnam ("Old Put"), Major-General in the Continental Army.* Boston, MA: Lockwood, Brooks, 1876.

Trask, David F. *The War with Spain in 1898.* Lincoln: University of Nebraska Press, 1996.

Ward, Christopher: *The War of the Revolution,* vol. 1. New York: Macmillan, 1952.

Ward, Harry M. *Between the Lines: Banditti of the American Revolution.* Westport, CT: Praeger, 2002.

Warren, Mercy Otis. *History of the Rise, Progress and Termination of the American Revolution,* 2 vols. Indianapolis, IN: Liberty Fund, 1994.

Webb, J. Watson. *Reminiscences of Gen'l Samuel B. Webb of the Revolutionary War.* New York: Globe Stationary, 1882.

Wheeler, Richard. *Voices of 1776: The Story of the American Revolution in the Words of Those Who Were There.* New York: Meridian, 1991.

Woodward, Ashbel. *Memoir of Col. Thomas Knowlton of Ashford, Connecticut.* Boston, MA: Henry W. Dutton, 1861.

Wright, Robert K. Jr. *The Continental Army.* Washington, DC: Center of Military History, United States Army, 1983.

ARTICLES

Boutin, Cameron. "Adversary and Ally: The Role of the Weather in the Life and Career of George Washington," *The Journal of Military History* 81, no. 3 (July 2017): 693–718.

Carter, Clarence E. "Some Aspects of British Administration in West Florida," *The Mississippi Valley Historical Review* 1, vol. 3 (December 1914).

Cray, Robert E. Jr. "Bunker Hill Refought: Memory Wars and Partisan Conflicts, 1775–1825," *Historical Journal of Massachusetts* 29, no. 1 (Winter 2001): 22–52.

Drury, David. "Connecticut in the French and Indian War." https://connecticuthistory.org.

Edwards, Andrew David. "Grenville's Silver Hammer: The Problem of Money in the Stamp Act Crisis." *Journal of American History* 102, no. 2 (September 2017): 337–62.

Friends and Neighbors of Putnam Park. "Park History," putnampark.org/park-history/.

Hamilton, Milton W. "Hero of Lake George: Johnson or Lyman?" *The New England Quarterly* 36, no. 3 (September 1963): 371–82.

Haynes, Robert V. "Mississippi Under British Rule: British West Florida," Mississippi History Now (September 2000), https://mhistorynow.mdah.state.us/articles/66/mississippi-under-british-west-florida. Accessed March 29, 2020.

Howard, Clinton L. "Colonial Pensacola: The British Period Part III: The Administration of Governor Chester, 1770–1781," *The Florida Historical Quarterly* 19, no. 4 (April 1941): 368–401.

Jones, T. Cole. "'The Rage of Tory-hunting': Loyalist Prisoners, Civil War, and the Violence of American Independence." *The Journal of Military History* 81, no. 3 (July 2017): 719–46.

Kingsley, Ronald F., and Harvey J. Alexander. "The Failure of Abercromby's Attack in Fort Carillon, July 1758, and the Scapegoating of Matthew Clerk," *The Journal of Military History* 72 (January 2008): 43–70.

Kochan, James L. "Joseph Frye's Journal and Map of the Siege of Fort William Henry, 1757," *The Bulletin of the Fort Ticonderoga Museum* 15, no. 5 (1993): 339–61.

Lender, Mark Edward, and James Kirby Martin. "Target New London: Benedict Arnold's Raid, Just War, and 'Homegrown Terror Reconsidered.'" *The Journal of Military History* 83, no. 1 (January 2019): 67–95.

Lepore, Jill. "Back Issues." *New Yorker* 84, no. 46 (January 26, 2009): 68–73.

McCulloch, Ian MacPherson. "'A blanket of inconsistencies . . .' The Battle of Fort Ticonderoga." *Journal of Military History* 72, no. 3 (July 2008): 889–900.

Menschel, David. "Abolition Without Deliverance: The Law of Connecticut Slavery 1784–1848." *The Yale Law Journal* 111 (September 2001): 183–222.

Myers, William Starr. "Log of an American Marine in 1762 on a British Fighting Ship." *Journal of American History* 3 (1909): 113–17.

Nelson, Paul David. "Legacy of Controversy: Gates, Schuyler, and Arnold at Saratoga, 1777." *Military Affairs* 37, no. 2 (April 1973): 41–47.

Priest, Claire, and Justin du Rivage. "The Stamp Act and the Political Origins of American Legal and Economic Institutions" (2015). *Faculty Scholarship Series* 4934, https://digitalcommons.law.yale.edu/fss_papers/4934.

Reinke, A. A. "Occupation of New York City by the British, 1776." *The Pennsylvania Magazine of History and Biography* 1, no. 2 (1877): 133–48, republished by the University of Pennsylvania Press, https://jstor.org/stable/20084272.

Soucier, Daniel S. "Where There Was No Signs of Any Human Being: Navigating the Eastern Country Wilderness on Arnold's March to Quebec, 1775." *The Journal of Military History* 81, no. 2 (April 2017): 369–93.

Starbuck, David R. "British Forts in Northern New York State." Chapter 1 in *British Forts and Their Communities: Archaeological and Historical Perspectives*, edited by Christopher R. DeCorse and Zachary J. M. Beier, 31–48. Gainesville: University Press of Florida, 2018.

NEWSPAPERS

Connecticut Courant and *Hartford Weekly Intelligencer*
Gazette of the United States (New York)
Marietta Times
Norwich (CT) Bulletin

Index

Abenaki tribe, 32

Abercromby, James: Amherst and, 60; Bradstreet and, 57–58; deputies of, 37–38; France to, 48–49; in French and Indian War, 25, 35, 37; Howe and, 46–48, 50; Loudon (lord) and, 45–46; Lyman, P., and, 51–52; Montcalm and, 50–51; Pitt and, 53, 57

Adams, Abigail, 152

Adams, John: Greene, N., and, 220; independence to, 101; leadership of, 126, 168; Tudor and, 171; Putnam and, 287, 290

Adams, Samuel, 126–27, 130

Adventurer (ship), 122

Africa, 7

Alexander, William. *See* Stirling

Allen, Abner, 144

Allen, Ethan, 162

America: American Duties Act, 98–99; Army Special Forces, U.S., 18; Board of War in, 240–41, 254, 257, 337n23; calendars in, 293n2; Canada and, 223–27; Civil War in, 318n32; as colony, 18, 64–65; Court of Enquiry in, 256–57; Cuba to, 81–82, 310n24; diplomacy in, 230–39; England and, 156–58, 163–64, 173–74, 188–92, 198–200, 209–10, 212–13, 269–70; espionage against, 217–19, 255, 268, 278, 286, 341n68; Europe and, 37–38; folklore in, 352n94; France and, 27–28, 313n27; in French and Indian War, 25–27, 30–34, 51–57; Militias for, 15; missionaries in, 66–67; monarchy to, 65, 98–108, 175; in Montreal Campaign, 1760, 65–68; politics in, 210–12, 248–50, 290–91, 310n24; "Powder Alarm" in, 128–29; Provincial troops in, 9; to Putnam, I., 9–10; quotas in, 12; Regulating Act to, 125–26; slave labor in, 7, 303n42; Spain and, 71–79; Stamp

Act to, 289; Ticonderoga to, 46–48; Treaty of Paris for, 84; in truce, 137; volunteers in, 9–10, 12–13. *See also specific topics*
American Revolution. *See* Revolutionary War
Amherst, Jeffery: appointment of, 57; Bradstreet and, 88; in England, 83–84; in French and Indian War, 60–69; history from, 311n31; Native Americans to, 87; Pitt and, 308n60; Putnam, I., and, 61
Anderson, Fred, 95
Angell, Israel, 215–16, 219
Antigua, 75
Army Special Forces, U.S., 18
Arnold, Benedict: at Fort Ticonderoga, 162; leadership of, 170, 224; Small and, 255; after treachery, 278, 341n68; to Washington, 213–14
Articles of War, 25–26
Atlee, Samuel, 182–83
Atwater, Caleb, 56
Augustus, George, 37–38
Avery, Ephraim, 104

Bagley, Jonathan, 23
Bagley, Philip, 144
"The Ballad of Maggie Lauder" (song), 170, 261, 278
Baltimore, Maryland, 204
Barré, Isaac, 101

Barrett, Isaac, 144
Battle of Bunker Hill, 138–45, *146*, 147–51, 287–88
Battle of Chelsea Creek, 135–37
Battle of Lake George, 15
Bayard, Rebecca, 259
Baylor, George, 260
Bayou Pierre, 116–20
Beaver (ship), 125
Belcher, Jonathan, 3
Billings, Roger, 23
biographies, 294n4, 299n25, 299n27, 301n23, 303n46
Black slaves, 75, 303n42
Black soldiers, 39
Blagden, Samuel, 247
Blanchard, Joseph, 16–17
Blomart, John, 123–24
Board of War, 240–41, 254, 257–58, 337n23
Bogue, Daniel, 26
Borland, John, 134
Boston: Boston Campaign, 1775-1776, *xii*; Boston Port Bill, 125–26; Boston Tea Party, 125–26; to Connecticut, 155; Hartford and, 294n8; Moncrieffe, T., in, 286; Putnam, I., in, 125–28, 131–35, 164; violence in, 128–31, 163–64, 325n88; Washington and, 162–64
Bouquet, Henry, 93–94
Braddock, Edward, 11, 13
Bradley, Philip Burr, 267

Hierlihy, Timothy, 75–76, 84
Hillsborough (lord), 108–9
Hispaniola, 76, 111
Hog Island, 135–36
Holden, John, 144
Holdridge, Hezekiah, 270–71
Holland, Joseph, 126
Horseneck escape, 269–71, *272*, 273
Hotham, William, 229
Howe, Jemima, 58
Howe, Richard, 178, 229–30
Howe, Viscount, 37–38, 46–50
Howe, William: Clinton, H., and, 192; leadership of, 143–44, 162–63, 181–82, 185–86, 195–97; in Philadelphia, 221; reputation of, 179–81, 183, 186–87, 199–200, 231, 234; before Revolutionary War, 72, 74–75, 77–78; Small and, 72; strategy of, 212–14, 224; tactics against, 243–44; Washington to, 178–79; Webb, S., on, 201
Hubbard, Nathaniel, 79–80
Hudson Highlands, *xiv*, 205, 213–15
Hughes, Hugh, 250
Humphreys, David: as biographer, 299n25, 299n27, 301n23, 303n46; on *Chesterfield*, 309n12; on Clinton, H., 339n46; on Farnsworth, 321n30; on French and

Indian War, 55; interviews with, 293n1; observations of, 191, 246, 276; Putnam, I., and, 50, 67, 124, 276–78, 297n9, 306n26, 308n62; on Putnam, R., 319n45; Rogers, Robert, to, 300n7, 306n29; Washington and, 1
Hunt, James, 245–47
Hunt, Samuel, 19
Huntington, Andrew, 216, 261
Huntington, Ebenezer, 163–64
Huntington, Jedediah, 134, 168–69, 182, 252, 261, 266, 349n55
Huntington, Joshua, 158–59, 168–69
Hutchins, Anthony, 117, 123–24
Hyde, Jedidiah, 81

illness, 62–63, 310n24
Independent soldiers, 36
Indians. *See* Native Americans
infrastructure, in New England, 62–63
Ingersoll, Jared, 100, 314n12
Inman, Elizabeth, 133, 139
Inman, Ralph, 133
Intrepid (ship), 75–77, 82
Iroquois tribe, 18, 91
Israel Putnam, John Trumbull sketch (circa 1780), *146*

James, Thomas, 117, 119–20
Jane & Elizabeth (ship), 82

63; in Cuba, 76, 78–82; Dalyell to, 87; death of, 281–83, *282*; discharge of, *43*, 44; Drake and, 245–47; Durkee and, 21–22, 88–89, 93, 340n67; early years of, 1–4, *2*, *5*, 7; England to, 159–60, 187, 325n88; ethics of, 209–10, 217–19, 247–48, 254–55, 265–68; family of, 9, 58, 227–28, 262, 276–77; Fellows and, 303n46; at Fort Edward, 23–24, 40; after French and Indian War, 69; with Gage, 65–66; Gates, H., and, 173–74, 242, 336n11; Goodrich and, 110–11, 113–15, 130, 133; grave of, *282*; Greene, N., and, 197, 273, 277–78; Green on, 147–48; Howe, V., and, 49; Humphreys and, 50, 67, 124, 276–78, 297n9, 306n26, 308n62; with Hunt, 19; Israel Putnam, John Trumbull sketch, *146*; Knowlton and, 144, 160–61, 193–94; at Lake George, 16–23; leadership of, 55–56, 139–42, 184, 188, 191–92; legacy of, 279–81, 289–91; Leonard to, 219–21; Livingston and, 211–12; Lyman, P., and, 84, 112, 309n12; middle years of, 97–106, *104*; Moncrieffe,

T., and, 175–78; Montcalm and, 306n30; with Native Americans, 68; in New Hampshire, 68–69; in New York, 128–29; as officer, 161; Parsons and, 222, 251, 264, 273; in Pensacola, 120–21; personality of, 170; in Philadelphia, 202–5; politics of, 256–58; Pomeroy, D., and, 137–38; Pomeroy, S., and, 143; Prescott and, 151; as prisoners of war, 56–57; promotions for, 152–53; Provincial Militia to, 242; Putnam, R., and, 109, 111–21, 124, 163, 195–96, 319n45, 345n17; Putnam birthplace, *2*; Putnam Homestead, *43*; "Putnam's Escape at Horseneck," *272*; Rangers with, 30–34, 46, 53–56; recruiting and, 65; Reed, Joseph, and, 206, 208–9; "The Reivers" to, 135–37; release of, 58; relief forces for, 75–76; religion to, 81, 97–98, 110; remarriage, 104–5; reputation of, 79–81, 154–56, 186, 190, 194–95, 198–99, 207, 285–87; Revolutionary War and, 250–55, *272*, 273–77; Rogers, Robert, and, 16–21, 27–28, 43–44, 46–48, 69, 72, 285;

"The Reivers," 135–37
relief forces, 75–76
religion, 81, 97–98, 110
remarriage, 104–5
van Rensselaer, John, 296n4
Revolutionary War: Battle of
    Bunker Hill in, 138–45, *146*,
    147–51; Battle of Chelsea
    Creek in, 135–37; Black slaves
    in, 303n42; Brooklyn after, 1;
    communication in, 232–39;
    Connecticut in, 132–33,
    268–71; culture during,
    175–78, 219–21, 245–48; after
    Declaration of Independence,
    174–75; ethics in, 286;
    General Assembly in, 132–33,
    266–68; in history, 288,
    290–91; Howe, W., before,
    72, 74–75, 77–78; Hudson
    Highlands in, 205, 213–15;
    leadership in, 170–72, 178–81,
    187–88, 192–94, 230–32,
    240–41; Massachusetts in,
    128–32; migration after, 121–
    22; neutral ground in, 217–19;
    New England and, 125–28,
    197–200, 210–12, 223–27,
    248–50; in New Jersey,
    201–2, 206–8; New York and,
    165–69, 221–23, 243–45; in
    Philadelphia, 202–5; politics
    of, 137–38, 155–60, 173–74,
    208–9, 241–42, 258–61,
    265–68; Provincial Militia in,
215–17; Putnam, I., and, 250–
55, *272*, 273–77; recruiting in,
256–58; retreat in, 188–92;
Rogers, Robert, in, 172–73;
Stamp Act and, 98–103; Stark
in, 140, 142–45, 147; strategy
in, 133–35, 152–55, 160–64,
173–74, 181–86, 194–96,
205–6, 228–30; veterans of,
287; violence in, 168–69,
197–98; weather in,
261–64
Rhode Island, 7, 14
Rivington, James, 255
Robertson, James, 255
Robinson, Beverly, 225–26, 255
Rogers, John, 17, 110
Rogers, Mary, 17
Rogers, Richard, 30
Rogers, Robert: in absence,
37–38; France to, 54–55; to
Humphreys, 300n7, 306n29;
leadership of, 51–52, 87;
with Loudon, 37; Putnam,
I., and, 16–21, 27–28,
43–44, 46–48, 69, 72, 285;
reputation of, 16–23, 33,
298n24, 329n21; return of,
40–41; in Revolutionary War,
172–73; scouting by, 25. *See
also* Rangers
Rogers Island, 41–43
Rohrbough, Malcolm, 316n5
Roosevelt, Theodore, 310n24
Rose (ship), 174